BEHIND-THE-BORDER POLICIES

One feature of globalization is that barriers to international competition have come to be associated with differences in regulatory policies that increase the costs of engaging in cross-border sales. Such non-tariff measures (NTMs) have attracted growing attention from policy makers and raise important questions for policy research. This book provides a valuable overview of key issues related to NTMs and domestic regulation. It covers the classification and definition of NTMs, new sources of data on NTMs, the impacts of (different types of) NTMs, the challenges that confront efforts to reduce the negative trade effects of NTMs and what can and should be done through international cooperation to promote good practices in the design and implementation of NTMs. The contributors comprise a mix of leading trade policy experts – both academics and practitioners – and younger researchers who have specialized in the analysis of NTMs.

JOSEPH FRANCOIS is Professor of Economics and Managing Director of the World Trade Institute, Universität of Bern, Switzerland. He is a Centre for Economic Policy Research (CEPR) research fellow, and co-founder of the European Trade Study Group (ETSG). He has published widely on trade, the role of services in growth and development, and sustainability aspects of globalization.

BERNARD HOEKMAN is Professor at the Robert Schuman Centre for Advanced Studies and Dean, External Relations, at the European University Institute, Florence, Italy. A Centre for Economic Policy Research (CEPR) research fellow, he has published widely on trade and development, trade in services and the multilateral trading system.

BEHIND-THE-BORDER POLICIES

Assessing and Addressing Non-Tariff Measures

Edited by

JOSEPH FRANCOIS
University of Bern
BERNARD HOEKMAN
European University Institute

CAMBRIDGE
UNIVERSITY PRESS

CAMBRIDGE
UNIVERSITY PRESS

University Printing House, Cambridge CB2 8BS, United Kingdom

One Liberty Plaza, 20th Floor, New York, NY 10006, USA

477 Williamstown Road, Port Melbourne, VIC 3207, Australia

314–321, 3rd Floor, Plot 3, Splendor Forum, Jasola District Centre, New Delhi – 110025, India

79 Anson Road, #06–04/06, Singapore 079906

Cambridge University Press is part of the University of Cambridge.

It furthers the University's mission by disseminating knowledge in the pursuit of education, learning, and research at the highest international levels of excellence.

www.cambridge.org
Information on this title: www.cambridge.org/9781108485531
DOI: 10.1017/9781108751698

First published 2019
Printed and bound in Great Britain by Clays Ltd, Elcograf S.p.A.

A catalogue record for this publication is available from the British Library.

Library of Congress Cataloging-in-Publication Data
Names: Francois, Joseph F., editor. | Hoekman, Bernard M., 1959– editor.
Title: Behind-the-border policies : assessing and addressing non-tariff measures / edited by Joseph Francois. Universität Bern, Switzerland; Bernard Hoekman, European University Institute, Florence.
Description: Cambridge, United Kingdom ; New York, NY, USA : Cambridge University Press, 2019. | Includes bibliographical references and index.
Identifiers: LCCN 2019021321 | ISBN 9781108485531 (hardback : alk. paper) | ISBN 9781108707244 (pbk. : alk. paper)
Subjects: LCSH: Non-tariff trade barriers–Law and legislation.
Classification: LCC K3942 .B44 2019 | DDC 382/.5–dc23
LC record available at https://lccn.loc.gov/2019021321

ISBN 978-1-108-48553-1 Hardback

CONTENTS

List of Figures vii
List of Tables ix
List of Boxes xi
List of Contributors xii

1 **Moving beyond the Border: Introduction and Overview** 1
JOSEPH FRANCOIS AND BERNARD HOEKMAN

PART I **Concepts and Measurement** 9

2 **Nontariff Measures: Data Concepts and Sources** 11
MARIE-LUISE RAU AND ACHIM VOGT

3 **Regulatory Bindings, Policy Uncertainty, and Market Access in Services** 48
PETER EGGER, JOSEPH FRANCOIS, BERNARD HOEKMAN, AND MIRIAM MANCHIN

PART II **Assessing and Benchmarking Policy** 63

4 **Non-tariff Measures in the Presence of Global Value Chains and Their Impact on Productivity** 65
MAHDI GHODSI AND ROBERT STEHRER

5 **Non-tariff Measure Estimations in Different Impact Assessments** 100
EDDY BEKKERS AND HUGO ROJAS-ROMAGOSA

6 **Gauging Procurement Policy Change during the Crisis Era: Evidence from the Global Trade Alert** 128
SIMON J. EVENETT AND ANIRUDH SHINGAL

7 **Preferences, Income Distribution, and the Burden of Non-tariff Measures** 150
IGOR BAGAYEV AND RONALD B. DAVIES

PART III Dealing with Non-tariff Measures: Legal and Institutional Contexts 177

8 Nontariff Measures Reforms: A Practitioner's Perspective 179
FABIO ARTUSO

9 Good Regulatory Practices and International Trade 193
ROBERT BASEDOW

10 Rules of Origin as Non-tariff Measures: Towards Greater Regulatory Convergence 209
BERNARD HOEKMAN AND STEFANO INAMA

11 Behind-the-Border Measures and the New Generation of Trade Agreements: Technical Barriers to Trade and Sanitary and Phytosanitary Measures Compared 246
MANFRED ELSIG AND SEBASTIAN KLOTZ

12 Nontariff Responses to China's Development Strategy: The WTO's Interface Challenge 277
CHAD P. BOWN

13 A Time for Action: The WTO Must Change to Promote Regulatory Cooperation 299
THOMAS J. BOLLYKY AND PETROS C. MAVROIDIS

References 339
Index 361

FIGURES

2.1 Geographical overview of NTM data availability (country coverage) 32
4.1 Country average IBRI – third channel 80
4.2 Country average indirect tariffs on inputs – third channel 81
4.A1 Country average indirect AVE for TBT on inputs – third channel 97
4.A2 Country average indirect AVE for SPS on inputs – third channel 98
4.A3 Country average indirect AVE for TBT STC on inputs – third channel 98
4.A4 Country average indirect AVE for SPS STC on inputs – third channel 99
5.1 Welfare changes in the EU as a function of changes in iceberg trade costs $\hat{\tau}_{ij}^{NTM}$ for various values of the trade elasticity 124
6.1 Evolution of all public procurement-related measures over time 140
6.2 Evolution of all public procurement-related measures over time by GTA classification 141
6.3 Public procurement-related measures imposed in non-US countries 141
6.4 Discriminatory procurement measures imposed in non-US countries 142
6.5 Distribution of US discriminatory procurement measures by implementation status 144
6.6 Distribution of non-US discriminatory procurement measures by implementation status 144
6.7 Distribution of non-discriminatory procurement measures by country and implementation status 146
6.8 G20 exports (% share, 2009 and change over 2009–15) potentially at risk through discriminatory public procurement policies 148
7.1 Average TBT coverage ratio 152
7.2 Average SPS coverage ratio 152
11.1 Requests for consultations referring to the WTO TBT and SPS Agreements, 1995–2016 248
11.2 TBT and SPS measures by sector 249
11.3 Evolution of TBT and SPS in PTAs, 1990–2016 256
11.4 TBT in CETA 260
11.5 SPS in CETA 261
11.6 TBT in TPP 262

11.7 SPS in TPP 265
11.8 TBT in USMCA 267
11.9 SPS in USMCA 268
11.10 TBT in EU and US TTIP draft proposals 269
11.11 SPS in EU and US TTIP draft proposals 270
12.1 US goods imports from China and bilateral import share subject to antidumping and countervailing duties, 1990–2015 286
12.2 US goods imports from China and bilateral import share subject to antidumping in 2015, by sector 288
12.3 US goods exports to China and bilateral export share subject to antidumping and countervailing duties, 1992–2015 293

TABLES

2.1 MAST NTM classification 15
2.2 Sources and databases of NTM information 17
2.3 Trade facilitation measures 30
2.4 Summary of NTM databases' time coverage 34
2.5 Number of countries and measures per MAST chapter 36
2.6 Goods NTMs per sector 38
2.7 Services NTMs per sector as defined in GATS 40
2.A1 Trade obstacle classification by ITC 47
3.1 Blended and extra-EU STRI for market access in EU 56
3.2 Gravity regressions, total bilateral services trade 57
3.3 Estimated trade cost savings (total services EBOPS 200) tariff equivalent from eliminating binding overhang, value expressed as a percentage of the cost of exporting services 59
3.4 Potential trade cost reduction equivalents by sector from bindings, as percentage points 60
4.1 Direct AVE statistics – first channel 79
4.2 Third channel of trade policy measures by type, global simple average by WIOD sector 82
4.3 Three BRI channels' impact on productivity growth 87
4.4 Direct and indirect policy measures impact on productivity growth 89
4.5 Bilateral direct and indirect policy measures impact on productivity growth 94
5.1 Trade-weighted average percentage iceberg trade cost reductions 118
5.2 Estimated TTIP welfare effects, with and without spillover effects 127
6.1 Discriminatory procurement measures imposed by countries other than USA, by type of measure 143
6.2 Distribution of 'green' procurement measures by type of measure and evolution over time 145
7.1 Top fifteen sectors ranked by cross-country variance in coverage ratio 160
7.2 Coverage rates across and within countries 162
7.3 Summary statistics 164
7.4 Baseline results: four-digit level 165

7.5 Baseline results: two-digit level 167
7.6 Baseline results: country level 168
7.7 Extended results: four-digit level 170
7.8 Manufacturing results: four-digit level 171
7.9 Non-manufacturing results: four-digit level 172
7.10 Manufacturing and non-manufacturing extended results: four-digit level 173
7.11 Tobit estimation: four-digit level 174
7.12 Poisson estimation: four-digit level 175
10.1 Evolution of the NAFTA percentage-calculation-based RoO 217
10.2 Comparison of six-digit PSRO: HWP, CETA, USA–Korea, EU–Korea and CPTPP 221
10.3 HRO, CETA, TPP, EU and US PTAs with South Korea: signs of convergence 222
10.4 HRO, CETA, TPP, EU and US PTAs with South Korea: signs of divergence 225
11.1 Evolution of TBT in PTAs by development group, 1990–2016 257
11.2 Evolution of SPS in PTAs by development group, 1990–2016 258
11.3 Text-as-data results by TPP country 263
11.4 US vs EU TTIP TBT: objective, scope and coverage 272
11.5 US vs EU TTIP TBT: standards and standardization 274
12.1 Factors the US Department of Commerce must consider in identifying a country as a nonmarket economy 281
12.2 US antidumping and countervailing duties applied in 2015 290
12.A1 Industry definitions and classifications 298

BOXES

8.1 The Standard Cost Model (SCM) 183
8.2 Reviewing export costs in Cambodia 188

CONTRIBUTORS

FABIO ARTUSO,
Senior Trade Specialist, World Bank Group

IGOR BAGAYEV,
Assistant Professor at the School of Economics, University College Dublin

ROBERT BASEDOW,
Assistant Professor in International Political Economy, European Institute, London School of Economics and Political Science

EDDY BEKKERS,
Research Economist, World Trade Organization

THOMAS J. BOLLYKY,
Senior Fellow for Global Health, Economics and Development, Council on Foreign Relations

CHAD BOWN,
Reginald Jones Senior Fellow, Peterson Institute for International Economics, Washington, DC

RONALD B. DAVIES,
Full Professor of Economics, Head of School, School of Economics, University College Dublin

PETER EGGER,
Professor of Applied Economics, ETH Zürich

MANFRED ELSIG,
Professor of International Relations, Deputy Managing Director and Director of Research, World Trade Institute, University of Bern, Switzerland

SIMON J. EVENETT,
Professor of International Trade and Economic Development, University of St. Gallen, Switzerland

JOSEPH FRANCOIS,
Professor of International Economics, Managing Director, World Trade Institute at the University of Bern, Switzerland

MAHDI GHODSI,
Economist, The Vienna Institute for International Economic Studies (wiiw)

BERNARD HOEKMAN,
Professor, Robert Schuman Centre for Advanced Studies, European University Institute, Florence, Italy

STEFANO INAMA,
Chief, Technical Assistance and Enhanced Integrated Framework section, UNCTAD

SEBASTIAN KLOTZ,
PhD candidate, International Political Economy, World Trade Institute, University of Bern, Switzerland

MIRIAM MANCHIN,
Associate Professor, Political Economy of European Union Integration, University College London

PETROS C. MAVROIDIS,
Edwin B. Parker Professor of Foreign and Comparative Law, Columbia Law School

MARIE-LUISE RAU,
Wageningen University and Research (WUR), the Netherlands

HUGO ROJAS-ROMAGOSA,
Independent Research Economist, Senior Research Fellow, World Trade Institute, University of Bern, Switzerland

ANIRUDH SHINGAL,
Senior Fellow, Indian Council for Research on Economic Relations (ICRIER), New Delhi and Programme Associate, European University Institute, Florence, Italy

ROBERT STEHRER,
Scientific Director, The Vienna Institute for International Economic Studies (wiiw)

ACHIM VOGT,
Economist at the World Trade Institute, University of Bern, Switzerland

1

Moving beyond the Border

Introduction and Overview

JOSEPH FRANCOIS AND BERNARD HOEKMAN

Over the last three decades, traditional barriers to trade – import tariffs and quantitative restrictions (QRs) – have fallen dramatically. Globally, average applied import tariffs are less than 10 percent, and are well below 5 percent in Organisation for Economic Co-operation and Development (OECD) countries. Quantitative import restrictions have become rare outside of agriculture and even there today mostly take the form of so-called tariff rate quotas where higher tariffs apply once a certain quantity of imports (the quota) has been exceeded. Many inputs used in production are duty-free if imported. The decline in tariffs and QRs was a driver of a boom in international trade flows in the 1990s and 2000s and supported major changes in the structure and composition of world production and trade as this came to be organized in global value chains (GVCs). Tariff reductions, complemented by technological and managerial advances, drive firms to specialize in specific tasks and activities. International supply chains and production networks are the mechanisms through which this process of specialization is organized, with production occurring – and value being added – in multiple countries that are part of a chain or network.

One consequence of global trade liberalization is that barriers to international competition today have come to be associated with differences in regulatory policies that increase the costs of engaging in cross-border sales. Increasingly, emphasis is placed on behind-the-border policies and their impact on cross-border economic activity. This change in emphasis can be seen in the evolution of trade agreements, where more recent agreements are far more comprehensive than earlier ones. (See Dür, Baccini, and Elsig, 2014.) It also can be seen in a shift in the work program of trade ministries and international organizations away from relatively simple analysis of tariffs and quotas to a more challenging set of questions tied to regulatory cooperation and regulatory diversion and regulatory heterogeneity. In addition, bilateral cooperation on regulatory matters poses challenges for third countries that are less clear-cut than discriminatory tariff policy. (See Francois, Hoekman, and Nelson, 2015.)

Lurking behind the impact of nontariff measures (NTMs) on cross-border integration is the underlying politics driving the relevant regulatory structures. To the extent these measures are designed deliberately to act as barriers to trade and investment, they are often referred to in the literature as nontariff barriers (NTBs). However, this is a narrow view on what is really the broader question of the impact of NTMs (both intended and unintended) on economic integration. Indeed, while tariffs, trade subsidies, and related policy instruments that are clearly discriminatory measures are usually driven by the politics of protecting domestic industry from foreign competition, domestic regulatory structures are driven instead by a desire to protect consumers from substandard products, to protect farmers from animal and plant pathogens, or to ensure prudent regulation of service providers. As such, the impact on foreign suppliers may be unintentional, or even seen as a necessary element of ensuring domestic policy goals. This in turn means there is scope for international cooperation to minimize unintended consequences of regulation (such as through mutual recognition or even common regulatory decisions).

The contents of this volume address many of the challenges posed by the heightened relevance of NTMs to the world economy. These challenges include basic questions of benchmarking policy in terms of NTMs, quantifying the impact of those NTMs on trade and investment, negotiating on NTMs, and finally approaches to regulatory cooperation and targeting regulatory divergence. The final chapters focus on challenges that NTMs pose for the ability of the rules-based trade and investment system to keep up with the evolution of the global economy itself.

In the first section of the volume (Part I) we focus on the basic issue of benchmarking NTMs and their impact on market access. In Chapter 2, Marie-Luise Rau and Achim Vogt focus on the availability of NTM data for goods, taking stock of the key NTM databases by elaborating on the kind of NTM information actually provided, and the advantages and disadvantage of the data and their interpretation. They also identify gaps in the data and explore options for reconciliation, mapping future directions for research in this area.

Compared to goods, the classification and benchmarking of market access in services is far less developed. Yet, it has become increasingly clear that restrictions on services trade and investment impact not only trade in services, but also trade in goods as well. Lack of detailed information poses unique challenges when identifying priorities for negotiation and regulatory cooperation. From the data we have, we know that in the case of services, there is a substantial gap between commitments made both in the General Agreement on Trade in Services (GATS) and in regional agreements compared to actual policy. For this reason, while Chapter 2 is focused on NTMs affecting goods, in Chapter 3 the spotlight is turned to services. Here, Peter Egger, Joseph Francois, Bernard Hoekman, and Miriam Manchin focus on the impact of policy uncertainty due to binding overhang, or the gap between bound commitments on policy and actual applied policy in international trade agreements as they relate to services, on effective market access. The authors argue that a renewed push to reduce binding overhang in a World Trade Organization (WTO) context may yield not only a basis for future negotiated gains, but also immediate gains in market access. Like goods, security of market access through effective bindings matters.

The next section of this volume (Part II) is concerned with the assessment and benchmarking of regulatory policy and the possible impact of negotiated agreements affecting NTMs. In Chapter 4, Mahdi Ghodsi and Robert Stehrer combine the type of data covered in Chapter 2 with recent data on global production linkages to examine the impact of policy when transmitted across GVCs. In the presence of GVCs, import policies affect not only the directly targeted trading partners, but also third countries through international industrial linkages. This is the case for both tariffs and NTMs. The chapter analyses the effects of NTM trade policy instruments in the global economy. Their integrated analysis of trade costs and global production linkages yields insight on the impact of NTMs on growth in labor productivity.

Chapter 5 focuses on the analysis of NTM trade impact assessments. In the chapter, Eddy Bekkers and Hugo Rojas-Romagosa provide a critical overview of the two main approaches used to estimate NTM reductions associated with the implementation of free trade agreements. They use recent assessments of the Trans-Atlantic Trade and Investment Partnership (TTIP) as a reference set, detailing the role that NTM-related cost reductions estimated in different impact assessments of the TTIP play in the findings of such studies. They compare and analyse the main differences in these estimations and how these differences affect the overall estimated economic impact of the TTIP. They find that accounting for differences in the expected NTM reductions explains much of the discrepancies regarding the overall potential economic effects between different impact assessments of the TTIP. This highlights the importance of future research to better map changes in NTMs in trade agreements into changes in trade costs, if we are to identify priorities in addressing trade impacts of NTMs through negotiated agreements.

Chapter 6 focuses specifically on government procurement. This is an area where governments traditionally use a mix of price preferences for domestic suppliers and localization (local content) requirements. The use of such policies is to some extent constrained for members of the WTO Agreement on Government Procurement and for countries that have included procurement policy disciplines in their preferential trade agreements. In Chapter 6, Simon Evenett and Anirudh Shingal provide an analysis of findings based on the data from the Global Trade Alert team on public procurement policy changes undertaken since November 2008. They focus in particular on policy changes that alter the relative treatment of domestic firms vis-à-vis foreign rivals and demonstrate that procurement policy is a frequently used NTM with adverse effects on foreign suppliers.

Chapter 7 examines methodological issues related to how we benchmark NTMs and their impact on market access. In the chapter, Igor Bagayev and Ronald Davies work with some of the datasets covered in Chapter 2, focusing on NTM coverage ratios for the 2008–14 period in the European Union. Trade-weighted coverage ratios are commonly used when estimating the effect of NTMs on trade flows and other outcomes. Because they weight by import shares, for a given sector they can vary across countries even when actual policies are the same. While trade shares can depend on several factors, here the authors link them to income distribution. They find not only that the variation in coverage ratios is linked to income inequality, but also that this relationship is consistent with NTMs primarily on luxuries. This points to the need to include a focus on income distribution when benchmarking the effects of NTMs.

The third section of the volume (Part III) is concerned with the legal and institutional contexts of NTMs. The focus here is not only on how context affects policy reform efforts, but also how NTMs are themselves a limiting factor in the operational effectiveness of multilateral and preferential cooperation and treaties.

In Chapter 8, Fabio Artuso describes how some Association of Southeast Asian Nations (ASEAN) countries have leveraged their commitments under the ASEAN Trade in Goods Agreement (ATIGA) and the WTO Trade Facilitation Agreement to collect, classify, and publish information on NTMs. The establishment of institutional mechanisms to promote interministerial coordination in view of establishing Trade Portals for the publication of NTMs is emphasized as a critical element. Interministerial collaboration, backed by a clear legal mandate, is also considered fundamental to tackle effectively review and streamlining of NTMs. A concerted effort to develop regulators' capacity is necessary to improve NTM design and enforcement, in order to limit their potentially negative impact on a country's competitiveness and/or on its population's welfare.

In Chapter 9, Robert Basedow evaluates the contribution of collaborative efforts to identify and agree on what constitutes Good Regulatory Practices – such as ex ante regulatory impact assessments, ex post evaluations, and stakeholder consultations – to reducing regulatory divergences across countries and reducing related trade costs. The chapter first offers a theoretical evaluation of the strengths and weaknesses of Good Regulatory Practices to deal with regulatory frictions and trade costs. While Good Regulatory Practices have the potential to make an important contribution to limit unnecessary regulatory differences and trade costs, they cannot and should not do away with certain types of regulatory differences. Second, the chapter then discusses how OECD countries actually use Good Regulatory Practices to identify and to limit regulatory divergence. The findings suggest that even OECD countries with highly developed regulatory systems still struggle to mainstream trade considerations in the rule-making process. The chapter concludes with a discussion of the potential contribution of the WTO and recent preferential trade agreements such as the Comprehensive and Progressive Agreement on Trans-Pacific Partnership (CPTPP) to enhance the use of Good Regulatory Practices.

Continuing with the issue of regulatory divergence (and convergence), Bernard Hoekman and Stefano Inama examine rules of origin (RoO) in Chapter 10. In their implementation, RoO can work as nontariff measures, neutralizing what might otherwise be trade liberalization efforts with other instruments (such as preferential tariff reductions or agreements to discipline the use of antidumping actions). The chapter examines the causes of the long-standing deadlock in the WTO on multilateral harmonization of nonpreferential RoO, and reviews trends in RoO included in recent preferential trade agreements (PTAs) involving the EU and/or the USA. These trends reveal a steady and substantial movement toward adoption of similar approaches and illustrate that cooperation to reduce the trade-impeding effects of differences in RoO across jurisdictions is feasible. The authors argue that from a trade facilitation perspective, such cooperation can and should pursue greater convergence between preferential and nonpreferential RoO, building on the developments observed in recent PTAs.

In Chapter 11, Manfred Elsig and Sebastian Klotz focus on sanitary and phytosanitary (SPS) measures and technical barriers to trade (TBT) in the new generation of PTAs. Using a text-as-data approach, they analyze the TBT and SPS chapters of the Canada–EU Trade Agreement (CETA), the TPP, and the TTIP, addressing three questions: First, how much does innovation versus imitation of the WTO characterize the CETA and the TPP? Second, to which extent do these two PTAs present templates for the TTIP? And third, in which areas do the EU and the USA converge and diverge? The authors find that in all three PTA initiatives, negotiators rely more heavily on texts from previous agreements when designing the TBT chapter in comparison to the SPS chapter. In both chapters in the TPP treaty, they identify a considerable prominence of legal texts from existing trade deals, predominantly from treaties the USA is a signatory to. By contrast, CETA negotiators relied less on previous PTAs and appear to have developed a more innovative approach to TBT and SPS. The EU draft proposals for the TBT and SPS chapters of the TTIP rely heavily on the CETA text. Interestingly, the TPP plays a fairly limited role in the US draft proposal for the TTIP, even though it was an agreement largely written by the USA and was virtually contemporaneous with the TTIP talks. Finally, the authors show that the EU and USA tend to converge on general topics such as the objective, scope, and coverage of TBT and SPS in the TTIP but diverge when it comes to more detailed items such as standard-setting processes and conformity assessment procedures.

China's entry into the WTO and its incomplete and uncertain transition into a market economy have reestablished the "interface question" as one of fundamental importance for the multilateral trading system – and one that illustrates the salience of NTMs and NTM-related multilateral disciplines. In Chapter 12, Chad Bown uses the USA–China relationship as a case study to examine how countries are only indirectly addressing the underlying issues. It introduces data on US use of nontariff barrier policies – antidumping and countervailing duties – to assess whether a potential change in China's nonmarket economy (NME) status reduces the United States' access to special trade policies in a way that might result in a sudden surge in imports from China. It then considers the potential consequences of a failure by the United States and the existing WTO membership to negotiate a solution to the NME issue with China.

It concludes by raising systemic concerns for the WTO of a failure to seriously address the long-run interface question.

Finally, in Chapter 13 Thomas Bollyky and Petros Mavroidis argue that institutional dimensions of the WTO need to be adjusted in order to reflect the decline in tariffs and other border restraints to commerce and the emerging challenges of advancing freer trade and better regulatory cooperation in a world economy dominated by GVCs. This chapter therefore builds on the findings of Chapter 4 linking NTMs along value chains to labor productivity trends and Chapter 9 on good regulatory practices. The authors argue that addressing these challenges requires an integration strategy that they refer to as the "new WTO Think." This strategy is more of an evolution rather than a revolution, as it remains rooted in the original rationale of the General Agreement on Trade and Tariffs (GATT) of reducing the negative externalities of unilateral action and solving important international coordination challenges. At the same time, they see it as more inclusive of regulators and nonstate actors and more flexible and positive in its means. Because it does not require fundamental rethinking of the current regime, their proposals are more likely to be feasible to implement by WTO members. In particular, Bollyky and Mavroidis advocate that the WTO should embrace the confluence of shared social preferences and trade, where it exists, as a motivation for advancing international regulatory cooperation. The WTO should also multilateralize the important regulatory cooperation occurring in smaller clubs of like-minded countries and better facilitate the use of plurilateral agreements where consensus across all WTO members is not yet possible.

PART I

Concepts and Measurement

2

Nontariff Measures: Data Concepts and Sources*

MARIE-LUISE RAU AND ACHIM VOGT

2.1 Introduction

Nontariff measures (NTMs) have become increasingly important in the context of trade liberalization. With declining tariffs, they have been widely discussed at the international level. Plurilateral and bilateral trade agreements have covered them in order to tackle these behind-the-border measures, while acknowledging public policy goals in the interest of individual countries. Given the proliferation of such trade agreements, the analysis of trade policies in particular aims to determine the effect of NTMs by applying different types of information about them. The results of such analysis are hardly comparable and tend to be inconclusive not only due to the different methodologies applied but also due to the different data employed.

NTMs take various forms ranging from requirements for market access, e.g., food safety standards and norms, certification, custom procedures, safeguard measures, including antidumping, rules of origin, and public procurement. UNCTAD (2009) defines NTMs as policy measures, other than ordinary customs tariffs, that can potentially have an economic effect on international trade in goods, changing quantities traded, or prices, or both. NTMs have been defined by concerted effort of the Multi-Agency Support Team (MAST) group that consists of international organizations[1] and experts. Applying the MAST classification,

* The authors kindly acknowledge that this chapter is produced as part of the project "Productivity, Non-tariff Measures, and Openness (PRONTO)" funded by the European Commission under its Seventh Framework Programme – contract no. FP7-SSH-613504. We would like to thank participants of the PRONTO workshop in Paris, Galbino summer school, the World Trade Forum in Grindelwald, and the European Trade Study Group (ETSG) in Florence for valuable feedback and comments.

[1] United Nations Conference on Trade and Development (UNCTAD), United Nations Industrial Development Organization (UNIDO), Food and Agriculture Organization of the United Nations (FAO), World Trade Organization (WTO), International Trade

UNCTAD and ITC, both part of the MAST group, and other institutions have been engaged in the collection of NTM data. While the MAST definition is widely accepted, the information collected in different initiatives is not comparable and cannot be easily matched across databases. Of course, NTMs that are very complex can be described in many different ways and at different levels of detail, which either paint a very broad picture or a very detailed picture about the respective measures. Furthermore, specific information contents on measures is provided by various data sources, for example complaints about measures, notification of regulations, or the information provided in regulations.

In this chapter, we systematically examine the NTM data commonly applied in trade policy analysis and present main characteristics that should be considered in their application. As stated, the results of the analysis of NTMs crucially depend on the data applied. Hence, knowing details about the data will help to interpret and compare results. Most importantly, the data best suited can be chosen in order to meet the purpose of the respective analysis. We take stock of the key NTM data for trade policy analysis by putting the data into the context of conceptually thinking about NTMs and assess which NTM information is actually available for a meaningful analysis. The ultimate goal of our endeavor would be to reconcile the NTM data available so as to provide comprehensive and compatible datasets about NTMs. This would facilitate the assessment of the impact of NTMs and provide new insights about the measures under review.

The chapter is structured as follows: First, we briefly introduce the classification of NTMs and databases for NTMs for goods and NTMs for services. Note that NTMs are generally distinguished between those for goods and those for services. While NTMs for goods have been well captured by applying a common classification, respective work on NTMs for services is currently under way. With this background, we present the different types of NTMs, data sources, as well as the implications of the data collection. Second, we present a comparative analysis in which we identify the differences and communalities of the key NTM data. Third, we elaborate on the challenges when applying the data to trade policy analysis. The chapter ends with concluding remarks that point out the possibilities of proceeding with NTM data work.

Centre (ITC), Organisation for Economic Co-operation and Development (OECD), World Bank (WB), and the International Monetary Fund (IMF).

2.2 Classification of NTMs

NTMs have been classified by defining the very different types of measures. Indeed, NTMs are all measures that can have an impact on trade but that are not import tariffs. This is a negative concept of the broad term covering all trade-related regulations that should best be interpreted in a wide sense. The measures being imposed by one country could affect the activities of firms of other countries, irrespective of whether the measures are applied at the border, in the imposing country, or in the exporting countries. NTMs are often referred to as "behind-the-border measures" that have a bearing on the production of foreign firms in other countries. Furthermore, the effect of measures can be manifold, interlinked, and different for different types of firms, distinct firm sizes, and so on. As mentioned, they have a potential economic effect by changing quantities traded, or prices, or both (see for example UNCTAD, 2015).

NTMs refer to policy measures and are thus directly linked to the legislation of a country. They are official governmental regulations with reference to legal texts. The emphasis on governmental regulation is particularly relevant for technical measures because some technical measures, like for example standards for products safety, product compatibility, or labels, are also set by the private sector. Private standards developed by the respective sector are not described in legal texts, while possibly referring to legal provisions and/or being endorsed by governments. Initially, private standards have been considered as being voluntary but de facto they have become mandatory since compliance with them is a prerequisite for products being sold (e.g., due to consumer demands or market power of retailers). The differentiation between governmental (public) and private standards has caused confusion and debates, especially on the international floor where governmental measures are subject to the WTO agreements but private standards are not.

Furthermore, the focus is on the measures, no matter whether they are barriers to trade or not. In fact, NTMs have often been referred to as nontariff barriers (NTBs). Using the term NTBs points out the negative trade-hampering effect of measures that would need to be determined in an analysis. The term NTMs is neutral in the sense that both the potential costs and benefits of these measures are considered. The benefits of measures would clearly need to be considered if measures are imposed for public policy goals and if they are not only identified as disguised protectionist measures. This is why it makes sense to look at NTMs in a wider cost-benefit framework, see for example van Tongeren, Beghin, and Marette (2009). It has been argued that some types of NTMs, especially those that convey information related to the respective product or those that impact the product quality, would facilitate international trade across partner countries, in addition to causing trade costs. NTMs could indeed open up markets, thereby functioning as "trade catalysts" even for producers in developing countries where the trade-restricting effect of NTMs has typically been emphasized (World Bank, 2010).

For classifying NTMs, services and goods are dealt with separately. Most effort has been made in defining NTMs and streamlining the classification and data collection for NTMs for goods. For NTMs relevant for trade in services, activities of other data collection efforts have made available rich databases using different categories of services sectors and measures. These disintegrated data make it difficult to compare the information provided by the various data collection methods and different underlying concepts. Experts involved in the topic have been working on merging the available information to a common classification that would help to conduct comparative analysis in order to assess the impact of NTMs in services trade. For example, the World Bank and the OECD have been engaged in large-scale data collections for NTMs for services. Their classifications could be the basis for a common classification that could then be linked to the structure of the General Agreement on Trade in Services (GATS).

Concerning NTMs for goods, a working group of international organizations, researchers, and users has developed a classification, henceforth referred to as the MAST classification. The MAST classification of NTMs is the outcome of intensive discussions, agreement by MAST members, as well as testing in the field through data collection. For the specific goals of the MAST classification, see UNCTAD (2009). The MAST classification has become the standard taxonomy for NTMs in the international trade community, including regional and international organizations. It is important to note that the MAST classification does not contain any judgment on legitimacy of measures, adequacy, or necessity nor does it provide information on the goals that the measures are supposed to achieve.

The current and latest MAST classification is version 2012; see UNCTAD (2015). In addition, UNCTAD (2016) describes the main measures in detail in order to guide data collectors in applying the classification. There is a continuous effort to update measure descriptions and further classify measures, thereby adapting to the realities of trade and meeting information needs. Hence, the MAST classification should

Table 2.1 *MAST NTM classification*

Category		Classification chapter
Imports	Technical measures	**A** Sanitary and Phytosanitary (SPS) Measures
		B Technical Barriers to Trade (TBT)
		C Pre-Shipment Inspection (PSI) and Other Formalities
	Nontechnical measures	**D** Contingent Trade-Protective Measures
		E Nonautomatic Licensing, Quotas, Prohibitions and Quantity-Control Measures Other Than for SPS or TBT Reasons
		F Price-Control Measures, Including Additional Taxes and Charges
		G Finance Measures
		H Measures Affecting Competition
		I Trade-Related Investment Measures
		J Distribution Restrictions
		K Restrictions on Post-Sales Services
		L Subsidies (Excluding Export Subsidies under P7)
		M Government Procurement Restrictions
		N Intellectual Property
		O Rules of Origin
Exports		**P** Export-Related Measures

Source: UNCTAD (2015).

be seen as evolving with updates of more detailed classifications, amendments, and additions to the existing structure.

Table 2.1 presents the MAST classification at the most aggregated of measures. For detailed description about which measures are included in the different chapters, see the Appendix. First of all, import and export measures are differentiated. Import measures target foreign products or foreign firms, as opposed to export measures that target domestic products or domestic firms, while having a bearing on international trade. Import measures are further classified as being either technical measures or nontechnical measures. In contrast, export measures comprise only one chapter, which is currently not further detailed.

Each chapter of the MAST classification is given a capital letter, presenting the broad category of measures. The chapters are then further divided into subcategories by numbering. The subcategories mainly contain details down to the three-digit level. In the definition of the subcategories, the same structure of further specifying measures is applied in order to add logic and to facilitate the comparison across the potentially very different measures. The parallel structure of the subcategories is most visible for SPS measures and TBT measures that are described in chapter A and chapter B, respectively.

Problems with NTMs are not necessarily due to measures per se but can be caused by their implementation and application. In this case, NTMs are referred to as procedural obstacles. When analyzing NTMs, it should be made explicit whether the measure (according to the MAST classification) under review or the implementation of the measure is causing the NTM issues. In the context of NTMs and developing countries, the ITC aims at identifying procedural obstacles in addition to measures that are relevant for developing countries. Surveys have been conducted in order to ask firms directly about NTMs and the related issues they face when exporting and developed a separate classification of NTM obstacles that distinguishes between regulatory obstacles due to measures and procedural obstacles due to the implementation of measures. In the appendix, Table 2.A1 provides the ITC classification; for details see ITC (2014).

2.3 NTM Data: Sources, Information Contents, and Databases

2.3.1 Data Sources

The information about NTMs comes from different sources that are used in the data collection. Table 2.2 provides an overview of different sources of NTM information that are respectively mapped to the databases for NTMs for goods and NTMs for services. In the following, we elaborate on the sources by ordering them according to their completeness and the details they provide about the measures identified:

- inventories of legislation;
- international agreements;
- review of legislation;
- notifications;
- surveys and complaint portals;
- import refusals;
- other sources.

2.3.1.1 Inventories of Legislation

NTM TRAINS. The most direct sources of NTM data are regulatory inventories in which national legislation is meticulously reviewed in

Table 2.2 *Sources and databases of NTM information*

Source	Goods	Services
Inventories of legislation	- NTM TRAINS - OECD PMR Database - WB Investing Across Borders - WB TTBD - OECD Export Restrictions - Global Trade Alert	- WB STRI Database - OECD STRI Database - OECD PMR Database - WB Investing Across Borders - Global Trade Alert
International agreements	- DESTA - UNCTAD BITs Database	- DESTA - GATS commitment schedule - WTO Services RTA - UNCTAD BITs Database
Review of legislation	- WTO Trade Policy Reviews - WTO DG Monitoring Reports - UNCTAD Investment Policy Reviews	- WTO Trade Policy Reviews - WTO DG Monitoring Reports - UNCTAD Investment Policy Reviews
Notifications	- WTO Notifications	- GATS Notifications
Surveys and complaint portals	- ITC NTM Surveys - ITC Trade Obstacle Alert - WTO STC - EU MADB - tradebarriers.org	
Import refusals	- EU RASFF - US FDA OASIS	
Other sources	- USITC CoRe	

Source: Authors' compilation.

order to identify which measures are specified in the legal body of a country and thus imposed by the country. Regulatory inventories require considerable knowledge of the rules and regulation that contain NTMs but also the governmental bodies/ministries making the legislation. For the regulatory inventories, collection methods range from scanning the entire legislation documents to approaching policy-makers or industry for their expert knowledge on specific regulations of detailed products. The latter of course may result in the inventory reflecting expert opinions and judgment to a certain extent. For example, the data on NTMs in the World Bank Investing Across Borders, the OECD Product Market Regulation (OECD PMR), the OECD Services Trade Restrictiveness Index (OECD STRI), and the World Bank (WB STRI) databases are collected by surveys of legal and industry experts as well as officials in the national ministries/administrations. In contrast, the NTM TRAINS database by UNCTAD and ITC involves desk research to identify and classify all legal texts that are published by governments. For the collection, UNCTAD and ITC have been engaging independent and specially trained data collection teams, preferably local people who are familiar with the legal structure of their country.

Mapping the existing body of regulations to the MAST classification, NTM TRAINS is the most comprehensive and rigorous regulatory inventory. The regulations covered have a clear relation to trade by mentioning imports, foreign firms, or the respective partner countries; information about regulations for domestic products and production is not collected.

In addition, international bilateral or plurilateral agreements have been scanned for information about NTMs as they increasingly contain provisions on measures other than tariffs and how they are dealt with by the respective partner countries. International agreements provide important information about NTMs, especially when considering that national legislations tend to refer equally to all foreign countries according to the most-favored nation (MFN) principle of the WTO. Thus, the provisions specified between countries are likely to give more insights into what types of measures are actually applied, including preferential access. Databases on international agreements are for example the Design of Trade Agreements (DESTA) database or WTO Services Regional Trade Agreement (RTA) database.

OECD Product Market Regulation (PMR) Database. The OECD collects data on regulations in order to conduct cross-country comparative analyses. The focus is on economic regulations that target product markets, thereby affecting domestic and foreign firms alike (Nicoletti, Scarpetta, and Boylaud, 1999). The regulatory environment of countries, i.e., the de jure policy settings, is of main interest and hence the regulatory body of the countries under review is not covered entirely. The core of the data collection is a regulatory database that consists of information of the OECD Regulatory Indicators Questionnaires about economy-wide or industry-specific regulatory provisions as well as administrative procedures. In surveys, these questionnaires are completed by country governments. Questions are of closed form leaving space to either answer with a numerical value or select a response from a predefined list. In contrast to open questions, the burden of interpretation thus lies with the respondent rather than with the OECD (Koske et al., 2014).

By applying the information collected in combination with other data (e.g., tariffs, World Bank Doing Business indicators, OECD index of restrictiveness for foreign direct investment; see Blanka, Palerm, and Thomsen, 2010), the OECD constructs the following indices (for details see Koske et al., 2014):

- economy-wide product market regulations (OECD PMR) that capture cross-sector horizontal regulation and indicators relevant for services and manufacturing sectors;
- nonmanufacturing sector regulations that comprise sector-specific regulations affecting entry and operations of professional services, retail distribution, and network sectors;
- internet regulations that cover a subset of regulations particularly relevant for the assessment of a country's approaches to the internet economy;
- indicators for sectors that focus on the governance performance of regulatory bodies: design, implementation, and enforcement of regulations.

OECD Services Trade Restrictiveness Index (OECD STRI). The OECD provides information about policies in eighteen broad services sectors. Next to sector-specific measures, there is also a broad group of general measures that apply horizontally. The following broad categories of measures are covered: restrictions on foreign entry, restrictions on the movement of people, other discriminatory measures, barriers to competition, and regulatory transparency. For each measure, information is provided about which mode of supply of the service, as defined by GATS, is affected, and whether a measure applies to foreign services suppliers only or whether it applies to all operators in the market. In the latter case, the measure is considered as being nondiscriminatory. In addition, it is identified whether a particular measure affects the establishment or operations of business.

Like the OECD PRM database, the data for services are collected by surveys for officials in governments or national administration and are used for the construction of an index. With the index, the qualitative answers about the respective measures are translated into quantitative information. For details about the construction of the index see Grosso et al. (2015).

World Bank Services Trade Restrictiveness Index (WB STRI). The World Bank STRI database contains information on services policies that apply to both domestic and foreign firms in five broad sectors, namely telecommunications, finance, transportation, retail, and professional services. Similar to the OECD databases, the World Bank does not include information about the implementation, the status, or the performance of measures. For each of the sectors, measures are structured along their most dominant mode(s) of supply. The supply of services through commercial presence (mode 3) is most prominent and we thus summarize the corresponding categories of measures collected as an example:

- *Legal form of entry and restrictions on foreign equity* (GATS Article XVI): Measures that affect the establishment of services activities of foreigners. For professional services these are further supplemented by measures that stipulate local licensing requirements linked to the establishment and ownership of businesses.
- *Licensing limits and transparency of licensing requirements* (GATS Article XVI, Article XVII [partly], and Article VI): Measures that limit the number of licenses issued leading to de facto quotas on the number of providers.
- *Restrictions on operations* (GATS Article XVII): Measures that affect the operations of a firm, e.g., national requirements for the board of directors and/or employees, restrictions on the repatriation of earnings. Other measures are sector-specific, e.g., restrictions of the number of ATMs.
- *Relevant aspects of the regulatory environment* (GATS Article VI and XVIII): Measures indicating the independence of the sector regulator, transparency of regulatory changes, and how firms can appeal decisions.

For non-OECD countries, the World Bank collects the respective data via questionnaires that local law firms specialized in or familiar with the policy issues and/or sector at hand are asked to complete. For OECD countries, the data are retrieved from publicly available sources including for example WTO Trade Policy Reviews. Finally, the government or WTO representatives/delegates of the countries under review are asked to validate the information collected.

After the data collection, the information is used to calculate a restrictiveness index. Since only the information about measures for foreign firms is used, the index clearly focuses on the discriminatory effect of the measures under review. In the calculation, the World Bank ranks the measures according to their relevance for the sector as well as according to their effect on firms. Borchert, Gootiiz, and Mattoo (2012) provide the details of the index calculation.

World Bank Investing Across Borders. The data on investment across borders come from surveys of experts such as law professors, professional service providers, export promotion authorities, or chambers of commerce that are asked about the laws affecting FDI. The information encompasses five themes as follows; for details see World Bank (2010):

- *Investing across sectors:* Limits of foreign equity ownership.
- *Starting a foreign investment:* Procedural burden of a company to establish a new business. This concerns questions on the administrational burden but also questions whether, for example, there are special incentive schemes for foreign investors, aspects of land acquisition and administration, or laws governing special economic zones (SEZs).
- *Arbitrating and mediating disputes:* Domestic and international arbitration regimes. The information provided is suitable to assess the quality of the legal environment in a given country. Information about the performance as well as cost estimates are also provided.
- *Converting and transferring currency:* Measures related to foreign exchange inflows, outflows, payments, and accounts. This includes possible limits to repatriation, requirements with respect to foreign service payments, or restrictions on capital gains outflows.
- *Employing skilled expatriates:* Measures that restrict the issuing of sponsored temporary work permits and that determine the procedural ease of or obstacle to receiving them.

UNCTAD Investment Policy Hub. The database is a repository of the investment policies that contain information about FDI policies affecting entry/establishment as well as treatment and protection. Furthermore, information about the general business environment and sectoral regulations is provided. The information is retrieved from bilateral investment treaties and other investment-related agreements, in addition to the WTO Investment Policy reviews conducted mainly for developing countries.

World Bank Temporary Trade Barriers Database (WB TTBD). The TTBD comprises five individual databases, namely the Global Antidumping Database, the Global Countervailing Duties Database (GCVD), the China-Specific Safeguards Database (CSGD), the WTO Disputes Database (DSUD), and the Global Safeguards Database (GSGD). The information is extracted from national legal texts and other governmental communications dealing with the respective measures. The information is mapped to the product codes of the harmonised system (HS) of trade data (HS codes). Combining national information with WTO information sources, in particular notifications, clearly links to reporting to the WTO.

In comparison with other NTM data sources, the time dimension is of course crucial for the TTBD since the measures under review are temporary, i.e., implying a start and an end date of measures being applicable. Indeed, the TTBD contains time series of the respective measures that allow time to be incorporated into the analyses of the measures.

The TTBD is the result of a data collection project for more than thirty countries. It was initiated by Brandeis University and that expanded further via funding by the Development Research Group of the World Bank, and the Global Trade and Financial Architecture (GTFA) project (sponsored by the UK Department for International Development, DFID). Bown (2007, 2016b) presents the detailed development of the TTBD.

Global Trade Alert (GTA). The GTA initiative (coordinated by the Centre for Economic Policy Research, CEPR) brings together experts from different research institutes in seven regions worldwide that examine potentially hampering trade measures, as found in newspapers, journals, and other news items. The GTA experts assess the measures identified according to their trade-related and economic effects and those that are actually found as being trade-hampering are recorded in the GTA. In addition to the information about the measure and the product affected, the country imposing the measure is also reported as well as the country affected. Note that the countries affected are made specific and hence the GTA provides country-specific NTM information rather than being bound to the MFN principle.

Overall, the GTA aims to increase the transparency about NTMs that matter. Identifying measures that are trade-hampering is also the first step of helping to reduce their impact by bringing forward policy options, like mutual recognition for example.

2.3.1.2 International Agreements

International bilateral or plurilateral agreements have been scanned for information about NTMs as they increasingly contain provisions on

NTMs and how they are dealt with by the respective partner countries. International agreements provide important information about NTMs, especially when considering that national legislations tend to equally refer to all foreign countries according to the MFN principle of the WTO. The provisions specified between countries tend to give more insights than regulatory inventories as they point out what type of measures are actually applied for pairs or groups of countries. They also provide information about preferential access for specific partner countries. Databases on international agreements are for example the DESTA database or WTO Services RTA database.

2.3.1.3 Review of Legislation

Information on NTMs can also be found in policy reviews of a country's trade policy and procedures. While WTO Trade Policy Reviews are embedded in the Trade Policy Review Mechanism (TPRM), UNCTAD Investment Policy Reviews are conducted upon request of a country's government. In general, for each of the reviews a screening of relevant policies is undertaken. These are by and large one-off activities, or with relatively large time intervals between reviews. In contrast, news, publications, and countries' policy initiatives are continuously screened in the GTA, thereby painting the "just-in-time" picture on policies that could have an effect on trade.

WTO Trade Policy Reviews. The reviews are a rich source of information about NTMs. The information is provided in text format with the MAST classification of measures or product codes not applied. Furthermore, country-pair-specific information is usually not reported on. This makes the application of the information in the trade policy reviews tedious and time-consuming. However, some information may directly clarify WTO notifications, helping to understand concerns and/or to simply provide background information about NTMs.

Note that the frequency of each WTO member being reviewed varies according to its worldwide trade position. For example, the four largest trading countries come under scrutiny once every two years, whereas other countries are reviewed less often. The reviews report on trade of goods as well as services and intellectual property. The latter expands the scope of the initial reviews as agreed under the WTO Uruguay agreements in 1995.

2.3.1.4 Notification

WTO Notifications. Notifications to the WTO constitute an important source of NTM data. WTO members are asked to notify their regulations as an important means of transparency and predictability of policies. The obligation of WTO members to notify measures is formulated and compliance has been encouraged throughout the years.[2] Bacchetta, Richtering, and Santana (2012) provide details on the development of WTO notifications. The notification obligations are formulated individually per topic, and the procedures of the notification, including information required, differ per topic.

Notifications are about changes of laws and regulations as well as their administration The measures notified are described as text, with NTM code defined by the MAST classification mentioned but not provided at the detailed level as in NTM TRAINS. Some kind of mapping and text mining could be used to assign the NTM codes as well as HS codes (see Ghodsi, Reiter, and Stehrer, 2015). The changes of the measures are supposed to be reported before their implementation by the reporting WTO member. Other WTO members could react, perhaps even influence the respective measure being proposed and notified, such that measures reported as WTO notifications may be implemented differently or may even be withdrawn. This information is not recorded, thereby leaving the question of implementation open.

Overall, countries seem to notify more measures than asked for. Notifications reflect the due diligence of countries' activities of policy-making as well as regulatory traditions. For those countries that are struggling to correctly notify, support measures and assistance have been made available by the WTO.

2.3.1.5 Surveys and Complaint Portals

Surveys or complaint portals gather the perceptions about the impact of NTMs from a business point of view. Such information is complementary to the inventory or listings of regulations or changes of regulations, that are generated by other collection initiatives. In surveys or complaint portals, the private sector can indicate if a certain measure poses challenges to trading activities and to what degree. Due to the complex nature of NTMs and the many combinations of measures and products affected,

[2] WTO members could also notify measures of other WTO members. These notifications are called reverse notifications as the reporting country does not implement the measures. With the establishment of committees for Special Trade Concerns (STCs), WTO members have increasingly made use of raising their concerns in these committees rather than notifying the measures of others to the WTO as reverse notifications.

data collections are large-scale, resource-intensive initiatives, usually embedded in other supporting activities (e.g., workshops).

In surveys, business sector representatives that are actually or potentially affected by the respective measures are asked about the measures and the impact of the measures on them. Such surveys are obviously crucial for understanding the effect of measures but also for identifying which measures actually matter. While surveys provide first-hand information about measures, survey results must carefully be dealt with due to potential biases and inconsistent replies. Surveys must be developed and conducted in a scientifically sound manner, otherwise they may become mere ad hoc opinion polls. The data collection by surveys should entail some kind of quality control in order to assure the data represent the measures and the corresponding issues correctly. This, for example, involves an appropriate selection of experts to conduct the reviews, the identification of suitable persons to complete the questionnaires, as well as the provision of training of those conducting the surveys, if necessary. Furthermore, testing a country's responses for internal consistency (e.g., whether responses to questions in a country survey contradict each other, or not), and cross-checking with results of other countries increase the likelihood of building a dataset enabling cross-country analyses.

Unlike NTM inventories or notifications, surveys about NTMs provide information about which particular measures cause difficulties for businesses or an entire sector and thus matter and have an economic impact. Note that surveys about NTMs shed light on perceptions about measures, and are not necessarily complete, since they focus on the measure that businesses actually report difficulties with. There are several initiatives of conducting NTM surveys in several countries organized by several organizations and institutions. However, NTM surveys often remain limited since they focus on one specific product/sector, one specific country/region, and results generate insights in a specific case study only.

ITC NTM Surveys. ITC has conducted (telephone and face-to-face) large-scale business surveys about exporters' and importers' experiences with trade-related regulations and procedures. They provide comparable information across twenty-three countries, where the survey has been conducted, mainly developing countries. Sectors are covered in a representative sample, whereby products are sometimes only described and thus appear without product code. NTMs are referred to by the MAST classification, while the difficulties reported are categories by the classification of trade obstacles. Note that obstacles of measures can be caused by the individual measure itself, by its implementation and procedures related to the implementation, as well as by the prevailing situation in the country that determines the capability and (technical) facilities necessary for meeting regulations and proving compliance with NTMs.

ITC (2015) presents an overview of the results of the ITC NTM surveys. Results depict the number of export and import businesses affected by NTMs of partner countries, as well as relevant trade-related domestic regulations. Given the sampling methods, shares with regard to the entire sector can be calculated in order to point out the impact and possibly costs caused by the respective measures. Furthermore, insights are provided about which measures cause problems and what kind of problems occur most frequently. For example, the lack of access to relevant information is often mentioned, and transparency and knowledge seems to be a crucial bottleneck for NTM compliance.

EU Market Access Database (MADB). The EU MADB of the European Commission contains a complaint register for EU firms that face NTMs when exporting to partner countries outside the EU. The complaints reported are systematically collected, evaluated, and made public if considered as being relevant from the perspective of the EU member states. Furthermore, the EC's efforts to remove the obstacles caused by the NTMs complained about are also reported and traced back. Information about the current state of affairs in the NTM matter is provided.

It should be noted that other groups of countries or individual countries have similar complaint registries in place; for example, the Tripartite Free Trade Area of Common Markets for East and Southern Africa (COMESA), the East Africa Community (EAC), and the Southern African Development Community (SADC).[3]

WTO Specific Trade Concerns (STC). The STC database comprises the WTO members' concerns about SPS and TBT measures. Any WTO member can raise a specific trade concern but usually groups of WTO members formulate concerns together. The WTO Secretariat collects the respective concerns mentioned in the minutes of the meetings of the members. Information on the concerns are thus scattered in WTO documents. From recent efforts of the WTO this information has been transferred to a database retrievable via the I-TIP portal (see WTO, 2015).

The information on the WTO STCs is provided for products, whereby the country or countries imposing the measure causing the concern are

[3] www.tradebarriers.org.

mentioned as well as the countries/countries affected and hence raising the respective concern.

The WTO STCs constitute information complementary to the WTO notification, as well as NTM inventories like NTM TRAINS. More specifically, STCs provide insights about measures that matter since WTO members would not raise their concerns if they were not relevant for them. As such, STCs can be considered to convey information about NTMs and the problems that they cause and that businesses share with their governments. Governments subsequently submit these business issues as concerns to the WTO.

2.3.1.6 Import Refusals

Governments monitor the entry of products by inspections and checks at the border. In addition to actual import refusals, alerts are used in order to inform about products that violate the rules of the importing country. In general, products for which alerts are given are held at the border until clearance or refusal, depending on the result of thorough inspections. Not all shipments of products can be checked in detail and hence risk-based criteria help to focus on which shipment of products and countries of origin should be examined in detail. Databases on the results of such border inspections, both alerts and refusals, provide insights if the origin actually complies with the requirements of the importing country.

Inspections are usually related to food products since food safety constitutes an important task of public policies by governments. With regard to NTMs, information about import alerts and refusals is thus generally on SPS measures that are used to ensure food safety and/or consumer protection. The latter for example includes issues of adulteration, misbranding by using misleading statements on labels, or lack of appropriate labeling and packaging.

Databases for example are the food-related import refusals of the US Food and Drugs Administration (FDA) or the EU Rapid Alert System for Food and Feed (RASFF).

2.3.1.7 Other

Other sources comprise government initiatives to provide an overview of NTMs that are relevant for the respective country. Usually, the exporting perspective is taken, and hence the measures of partner countries are covered. Such initiatives may bring together national experts on specific measures in order to assemble the legislation that is relevant for supplying foreign markets.

The United States International Trade Commission (USITC) has been engaging in the collection of existing NTM information that is made publicly available as a compilation of reported NTMs in the so-called CoRe NTM database. The CoRe database draws on the existing documentation of measures, specifically the WTO Trade Policy Reviews, the US reports on foreign trade barriers, the EU MABD complaint register as well as the Japanese government reports on compliance by major trade partners with trade agreements (JEMETI reports). The database thus includes 109 countries worldwide and covers all types of reported NTMs for all products, but the link to the product level is not always made. The CoRe database is about information on issues of NTMs that are reported. It is not an inventory of regulations, like the NTM TRAINS database. Reviewing the source documentation of measures by the respective countries, the different types of measures and information on the issues, i.e., type of barrier, are coded according to the specific CoRe classification; see Eaton et al. (2013).

2.3.2 Type of NTM Information

The information provided in the database consists of four main elements: the measure of course, the product affected, the country imposing the measure, and the country affected by the measure. The details about the measures under review range from noting down their mere presence to information on the actual provisions. Typically, they take the following form:

- *Binary* variables that indicate whether a measure is there or not. These can be simply in the form of 1/0, or yes/no.
- *Numerical* variables reflecting quantitative attributes of an NTM, e.g., percentage of foreign equity ownership, maximum residual limits, or maximum weight.
- *Text* that can be a plain description of a regulation (required info on a label, container clearance procedures, etc.); usually the link to the regulatory text is provided. Sometimes also the date of entry into force is provided, which adds important information in particular for ad hoc emergency or temporary measures.
- *Categorical* variables are used to classify measures, e.g., whether a measure is discriminatory or not.
- *Ordinal* variables indicating a ranking along a chosen dimension, e.g., a five-point scale of openness from “open without restrictions” to

"completely closed" or to signal the status of implementation (not/partially/fully implemented), as well as the perceived restrictiveness of a measure in business surveys.
- *Computed indicators* combining different information contents, e.g., restrictiveness indexes, count, or frequency ratios.

The information provided per measure varies in the different databases. While some databases provide considerable details, e.g., numerical information about maximum residue levels, others state if a measure is present or has changed. For example, a quota on intra-corporate transferees can be a binary piece of information (country A has a quota), a numerical statement (three transferees per company), or an ordinal variable (ten-point scale indicating the degree of restrictiveness of such a quota).

2.3.3 *Trade Facilitation and Compliance*

Since the impact of NTMs on trade is not only determined by the characteristics of the measure itself but also by the importers' and exporters' compliance capacity (or their trade/institutional environment more generally) information about different dimensions of trade facilitation is a useful complement to the available NTM data. Table 2.3 summarizes the main data sources for such indicators and highlights that these data are by and large available for a wide range of countries. Particularly, efforts by the OECD as well as World Bank have led to rich sets of indicators allowing creation of a comprehensive picture of a country's trading environment in this context. The data are mainly generated via desk research (e.g., most of the OECD indicators) or surveys among experts, practitioners, and academics in the field of logistics (e.g., World Bank Logistics Performance Index (LPI) or Global Express Association). Furthermore, the World Bank Doing Business indicators are available in time-series (starting in 2006), while other data sources provide a limited number of years. Sometimes data are only available for one or two years. Table 2.3 actually combines data availability for 2014 and 2015.

In a few cases, trade facilitation indicators could be directly linked to NTMs. For example, the quality of infrastructure section of the World Bank LPI contains a question with regard to the competence of domestic health and SPS authorities, and the United Nations Economic and Social Commission for Asia and the Pacific (ESCAP) asks about the state of

Table 2.3 *Trade facilitation measures*

Source	Category	No. indicators	Max no. countries
Global Express Association	Customs Efficiency	16	127
	Post-release Processes	9	120
	Transparency	3	122
OECD Trade Facilitation Indicators	Advance rulings	12	152
	Appeal procedure	13	171
	External border agency cooperation	6	152
	Fees and charges	6	152
	Formalities – Automation	6	152
	Formalities – Documents	6	151
	Governance and impartiality	11	165
	Information availability	26	165
	Internal border agency cooperation	4	152
	Involvement of the trade community	6	163
	Formalities – Procedures	17	153
ESCAP	Trade Facilitation and Paperless Trade	23	117
WB Logistics Performance Index	Changes in the logistics environment	8	117
	Competence and quality of services	13	117
	Efficiency of processes	7	117
	Level of fees and charges	10	117
	Quality of infrastructure	7	117
	Sources of major delays	5	117
	Domestic Performance	29	116
	International LPI	8	160
WB Doing Business	Trading Across Borders	17	189

Source: Compiled by authors as of 2015.

implementation of electronic SPS certificate exchange. In addition, the United Nations Industrial Development Organization (UNIDO) collects measures (not listed in Table 2.3) related to the trade standards compliance capacity of forty-nine countries (mainly developing countries).

These indicators reflect the different areas of a modern infrastructure (e.g., metrology, inspection, accreditation, or testing) that support the compliance with standards. Such information would be useful to better understand and explain the NTM impact.

2.4 Official NTM Database - Availability, Scope

2.4.1 Geographic Coverage

NTM data have been collected for many countries. Comprehensive cross-country analyses require a sufficiently large number of countries such that the results about measures can be generalized or consistently reported for groups of countries. In such analyses, the question of whether NTMs affect developing countries more than developed countries, for example, may be of particular interest. In addition, certain countries or groups of countries may impose NTMs more frequently than other countries or may impose specific NTMs that other countries do not apply.

Figure 2.1 illustrates the country coverage of the main NTM databases. For goods, the largest country coverage is available for the WTO notifications (138 countries) and the NTM TRAINS database (77 countries). For services, the country coverage is largest for the GATS schedules of commitments (160 countries) and the World Bank STRI database (103 countries). Comprising information about NTMs for both goods and services, the Global Trade Alert (169 countries) and the WTO Trade Policy Reviews (120 countries) show a large country coverage. In comparison, other databases cover considerably smaller numbers of countries. For example, the EU Market Access Database (MADB) provides complaints for 43 countries, and data for ITC's business surveys is available for 23 countries. It should be noted that Figure 2.1 adds the number of countries for which information is reported across the available years. This means that a country is included in the calculation of the country coverage if at least one data point is reported at one point in time.

As illustrated, data gaps with respect to the country coverage are significant, despite large-scale data collection efforts. This is particularly true for databases with complex, resource-intensive data collection projects such as the ITC surveys or regulatory inventories of the NTM TRAINS database. The country coverage tends to be higher for data collection efforts that have been institutionalized (i.e., the WTO) and/or

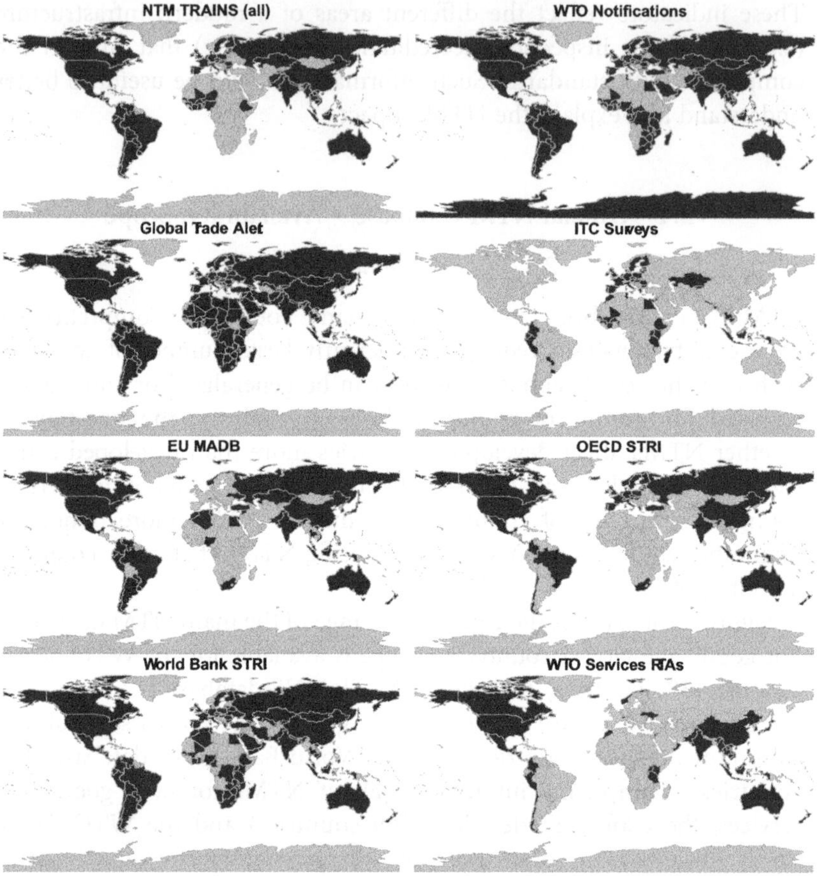

Figure 2.1 Geographical overview of NTM data availability (country coverage).

that have been applied in some kind of routine of regular collection mechanisms (e.g., the GTA). In addition, some databases have been constrained by whether countries actually have certain policy instruments in place (e.g., regional trade agreements (RTAs) with a services component), by their institutional focus (e.g., OECD databases), or by the participation of the business community (i.e., a complaint portal like the EU MADB).

There is usually differentiation between the imposing country and countries affected. The databases reviewed show that measures are often imposed on all countries, thereby reflecting the MFN principle of treating all partner countries equally. Information about NTMs between two specific countries or groups of countries is not always provided. By definition, some databases exclusively contain information about one country imposing NTMs on one or several specific partner countries. They, for example, include the measures reported under the MFN exemptions of the GATS, RTAs, as well as the complaints about NTMs affecting specific countries. In addition, the GTA, the WTO notifications, and NTM TRAINS identify the countries affected, where possible. However, the total share of country-specific bilateral or country-specific plurilateral information appears to be relatively small in the WTO notifications (about 15 percent of the measures). In NTM TRAINS, about 34 percent of the measures are reported for specific partner countries (or groups thereof), while 66 percent of the measures apply to all partner countries (MFN). NTM data are usually collected on a country level.

2.4.2 *Time Coverage*

Table 2.4 presents the availability of NTM data over time. We find the longest time coverage for the WTO Notifications, NTM TRAINS, and databases of trade and investment agreements (i.e., Design of Trade Agreements Database [DESTA] and the UNCTAD database of Bilateral Investment Treaties [UNCTAD BITs]). The scope of the data differs, though. For example, while the first fifteen years of the WTO Notifications exclusively contain temporary trade barriers (antidumping and countervailing measures), the number of measures has significantly increased since 1995, partly due to the notification requirements under the WTO SPS and TBT Agreement (i.e., members started notifying policy changes to the WTO). NTM TRAINS data, where the date of when the measure entered into force is recorded, only include those measures that are still in force today. It is only in very rare cases nonactive measures that have been withdrawn are found in any of the databases.

Additionally, information for a relatively large number of years can also be found in the WTO Trade Policy Reviews and Services RTA databases as well as the EU MADB. However, it should be noted that the information on all measures and all countries is not necessarily available for each year. The time coverage also depends on reporting cycles and/or the conclusion of agreements that include reporting commitments, provisions for NTM inventories, and maybe even solutions to overcome NTM issues.

The OECD and World Bank STRI databases cover a limited number of years only. They can hence be considered as providing a snapshot of the

Table 2.4 *Summary of NTM databases' time coverage*

Collection framework	Database	Time coverage	Comment
Inventories of legislation	- NTM TRAINS	1960–2016	Date of measure into force
	- OECD PMR Database	1998–2013	Inventory (1998, 2003, 2008, 2013)
	- WB Investing Across Borders	2011–12	Policy inventory as of data collection
	- WB TTBD	1980–2015	Date of measure into force
	- OECD Export Restrictions	1996–2014	Year of policy inventory
	- Global Trade Alert	2008–16	Date of measure into force
	- WB STRI Database	2008–12	Policy inventory as of data collection
	- OECD STRI Database	2014–16	Year of policy inventory
International agreements	- DESTA	1949–2016	Year of agreement
	- UNCTAD BITs Database	1957–2016	Year of agreement
	- GATS schedule	1995	Year of agreement
	- WTO Services RTA	1994–2016	Year of agreement
Review of legislation	- WTO Trade Policy Reviews	1996–2016	Year of policy review
	- WTO DG Monitoring Reports	2008–16	Date of implementation
	- UNCTAD Investment Policy Reviews	1999–2016	Year of report
Notifications	- WTO Notifications	1960–2016	Date of measure into force
	- GATS Notifications	2001–16	Date of notification
Surveys and complaint portals	- ITC NTM Surveys	2010–16	Year of survey data collection
	- ITC Trade Obstacle Alert	2014–16	Date of complaint
	- WTO STC	1995–2016	Date of STC raised
	- EU Market Access Database	1996–2016	Date of complaint
	- tradebarriers.org	2004–16	Date of complaint

Table 2.4 (*cont.*)

Collection framework	Database	Time coverage	Comment
Import refusals	- EU RASFF	1979–2016	Date of border refusal
	- US FDA OASIS	2002–16	Date of border refusal
Other sources	- USITC CoRe NTM Database	2009–12	Year of measure into force

Source: Compiled by authors as of 2016.

NTMs in services in a certain year. The OECD started to provide annual updates of its STRI measures and underlying regulatory information. Since 1998, the OECD PMR database has been updated every five years. While the most recent data may not be readily available, a comprehensive account of the regulations is available for specific years (namely, 1997, 2003, 2008, and 2013), in which the NTM data were updated. Lacking information for consecutive years, the data remain available for intervals only. However, given that the recorded policy measures do not change very frequently, interval data may be preferred for panel data estimations anyway.

2.4.3 Coverage of Type of Measures per MAST Chapter

Table 2.5 summarizes the data availability of measures classified by the respective MAST chapter for three databases: NTM TRAINS, WTO Notifications, and the GTA. The measures are summed over measure IDs and do not take into account any metric of stringency (e.g., number of HS codes affected by measure). Note that in the case of NTM TRAINS data MAST chapters included in the collection exercise may differ per country. Thus, a limited country coverage may simply be due to the fact that data for a particular MAST chapter were only collected for a few countries (e.g., finance measures) and not necessarily because of a limited application of the measure itself.

Keeping this in mind, the number of measures per MAST chapter differs considerably between the three databases. According to the NTM TRAINS data, the fifty-nine countries[4] reviewed have predominantly

[4] In this case the EU is counted as one entity.

Table 2.5 *Number of countries and measures per MAST chapter*

	NTM TRAINS		WTO Notifications		GTA	
Chapter	Total no. of measures	Countries	Total no. of notification	Countries	Total no. of measures	Countries
A SPS	18,165	59	15,084	123	451	17
B TBT	14,645	59	21,926	138	482	15
C Pre-Shipment Inspection	524	49				
D Contingent Trade Protection	484	20	5,472	65	10,881	86
E Nonautomatic Licensing	839	56	2,252	59	25,494	92
F Price-Control Measures	646	54			2,379	27
G Finance Measures	42	17			547	11
H Competition	57	24	279	37		
I Trade-Related Investment	13	7			9,523	62
J Distribution Restrictions	9	6				
L Subsidies	1	1			33,495	80
M Government Procurement	1	1			25,657	30
N Intellectual Property					113	6
O Rules of Origin	2	2				
P Export-Related Measures	2,786	59	409	24	44,868	99

Source: Compiled by authors as of 2016.

imposed SPS and TBT measures. Measures falling in other MAST chapters have been found far less frequently – even when country coverage was comparable to SPS and TBT measures. This also holds when considering that typically measures relating to preshipment inspections, licensing, or finance cover a wider array of products.

In comparison, due to the underlying reporting framework, WTO notifications are limited to fewer MAST chapters. Similar to NTM TRAINS the vast number of measures are SPS and TBTs, however with a much higher country coverage. Since the underlying collection methodology is different, it is uncertain to what degree measures in the two databases overlap.

In contrast to NTM TRAINS and the WTO notifications, GTA data contain a significant amount of measures related to government procurement and subsidies, with relatively high country coverage. The same holds for licensing, export, and trade-related investment measures.

2.4.4 *Coverage of Sectors*

Information about NTMs for goods is collected on the product level (HS codes). On the basis of these product codes Table 2.6 presents the number of NTMs reported on the sector level for all available years. Obviously, the number of total measures is much higher compared to Table 2.5 since a measure can apply to products across different sectors. Note that only those observations that contain a product code are considered. This means that only c. 40 percent of the notifications to the WTO are included. About 60 percent of the WTO notifications do not have an assigned HS code (Ghodsi et al., 2015). In contrast, NTM TRAINS and the GTA report their measures with the corresponding HS code (six-digit or even more detailed), which enables product-level analysis without worrying whether missing product codes are random or to some degree systematic.

As shown, in the UNCTAD and WTO databases most incidences of NTMs are found in animal and vegetables products (I and II), prepared foodstuffs (IV), and products of the chemical and allied industries (VI). It is interesting to note that for WTO notifications on average more countries notify NTMs in the primary and food sectors than in the manufacturing sectors. In that sense UNCTAD's data are more consistent in that the legislative inventory systematically captures measures across all product groups. In the GTA, the number of alerts is comparatively high for metals (XV), mineral products (V), machinery (XVI), and

Table 2.6 *Goods NTMs per sector*

	UNCTAD		WTO		GTA	
HS section	Countries	Measures	Countries	Measures	Countries	Measures
I Live animals; animal products	59	8,152	115	9,095	146	468
II Vegetable products	59	14,365	117	7,121	136	570
III Animal or vegetable fats and oils	59	2,611	76	658	119	153
IV Prepared foodstuffs	59	7,599	118	4,250	157	468
IX Wood and articles of wood	57	1,442	65	438	109	159
V Mineral products	59	3,035	77	692	147	954
VI Products of the chemical or allied industries	59	8,720	90	3,248	148	888
VII Plastics and articles thereof	59	2,657	69	1,047	139	439
VIII Raw hides and skins	57	1,028	43	247	103	147
X Pulp of wood, waste, and scrap	55	1,019	49	343	127	198
XI Textiles	59	1,946	55	1,222	129	413
XII Footwear, etc.	54	794	38	208	111	96
XIII Articles of stone, cement, etc.	55	1,258	59	539	121	287
XIV Natural or cultured pearls	55	994	23	136	82	118
XIX Arms and ammunition	57	843	23	78	70	52
XV Base metal and articles thereof	58	2,238	71	2,127	139	1,416
XVI Machinery and mechanical appliances	58	3,613	75	2,325	147	904
XVII Vehicles, aircraft, vessels	57	2,236	56	843	144	759
XVIII Optical, medical, or surgical	59	1,915	53	527	121	226
XX Misc. manufactured articles	57	2,161	51	602	128	202
XXI Works of art	51	619	19	59	26	14

Source: Compiled by authors as of 2016.

chemicals (VI). Similar to NTM TRAINS country coverage is more consistent across sectors.

Table 2.7 presents the number of observations for services by mapping the available data to the first level of the Services Sectoral Classification List (SSCL/W/120) covered under the GATS. As mentioned, the information provided in the different databases varies and thus the figures presented are hardly comparable across databases. Furthermore, the number of subsectors that differ according to classification influences the number of observations per SSCL sector. For example, the relatively high number of commitments and reservations as well as GTA measures in business and transport services could be partly explained by the various subchapters that are defined in the sectoral classification. The more subchapters, the more observations are expected at the aggregate level.

Overall, most observations are reported for business, communication, distribution, financial, and transport services. These sectors are relatively comprehensively covered by the GATS commitments, by the applied MFN policy (reported by the World Bank and OECD STRIs respectively) as well as by bilateral preferences (reported by the WTO Services RTA). In combination, these databases provide important insights on NTMs for services.

2.5 Challenges When Applying the NTMs Databases

Analyzing NTMs is not straightforward due to the complexity of measures. Usually, gravity estimations are used to gauge the impact of measures on trade by generating estimates of NTMs in terms of ad valorem equivalents. These estimates for NTMs can subsequently be used in simulation models in order to derive the economic and welfare effects of NTMs. In most studies, all NTMs are investigated in such a standard analysis. All sectors or broad categories of sectors and all countries or broad categories of regions are considered. There are also more detailed studies focusing on certain measures, sectors, and countries, e.g., the effect of SPS measures on the agri-food sector in developing countries.

In addition to limits of the analytical methodology, the studies in the literature show that the data constitute a common challenge for the analysis of NTMs. First of all, the data provided may be not complete or may not be coded according to the agreed categories and classifications, e.g., product and country codes as well as the NTM codes according to the MAST classification. Text mining in the regulatory

Table 2.7 *Services NTMs per sector as defined in GATS**

GATS sector	WTO Services RTA		World Bank STRI		OECD STRI		GTA
	Countries	Commitments / reservations	Countries	Indicators per country	Countries	Indicators per country	Measures
1 Business	45	4,124	103	67–70	40	46–63	517
2 Communication	41	1,901	103	51–3	40	1–61	106
3 Construction	31	600			40	59	241
4 Distribution	38	1,001	103	53	40	4–68	143
5 Education	38	486					33
6 Environmental	34	577					42
7 Financial	43	1,344	103	56–62	40	3–91	408
8 Health	28	241					53
9 Tourism	45	706					40
10 Recreation	36	916					102
11 Transport	43	3,322	103	46–58	40	0–20	404
12 Other	29	224					45

* The World Bank and OECD STRI, and GTA database do not use the SSCL sectoral classification. The sector mapping has been approximated.

Source: Compiled by authors as of 2015.

documents can help to retrieve and complete the missing information. However, in some cases challenges remain. From a conceptual point of view, the main challenges in the NTM analysis are identified as follows:

Regulatory Systems of NTMs. The relations between measures are often not appropriately reflected in the data. In most cases, many measures are imposed on one product or service, and measures imposed on this product/service could mean that another product may be less regulated. The set of measures imposed in a regulatory system are linked and interdependent, such that one measure can influence the outcome of another measure and the other way around. In conclusion, measures cannot be evaluated in isolation and the regulatory system should somewhat be considered when analyzing NTMs. The OECD and the World Bank, for example, have taken the "hierarchy of measures" into account for deriving their respective indices measuring the trade restrictiveness of NTMs for services.

Following the idea of regulatory systems of NTMs raises the question about how they are governed at the international, national, and local level. National authorities, for example, seem to regulate most NTMs, but some NTMs may be governed on the regional or local level. While some indication may be drawn from the OECD PMR data, data on the governance of NTMs are not systematically collected but would be relevant for understanding NTMs and their impact.

Implementation and Enforcement. Information about the implementation and enforcement of measures is not readily available. In addition to details about the measures, it is equally important to collect information about whether measures are applied and how they are applied. The NTM impact crucially depends on if the measures under review are actually implemented and enforced. Besides, the implementation and not the measure per se could cause the NTM impact. Some idea about implementation and enforcement is provided by those databases that report the beginning date and end date of a measure, or the date of enforcement of the regulation that describes the measure. Sometimes surveys provide information about procedural obstacles relating to the implementation of measures rather than the measures themselves.

In the context of procedural obstacles, institutions are often mentioned as being unsatisfactorily equipped or lacking the capacity to deal with NTMs. For example, it can be argued that the impact of NTMs on exporters and importers of a country is to a large degree influenced by the country's institutions related to the official national quality infrastructure engaged in technical regulations (both SPS and TBT), e.g., standard setting, conformity assessment, and custom authorities of a country. The World Bank reports on domestic LPI and UNIDO reports on compliance with standards thereby shedding some light on these institutional matters. However, information is neither systematically collected nor reported for specific measures.

Restrictiveness of Measures. Determining the restrictiveness of measures can be considered a main issue in the analysis of the impact of NTMs. Restrictiveness is essentially a relative concept, that is regulations are somehow compared when determining their restrictiveness and impact. The impact of measures imposed by a trade partner depends on whether they are more restrictive than domestic regulations, as well as more restrictive than the measures imposed by other countries. Comparable information in details is needed for measuring the restrictiveness across countries, e.g., numerical values of maximum residue levels, fees, tax rates, or service charges as well as the size of quotas imposed. This goes far beyond the commonly provided information about whether a measure is in place or not. Note that it could be argued that the NTM impact is caused by the mere differences of measures rather than by how much they actually differ. Following this line of thought, regulatory differences (rather than the restrictiveness of measures) could be investigated by comparing qualitative information on regulatory systems.

Beyond the Economic Effects of NTMs. Applying the available NTM data, research has been focusing on the economic effects of NTMs. In a few studies, public good aspects have been included by applying a cost-benefit framework. Other studies have looked at welfare effects that are economically defined. From a policy point of view, it would be interesting to know more about the effects of NTMs on aspects broader than the economic impact, e.g., the effects on market structure, different types of business and households, as well as health and/or environmental effects. Such kinds of analyses require additional data and (outcome) indicators in relation to NTMs and possibly the policy objectives behind them.

2.6 Conclusion

NTMs have been widely discussed and investigated, but information on them still limits their analysis. A main challenge for the analysis is related to the NTM data available. Often, details about the NTM data applied is not reported although such details are paramount for ensuring the quality and an appropriate interpretation of results. This chapter brings together information about NTMs and data sources that are officially available. We assess the available NTM data systematically in order to provide information about their characteristics and the conceptual background that needs to be considered in NTM analyses.

Data sources of NTMs usually provide information about the measures, products, and the countries imposing the measure as well as the countries being affected by the measure. NTMs for goods and NTMs for services are dealt with separately. NTMs for goods have been classified according to the international MAST classification, which was initiated by international organizations and experts working on NTM-related topics. For NTMs for services, the first steps of mapping different classifications have been undertaken and will facilitate the analysis in the near future.

The level of detail about measures differs considerably. Information provided comprises binary variables that indicate whether a measure is in place or not, ordinal variables indicating a ranking along a chosen dimension or numerical variables reflecting quantitative attributes of an NTM, e.g., percentage of foreign equity ownership, maximum residual limits, or maximum weight. In addition, detailed texts that describe measures and their implementation may be provided in some databases. In databases of goods NTMs, the main focus is on information about whether a measure is in place or not (binary variable). However, links to further information and original texts are frequently provided. Databases of NTMs for services in addition provide information about the ranking sequence and/or indication of restrictiveness of measures. This adds a dimension to NTM data for services allowing for a more detailed analysis.

Moreover, there have been gaps in the country and product coverage. This means that in some databases the NTM information is missing for certain countries and NTMs may also not be reported for all products. Furthermore, databases as well as studies do not necessarily apply existing definitions of measures. In the case of NTMs for goods, some surveys for example do not apply the MAST classification. Similarly, products are not always assigned to proper product classification codes. This makes the combined use of databases difficult and often unfeasible, given time and budget constraints. Thus, researchers usually omit those observations for which the full information is not available.

Another main challenge of the NTM data relates to the question whether measures are specific to countries or specific to products. Often countries impose NTMs on all partner countries, or measures could be horizontally applicable on all products or certain groups of products.

In addition, information about the implementation and enforcement of measures is by and large missing. As the NTM impact crucially depends on whether the measures under review are actually implemented and enforced, such information would need to be added or assumptions need to be made.

Since the various NTM databases contain different information contents and details about measures, using different NTM data in combination would bring forward the analysis and interpretation of results. Linking the information contents of different NTM data would involve considerable data work and text mining, and assumptions would need to be made in order to bring the different pieces of information together. Furthermore, measures are not always uniquely identified, which could easily lead to the double counting of measures. Special attention and a careful merging by experts that understand the data are prerequisite to ensure consistency.

Combined and integrated NTM data would not only help to provide a more complete picture of which measure is imposed on which product by which country and for what purpose, but would also give an indication about the enforcement of the measure. Furthermore, adding information about complaint registers, for example, could point out which measures actually matter in international trade, in addition to identifying the difficulties that businesses face due to the presence per se. Information beyond the mere existence of measures would add content and hence value to the analysis of NTMs, thereby building up knowledge about the many aspects of NTMs.

Appendix: Description of NTMs for Goods According to the MAST Classification

Chapter A deals with sanitary and phytosanitary measures, which are generally referred to as SPS. It gathers measures such as restriction for substances and ensuring food safety, and those for preventing dissemination of disease or pests. Chapter A also includes all conformity-assessment measures related to food safety, such as certification, testing and inspection, and quarantine.

Chapter B collects technical measures, also called TBT. It refers to measures such as labeling, standards on technical specifications and quality requirements, and other measures protecting the environment. As in the case for SPS, chapter B also includes all conformity-assessment measures related to technical requirements, such as certification, testing, and inspection.

Chapter C classifies the measures related to preshipment inspections and other customs formalities.

Chapter D groups the contingent measures, i.e., those measures implemented to counteract particular adverse effects of imports in the market of the importing country, including measures aimed at unfair foreign trade practices. They include antidumping, countervailing, and safeguard measures.

Chapter E includes licensing, quotas, and other quantity control measures, including tariff rate quotas. Chapter F lists price-control measures implemented to control or affect the prices of imported goods. Among the examples are those to support the domestic price of certain products when the import prices of these goods are lower; to establish the domestic price of certain products because of price fluctuation in domestic markets, or price instability in a foreign market; or to increase or preserve tax revenue. This category also includes measures other than tariffs measures that increase the cost of imports in a similar manner (para-tariff measures).

Chapter G refers to measures restricting the payments of imports, for example when the access and cost of foreign exchange is regulated. It also includes measures imposing restrictions on the terms of payment.

Chapter H includes those measures affecting competition – those that grant exclusive or special preferences or privileges to one or more limited group of economic operators. They refer mainly to monopolistic measures, such as State trading, sole importing agencies, or compulsory national insurance or transport.

Chapter I deals with trade-related investment measures, and groups the measures that restrict investment by requiring local content or requesting that investment be related to export in order to balance imports.

Chapters J and K relate to the way products, or services connected to the products, are marketed after imports. Chapter J, on distribution restrictions, refers to restrictive measures related to the internal distribution of imported products.

Chapter K deals with restrictions on postsales services, for example, restrictions on the provision of accessory services.

Chapter L contains measures that relate to the subsidies that affect trade.

Chapter M, on government procurement restriction measures, refers to the restrictions bidders may encounter when trying to sell their products to a foreign government.

Chapter N gathers restrictions related to intellectual property measures and intellectual property rights.

Chapter O, on rules of origin, groups the measures that restrict the origin of products or their inputs.

Chapter P is on export measures. It groups the measures a country applies to its exports. It includes export taxes, export quotas, and export prohibitions.

Table 2.A1 *Trade obstacle classification by ITC*

Category	Obstacle
Administrative burdens	Large number of different documents
	Documentation is difficult to fill out
	Difficulties with translation of documents from or into other languages
	Numerous administrative windows/organizations involved
Information or transparency issues	Information on selected regulation is not adequately published and disseminated
	No due notice for changes in selected regulation and procedures
	Regulations and procedures change frequently
	Requirements and processes differ from information published
Discriminating behavior of officials	Arbitrary behavior of officials regarding classification and valuation of the reported product
	Arbitrary behavior of officials with regards to regulations or procedures
Delays or time constraints	Delay related to the implementation of regulations or procedures
	Deadlines set for completion of requirements are too short
Problem of payment	Unusually high fees and charges for the implementation of regulations or procedures
	Informal payment (e.g., bribery)
Limited facilities	Limited or inappropriate facilities for trade procedures (e.g., inspections)
	Limited or inappropriate facilities for transport and storage (e.g., refrigerated trucks)
	Other types of problems related to limited or inappropriate facilities
Lack of international recognition	Facilities lacking international accreditation or recognition (e.g., testing laboratory)
	Lack of international accreditation or recognition of procedures or regulations (e.g., lack of recognition of national certificates)
Other obstacles	Other obstacles

Source: ITC (2016).

3

Regulatory Bindings, Policy Uncertainty, and Market Access in Services*

PETER EGGER, JOSEPH FRANCOIS,
BERNARD HOEKMAN, AND MIRIAM MANCHIN

3.1 Introduction

Unlike trade in goods, market access commitments for services usually comprise regulatory measures as opposed to trade taxes. In other words, they are generally about non-tariff measures (NTMs). In some sectors foreign access may be limited or completely prohibited through quantitative restrictions, e.g. bans on foreign provision of broadcasting or transport services, or requirements that government officials fly on the national airline. More generally, services activities are often regulated. Differences in regulation may then result in additional costs for foreign providers when they contest a market. Because they involve sale of intangibles in the form of service flows rather than physical goods, there is usually some form of direct interaction between service producers and customers. This means that establishment is more likely to be important for service exports than goods exports, resulting in an effective mix of cross-border and FDI related regulatory measures when we discuss market access in services.[1]

While most trade agreements concluded since the mid-1990s reference trade in services and many include substantive provisions,[2] analysts have

* This chapter is based closely on (and in some parts borrows from and/or updates) our earlier paper summarizing analysis of TiSA for a project assessing TiSA for the European Commission (Trade Sustainability and Impact Assement (SIA) in support of negotiations on a plurilateral Trade in Services Agreement – TiSA). Updated data are from Francois and Manchin (2016), which received support from the European Union's Seventh Framework Programme for research, technological development and demonstration under grant agreement no. 61350. While we acknowledge the support, all opinions are strictly those of the authors themselves.

[1] See Francois and Hoekman (2010) for more extensive discussion on these points.

[2] Virtually all agreements to liberalize trade in services include goods trade as well. Dür, Baccini and Elsig (2014) find that only 1 per cent of extant agreements are pure services

found that frequently these do little to liberalize trade (Roy, 2011; Miroudot and Shepherd, 2014). Negotiations to expand the General Agreement on Trade in Services (GATS) as part of the World Trade Organization (WTO) Doha Round (launched in 2001) failed. A subsequent initiative launched in 2012 by a group of WTO members to conclude a plurilateral Trade in Services Agreement (TiSA) is in limbo at the time of writing following the cessation of negotiations after the election of President Trump. The Comprehensive and Progressive Agreement on Trans-Pacific Partnership (CPTPP) includes services but does relatively little to go beyond the GATS commitments of participating countries (Gootiiz and Mattoo, 2017).[3] Services have also been controversial in negotiations between high-income countries: in the context of the Transatlantic Trade and Investment Partnership (TTIP), civil society groups expressed strong concerns about opening public services sectors to greater foreign competition (Young, 2016).

Overall, trade agreements that include services are largely limited to commitments that 'lock in' prevailing policies as opposed to liberalization. Why this is the case is an important question given that services trade barriers are significant and services account for the majority of economic activity in more advanced countries – over 70 per cent of GDP and employment in the European Union (EU) is created by services sectors. A significant share of value added embodied in goods reflects services, and the productivity of firms across a broad range of sectors depends on access to high-quality, competitively priced services (Lanz and Maurer, 2015). Various hypotheses have been put forward to explain the limited extent of services liberalization commitments observed in the GATS and trade agreements (Hoekman, 2008). A common feature of these hypotheses is the complex political economy of services liberalization that arises because trade often requires cross-border movement of service suppliers and the fact that many services are regulated.

In this chapter, we abstract from the reasons why liberalization is limited in trade agreements. Instead, we focus on another feature of trade agreements, one that is particularly prevalent in agreements covering services: they are instruments through which governments make commitments not to exceed a specified threshold level of trade

agreements and report that of a total of 587 agreements concluded since the late 1950s, 17 per cent include substantive provisions on services trade. Agreements covering services began to be negotiated in the early 1990s.

3 See Ciuriak, Dadkhah and Xiao (2017) for an analysis of the CPTPP.

restrictions. That is, we are interested in market access in services as it is related to reducing the policy uncertainty that confronts traders. In particular, we focus on the market access impact of policy uncertainty arising from binding overhang, or the gap between bound commitments on policy and actual applied policy in international trade agreements as they relate to services. Binding overhang is a well-documented feature of the WTO system for both goods (Blackhurst, Enders and Francois, 1996; Francois and Martin, 2003) and for services (Hoekman, 1996; Borchert, Gootiiz and Mattoo, 2011). In the case of services, there is a substantial gap between commitments made both in the GATS and in preferential trade agreements and actual applied policy. This implies that governments retain substantial discretion to increase the restrictiveness of trade policies without violating the obligations they have undertaken in their trade agreements.[4]

Our analysis is limited to the effects of binding overhang for discriminatory policies, i.e. measures that target foreign services suppliers and restrict their market access. We abstract from the effects of domestic regulation and differences in domestic regulatory regimes. In practice regulatory heterogeneity will have trade effects that may be substantial, but to date trade agreements have done little to address this dimension of international services trade costs.

3.2 Uncertainty and Market Access

There are valid reasons to expect that policy uncertainty may itself suppress general macroeconomic conditions, including the incentives for international trade. One reason is that investors are in reality averse to risk. As such, increased risk, including from policy uncertainty, reduces the willingness of investors to commit resources. The end result is that, like a tax on investment returns, uncertainty about market conditions can drive reallocation of resources to other sectors. Indeed, while for this chapter we focus on the relatively narrow question of uncertainty linked to guaranteed conditions for market access in services, the linkages between macroeconomic conditions and trade barriers are deeper, and include both tariff and non-tariff measures. For example,

[4] Discussion on the salience of this feature of services trade agreements and options on how to close the gap between actual market access policies and bound commitments under the GATS began even before the Uruguay Round Agreements were signed (see Sauvé, 1995; Hoekman, 1996).

Rodrik (1991, 1992), Francois (1997, 2001), Baldwin, Francois and Portes (1997), Gulen and Ion (2015), and Baker, Bloom and Davis (2016) all emphasize macroeconomic effects (e.g. the impact on incentives for investment) from policy uncertainty, while Francois and Martin (1997, 2004) and Handley (2014) focus specifically on the benefits of tariff bindings. In the context of policy commitments and investor protection, increased certainty of commitments can be seen as beneficial on several levels (again see Rodrik, 1992). Examples include both the Eastern Enlargement of the EU, and Mexico's simultaneous joining of the General Agreement on Tariffs and Trade (GATT) and North American Free Trade Agreement (NAFTA) as signalling a commitment to more stable policy regimes.[5] In the context of the WTO, developing countries were given negotiating credit in the Uruguay Round specifically for entering ceiling bindings on tariffs even when those were well above applied rates (Blackhurst et al., 1996), again signalling that WTO Members value bindings. The same concept of credit for bindings, even when applied policies do not actually have to change, was also contemplated for the Doha Round (Francois and Martin, 2003).

In the context of services commitments in the GATS, gaps between bound and applied measures are the norm rather than the exception (Hoekman, 1996; Borchert et al., 2011, 2014). The 'GATS structure allows Members not to bind the status quo in many sectors. The fundamental question is whether GATS will induce Members to go further in future negotiating rounds' (Hoekman, 1996, p. 117). The challenge in negotiating trade agreements, including the recent TiSA negotiations, is in part to find a way to close this gap. Based on the assessment of Borchert et al. (2011), tabled commitments under the Doha agenda did not represent any real substantive change in this situation. While the question remained open in the case of the TiSA talks, the CPTPP does include some features that close the gap between bound commitments and actual policy (Ciuriak et al., 2017).

3.3 Data and Methodology

The approach we follow here is to estimate a reduced form trade cost following from the gap between bound policy commitments under the GATS and actual applied policy, using a gravity model.

[5] See the discussion in Baldwin et al. (1997) and Francois (1997).

3.3.1 Data

Our data come from a number of sources. Trade data come from an updated version of the Trade in Services Database available from the World Bank.[6] Pairwise variables also come from a number of sources. Distance comes from the CEPII database, as do several other pairwise variables pertaining to colonial history, common border, etc. (Mayer and Zignago, 2006).

For services trade policy, we work with the World Bank Services Trade Restrictiveness Index (STRI) database. In the database, regulatory data are used to assign numerical scores indicating relative degrees of impact on openness. This may include for example ownership share restrictions when establishing an affiliate operation, or limits on the right to provide professional services based on nationality. Such scoring of regulatory measures is then classified based on the GATS modes of supply.[7] The scores are then combined to yield STRIs by mode, and then also overall (Borchert et al., 2011, 2014).[8] The STRI data provide valuable information linking regulation (inherently qualitative) to quantitative market access measures.[9]

We work here with an extension of the STRI data from Francois and Manchin (2016), who report both intra-EU and extra-EU index values for the EU Member States. In the case of EU Member States, the data from the World Bank report a blended index, reflecting a weighted average of intra-EU and extra-EU market access conditions. The extended data reflect a process of revisiting the original classification and scoring of regulatory measures as reported by the World Bank, and

[6] http://data.worldbank.org/data-catalog/trade-in-services.

[7] The GATS defines four modes through which services trade may occur: cross-border exchange of products; through movement of the consumer to the location of a foreign provider; through establishment (direct investment) by foreign suppliers in a market; and through the temporary cross-border movement of services suppliers.

[8] Further documentation and the underlying regulatory data are available online: http://data.worldbank.org/data-catalog/services-trade-restrictions.

[9] While the emphasis of the World Bank database is on market access (i.e. discriminatory measures), the Organisation for Economic Co-operation and Development (OECD) has a similar project supplying data that includes not only measures that are discriminatory, but also measures that impact on performance of domestic and foreign firms alike. In this sense, they blend market access and overall regulatory efficiency concepts. The OECD data and background documentation are also available online: www.oecd.org/tad/services-trade/services-trade-restrictiveness-index.htm These data are for fewer countries, however, while the World Bank also provides an easier route to the intra- and extra-EU STRI margins discussed below.

re-scored them for both intra-EU market access and extra-EU market access. This means that for the EU Member States, we have indicators of market access for other EU firms, as distinct from providers from third countries accessing the market of a Member State. This extension is needed because EU firms benefit from the Single Market in selling services within the EU. The Single Market is not complete, however, as EU Member States continue to maintain some restrictions on intra-EU trade in services. EU monitoring reveals there is still a substantial gap between the vision of a single EU-wide market for services and the reality reflected in restrictions that continue to be imposed by Member States on intra-EU trade reflecting public interest objectives (Monteagudo, Rutkowski and Lorenzani, 2012).

In addition to scoring the level of market access commitments in the GATS, the World Bank has also produced a separate breakdown of applied policies vs actual GATS commitments for the 103 countries in the database (Borchert et al., 2011). These data have been published for overall STRI levels at sector level, and not by mode.[10] As part of the same project, the World Bank has also released recent estimates of trade costs. These trade costs are expressed as tariff equivalents, for all 103 countries in the database (Jafari and Tarr, 2017). These represent estimates of trade costs for applied market access. In other words, they are estimates of the costs of restrictions on market access for services, as a percentage of the cost of delivery of those services. As Jafari and Tarr note, there are two approaches followed in the literature when estimating ad-valorem equivalents (AVEs) for services. The first is the gravity approach to AVE estimation, which has been employed, for example, by Francois and Hoekman (1999), Kimura and Lee (2006), Walsh (2006), and Francois, Hoekman and Woerz (2007). While this approach allows for estimation of overall levels of trade costs, it fails to link these to specific sets of policies and regulations. The second approach, pioneered by the Australian Productivity Commission, involves linking underlying regulatory measures to evidence on sectoral pricing and general market access. This second approach is the one followed for the World Bank estimates. Basically, the World Bank AVE estimates follow from the underlying regulatory data that form the basis for the World Bank indexes, which are processed using updates to the methodologies employed for the Productivity Commission–based estimates. The end results are AVEs that reflect

[10] The OECD has released a version of its own data from a similar exercise for the OECD countries (Miroudot and Pertel, 2015).

the underlying structure of regulation. It should be stressed that because the data used to estimate the AVEs only provide information on discriminatory policy measures, the estimates of the AVEs themselves are also strictly for discriminatory barriers. They do not reflect costs faced by foreign firms because of regulatory policies (i.e. regulatory costs that also affect domestic firms).[11]

In essence, using a measure of the gap between bound market access and actual market access as a metric for sector-specific policy uncertainty linked to market access (i.e. how secure are current market access conditions) we estimate the iceberg trade cost necessary to yield the same identified impact on trade from this uncertainty. In effect, we use the binding overhang, or the policy space allowing for replacing current policy with a more protectionist one, as a metric for policy uncertainty.

3.3.2 *Estimating Equations*

We work with a gravity equation of cross-border services trade. The gravity model itself follows from a range of standard models (Deardorff, 1998; Head and Mayer, 2014). For bilateral trade in services, we have estimated a gravity equation using Poisson quasi-maximum likelihood (so allowing for zeroes in trade).[12] This means we model bilateral trade in services as taking the following basic form:

$$E\left(v_{i,j,t}|X\right) = e^{\theta' X_{i,j,t}} \tag{3.1}$$

where

$$\theta' X_{i,j,t} = \theta^{X}{}_{i,t} + \theta^{M}{}_{j,t} + \sum\nolimits_{k} \theta_k z_{i,j,k,t}. \tag{3.2}$$

In Equation (3.1) the term $v_{i,j,t}$ represents bilateral trade flows from exporter i to importer j in time period t, while in Equations (3.1) and (3.2), θ is the vector of coefficients applied to explanatory variables X, and the explanatory variables can themselves be broken down into time-varying exporter fixed effects $\theta^{X}{}_{i,t}$, time-varying importer fixed-effects

[11] See Christen, Francois and Hoekman (2012) for further discussion on discriminatory vs non-discriminatory barriers to services trade and Crozet, Milet and Mirza (2016) for an empirical analysis of the trade effects of non-discriminatory regulation.

[12] While with Poisson one does not discard zeroes from the data, we should note that Poisson assumes 'proportionality' about all numbers. Hence, an excess mass at zero is not accommodated. Only the heteroscedasticity of the residuals flowing from it is (where the heteroscedasticity is associated with parameter bias).

$\theta^{M}{}_{j,t}$, and pairwise variables (some time-varying, some not) $z_{i,j,k,t}$. The time-varying importer and exporter fixed effects capture annual supply and demand related variables that are country specific. These variables are all discussed in more detail in what follows.

In estimating Equations (3.1) and (3.2), importer fixed effects will capture average or most-favoured nation (MFN) levels of market access. At the same time, as we are able to distinguish between intra-EU and extra-EU market access, we have a measure of the margin of preference between EU Member States. This is measured as the difference from the average or MFN rate of protection captured by importer fixed effects. As this difference has the same coefficient as the MFN rate, and is the price elasticity (with AVEs) or STRI elasticity, it can be used when estimating the value of the price coefficient. This same approach is followed in Egger et al. (2015) for estimation of tariff elasticities. We include two measures of trade restrictions for this purpose. Both are based on differences between external (MFN) and internal (intra-EU) market access measures.

Starting from Francois and Manchin (2016), the first measure is based on the extended STRI database. Since WTO commitments involve commitments on extra-EU market access, to examine the impact of overhang we focus on the difference between extra-EU actual market access, and the STRI values for GATS commitments, both measured in terms of STRI values. The second measure combines the STRI data with the Jafari and Tarr (2017) AVE estimates. Here we use the relative difference between intra- and extra-EU indexes to rescale the World Bank AVEs (based on the STRI data also as described above) to arrive at estimated intra-EU and extra-EU AVEs. For example, if the extra-EU STRI is twice the intra-EU STRI, this means the extra-EU AVE is then also scaled at twice the intra-EU AVE. In this second case, the coefficient applied to the AVE margin is theoretically identical to the price elasticity for services, just as it is when working with tariff data for goods. (Again, see for example Egger et al., 2015; ECORYS, 2009 for examples in the case of goods). While the regressions based on AVEs provide us directly with price elasticities, the STRI regressions serve as a robustness check. In both cases we treat intra-EU market access as bound at applied rates (based on EU policy related to the Single Market), and extra-EU market access as bound based on GATS bindings. In both cases, the average value of service restriction related trade costs is captured by the importer fixed effects for the full sample, while we obtain pairwise variation based on intra-EU and extra-EU levels of bindings (and AVEs) relative to actual market access, based on the World Bank data as discussed

Table 3.1 *Blended and extra-EU STRI for market access in EU*

Sector	Original STRI	External STRI
Overall	17.97	25.25
Financial	4.36	8.71
Banking	1.82	3.75
Lending by banks	1.82	3.63
Acceptance of deposits by banks	1.82	3.63
Insurance	8.38	16.50
Automobile insurance	8.63	16.75
Life insurance	10.50	21.25
Reinsurance	6.00	11.50
Telecommunications	1.88	2.50
Fixed-line telecommunications	2.50	3.75
Mobile telecommunications	1.25	1.25
Retail	8.75	7.50
Transportation	25.35	41.57
Air passenger international	27.63	43.50
Maritime shipping international	9.26	14.56
Maritime auxiliary services	8.82	14.71
Road freight domestic	35.00	70.00
Rail freight domestic	36.25	38.75
Professional	45.15	59.41
Accounting and auditing	43.25	55.00
Accounting	33.25	44.75
Auditing	53.25	65.25
Legal	46.42	62.35
Legal advice foreign law	29.25	42.38
Legal advice domestic law	56.25	73.75
Legal representation in court	53.75	70.94

Source: Francois and Manchin (2016). Values are based on averages of EU Member State values from the extended STRI database.

above.[13] The average STRI values for intra- and extra-EU trade are reported in Table 3.1. In the table an index value of 0 means no restrictions, while an index of 100 means a market is fully closed.

[13] As a robustness check, we also included various pairwise dummies for other PTAs, but the EU is the only one for which we identify significant differences in market access linked to preferential trade agreements (PTAs) and customs unions for services. Therefore the specification reported here includes only the EU trade effects.

3.4 Results and Discussion

Our regression results are reported in Table 3.2 for total services trade. The first specification is based on the AVEs for trade costs in services from Jafari and Tarr (2017) while the second instead uses the STRI indexes themselves as discussed above. Both specifications have the same basic overall fit, with the model explaining roughly 86 per cent of the sample variation in bilateral services trade in our 2005–11 panel (based on the pseudo R-squared statistic). Both the AVE and STRI coefficients are statistically significant. Our interpretation is that the AVE estimates provide the same overall fit as the underlying STRI data.

Table 3.2 *Gravity regressions, total bilateral services trade*

	Specification 1	Specification 2
ln(distance)	−0.536	−0.537
	(45.09)**	(45.46)**
Common colonial history	−0.676	−0.675
	(4.38)**	(4.38)**
Shared ethnic language	0.467	0.456
	(19.51)**	(19.09)**
Shared border	0.194	0.207
	(7.95)**	(8.52)**
Former colonial relationship	0.305	0.306
	(12.68)**	(12.70)**
ln(1+AVE)	−4.775	
	(14.04)**	
Binding overhang (STRI based 0–100)	0.006	−0.006
	(3.33)**	(3.28)**
Applied STRI (STRI based 0–100)		−0.026
		(13.97)**
N	34,457	34,457
pseudo R2	0.8619	0.8618

Notes:

1. Bilateral services trade 2005–11.
2. Poisson quasi-maximum likelihood estimates.
3. AVE estimates are from Jafari and Tarr (2017).
4. Policy variables are estimated based on intra-EU vs extra-EU values, as these vary with dyad and so are not subsumed by importer fixed effects.
5. Regressions include importer and exporter time-varying fixed effects.

The AVE coefficient is −4.775, and can be interpreted as the trade price elasticity. While it has different interpretations depending on the underlying model for the gravity equation (Armington, Eaton-Khortum, etc.), the estimated value of this coefficient is in line with trade elasticity estimates for goods.

We are particularly interested in the overhang coefficient in Table 3.2. By construction, this is a semi-elasticity, where each index point change in binding overhang based on the STRI values implies a −0.006 per cent change in the log value of trade. These can be interpreted as follows. Assume we have a fifteen-point difference between the bound and applied STRI values. We would like to know how the estimated trade volume effect from this gap compares to the impact of applied trade restrictions, as a trade cost equivalent. Basically, defining the log of the estimated volume effect of overhang as G_j, this means we want to know the log AVE equivalent $\tilde{t}_j$ such that the log volume effect from the overhang (represented below as G_j) should equal the log volume effect from the log AVE equivalent $\tilde{t}_j$. This involves a two-step calculation. The overhang coefficient identifies the change in the log of trade (or the percentage change in trade) when the overhang itself changes (measured in units of the STRI). This is a measure in volume terms. We use this to identify the corresponding trade cost, given our price elasticity estimate from Table 3.2, consistent with this change in volume. To do this, note that the price coefficient (from the AVE term in Table 3.2) gives us the change in the log of trade when the AVE is increased by a certain amount. Taken together, these two coefficients let us determine the additional trade cost (as an AVE) needed to give us the same volume effect as we get from change in overhang.

$$-0.006\ G_j = -4.775\ \tilde{t}_j. \qquad (3.3)$$

Rearranging Equation (3.3), we can obtain the AVE itself for our example.

$$\tilde{t}_j = \ln\left(1 + 0.01\ AVE_j\right) = \frac{0.006}{4.775} G_j. \qquad (3.4)$$

From Equation (3.4), given the coefficient estimates in Table 3.2, the estimated AVE for a fifteen-point STRI overhang is 1.9 per cent. In other words, bringing the bindings in line with actual market access (binding at current market access) yields estimated trade volume effects in this case comparable to a 1.9 per cent reduction in trade costs, measured as a share of the cost of exports.

Table 3.3 *Estimated trade cost savings (total services EBOPS 200) tariff equivalent from eliminating binding overhang, value expressed as a percentage of the cost of exporting services*

	Bound STRI	Applied STRI	AVE: estimated cost savings (see text)
Australia	0.46	0.22	2.99
Canada	0.53	0.26	3.51
Chile	0.73	0.25	6.15
China	0.51	0.48	0.32
Chinese Taiwan	0.62	0.33	3.70
Colombia	0.81	0.27	7.04
Costa Rica	0.95	0.49	5.93
European Union	0.55	0.25	3.76
Japan	0.57	0.33	3.05
Korea	0.62	0.33	3.70
Malaysia	0.68	0.60	0.90
Mauritius	0.76	0.23	6.84
Mexico	0.70	0.40	3.89
New Zealand	0.32	0.15	2.16
Norway	0.55	0.27	3.68
Pakistan	0.84	0.32	6.79
Panama	0.65	0.40	3.24
Peru	0.72	0.33	5.01
Philippines	0.80	0.57	2.95
Thailand	0.78	0.59	2.29
Turkey	0.56	0.37	2.39
United States	0.50	0.28	2.75
Vietnam	0.42	0.32	1.24

Source: Own estimates as described in text.

For a selection of countries, based on Equation (3.4) and coefficients in Tables 3.1 and 3.2, Table 3.3 summarizes, for total trade in services, the estimated value of trade cost reductions linked to moving bindings to actual market access levels. These are to be interpreted as eliminating a trade cost expressed as a percentage of the cost of exporting services, and not as an estimate of total underlying trade costs. (Also recall these are averages for all services.) They represent potential cost savings, scaled as a percentage of the current value of services traded. Table 3.4 presents estimates for the same countries and for a more detailed set of sectors. In

Table 3.4 *Potential trade cost reduction equivalents by sector from bindings, as percentage points*

	Water transport	Other transport	Communications	Trade, distribution	Finance	Insurance	Business, professional services
Australia	1.3	6.7	0.0	0.0	6.5	2.7	2.6
Canada	6.5	3.2	0.0	0.0	6.5	3.2	3.1
Chile	11.3	9.9	3.2	9.9	8.2	1.6	6.3
China	0.6	0.0	0.0	0.0	1.6	0.0	1.1
Chinese Taipei	5.2	4.8	0.0	6.5	6.5	2.1	3.4
Colombia	12.7	13.4	0.0	13.4	8.2	2.1	7.9
Costa Rica	9.9	6.5	8.2	13.4	3.2	7.0	4.1
EU	9.0	5.0	0.3	1.1	6.0	3.0	1.1
Japan	8.5	4.8	0.0	0.0	6.5	3.2	0.7
Korea	5.2	4.8	0.0	6.5	6.5	2.1	3.4
Malaysia	0.6	3.2	3.2	9.9	3.2	2.7	0.0
Mauritius	11.3	6.7	0.0	13.4	8.2	1.1	8.6
Mexico	6.5	0.0	0.0	0.0	4.8	3.2	5.0
New Zealand	3.8	0.0	0.0	0.0	6.5	2.7	0.9
Norway	8.6	6.6	0.0	1.6	5.5	2.5	1.1
Pakistan	9.2	13.4	0.0	13.4	4.8	2.7	8.9
Panama	10.6	4.9	9.9	0.0	0.0	0.5	2.9
Peru	10.6	13.4	0.0	6.5	0.0	0.0	7.6
Philippines	0.0	0.0	3.2	6.5	3.2	1.1	4.7
Thailand	3.2	4.8	3.2	9.9	1.6	1.6	1.3
Turkey	6.5	0.0	0.0	13.4	2.4	4.3	0.0
United States	10.6	6.7	0.0	0.0	6.5	1.1	0.3
Vietnam	0.6	1.6	0.0	0.0	2.4	1.6	1.6

Source: Own calculations as discussed in text.

Table 3.4, we continue to use the overall service price elasticity estimate from Table 3.2. Note that the STRI data on bindings are more limited than the applied policy STRI data, in terms of sector coverage. As such we have fewer sectors in Table 3.4 than we do in Table 3.1.

The pattern of estimates in Tables 3.3 and 3.4 reflects a number of factors. One is that, because of the process of Chinese accession to the WTO, existing WTO Members were quite aggressive with China. As a result, bindings are generally at the actual applied policy, in terms of MFN-based market access conditions. This means there is no real gain to be had in the case of removing binding overhang in China.[14] A similar case, though not quite as extreme, applies to Vietnam. On the other hand, for many of the other CPTPP countries included in Tables 3.3 and 3.4 there should be gains from simply binding market access at current levels (e.g. Australia, New Zealand, Japan . . .).

3.5 Concluding Remarks

A stylized fact that emerges from the literature assessing and analysing trade agreements spanning services is that these generally do relatively little to liberalize trade. Instead, their main purpose seems to be to provide a mechanism through which states agree to reduce policy uncertainty by making commitments not to exceed a threshold level of trade restrictiveness. These policy bindings usually leave a substantial degree of discretion to raise barriers – there is significant water in the bindings – but nonetheless have value from a market access perspective by defining an upper bound on the level of protection that a firm may confront. The estimates discussed above suggest that a renewed push for more effective market access policy bindings in the WTO context may yield not only a basis for future negotiated gains, but also immediate gains in market access. Like goods, security of market access through effective services policy bindings matters.

[14] Analysis of the effects of the very limited water in China's WTO tariff bindings for goods has shown that this acted as an effective constraint on trade policy choices during the 2008–9 global financial crisis. See Gawande, Hoekman and Cui (2015).

PART II

Assessing and Benchmarking Policy

4

Non-tariff Measures in the Presence of Global Value Chains and Their Impact on Productivity*

MAHDI GHODSI AND ROBERT STEHRER

4.1 Introduction

There are certain legitimate motives for the imposition of non-tariff measures (NTMs). When a foreign imported product potentially harms the domestic consumers' health, safety, animal health, environmental quality, etc. countries are allowed to restrict or regulate the importation of that product. Specifically, non-discriminatory standards are regulated across trading partners by qualitative NTMs such as sanitary and phytosanitary (SPS) measures, and technical barriers to trade (TBTs) to assure certain standards and characteristics of imported products. Such regulations affect trade flows and prices of products at different stages of production in various ways. For instance, chemicals used in the first stages of production can be the focus of a prohibitive TBT, which can influence the cost of production for downstream products where this product is used as intermediary input. In contrast, some market efficiency regulations such as mandatory labelling set within TBTs can improve the transparent information to the consumers and producers who can utilize the intermediates to their production with lower transaction costs.

The ability of the exporters to comply with such non-discriminatory NTMs differs across countries. It might be the case that certain countries that are already producing in line with the imposed regulations are not harmed or even can increase their exports (due to redirection effects or a general increase in demand due to quality improvements caused by the NTM). In contrast, some other countries' exports that are not in line with

* This chapter was produced as part of the project 'Productivity, Non-tariff Measures and Openness' (PRONTO) funded by the European Commission under the Seventh Framework Programme, Theme SSH.2013.4.3-3 'Untapped Potential for Growth and Employment Reducing the Cost of Non-tariff Measures in Goods, Services and Investment', grant agreement no. 613504.

the measures in the destination market might be restricted. The consequence of a specific qualitative NTM might even result in absolute prohibition until the product complies with the implemented standards. Domestic producers in need of intermediate inputs from abroad then alter their demand to those import sources who comply with the new regulations. Therefore, responses of the domestic producers to the NTMs affecting their inputs are heterogeneous across sourcing countries depending on the exporters' capabilities to cope with the standards.

Countries can raise specific trade concerns (STCs) on the TBT and/or SPS measures imposed by other World Trade Organization (WTO) members. These STCs are mainly raised due to the discrimination or the trade restrictiveness of special cases of TBT or SPS measures. Some parts of these STCs are already notified by the imposing country to the WTO notifications. However, some STCs are not directly notified by the maintaining member. It is argued that governments sometimes are reluctant to notify their implemented NTMs to avoid trade conflicts, which reduces the transparency of trade policies. Therefore, the WTO established TBT and SPS committees to allow member states to discuss the policy measures imposed by other countries. These STCs have certain impacts on bilateral trade flows, which sometimes lead to Dispute Settlement cases within the WTO (Ghodsi and Michalek, 2016).

Firms and industries are affected by trade policy measures through three channels. The first channel can be identified as a protectionist measure imposed against the competitors of an industry within the domestic market, which is imposed by the domestic government. The second channel comprises those measures that the industry faces while exporting to the foreign destinations. The third channel can refer to measures levied against the inputs of production of an industry, which usually imposes extra costs on the intermediate inputs of production in previous stages of production. Depending on the type of measures implemented within each channel, industries are affected differently. Unlike traditional tariffs, some regulatory NTMs might promote trade instead of prohibiting it in any of the three channels. Therefore, some NTMs in the first channel are not necessarily protectionist measures. In addition, in the third channel, those NTMs might reduce the costs of intermediate inputs when they are promoting trade.

Considering global value chains (GVCs), one can track NTMs' traces of the third channel of trade policy (TP) using measures of backward and forward linkages. Diverse impacts of various types of NTMs need to be carefully taken into consideration while studying their role in GVCs.

Usually, tariffs and NTMs levied on the first-stage inputs of production exhibit a direct impact on the cost of production. However, heterogeneous effects of NTMs at previous stages of production might affect costs and trade patterns of downstream sectors.

Against this backdrop the chapter studies such measures and the way they trickle through GVCs by assessing their role in sectoral performance across forty economies in the world. The main goal of this chapter is to study the direct and indirect effects of NTMs through backward and forward linkages within GVCs, and assess their role in the growth of labour productivity of services and non-services sectors. In order to achieve this, the methodological approach is divided into four stages. In the first stage, the bilateral import demand elasticities are estimated. At the second stage, the bilateral impacts of aforementioned types of NTMs on the import flows are assessed allowing one to calculate ad valorem equivalents (AVEs) of the NTMs using the above elasticities. The third stage provides the calculation of bilateral-trade restrictiveness indices (BRIs) that are levied against the upstream input sectors of production for each sector. The fourth stage then analyses the impact of three channels of such measures on the labour productivity growth during the period.

This chapter contributes to the literature by using a comprehensive set of NTMs, calculating import elasticities and AVEs in a bilateral setting and considering the effect of backward and forward linkages of NTMs on labour productivity. The rest of the chapter is organized as follows. In Section 4.2 we briefly overview the literature on the topic. Section 4.3 discusses the first three stages of the methodological approach and the data applied in the analysis. Section 4.4 presents selected descriptive results. Section 4.5 presents the fourth stage of the analysis, i.e. the impact of NTMs on labour productivity growth and Section 4.6 discusses the results of the fourth stage. Finally, Section 4.7 concludes.

4.2 Literature

Already a large number of recent studies exist acknowledging the opaque nature of NTMs. The complex nature of NTMs is explained by the diversity of the motives of the governments in addition to their various consequences. Safety, health, and environmental issues (Otsuki, Wilson, and Sewadeh, 2001; Ghodsi, 2018) and technological advancement and innovation are the qualitative issues that might have a short-term hampering impact on trade but a positive long-run effect due to positive externalities (Beghin et al., 2012). Additionally, substitutability for tariffs

(Moore and Zanardi, 2011; Ghodsi, 2018), substitutability for other NTMs (Rosendorff, 1996), and policy retaliation (Vandenbussche and Zanardi, 2008; de Almeida, Da Cruz Vieira, and Da Silva, 2012) are political motives behind the imposition of NTMs that might lead to trade disturbances and prohibitions. The various causes of NTMs left no solid consensus for the general impact of each type of NTM among scholars. Hence, it might be more appropriate to analyse the causes and effects of each measure separately instead of giving a general conclusion regarding the diverse effect of NTMs given their complexity and ambiguous effects.

A common way to assess the impact of NTMs is to calculate AVEs. The estimation of the AVE for NTMs was first proposed by Kee, Nicita, and Olarreaga (2009) using cross-sectional trade data at the six-digit level of the Harmonized System (HS) for 2002. They constrained their results to only the positive AVEs thus assuming a hampering effect on trade. This approach was then applied by Beghin, Disdier, and Marette (2015) and Bratt (2017), however, allowing for negative AVEs representing promotive behaviour of the NTM as well. In these studies, however, all various types of NTMs were included as a single dummy variable indicating whether any type of NTM impacted on the respective trade flow. Moreover, the estimates at the product level provided only one (average) estimator of the impact of NTMs across all countries. The unilateral elasticities used in those studies were borrowed from Kee, Nicita, and Olarreaga (2008), which by construction vary across countries only through variations of the share of import in GDP of the product under consideration across countries. The shortcoming of those approaches is that the impact of the imposed NTMs by various countries on a single product is assumed to be uniform and is captured by a single estimator. Ghodsi, Gruebler, and Stehrer (2016a) extend the approach allowing the impacts of NTMs to vary by the importing countries. In this chapter, we extend this empirical strategy differentiating the impact of NTMs by types, by products, by the imposing country, and by the exporting country facing them.

The second building block of our approach is the concept of GVCs. During the 1980s in a research proposal on *the modern world system*, Hopkins and Wallerstein (1977) elaborated the concept of *commodity chains* in a macro and holistic perspective as whatsoever inputs that a final consumable good needs to reach the final consumer. The process in which any types of raw materials, services, transportation mechanisms, or even food inputs consumed by the labour at any stages of production of all inputs used for an ultimate consumable item was termed as commodity chains. Later on, Gereffi (1994) established a study framework on *global commodity chains* (GCCs) in a meso or micro perspective. Industrial organization and structural governance in the economic literature of international business discussed in various studies such as Porter (1985b) shifted the concept towards GVCs, which is not conceptually far from GCCs. Studies such as Gereffi, Humphrey, and Sturgeon (2005), and Gereffi and Sturgeon (2013), however, use GVCs in explaining the industrial characteristics and performances through inter-firm and inter-industry relations.[1]

Trade liberalization, decreasing tariff rates, and reduction of other trade barriers forced by international and multilateral agreements led to an increasingly important role of GVCs in the world economy. Moreover, existing offshoring strategies, outsourcing of activities, and global fragmentation of production of goods and services are emerging due to the reduced transaction costs by technological development in recent decades, such as the improvement in the information and telecommunication (ICT) services. In fact, ICT services advancement replaced the traditional transport costs, which are also parts of the GVCs as major services sectors (Backer and Miroudot, 2013).

The importance of GVCs was emphasized more recently in efforts compiling inter-country input-output databases such as the World Input-Output Databases (WIOD) by Timmer et al. (2012). Many scholars have proposed and used frameworks to track GVCs through WIOD. Antràs et al. (2012) established a framework to calculate the upstreamness of sectors as the stages of production within GVCs to the ultimate consumable item. Using the same methodology and considering the whole world as a single economy, Chor, Manova, and Yu (2014) and Miller and Temurshoev (2017) find that upstreamness across countries has increased due to liberalization in trade. Backer and Miroudot (2013) also show that the number of stages within GVCs increased during 1995–2008, which indicates a dominant role of trade liberalization in global fragmentation of production. This further implies that services and manufacturing are more intertwined, and their shares of value-added in each other's value-added are becoming increasingly important in the globalization process (Organisation for Economic Co-operation and Development (OECD), 2013b).

[1] For further study on the conceptual evolution of GVCs, see Bair (2005).

The intertwined sectors within GVCs can be referred to as a network of industries, in which a simple shock in one node is transmitted to pther nodes along GVCs. Considering tariffs as a policy shock to a specific sector, all users of that sector are affected along GVCs. Rouzet and Miroudot (2013) proposed a framework to calculate the cumulative effect of such a shock. In fact, their approach calculates the cumulative costs of tariffs against the inputs of a given sector. Miroudot, Rouzet, and Spinelli (2013) use the same methodology to estimate the cumulative tariffs on the inputs of services sectors. In fact, they track the effects of tariffs against non-services industries on the production and exports of services. They find a downward trend of cumulative tariffs on services sectors for a majority of countries from 2000 to 2009 due to liberalization through WTO commitments.

Third, the relationship between productivity growth and trade openness is also widely studied in the literature (e.g. Harrison, 1996; Edwards, 1998; Frankel and Romer, 1999; Rodriguez and Rodrik, 2001). Grossman and Helpman (1993) argue that diffusion of knowledge through the inputs of production traded to a country increases the innovative capacities and consequently productivity. Coe, Helpman, and Hoffmaister (1997) identify channels through which R&D spillovers affect productivity. Among those channels, imports of intermediate inputs and capital goods transfer the embodied technology of products made in a country to another affecting the productivity of the producers in the destination. In addition to this direct link, other scholars found such technology spillovers from a third country in the middle of the supply chain. Lumenga-Neso, Olarreaga, and Schiff (2005) find evidence of such an indirect effect of technology spillover from a country to another country that has no trade relationship on the given sector. Thus, similar to tariff shocks discussed above, it would be possible to have the effects of technology shocks along GVCs. Nishioka and Ripoll (2012) tested the direct and indirect effects of technology spillovers through intermediate inputs using input-output tables. Using WIOD, Foster-McGregor, Pöschl, and Stehrer (2014) find a positive relationship between the growth of the R&D contents of the intermediate inputs and labour productivity growth.

Going through the selected studies within the literature there are still some gaps to be filled. Specifically, despite the existing studies on the effects of cumulative tariffs using the backward linkages, the literature still lacks the measurement of NTM impacts along GVCs. This contribution aims at filling this gap by discussing the impact of NTMs along GVCs on productivity.

4.3 Methodology

As already sketched in the introduction the methodological approach followed in this chapter consists of four stages, three of which will be elaborated in the following subsections, and the fourth stage will be presented in Section 4.5.

The methodological contributions of this chapter to the literature summarized above are: the first step is to provide bilateral import demand elasticities. These elasticies are an extension to previous unilateral demand elasticities provided by Kee et al. (2008) and which is calculated for a more recent period from 2002 to 2011. Second, based on this we provide new AVEs for four types of NTMs capturing the effects of these policy measures' intensity varying across sectors, importers, and exporters during the period. Third, taking externalities associated with some NTMs in addition to their trade restrictiveness into account, we provide cumulative AVEs summed up to BRIs levied on the inputs of industrial production. Fourth, having these measures, we assess the impact of encompassing trade policy measures on the growth of labour productivity consistent with the WIOD classification (which is reported in Section 4.5).

4.3.1 Bilateral Import Demand Elasticities

In order to calculate AVEs characterizing the impact of NTMs on the quantity of the imported products, one needs to estimate the respective import demand elasticities. These import demand elasticities determine how much a one-percentage variation in the price of the imported product changes the quantity of the imported product in percentage. Such import demand elasticities were estimated by Kee et al. (2008) for the period 1988–2002, which were however assumed to be unilateral across countries. In contrast, this analysis considers bilateral trade flows at the level of HS six-digit products over the period 2002–11. In doing so, we extend the approach proposed by Kee et al. (2008) allowing for bilateral estimates of elasticities. Starting from a flexible gross domestic product (GDP) function including prices of imported products differentiated by the country of origin j and factors of production one can extend the GDP function into a semi-flexible function including only one price indicator for the estimation. This price indicator is a ratio of the price of the imported good h in country i from country j, relative to the average price of all other goods demanded in the GDP of country i. Hence, the resulting benchmark equation to be estimated by product-exporter hj is as follows:

$$\begin{aligned} & s_{hij}^{t}\left(p_{hij}^{t}, p_{-hi}^{t}, v_{hi}^{t}\right) \\ & \quad = a_{0h} + a_{hij} + a_{h}^{t} + a_{hhj}^{t} \ln \frac{p_{hij}^{t}}{p_{-hi}^{t}} + \sum_{m \neq l, m=1}^{M} c_{hm}^{t} \ln \frac{v_{mi}^{t}}{v_{li}^{t}} + u_{hij}^{t}, \qquad (4.1) \\ & \quad \forall h = 1, \ldots, H, \ \forall i = 1, \ldots, I, \ \forall j = 1, \ldots, J, \\ & \quad \kappa_{hij}^{t} = a_{hi} + a_{h}^{t} + a_{hj} + u_{hi}^{t} \end{aligned}$$

where s_{hij}^{t} is the share of value of product h shipped from country j to country i in the GDP of the country i at time t; p_{hij}^{t} is the price (unit value) of the imported product; v_{mi}^{t} and v_{li}^{t} refer to the factors m and l in the production of GDP of country i; and p_{-hi}^{t} is the Tornqvist price index (Caves, Christensen, and Diewert, 1982) of all other goods constructed using the GDP deflator p^{t} as follows:

$$\ln p_{-h}^{t} = \left(\ln p^{t} - \bar{s}_{h}^{t} \ln p_{h}^{t}\right) \Big/ \left(1 - \bar{s}_{h}^{t}\right), \quad \bar{s}_{h}^{t} = \left(\bar{s}_{h}^{t} + \bar{s}_{h}^{t-1}\right) \Big/ 2 \qquad (4.2)$$

However, estimating Equation (4.1) by each product-exporter pair would reduce the consistency of the estimates due to the small number of observations, which vary only across importing countries. In order to increase the efficiency of the estimates, estimation can be run by each product. In order to differentiate the countries of origins it is required to have the interaction of the price indicator $\frac{p_{hij}^{t}}{p_{-hi}^{t}}$ with the exporter dummies. Thus, Equation (4.1) is transformed into the following equation:

$$\begin{aligned} & s_{hij}^{t}\left(p_{hij}^{t}, p_{-hi}^{t}, v_{hi}^{t}\right) \\ & \quad = a_{0h} + a_{hij} + a_{h}^{t} + \sum_{j=1}^{J} a_{hhj} \ln \frac{p_{hij}^{t}}{p_{-hi}^{t}} a_{hj} + \sum_{m \neq l, m=1}^{M} c_{nm}^{t} \ln \frac{v_{mi}^{t}}{v_{li}^{t}} + u_{hij}^{t}, \qquad (4.3) \\ & \quad \forall h = 1, \ldots, H, \ \forall i = 1, \ldots, I, \ \forall j = 1, \ldots, J, \\ & \quad \kappa_{hij}^{t} = a_{hi} + a_{h}^{t} + a_{hj} + u_{hi}^{t} \end{aligned}$$

For the purpose of the calculation of accumulated AVEs at a level allowing one to assess the effects of backward and forward linkages, we are bound to use the WIOD industry classification in our analysis. Assuming homogeneous functional forms of parameters for the HS six-digit products within each WIOD category, and controlling for their heterogeneity using the country-pair product fixed effects (FE) κ_{hij}^{t}, we estimate Equation (4.3) for each WIOD industry encompassing all six-digit products via the relevant concordance tables. This first gives us a large number of observations with a larger number of statistically significant estimators. Second, capturing the variations across products it controls for cross-price elasticities within each WIOD category. Therefore, parameters a_{hhj} – as many as the number of exporters J – are estimated for each sector. Kee et al. (2008) suggested another method to calculate elasticities of sectorial levels using the elasticities at disaggregated levels.[2] By construction, the share of imports in GDP is negative, which gives the import demand elasticity of good hj derived from its GDP maximizing demand function as follows:

$$\hat{\varepsilon}_{hhij} \equiv \frac{\partial q^t_{hij}(p^t, v^t)}{\partial p^t_{hij}} \frac{p^t_{hij}}{q^t_{hij}} = \frac{\hat{a}_{hhj}}{\bar{s}_{hij}} + \bar{s}_{hij} - 1, \; s^t_{hij} < 0; \varepsilon^t_{hhij} \begin{cases} < -1 \; if \; a^t_{hhj} > 0 \\ = -1 \; if \; a^t_{hhj} = 0 \\ > -1 \; if \; a^t_{hhj} < 0 \end{cases} \tag{4.4}$$

4.3.1.1 AVE for NTMs

In the second step we use a gravity framework to estimate the impact of four types of NTMs on the bilateral import quantity extending the approach proposed by Kee et al. (2009)[3] as outlined in Section 4.2. The estimated specification is

$$\ln(q_{ijht}) = \alpha_{1h} + \sum_k \alpha_{1k} C^k_{ijt} + \alpha_{1ht} \ln(1 + T_{ijht}) + \sum_{ij=1}^{IJ} \sum_{n=1}^{N} \omega_{ij} \beta_{1nh} NTM_{nijht} + \omega_{1ijh} + \omega_{1t} + \mu_{1ijht}, \; \forall n \in \{SPS, TBT, TBT\,STC, SPS\,STC\} \tag{4.5}$$

where $\ln(q_{ijht})$ is the natural logarithm of the import quantity of product h to country i from country j at time t; C^k_{ijt} is the vector of country-pair characteristics and consists of classical gravity variables and factor endowments. It includes traditional market potential of trade partners that is the summation of both countries' GDP:

$$Y_{ijt} = \ln(GDP_{it} + GDP_{jt}) \tag{4.6}$$

[2] Such sectorial aggregates of elasticities can be provided upon request.

[3] This approach has been extended by Ghodsi et al. (2016a) differentiating NTM types and importers.

and the economic development distance similarly used by Baltagi, Egger, and Pfaffermay (2003):

$$y_{ijt} = \left(\frac{GDPpc_{it}^2}{\left(GDPpc_{it} + GDPpc_{jt}\right)^2} + \frac{GDPpc_{jt}^2}{\left(GDPpc_{it} + GDPpc_{jt}\right)^2} \right) - \frac{1}{2}, y_{ijt} \in (0, 0.5) \tag{4.7}$$

In addition, C_{ijt}^k includes distance between the trading partners in three relative factor endowments: labour force L, the capital stock K, and agricultural land area A_l as follows:

$$f_{\varsigma ijt} = \ln\left(\frac{F_{\varsigma jt}}{GDP_{jt}}\right) - \ln\left(\frac{F_{\varsigma it}}{GDP_{it}}\right), F_{\varsigma} \in \{L, K, A_l\} \tag{4.8}$$

Further variables that enter our regressions are dummy variables indicating whether both trade partners are EU or WTO members, or having a Preferential Trade Agreement (PTA).[4] ω_{1ijh} and ω_{1t} are respectively country-pair product and time fixed effects capturing multi-resistances. Similar to the estimation of elasticities, the estimations are run at the WIOD industry level encompassing all corresponded six-digit products of the HS. In order to achieve unbiased estimators robust to heteroscedasticity, we cluster the variance-covariance vectors of the error terms μ_{1ijht} by the country-pair products.

Equation (4.5) incorporates the coefficients capturing the impacts of tariffs α_{1ht} and non-tariff measures on imports $\omega_{ij}\beta_{1nh}$, which in a final step are transformed to AVEs. For tariffs T_{ijht} we prioritize the data on AVEs (using UNCTAD 1 methodology[5]) on preferential tariff (PRF) rates, then AVEs on most-favoured nation (MFN) rates, and then effectively applied (AHS) rates. NTM_{nijht} are count variables for four different groups of NTMs, i.e. $\forall n \in \{SPS, TBT, TBT\ STC, SPS\ STC\}$. For instance, $NTM_{TBTijht}$ shows the number of TBTs in force at time t (since the beginning) maintained by country i on product h against trade partner j. This in fact is one of the major contributions of this chapter capturing the intensity of each type of NTM. In order to obtain bilateral-product-specific

[4] We could use other gravity variables such as distance, contiguity, common languages, common colonial history, and same countries in the regressions. However, using the country-pair product fixed effects would drop out these time-invariant variables.

[5] wits.worldbank.org/wits/wits/witshelp/Content/Data_Retrieval/P/Intro/C2.Ad_valorem_Equivalents.htm.

AVEs of NTMs, we interact NTM variables with country-pair dummies ω_{ij}. However, including all country-pair interactions with all NTMs would exhaust all degrees of freedom. Therefore, we run the regression four times (for each NTM type) for each sector. Each time one of the NTMs is interacted with the bilateral dummy whereas the rest of the NTMs are kept as control variables.

In a last step, we consider all coefficients of NTMs ($\omega_{ij}\beta_{2nh}$) to derive their corresponding AVEs. For this purpose, bilateral import demand elasticities ε_{ijh} from the previous stage are used. AVEs are obtained by differentiating import Equation (4.5) with respect to each of the count variables for NTMs:

$$ave_{nijh} = \frac{1}{\varepsilon_{ijh}} \frac{\partial \ln\left(q_{ijh}\right)}{\partial NTM_{ijh}} = \frac{e^{\omega_{ij}\beta_{1nh}} - 1}{\varepsilon_{ijh}} \tag{4.9}$$

Summarizing, as discussed earlier, this approach improves the estimates of the impact of NTMs and the calculations of AVEs compared to previous studies by additional information on the intensity of various types of NTMs. The reason for this is that variations in ave_{nijh} are not only due to the variations in the imports share to GDP across countries within the estimated bilateral import demand elasticities, but also by the variations in the diverse effect of each NTM imposed against a specific trade partner.

After estimation of AVEs for each type of NTM, we calculate the bilateral restrictiveness index (BRI_{ijh}) as the summation of AVE for all trade policy measures τ (i.e. all NTMs and weighted average tariffs during 2002–11) imposed by country i against product h imported from country j.

$$\overline{BRI_{ijh}} = \sum_{\tau} \overline{ave_{\tau ijh}}, \quad \tau \in \{T, SPS, TBT, TBT\ STC, SPS\ STC\} \tag{4.10}$$

where $\overline{ave_{\tau ijh}}$ stands for the period-averaged AVEs. The estimation of Equation (4.5) results in the average impact of NTMs during the period as AVEs. To have a consistent measurement of BRI for the period, we take the average of AVE for annual tariffs over the period and use it in Equation (4.10).

4.3.1.2 Cumulative AVEs in GVCs

Following Miroudot et al. (2013) the cumulative AVEs of NTMs and tariffs along GVCs can then be tracked. For notational convenience, denote the various types of AVEs calculated in the previous stage for the period 2002–11 by τ_{ijh}. Each industry h in a given country i is influenced by three channels.

The **first channel** of trade policy is comprised of the direct trade policies (τ_{1ijh}) that the government of country i imposes on imports of industry h from country j. Traditional tariffs and prohibitive NTMs with positive AVEs are often implemented to support the domestic industry producing this product h. In fact, these measures protect the domestic industry by reducing the fierce competition. This is expected to reduce imports of these products. However, some qualitative NTMs with negative AVEs stimulate imports of products increasing the competition in the domestic market. When country i imposes a tariff τ on a specific product h imported from country j, domestic production of the sector producing this product might benefit from the direct τ_{1ijh} as the price of the imported product increases by τ_{1ijh}, while consumers lose (due to higher prices). However, as this sector – given the level of aggregation in the data – also sources these products from abroad ('narrow offshoring') it also faces higher costs making the sector less competitive (depending on the cost share of the imported product).

The **second channel** includes the trade policy measures that an industry h in country i is facing while exporting to other destinations j, i.e. by trade policy of the export destination country j against products of industry h from country i (τ_{2ijh}). According to the 'new new trade theories', the relatively more productive firms are able to afford higher costs of exports incurred by tariffs or qualitative regulations, which therefore leads to higher productivity at the industry level.

Finally, the **third channel** affects the intermediate inputs of a given industry h', which is captured by indirect trade policy measures τ_{3ijh} (named BRI_3 for aggregate trade policy measures). Trade policies in country i against imports of product h (from country j) affect the industry's h' using product h in their production process (as intermediate input). Like a tariff, this might result in higher costs for the industries using this product intensively (even including industry h itself). However, depending on the type of trade policy tool in this channel, a given industry h' can be affected diversely because a trade policy measure might affect the quality of imports, thus, increasing both the costs and quality of the inputs along backward linkages of GVCs.

Further, there is an indirect effect on the respective downstream industries $h' \neq h$ which (indirectly) use the importing products from other sectors h' as intermediate inputs for sector h, as these also bear costs from the $\tau_{1ijh'}$. Thus, the impact of the indirect *cumulative* $\tau_{1ijh'}$ is reflected as costs along later stages of production utilizing the affected sectors' output as inputs.

In order to calculate τ_{3ih} we follow Miroudot et al. (2013). The amount τ paid for the trade policies in the production of one unit of good h in country j is $\sum_{ks} a_{ksjh}\tau_{jks}$, where $a_{ks,jh}$ denotes the technical coefficient of the sector s from country k that is used in the production of sector h in country j as input, and τ_{jks} is the imposed trade policy τ by country j on the import of industry s from country k. Going one stage further backward, one needs to take into consideration the τ imposed on the inputs of the above-calculated stage as $\sum_{xz}\sum_{ks} a_{ksjh}\tau_{jks}a_{xzks}\tau_{kxz}$, where a_{xzks} is the amount of sector z from country x used in the production of sector s in country k. Adding up all other imposed τ at previous stages of production, one obtains the required measure of $I\tau$. Using matrix algebra, this measure can be summarized as follows:

$$\tau_3 = \left[e \times B \times \sum_{n=0} A^n\right]' = \left[e \times B \times [I - A]^{-1}\right]' \qquad (4.11)$$

where A^n is a J by J matrix of technical coefficients, e is a row vector of ones, B is a J by J matrix of element-by-element multiplication of technical coefficients and τ; $B = A : \times\tau$. At the end, τ_3 is a column vector indicating the τ_3 for the inputs of production of each country-sector. Technical coefficients are calculated using the Leontief inverse based on the world input-output tables (WIOT).

The AVEs calculated in the previous stage are for the period 2002–11, which indicate the impact of NTMs over time. Therefore, in order to have τ_3 over the whole period, the average of technical coefficients over the period, i.e. $A = \frac{1}{10} \times \sum_{t=2002}^{2011} A_t$ is used. As mentioned above, for bilateral tariffs, we use the import weighted average bilateral tariffs during the period.

4.3.2 *Data*

At the heart of the data set is the WTO I-TIP notifications database on NTMs as documented in Ghodsi et al. (2016b). Import data for all WIOD economies except Taiwan as the importing country were taken from the UN COMTRADE database and complemented by the TRAINS database. Thus, the data for the rest of the world (ROW) are the aggregation of all other economies in the world. We consider AVEs of tariffs at the HS six-digit level from TRAINS. Wherever AVEs for tariffs are not available, PRF rates, MFN tariff rates, and AHS rates are included in respective orders. These data are corresponded to WIOD classification using relevant concordance tables. It is important to note that for the intra-EU trade, tariffs and NTMs are set to zero reflecting the common trade policy within the EU. This allows the trade observations to be kept between the EU members.

Data on factor endowments (labour force, capital stock) as well as GDP are retrieved from the Penn World Tables (PWT 8.1); see Feenstra et al. (2015). The latest update of the PWT includes data for 2011, which constrain the AVEs for NTMs to the period 2002–11. Output-side real GDP per capita at chained purchasing power parity (PPP) in 2005 USD is used for the computation of the similarity index, while expenditure-side real GDP at chained PPP in 2005 USD was considered for representing the traditional market (demand) potential. Information on agricultural land was taken from the World Development Indicator (WDI) of the World Bank and wherever not available is obtained from Food and Agriculture Organization of the United Nations Statistics (FAOSTAT).[6] CEPII provides data on commonly used gravity variables as mentioned above. As stated above, technical coefficients are calculated using the inverse Leontief of the WIOD.

4.4 Selected Descriptive Results

Let us recapitulate. Our analysis results in several data sets for the period 2002–11. First, we provide a data set on bilateral import demand elasticities estimated at each WIOD industry including all corresponding HS six-digit products. Second, by estimating the AVE for NTMs, we have a data set of direct bilateral AVE for four types of NTMs imposed against six-digit products within each WIOD industry level imported to a country (τ_{ijh}). Moreover, the summation of all AVEs and average tariffs within each WIOD industry gives a data set on BRI_{1ijh} and/or BRI_{2ijh}. Third, using the matrix algebra, we construct a data set of τ_{3ih} and BRI_{3ih} indicating the restrictiveness of a trade policy measure τ on trade of the inputs to a specific country-sector within WIOD classification. Of course, summing up all τ_{3ih} for a given industry h in country i (similar to Equation 4.10) gives the aggregate BRI on the inputs of production in the

[6] http://faostat.fao.org/site/377/DesktopDefault.aspx?PageID=377#ancor.

Table 4.1 *Direct AVE statistics – first channel*

NTM	Sample mean (%)	Mean AVE>0 (%)	No. AVE>0	Mean AVE<0 (%)	No. AVE<0
SPS	0.061	11.632	2,653	−11.126	2,629
SPS STC	−0.060	15.000	399	−23.330	324
TBT	0.205	10.461	3,526	−9.290	3,391
TBT STC	0.039	11.912	1,033	−12.658	892

Source: Authors' calculations.

focal country-industry (BRI_{3ih}). Such a data set is constructed on the AVE for each type of NTM affecting the trade of inputs of production during the period. The elasticity and direct AVE data sets are available for only manufacturing industries. An indirect restrictiveness indices data set is compiled for both services and non-services WIOD sectors using the input-output linkages.

In the following, only the estimation results that are statistically significant at the 10 per cent level are included in the analysis. It is important to note that the AVEs are not constrained to only positive ones indicating restrictiveness, and positive elasticities are not dropped out. This means that for some bilateral flows, some NTMs promoted trade resulting in negative AVE. Besides, AVEs are constrained to 100 in absolute terms. The intuition behind this is that an NTM that works as a subsidy rather than a tariff cannot reduce the price of a given imported product by more than 100 per cent.

Table 4.1 provides summary statistics of the direct AVEs (first channel). Both positive and negative AVEs are included. For instance, TBT in average works as a tariff of 0.21 per cent, while there are 3,526 positive AVEs for TBTs with the magnitude average of a 10.46 per cent tariff, and there is 3,391 negative AVE for TBTs with the average subsidy-equivalent of 9.29 per cent.

Next, we present the indirect bilateral restrictiveness indices (BRI_3) levied against the inputs of production along GVCs showing ad valorem restrictiveness of all NTMs and tariffs in percentages of export values. These results are country aggregates using simple averages over all sectors. In the Appendix the τ_3 for each of the four types of NTM considered in this chapter on the inputs of production are presented by country.

Figure 4.1 indicates that these BRI_3s for manufacturing sectors range from −0.37 per cent for Hungary to 4.7 per cent for India as

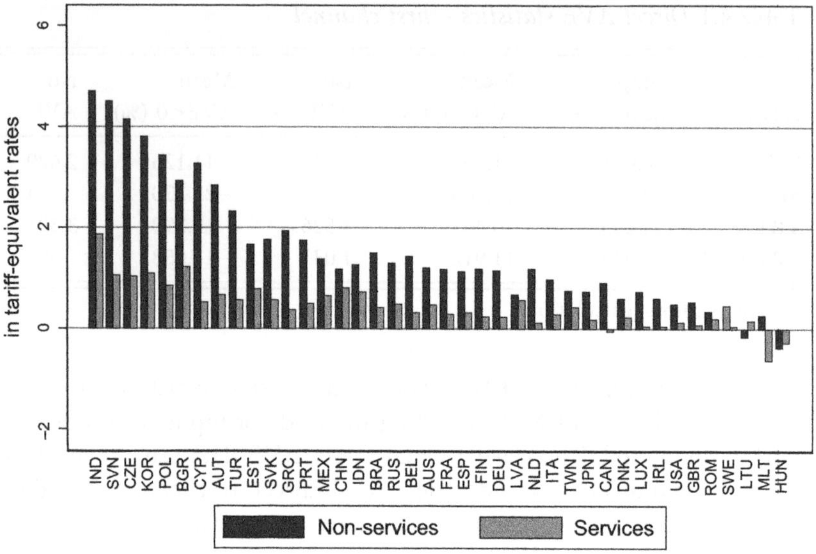

Figure 4.1 Country average IBRI – third channel.
Source: Authors' calculations; sorted by average BRI_3 across all sectors

tariff-equivalent rates and are generally larger for manufacturing industries as compared to services industries which are affected only indirectly. The highest BRI_3s in manufacturing are for India (4.7 per cent), Slovenia (4.5 per cent), Czech Republic (4.14 per cent), Korea (3.8 per cent), and Poland (3.43 per cent).

Despite positive indirect accumulative tariffs on inputs (see Figure 4.2) the average BRI_3s are negative for two countries (Figure 4.1). Hungary and Lithuania on average benefit from their trade policy measures with average negative BRI_3s including AVEs from both tariffs and NTMs. This suggests that producers in these countries benefit from trade policies which promote the trade of their inputs of production along GVCs. This happens for both Hungarian services and non-services sectors. In fact, BRI_3 for the intermediate inputs of Hungarian services is equivalent to a −0.27 per cent tariff. On the other hand, Indian suppliers incur larger losses for more expensive inputs of all sectors due to trade-restrictive policies. While normal tariffs induce around 2 per cent indirect tariffs (Figure 4.2) to the Indian inputs for manufacturing sectors tariffs accumulated along previous stages of GVCs incur 0.85 per cent for the inputs of Indian services sectors. This suggest that NTMs induce around 2.7 per cent cost to non-services Indian sectors on average, which in total

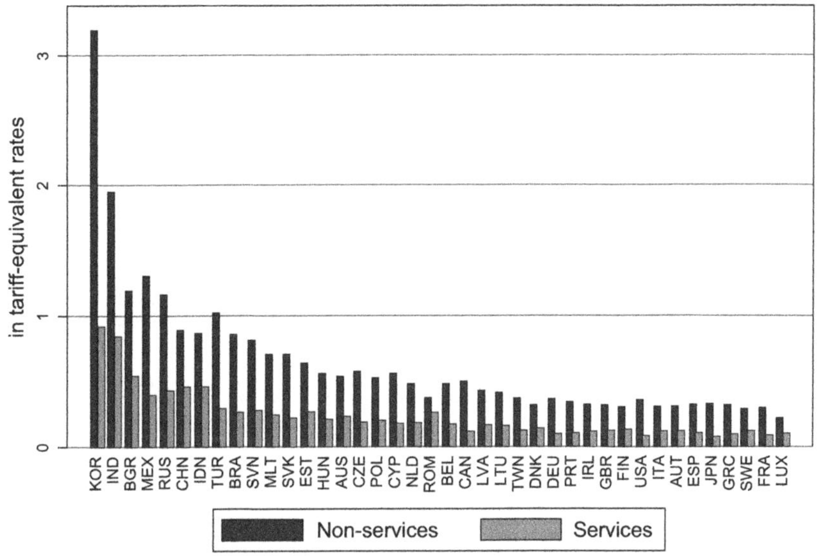

Figure 4.2 Country average indirect tariffs on inputs - third channel.

makes the average BRI_3 on Indian inputs equal to 4.7 per cent. The accumulated impact of global NTMs on the inputs of the Indian services sector is thus around 1 per cent.

As mentioned above, no tariffs are levied against trade flows of services. However, service providers are indirectly affected by the policy measures imposed against the non-services inputs for their production. In general, without a direct trade policy measure imposed on services and only due to their weaker linkages to non-services, they are less affected. For a few economies, service inputs are promoted on average by the global trade policy measures while the inputs for the manufacturing have become expensive due to such measures. BRI_3 of all trade policy measures on services in the rest of the world economy (RoW) is −4 per cent while on manufacturing it is about 2.5 percent. Malta and Canada are also enjoying negative indirect BRI for their services sectors while facing a positive accumulated cost on the inputs of their manufacturing production.

Table 4.2 presents the third channel of trade policy measures that are estimated as the effects of the respective trade policy measures accumulated on the inputs of production along GVCs by sector. For instance, TBTs improve the cost efficiency of the inputs for the production of 'coke and petroleum' and 'electrical and optical equipment' with negative

Table 4.2 *Third channel of trade policy measures by type, global simple average by WIOD sector*

Sector	Sector description	BRI (%)	Tariffs (%)	SPS (%)	TBT (%)	TBT STC (%)	SPS STC (%)
1	Agriculture, Hunting, Forestry and Fishing	0.66	0.54	0.15	0.00	0.11	−0.14
2	Mining and Quarrying	0.76	0.27	0.45	−0.07	0.12	0.00
3	Food, Beverages, and Tobacco	0.97	1.08	0.05	0.05	0.11	−0.31
4	Textiles and Textile Products	2.18	1.02	0.83	0.38	0.00	−0.06
5	Leather and Footwear	1.29	1.04	0.43	0.05	0.09	−0.32
6	Wood and Products of Wood and Cork	0.91	0.82	0.06	0.19	0.06	−0.22
7	Pulp, Paper, Printing and Publishing	0.69	0.50	−0.07	0.24	0.04	−0.01
8	Coke, Refined Petroleum, and Nuclear Fuel	2.91	0.56	2.25	−0.22	0.33	−0.02
9	Chemicals and Chemical Products	1.50	0.62	0.48	−0.03	0.28	0.14
10	Rubber and Plastics	1.81	0.76	0.42	0.18	0.32	0.14
11	Other Non-Metallic Mineral	1.05	0.41	0.53	0.01	0.10	0.01
12	Basic Metals and Fabricated Metal	3.21	0.62	2.06	0.06	0.47	−0.01
13	Machinery, n.e.c.	2.00	0.67	0.88	0.07	0.38	0.00
14	Electrical and Optical Equipment	1.34	0.78	0.05	−0.16	0.68	0.00
15	Transport Equipment	2.19	0.94	0.63	0.15	0.42	0.05
16	Manufacturing, n.e.c.; Recycling	1.52	0.72	0.44	0.20	0.27	−0.11
17	Electricity, Gas, and Water Supply	1.21	0.35	0.86	−0.16	0.16	−0.01
18	Construction	1.06	0.47	0.41	0.03	0.19	−0.04
19		0.35	0.27	−0.01	−0.03	0.12	0.00

	Sale, Maintenance, and Repair of Motor Vehicles and Motorcycles; Retail Sale of Fuel						
20	Wholesale Trade and Commission Trade, Except of Motor Vehicles and Motorcycles	0.11	0.21	−0.11	−0.05	0.08	−0.03
21	Retail Trade, Except of Motor Vehicles and Motorcycles; Repair of Household Goods	0.10	0.18	−0.07	−0.05	0.06	−0.02
22	Hotels and Restaurants	0.25	0.66	−0.02	−0.04	0.04	−0.40
23	Inland Transport	0.66	0.34	0.29	−0.09	0.11	0.00
24	Water Transport	0.58	0.36	0.20	−0.07	0.09	−0.01
25	Air Transport	0.71	0.47	0.24	−0.15	0.18	−0.03
26	Other Supporting and Auxiliary Transport Activities; Activities of Travel Agencies	0.22	0.25	0.00	−0.08	0.09	−0.05
27	Post and Telecommunications	0.06	0.22	−0.23	−0.08	0.17	−0.01
28	Financial Intermediation	−0.08	0.11	−0.15	−0.07	0.05	−0.02
29	Real Estate Activities	0.15	0.10	0.02	−0.01	0.04	−0.01
30	Renting of M&Eq and Other Business Activities	−0.06	0.23	−0.33	−0.10	0.15	−0.02
31	Public Admin and Defence; Compulsory Social Security	0.16	0.20	−0.04	−0.04	0.07	−0.03
32	Education	0.10	0.14	−0.04	−0.02	0.05	−0.03
33	Health and Social Work	0.43	0.33	0.03	−0.05	0.14	−0.02
34	Other Community, Social, and Personal Services	0.26	0.28	−0.05	−0.04	0.12	−0.05
35	Private Households with Employed Persons	−0.23	0.27	−0.53	−0.16	0.21	−0.02

Source: Authors' calculations.

accumulated AVE for TBT. However, SPS measures largely increase the costs of inputs for the former sector. Another sector that is largely affected by higher costs of inputs induced by global SPS measures is 'basic metals' that is also affected by TBT in the same direction but with much lower magnitude.

An interesting pattern emerges for the services sectors (sectors 17 through 35), where the majority of BRI_3s and τ_{3ih} for NTMs show negative signs. In fact, while tariffs levied on manufacturing products increase the costs of inputs for service providers, regulated NTMs reduce these costs. Market efficiency regulations enhancing the information symmetries, which are directed within TBTs, are good examples that can act in the opposite direction of tariffs. Another interesting result in Table 4.2 is that all sectors are on average facing costs on their inputs induced by TBT STCs represented by positive AVEs. In contrast, the majority of sectors benefit from SPS STCs imposed along previous stages of production of intermediate inputs.

4.5 Impact of NTMs on Industrial Productivity Performance

In this section, the impact of BRIs (first and second channel) and BRI_3s (third channel) on productivity growth is studied as the last step of our investigation. The bilateral AVEs of NTMs imply different cost structures for the direct but also indirect users of intermediate inputs as outlined in the previous section.[7] Higher costs of intermediate inputs do not necessarily harm production. For instance, as argued earlier, a higher quality induced by qualitative regulations embodied within NTMs along GVCs, could result in inputs of production with higher prices. However, such a higher quality can reflect either higher quality of final product or production processes that are more efficient. Both will result in higher gross output; while the latter is caused by higher value-added in the presence of price-cost margin, the former is caused by the higher price for higher quality of final goods.

4.5.1 Methodological Outline and Data

As discussed above, BRI_3 indicates the extent to which intermediate inputs are affected by trade policy measures. Starting from a simple

[7] NTMs also affect trade flows as such which are not considered here.

Cobb-Douglas function $Y_{iht} = \Psi_{iht} K^{\alpha}_{iht} L^{\alpha}_{iht}, \Psi > 0, 0 < \alpha < 1$ (where, Y, Ψ, K, and L are output, technology (TFP), capital, and labour, respectively), and taking first differences of the logarithmic labour-intensive form, we can obtain labour productivity growth as:

$$\Delta y_{iht} = \Delta \psi_{iht} + \alpha \Delta k_{iht} \tag{4.12}$$

where y_{iht} and k_{iht} are respectively logarithmic forms of output to labour (productivity) and capital to labour ratios, and $\Delta \psi_{iht}$ is the technological progress of industry h in country i at time t, which we hypothesize to be a function of TP channels and the share of high-skill labour in the given industry $\Delta \psi_{iht} = \gamma_0 TP_{ijht} + \gamma_1 HS_{iht}$.

Since the aforementioned AVE for an NTM on a given industry is a constant effect over the period, we will analyse its impact on the period-averaged annual productivity growth. Plugging the hypothesized technology growth function into Equation (4.12), and using the initial productivity levels to account for convergence, we use the following growth model in our econometric analysis:

$$\begin{aligned}\overline{\Delta y_{ih}} = {} & \beta_0 + \beta_1 y_{ih,t0} + \beta_2 \overline{\Delta k_{ih}} + \beta_3 \overline{HS_{ih}} + \beta_4 \overline{BRI_{1ih}} + \beta_5 \overline{BRI_{2ih}} \\ & + \beta_6 \overline{BRI_{3ih}} + \gamma_{ih} + \mu_{ih}\end{aligned} \tag{4.13}$$

$$\text{where } \overline{BRI_{1ih}} = \overline{\sum_{j=1}^{J} \frac{v^m_{ijh}}{\sum_{j=1}^{J} v^m_{ijh}} BRI_{ijh}}$$

$$\text{and } \overline{BRI_{2ih}} = \overline{\sum_{j=1}^{J} \frac{v^x_{ijh}}{\sum_{j=1}^{J} v^x_{ijh}} BRI_{jih}}$$

where $\overline{\Delta y_{ih}}$ is the average annual labour productivity growth of industry h in country i from 2002 to 2009, $y_{ih,t0}$ is the initial level of productivity in logarithmic form, $\overline{\Delta k_{ih}}$ is the average annual growth of capital to labour ratio. $\overline{BRI_{1ih}}$ and $\overline{BRI_{2ih}}$ refer to the period averaged of first and second channels of trade policy measures discussed before, respectively, which include the summation of all AVEs of NTMs and tariffs. These channels are included in the regression as trade-weighted averages over all bilateral partners for each importing country. $v^m_{ijh}(v^x_{ijh})$ is the imports (exports) of industry h from (to) partner j to (from) country i, and J is the total number of partners to i. Thus, $\overline{BRI_{3ih}}$ refers to the third channel of TP measures discussed before, which is the accumulated AVE of four types of NTMs and tariffs on the inputs of industry h in country i during the period. γ_{ij} denotes a set of industry and/or country-pair-specific effects, and μ_{ih} is the error term. We have two estimations specifications (4.13). The first specification includes BRIs as the summation of AVEs for NTMs and tariffs as in Equation (4.10). The second specification will estimate the productivity growth over all types of NTMs and tariffs instead of their summations as BRIs for each channel. Since the analysis results in cross-section data, we use normal ordinary least square (OLS) for the estimation of Equation (4.13) with robust standard errors to correct for possible heteroscedasticity.

Data on gross output (GO), value-added (VA), employment (l), and sectorial deflator for the fourth stage of analysis are obtained from the WIOD SEA data. Finally, data for PTAs are taken from the WTO. For labour productivity, we use two measurements to study the issue. The first is real gross output divided by employment, and the second is real value added divided by employment. Sectorial value-added deflators and exchange rates are used to calculate the real values from the national currency units. This constrains the period of analysis to 2009.

4.6 Results

Let us summarize the results of this investigation. The estimation of Equation (4.13) is separated into two categories, services and non-services sectors. This separation is mainly done because neither tariff nor NTM data are available for services which are therefore only affected indirectly. Due to production linkages, BRI_3 affects the intermediate inputs of production of services sectors as well as non-services sectors. Stepwise inclusion of sector and country fixed effects is considered in the estimations.

Table 4.3 presents the estimation results of the first specification concerning the impact of three channels of trade policy measures on the average annual labour productivity growth. Control variables show the expected effects on productivity growth in some of the regressions with different fixed effects. Including sector fixed effects γ_h captures the variations across sectors within a country that leads to insignificant coefficients for initial labour productivity in non-services. Country fixed effects γ_i explaining large variations in the dependent variables make the initial productivity of value-added in non-services statistically significant and negative, pointing at convergence. Inclusion of both sector and country fixed effects make the convergence statistically significant for gross output productivity in non-services and for value-added

Table 4.3 *Three BRI channels' impact on productivity growth*

Sectors:	Non-services						Services					
Dep. Var.:		$\overline{\Delta y_{ih}^{VA}}$			$\overline{\Delta y_{ih}^{GO}}$			$\overline{\Delta y_{ih}^{VA}}$			$\overline{\Delta y_{ih}^{GO}}$	
$y_{ih,2002}$	−0.014**	0.00041	−0.0094	−0.017	−0.0022	−0.031**	−0.00083	0.0028*	−0.012*	0.0030	0.0025	−0.011
	(0.0053)	(0.0023)	(0.0069)	(0.013)	(0.0038)	(0.016)	(0.0030)	(0.0016)	(0.0071)	(0.0029)	(0.0016)	(0.0075)
$\overline{HS_{ih}}$	0.20***	0.030	0.21***	0.19*	0.061	0.21**	−0.022*	−0.033*	0.0023	−0.023**	−0.017	−0.00095
	(0.063)	(0.036)	(0.072)	(0.099)	(0.052)	(0.088)	(0.011)	(0.020)	(0.023)	(0.0099)	(0.021)	(0.023)
$\overline{\Delta k_{ih}}$	0.085**	0.14***	0.092***	0.046	0.088**	0.048	0.21***	0.22***	0.19***	0.11**	0.12**	0.098**
	(0.034)	(0.029)	(0.031)	(0.040)	(0.037)	(0.045)	(0.059)	(0.061)	(0.057)	(0.051)	(0.048)	(0.045)
$\overline{BRI_{1ih}}$	−0.000052	−0.00024	−0.00011	−0.00029	−0.00033	−0.00029						
	(0.00014)	(0.00018)	(0.00015)	(0.00022)	(0.00023)	(0.00024)						
$\overline{BRI_{2ih}}$	−0.000054	0.00031	−0.00014	−0.00033	0.00020	−0.00030						
	(0.00022)	(0.00031)	(0.00024)	(0.00029)	(0.00034)	(0.00031)						
$\overline{IBRI_{3h}}$	0.0018	0.0040**	0.0029	0.0038	0.0038	0.0039	−0.0054**	−0.0014	−0.0053*	0.00052	0.00026	0.00026
	(0.0016)	(0.0016)	(0.0018)	(0.0029)	(0.0027)	(0.0030)	(0.0026)	(0.0026)	(0.0028)	(0.0029)	(0.0027)	(0.0032)
Constant	−0.0053	0.039***	0.024	0.019	0.044***	0.0056	0.042***	0.049***	0.031***	0.056***	0.054***	0.060***
	(0.018)	(0.0085)	(0.022)	(0.026)	(0.011)	(0.036)	(0.0084)	(0.0067)	(0.012)	(0.0079)	(0.0071)	(0.011)
N	627	627	627	627	627	627	709	709	709	709	709	709
R-sq	0.368	0.127	0.400	0.279	0.060	0.318	0.382	0.225	0.451	0.315	0.159	0.423
adj. R-sq	0.319	0.096	0.336	0.224	0.027	0.246	0.342	0.200	0.399	0.270	0.132	0.369
AIC	−1,821.6	−1,619.1	−1,824.5	−1,530.0	−1,363.2	−1,534.6	−2,254.3	−2,093.8	−2,302.2	−2,262.4	−2,116.7	−2,348.2
BIC	−1,790.6	−1,588.0	−1,726.8	−1,498.9	−1,332.1	−1,436.9	−2,231.5	−2,071.0	−2,197.3	−2,239.6	−2,093.9	−2,243.2
γ_i	Yes	No	Yes	Yes	No	Yes	Yes	No	Yes	Yes	No	Yes
γ_h	No	Yes	Yes	No	Yes	Yes	No	Yes	Yes	No	Yes	Yes

Notes: Robust standard errors in parentheses.
* $p < 0.1$, ** $p < 0.05$, *** $p < 0.01$.
Source: Authors' calculations.

productivity in services sectors. Non-services sectors with larger average share of high-skill labour enjoy larger productivity growth. Statistically positive significant coefficients of the physical capital to labour ratio growth indicate that labour productivity is enhanced by capital. With the large coefficients of growth of high-skill labour share, we observe that the contribution of human capital in labour productivity growth is larger than the contribution of physical capital growth in manufacturing sectors.

With respect to the variables of interest, the results indicate that there is no statistically significant impact of the first and the second channels (i.e. BRI_{1ih} and BRI_{2ih}) on productivity growth of domestic industries. It indicates that neither BRI faced by the exporting sector nor by the foreign competitors of the given sector influences the growth of labour productivity in that sector. However, the third channel (i.e. BRI_{3ih}) which includes all trade policy measures on the inputs of production accumulated along the upstream stages of GVCs, has statistically significant impact on the labour value-added productivity growth though not in all specifications. Further, these differ with respect to directions for services and non-services sectors.

BRI_3 is statistically significant and positive for commodities (non-services) only when country fixed effects are not controlled for with respect to value-added productivity growth. Thus, countries that have higher costs of intermediate inputs for their manufacturing sectors enjoy larger value-added productivity growth. While gross output productivity is not affected by the third channel, the results indicate that global trade policy measures imposed along the backward linkages of production enhance production procedures of countries in manufacturing, resulting in higher value-added productivity growth rather than gross output productivity growth. However, this third channel of trade policy is negatively related to the value-added productivity growth of services when country-specific effects are controlled using fixed effects. Thus, services sectors with larger costs of intermediate inputs induced by global trade policy measures along the previous stages of production have lower value-added productivity growth.

As discussed earlier, different types of trade policy measures have diverse impact on trade flows for various reasons and consequently affect the productivity differently. In Table 4.4, we present the second specification estimation results of labour productivity growth over various types of policy measures. Many of these policies do not have any statistically significant impact on the labour productivity via the

Table 4.4 *Direct and indirect policy measures impact on productivity growth*

Sectors:	Non-services						Services					
Dep. Var.:	$\overline{\Delta y_{ih}^{VA}}$			$\overline{\Delta y_{ih}^{GO}}$			$\overline{\Delta y_{ih}^{VA}}$			$\overline{\Delta y_{ih}^{GO}}$		
$y_{ih,2002}$	−0.016***	−0.0020	−0.011	−0.019	−0.0039	−0.032**	−0.00048	0.0020	−0.011	0.0028	0.0018	−0.012
	(0.0060)	(0.0023)	(0.0071)	(0.014)	(0.0036)	(0.016)	(0.0030)	(0.0018)	(0.0071)	(0.0030)	(0.0017)	(0.0075)
$\overline{HS_{ih}}$	0.20***	0.045	0.21***	0.18*	0.063	0.19**	−0.019*	−0.032	−0.00012	−0.021**	−0.021	−0.0035
	(0.067)	(0.035)	(0.077)	(0.10)	(0.048)	(0.089)	(0.011)	(0.020)	(0.023)	(0.0097)	(0.021)	(0.023)
$\overline{\Delta k_{ih}}$	0.089***	0.14***	0.099***	0.053	0.093***	0.058	0.21***	0.22***	0.20***	0.11**	0.12**	0.100**
	(0.034)	(0.028)	(0.031)	(0.039)	(0.036)	(0.044)	(0.060)	(0.063)	(0.058)	(0.052)	(0.050)	(0.046)
$\overline{SPS_{1ih}}$	−0.00029	−0.000025	−0.00026	−0.00063**	−0.00018	−0.00053*						
	(0.00021)	(0.00025)	(0.00022)	(0.00030)	(0.00032)	(0.00032)						
$\overline{TBT_{1ih}}$	0.000071	−0.00035	0.000045	−0.000034	−0.00043	−0.000024						
	(0.00023)	(0.00033)	(0.00022)	(0.00031)	(0.00035)	(0.00029)						
$\overline{TBTSTC_{1ih}}$	0.00085	0.0011*	0.00086	0.0012	0.0015	0.0013						
	(0.00053)	(0.00066)	(0.00055)	(0.0010)	(0.0011)	(0.00097)						
$\overline{SPSSTC_{1ih}}$	−0.00014	−0.00031	−0.00036	0.00029	0.000022	0.00038						
	(0.00030)	(0.00048)	(0.00035)	(0.00048)	(0.00051)	(0.00055)						
$\overline{T_{1ih}}$	0.00027	−0.0018**	0.00011	−0.00067	−0.0023**	−0.00083						
	(0.00066)	(0.00085)	(0.00068)	(0.00089)	(0.00094)	(0.00093)						
$\overline{SPS_{2ih}}$	−0.00049	0.00026	−0.00035	−0.0015**	−0.000091	−0.00091						
	(0.00047)	(0.00054)	(0.00045)	(0.00059)	(0.00054)	(0.00061)						
$\overline{TBT_{2ih}}$	0.00010	0.00076*	0.00020	−0.00031	0.00051	−0.000086						
	(0.00032)	(0.00043)	(0.00034)	(0.00044)	(0.00041)	(0.00041)						
$\overline{TBTSTC_{2ih}}$	−0.0000035	0.00066	−0.000072	0.00015	0.00076	0.00011						
	(0.00022)	(0.00045)	(0.00025)	(0.00021)	(0.00048)	(0.00025)						
$\overline{SPSSTC_{2ih}}$	0.0012*	0.0010	0.00068	0.0017**	0.00065	0.00100						
	(0.00064)	(0.00088)	(0.00075)	(0.00077)	(0.00097)	(0.00072)						
$\overline{T_{2ih}}$	−0.0010	−0.0017	−0.0023	−0.0013	−0.0015	−0.0026						
	(0.0014)	(0.0015)	(0.0018)	(0.0016)	(0.0016)	(0.0020)						

Table 4.4 (*cont.*)

Sectors:	Non-services						Services					
Dep. Var.:		$\overline{\Delta y_{ih}^{VA}}$			$\overline{\Delta y_{ih}^{GO}}$			$\overline{\Delta y_{ih}^{VA}}$			$\overline{\Delta y_{ih}^{GO}}$	
$y_{ih,2002}$	−0.016***	−0.0020	−0.011	−0.019	−0.0039	−0.032**	−0.00048	0.0020	−0.011	0.0028	0.0018	−0.012
$\overline{SPS_{3ih}}$	0.0039**	0.0063***	0.0059***	0.0072**	0.0064**	0.0076**	−0.010**	0.0015	−0.0099**	−0.0047	0.0052	−0.0056
	(0.0019)	(0.0017)	(0.0020)	(0.0033)	(0.0031)	(0.0036)	(0.0042)	(0.0044)	(0.0042)	(0.0056)	(0.0048)	(0.0063)
$\overline{TBT_{3ih}}$	0.0010	0.0082***	0.0016	−0.0000092	0.0077***	0.00070	−0.016**	−0.0059	−0.0086	−0.019***	−0.017***	−0.012*
	(0.0023)	(0.0023)	(0.0025)	(0.0036)	(0.0028)	(0.0034)	(0.0065)	(0.0081)	(0.0065)	(0.0065)	(0.0067)	(0.0066)
$\overline{TBTSTC_{3ih}}$	−0.0085*	−0.0094*	−0.0096**	−0.013	−0.014	−0.015	0.010	0.015	−0.0037	0.032**	0.022	0.017
	(0.0049)	(0.0052)	(0.0047)	(0.0099)	(0.011)	(0.0095)	(0.015)	(0.016)	(0.014)	(0.014)	(0.014)	(0.013)
$\overline{SPSSTC_{3ih}}$	0.015**	0.018**	0.012	0.025*	0.029***	0.019	−0.000074	0.0073	−0.028	0.031	0.019	−0.0032
	(0.0072)	(0.0071)	(0.0076)	(0.013)	(0.010)	(0.012)	(0.026)	(0.032)	(0.027)	(0.031)	(0.029)	(0.028)
$\overline{T_{3ih}}$	−0.00017	−0.00081	−0.00098	0.0054	0.0037	0.0055	0.0019	−0.012	0.0058	0.0060	−0.0061	0.013**
	(0.0022)	(0.0023)	(0.0022)	(0.0045)	(0.0025)	(0.0047)	(0.0060)	(0.0098)	(0.0053)	(0.0056)	(0.0071)	(0.0058)
Constant	−0.0060	0.045***	0.033	0.021	0.054***	0.017	0.040***	0.049***	0.031**	0.053***	0.053***	0.056***
	(0.019)	(0.0092)	(0.025)	(0.028)	(0.011)	(0.038)	(0.0086)	(0.0071)	(0.012)	(0.0083)	(0.0074)	(0.012)
N	627	627	627	627	627	627	709	709	709	709	709	709
R-sq	0.379	0.170	0.416	0.303	0.096	0.340	0.385	0.229	0.454	0.323	0.168	0.429
adj. R-sq	0.316	0.124	0.340	0.233	0.046	0.254	0.341	0.199	0.399	0.275	0.136	0.371
AIC	−1,808.5	−1,627.1	−1,817.6	−1,527.0	−1,363.9	−1,531.2	−2,249.7	−2,089.1	−2,297.6	−2,263.3	−2,116.8	−2,347.2
BIC	−1,724.1	−1,542.7	−1,666.6	−1,442.7	−1,279.5	−1,380.2	−2,208.7	−2,048.1	−2,174.4	−2,222.2	−2,075.7	−2,224.0
γ_i	Yes	No	Yes	Yes	No	Yes	Yes	No	Yes	Yes	No	Yes
γ_h	No	Yes	Yes	No	Yes	Yes	No	Yes	Yes	No	Yes	Yes

Notes: Robust standard errors in parentheses.
* $p < 0.1$, ** $p < 0.05$, *** $p < 0.01$.
Source: Authors' calculations.

first and second channel, which is similar to the results obtained in the first specification.

Among these measures, controlling for country fixed effects, SPS measures in the first and the second channels are linked with lower gross output productivity growth. These two results can be interpreted as follows: From the first channel one can argue that sectors within a country that are protected with SPS measures that are more trade restrictive have lower average annual gross output productivity growth. Productivity in value-added is also negatively affected by the domestic SPS measures but not statistically significantly. For the second channel, it can be interpreted that an industry that faces larger average costs of export due to the imposed SPS measures abroad has lower growth of productivity in gross output.

TBT STC in the first channel imposed by a country that prohibits imports with a high tariff equivalence can be linked with high annual growth of productivity, which is statistically significant for value-added regression controlling for only sector fixed effects. It means countries with restrictive TBT STCs enjoy higher value-added productivity growth in their sectors.

When controlling only for the sector fixed effects, tariffs in the first channel become statistically significant and negative. This first indicates that the differences in tariffs are largely across the countries imposing them. Second, it implies that countries that are protected by tariffs more than others have lower annual growth of labour productivity, which might be due to lack of competition in their domestic industries.

TBT in the second channel has positive coefficients in the regressions on value-added productivity but is statistically significant when excluding country fixed effects. This indicates that countries that are facing TBTs that are more restrictive have larger productivity growth in value-added. This might relate to the nature of these technical regulations that are usually enforced to increase the quality of products and improve the production procedures.

SPS STCs in the second channel are linked with the larger average annual productivity growth. Controlling for only country fixed effects, the results suggest that sectors that are facing very restrictive SPS STC measures have had larger productivity growth. Since these policy measures are special cases of SPS measures that are more restrictive and discriminative, it could indicate that only more productive sectors could pass those barriers.

The third channel of policy measures has a larger number of statistically significant coefficients. SPS measures in this channel have statistically significantly positive coefficients in all regressions of non-services sectors. It suggests that the accumulated costs on the inputs of production in previous stages of production by SPS measures are positively linked to large productivity growth of manufacturing. However, such costs are associated with lower average annual productivity growth in value-added of services sectors.

Controlling for only sector fixed effects gives positive and statistically significant coefficients of TBTs in the third channel for manufacturing. This suggests that countries that are sourcing intermediate inputs with higher costs associated with TBTs enjoy higher productivity growth in their manufacturing sectors. However, higher TBT costs on inputs of services production are associated with lower gross output productivity growth.

Induced costs of intermediate inputs by TBT STCs have a negative impact on the average annual value-added growth in manufacturing sectors. This can indicate the trade restrictiveness of these measures that are unnecessary by nature, which accumulate inefficient costs along GVCs. However, SPS STCs in the third channel are positively linked to the average annual growth of productivity in manufacturing when both sector- and country-specific effects are not controlled at the same time.

Accumulated costs induced by tariffs along the previous stages of production are affecting only gross output productivity growth in services while controlling for sector-country fixed effects. While no tariff is levied against services, these traditional policy tools increase the costs and gross outputs of services.

4.6.1 Bilateral Impacts

As discussed earlier, in the introduction, the impact of trade policy measures not only varies by types of instruments but also by the countries imposing or facing them. For instance, assume that two countries have similar sets of high regulatory standards, while a third country produces within a lower qualitative standards framework. Thus, a new regulatory measure imposed by one of the two similar countries might have positive influence on the other while having a negative impact on the trade patterns with the third country. Thus, performance of sectors might be affected differently taking the heterogeneous partners into consideration. Here, we use a similar framework to Equation (4.13) differentiating the first and second trade policy measures by partner countries. Thus, we estimate the following equation:

$$\begin{aligned}\overline{\Delta y_{ih}} &= \beta_0 + \beta_1 y_{ih,t0} + \beta_2 \overline{\Delta k_{ih}} + \beta_3 \overline{HS_{ih}} + \beta_4 \overline{\tau_{1ijh}} + \beta_5 \overline{\tau_{2ijh}} \\ &\quad + \beta_6 \overline{\tau_{3ih}} + \gamma_{ij} + \gamma_h + \mu_{ijh}\end{aligned} \tag{4.14}$$

where $\overline{\tau_{1ijh}}$ includes the trade policy measures in the first channel that are imposed by country i against the imports of sector h from country j, and $\overline{\tau_{2ijh}}$ includes the trade policy measures in the second channel that are imposed by country j against the imports of sector h from country i. γ_{ij} and γ_h are respectively country-pair and sector fixed effects. It is important to mention that the dependent variable is repeated across partners, which can potentially inflate the t-statistics of other variables that are also repeated across partners, making them statistically significant.

The estimation results are presented in Table 4.5. Both TBT and TBT STCs in the first channel are associated with higher average annual productivity growth of manufacturing. This indicates that when a country maintains these qualitative NTMs against the imports, making the imports more expensive, the domestic industries benefit by improving their productivities. This reflects that those country-sectors in which the majority of exporting partners have faced higher costs of entry by TBTs have larger productivity growth.

As it is observed, protecting the domestic industry by SPS measures do not affect the productivity growth of manufacturing sectors statistically significantly. However, SPS measures for which partner countries have raised STCs affect the domestic average annual growth of value-added negatively. This might be due to lack of qualitative improvement by these measures but by reducing the domestic competition. On the other side of trade, SPS STCs maintained by the partner countries, i.e. in the second channel, are associated with higher productivity growth. While these specific measures could be very restrictive and discriminative in nature, only industries with higher productivity are able to afford the high costs of exports to the country maintaining them.

Tariffs imposed by the domestic countries against exporting partners discourage the productivity growth of gross output statistically significantly. The impact on value-added productivity growth is not statistically significant. This indicates that due to larger tariff protection and reduced market competition, productivity in value-added in domestic manufacturing is not affected, while domestic industries could potentially reduce their prices resulting in lower gross output productivity. However,

Table 4.5 *Bilateral direct and indirect policy measures impact on productivity growth*

Sectors	Non-services		Services	
Dep. Var.:	$\overline{\Delta y_{ih}^{VA}}$	$\overline{\Delta y_{ih}^{GO}}$	$\overline{\Delta y_{ih}^{VA}}$	$\overline{\Delta y_{ih}^{GO}}$
$y_{ih,2002}$	−0.0097***	−0.031***	−0.011***	−0.012***
	(0.0010)	(0.0024)	(0.0011)	(0.0011)
$\overline{HS_{ih}}$	0.21***	0.21***	−0.00012	−0.0035
	(0.011)	(0.014)	(0.0035)	(0.0036)
$\overline{\Delta k_{ih}}$	0.097***	0.056***	0.20***	0.100***
	(0.0048)	(0.0069)	(0.0089)	(0.0071)
$\overline{SPS_{1ih}}$	−0.000018	−0.000042		
	(0.000025)	(0.000036)		
$\overline{TBT_{1ih}}$	0.000062***	0.000058**		
	(0.000019)	(0.000025)		
$\overline{TBTSTC_{1ih}}$	0.000052*	0.000078**		
	(0.000028)	(0.000035)		
$\overline{SPSSTC_{1ih}}$	−0.000054*	−0.000026		
	(0.000031)	(0.000041)		
$\overline{T_{1ih}}$	−0.000053	−0.00033***		
	(0.000061)	(0.000090)		
$\overline{SPS_{2ih}}$	0.0000045	0.000017		
	(0.000021)	(0.000024)		
$\overline{TBT_{2ih}}$	−0.000016	−0.000033		
	(0.000023)	(0.000031)		
$\overline{TBTSTC_{2ih}}$	−0.000043	−0.0000088		
	(0.000031)	(0.000034)		
$\overline{SPSSTC_{2ih}}$	0.00014***	0.00016***		
	(0.000029)	(0.000033)		
$\overline{T_{2ih}}$	0.000032	0.000035		
	(0.000046)	(0.000060)		
$\overline{SPS_{3ih}}$	0.0053***	0.0064***	−0.0099***	−0.0056***
	(0.00030)	(0.00054)	(0.00064)	(0.00097)
$\overline{TBT_{3ih}}$	0.0015***	0.00034	−0.0086***	−0.012***
	(0.00030)	(0.00040)	(0.0010)	(0.0010)
$\overline{TBTSTC_{3ih}}$	−0.0057***	−0.0086***	−0.0037*	0.017***
	(0.00054)	(0.0010)	(0.0021)	(0.0020)
$\overline{SPSSTC_{3ih}}$	0.0099***	0.018***	−0.028***	−0.0032
	(0.0011)	(0.0018)	(0.0042)	(0.0044)
$\overline{T_{3ih}}$	−0.0011***	0.0041***	0.0058***	0.013***
	(0.00031)	(0.00063)	(0.00081)	(0.00089)

Table 4.5 (*cont.*)

Sectors	Non-services		Services	
Dep. Var.:	$\overline{\Delta y_{ih}^{VA}}$	$\overline{\Delta y_{ih}^{GO}}$	$\overline{\Delta y_{ih}^{VA}}$	$\overline{\Delta y_{ih}^{GO}}$
Constant	0.023***	0.0046	0.031***	0.056***
	(0.0035)	(0.0057)	(0.0019)	(0.0018)
N	25,707	25,707	29,069	29,069
R-sq	0.409	0.329	0.454	0.429
adj. R-sq	0.368	0.282	0.421	0.394
AIC	−76,941.4	−65,052.7	−96,363.0	−98,395.3
BIC	−76,664.1	−64,775.4	−96,139.5	−98,171.8
γ_{ij}	Yes	Yes	Yes	Yes
γ_h	Yes	Yes	Yes	Yes

Notes: Robust standard errors in parentheses.
* $p < 0.1$, ** $p < 0.05$, *** $p < 0.01$.
Source: Authors' calculations.

statistically insignificant coefficients of tariffs in the second channel suggest that tariffs imposed by the destination countries do not relate to the productivity of an exporting sector.

As mentioned above, third channel coefficients could become statistically significant in these results due to repeated observations across partners. Coefficients of SPS in the third channel indicate similar results as those in Table 4.3 controlling for both sector and country fixed effects. A similar result also goes to TBT in the third channel with the coefficients being significant for the value-added productivity growth due to inflation of *t*-statistics. Yet, the TBT coefficient for manufacturing gross output productivity growth remains insignificant, which reassures no statistical relation between induced costs of inputs by TBTs and gross output productivity. A similar conclusion could be drawn from the coefficient of SPS STCs in the gross output productivity growth of services that remains statistically insignificant.

4.7 Conclusions

In this chapter we track how NTMs trickle through the GVCs and study their impact on industry productivity. The importance of the NTMs as complex trade policy measures is highlighted in various studies of the international trade policy literature. The opaque nature of NTMs distinguishes them from normal tariffs since they have qualitative impact on product flows in addition to price effects. While price effects incurred further up the value chains can be easily tracked along GVCs, the impact of NTMs on the quality of the upper stream sectors influences the production processes along GVCs. In this contribution, we present a framework to quantify such impacts.

The contribution of this chapter is two-fold. We first provide a database for bilateral AVEs of NTMs. This contributes to the existing literature in different ways: a data set on bilateral AVEs for four types of qualitative NTMs notified to the WTO during a period based on their intensity is a major contribution of this chapter. Second, we explain labour productivity growth by various types of global trade policy measures incorporated along GVCs.

In a four-stage methodology we estimate the trickling-down effect of NTMs and tariffs on labour productivity growth. The first stage estimates the bilateral import demand elasticities using detailed six-digit bilateral trade flows. The second stage quantifies the bilateral AVE of four types of qualitative NTMs notified to the WTO until 2011 applying a structural gravity model on traded quantities and using the elasticities calculated in the previous stage for the period 2002–11. The third stage uses these estimated AVEs of the four types of NTMs and the average tariffs for the period to calculate the cumulative indirect bilateral trade restrictiveness indices (BRI_{3ih}) for the inputs of production applying the Leontief technical coefficients consistent with WIOD. Three channels of trade policy measures are discussed as possible channels affecting the performance of industries. The first channel affects the foreign competitors of a given industry through direct trade protectionism measures (BRI_{1ijh}). The second channel is discussed as trade policy measures faced by the exports of a given sector (BRI_{2ijh}). The third channel is considered as BRI_{3ih} that are accumulated along previous stages of production of intermediate inputs. The final stage of the chapter analyses the impact of these three channels of trade policy measures on the average annual labour productivity growth.

The results point towards a positive influence of regulations embodied within TBTs and SPS measures further up the value chains on the performance of non-services industries. Moreover, the diverse effects of different types of NTMs are in line with the existing argument within the literature on the complexity of these trade policy tools.

Appendix

Note that all the trade policy measures in the third channel presented below are sorted by the AVE averaged across all sectors.

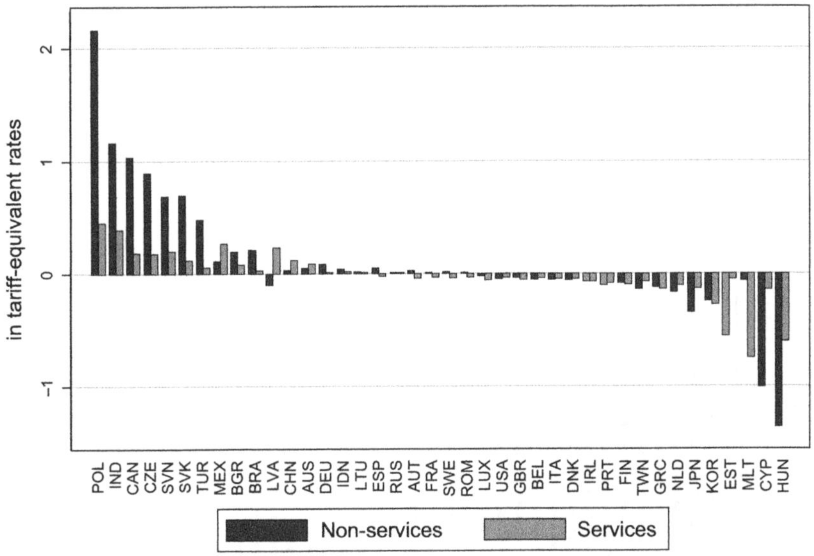

Figure 4.A1 Country average indirect AVE for TBT on inputs – third channel.

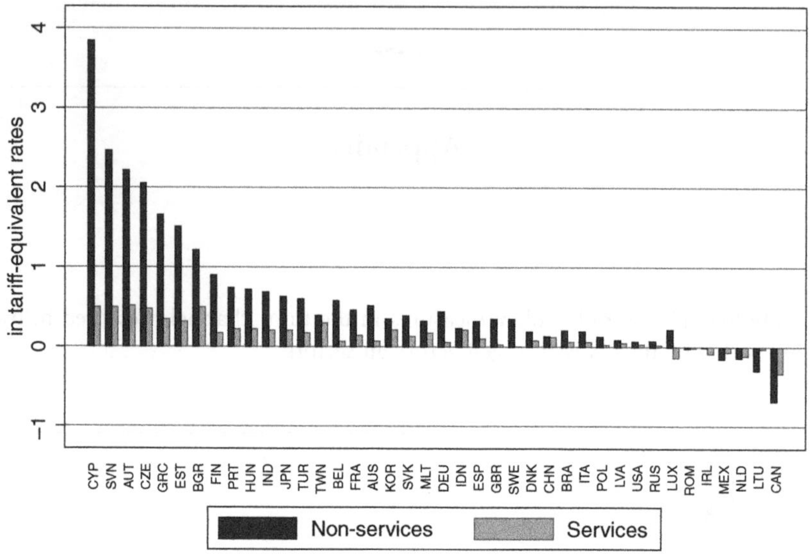

Figure 4.A2 Country average indirect AVE for SPS on inputs – third channel.

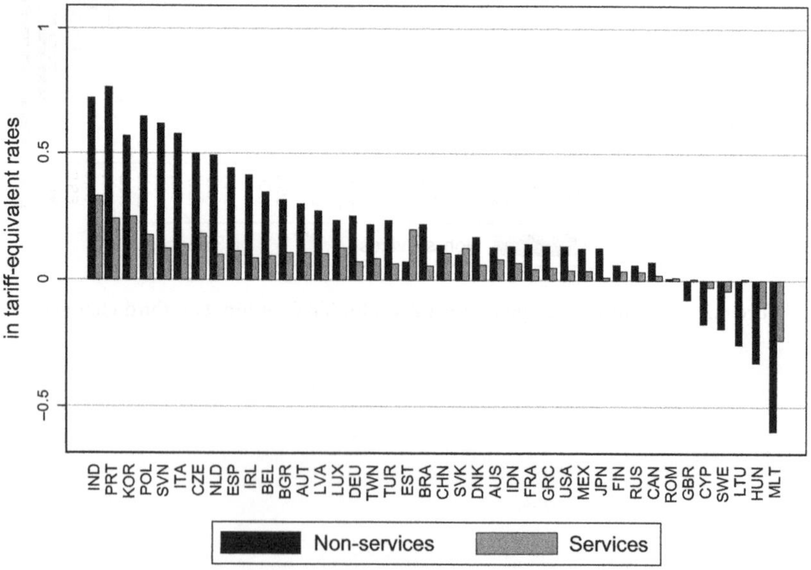

Figure 4.A3 Country average indirect AVE for TBT STC on inputs – third channel.

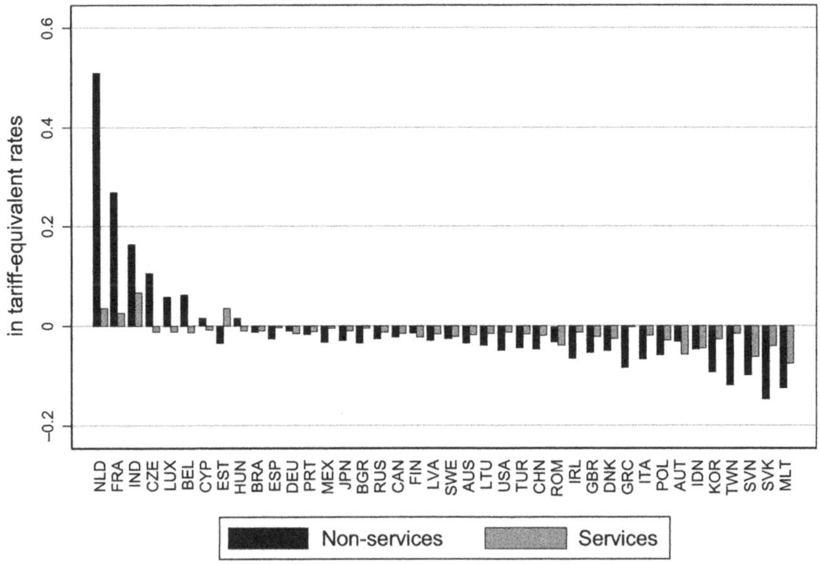

Figure 4.A4 Country average indirect AVE for SPS STC on inputs – third channel.

5

Non-tariff Measure Estimations in Different Impact Assessments

EDDY BEKKERS AND HUGO ROJAS-ROMAGOSA*

5.1 Introduction

Many recent free trade agreements (FTAs) are deep or comprehensive agreements that contain a large number of provisions on non-tariff measures (NTMs). This contrasts with the traditional shallow trade agreements that focused mainly on tariff reductions. Therefore, one of the main tasks of trade economists asked to predict the welfare effects of deep FTAs is to translate the NTM provisions into overall welfare effects. This can be achieved in two steps. First, the particular NTM provisions need to be translated into trade cost reductions, and second, welfare effects of the trade cost reductions are calculated with a general equilibrium model.

In this chapter we provide a detailed overview of the different approaches to calculate the trade cost reductions of NTM provisions in FTAs and their associated welfare effects. Moreover, we focus our analysis on different impact assessment studies over the Transatlantic Trade and Investment Partnership (TTIP) between the USA and the EU. In the different studies three types of reductions in trade costs are identified: first, a reduction or full elimination of tariffs; second, a reduction in NTMs between the EU and the USA; and third, a reduction in NTMs between the EU and the USA with third countries as a result of regulatory harmonisation – the so-called spillover effects.

* This chapter was produced as part of the project 'Productivity, Non-Tariff Measures and Openness' (PRONTO) funded by the European Commission under the Seventh Framework Programme, Theme SSH.2013.4.3-3 'Untapped Potential for Growth and Employment Reducing the Cost of Non-tariff Measures in Goods, Services and Investment', grant agreement no. 613504. The chapter represents the personal opinions of the authors and in no way reflects the official opinions or positions of any organisation or its employees with which the authors are or have been affiliated.

We distinguish between the two main approaches to calculate the reductions in NTMs: the bottom-up approach and the top-down approach. The bottom-up approach identifies the NTMs already in place between FTA partners and specifies scenarios for the expected trade cost reductions associated with a specific FTA. The top-down approach estimates the trade cost reductions from past FTAs, imposing that the expected trade cost reductions of the specific FTA analysed, will be similar as in comparable agreements from the past. In general, most studies use the concept of ad valorem equivalent (AVE) of an NTM, which is the equivalent ad valorem trade cost for a particular NTM. Some studies allow for differences in expected overall AVE trade cost reductions conditional on the depth level of the agreement. Some studies account separately for the reductions in tariffs and NTMs, whereas other studies do not explicitly model tariffs, calculating the expected overall AVE trade costs reductions associated with the FTA without distinguishing between tariffs and NTMs.

We start this chapter with an outline of the different approaches to the estimation of trade cost reductions associated with NTM provisions in FTAs in Section 5.2. Then we introduce the different TTIP impact assessment studies in Section 5.3, while in Section 5.4 we compare the predicted trade cost reductions for all studies. In Section 5.5 we then explore the impact of trade cost reductions on predicted welfare effects, the influence of the employed trade elasticities and we discuss the sensitivity of the results to different modelling assumptions. We conclude in Section 5.6.

5.2 Calculating NTM Reductions Associated with FTAs

Since tariff levels are low for many countries negotiating deep FTAs like the Trans-Pacific Partnership (TPP), TTIP and the EU–Canada Comprehensive Economic Trade Agreement (CETA), the largest impact in these agreements will come from changes in NTMs. Thus, the proper estimation of expected trade cost reductions associated with provisions on NTMs has become a critical element for assessing the potential economic impacts of modern FTAs. To determine the welfare effects of deep FTAs with provisions on NTMs, researchers first have to calculate the associated reductions in trade costs. In this section we explain the two approaches to map the NTM provisions into associated reductions in trade costs. Before discussing the two approaches to calculating the trade cost reductions, we first point out how NTMs are modelled as trade costs.

5.2.1 *Modelling Trade Costs Caused by NTMs*

The typical approach in the literature is to assume that NTMs generate resource-dissipating costs. Firms have to spend resources – i.e. time, working hours, financial resources – to comply with differences in national regulations and with barriers to trade. Such resource-dissipating costs are modelled in international trade using the concept of iceberg trade costs, where a fraction of goods 'melts away' in transit from one country to another, and this fraction corresponds with the resources used or dissipated to deal with the particular NTM.

More formally, denoting iceberg trade costs for goods exported from i to j as τ_{ij} means that τ_{ij} units have to be exported by country i to deliver one unit in country of destination j. Hence, $\tau_{ij} - 1$ units are lost or 'melted away' when transporting the good. The implication is that the cost of selling a good from i to j is given by $\tau_{ij}c_i$, where c_i is the marginal cost of production in exporter i.

We define iceberg trade costs without any NTMs in place as $\tau_{ij}^{noNTM} = 1 + C_{ij}$, where C_{ij} encompasses all trade costs except for tariffs and non-tariff measures, such as international transport costs and other costs related to distance, language and other barriers to trade. Iceberg trade costs inclusive of an NTM are defined as $\tau_{ij}^{NTM} = \left(1 + C_{ij}\right)\left(1 + AVE_{ij}^{NTM}\right)$, where AVE_{ij}^{NTM} is the ad valorem equivalent of an NTM, a concept often used to express the size of trade costs associated with an NTM. The AVE of an NTM is defined as the percentage increase in trade costs because of the NTM being present:

$$AVE_{ij}^{NTM} = \frac{\tau_{ij}^{NTM}}{\tau_{ij}^{noNTM}} - 1 \qquad (5.1)$$

To calculate the AVE of an NTM, the empirical literature has employed two methods (Berden and Francois, 2015). First, the price-based method relates the price difference between countries to NTMs, controlling for other observable variables and fixed effects. Second, the value-based method estimates a gravity equation relating the value of trade between countries to NTMs, controlling again for other observable variables and fixed effects. Since all studies on TTIP discussed in this chapter employ value-based methods, we explain how the iceberg trade costs associated with an NTM, τ_{ij}^{NTM}, can be calculated with this method.

Starting with a generic theoretical gravity equation, the bilateral trade value between country i and j inclusive of bilateral tariffs, V_{ij}, can be expressed as follows:[1]

$$V_{ij} = \frac{\left(\left(1 + t_{ij}\right)\tau_{ij}\right)^{-\theta} Y_i E_j}{\Pi_i \Omega_j} \tag{5.2}$$

where t_{ij} is the ad valorem tariff rate, Y_i the total output of exporter i, E_j is total expenditures in country j, θ is the trade elasticity and Π_i and Ω_j are the outward and inward multilateral resistance terms, respectively. The outward term denotes the attractiveness for exporter i to export to other destinations, and the inward term expresses the attractiveness for importer j to import from other sources. Failure to control for multilateral resistance leads to omitted variable bias (cf. Yotov et al., 2016).

From the theoretical formulation in Equation (5.2), the empirical gravity specification can be written as:

$$V_{ij} = \exp\left(\beta' C_{ij} - \theta \ln\left(1 + t_{ij}\right) + \gamma_c \ln NTM_{ij}^c + \gamma_d NTM_{ij}^d + \eta_i + \nu_j\right)\varepsilon_{ij} \tag{5.3}$$

NTMs can consist of both continuous variables, NTM_{ij}^c, which are included in logs in the estimation and discrete variables, NTM_{ij}^d, which are included in levels. C_{ij} is captured by the standard gravity bilateral variables affecting the value of trade (e.g. distance, tariffs, common border, common language and colonial past). η_i and ν_j are the exporter and importer fixed effects and ε_{ij} is an error term.

Comparing Equations (5.2) and (5.3), we see that iceberg trade costs can be written as $\tau_{ij} = \exp\left(-\frac{\beta' C_{ij} + \gamma_c \ln NTM_{ij} + \gamma_d NTM_{ij}}{\theta}\right)$.[2] We can now define the AVE of an NTM – i.e. the percentage change in iceberg trade costs as a result of the presence of this NTM – for both continuous and discrete variables. For continuous variables the AVE of an NTM is defined as the percentage change in iceberg trade costs as a result of increasing the NTM variable by 1%:

[1] As shown by Head and Mayer (2014) many theoretical trade models can be expressed using this generic gravity equation.

[2] When running simulations the importer and exporter fixed effects in the theoretical gravity equations will change as a result of changing the values of the NTM variable, but this does not affect the calculation of the change in iceberg trade costs as a result of the NTM.

$$AVE_{ij}^{NTM^c} = \frac{d \ln \tau_{ij}}{d \ln NTM_{ij}^c} \tag{5.4}$$

If the NTM_{ij} is a dummy variable, the associated AVE is defined as the change in iceberg trade costs by switching the value of the NTM dummy (NTM_{ij}) from 0 to 1:

$$AVE_{ij}^{NTM^d} = \frac{\tau_{ij}\big|NTM_{ij}^d = 1 - \tau_{ij}\big|NTM_{ij}^d = 0}{\tau_{ij}\big|NTM_{ij}^d = 0} \tag{5.5}$$

We can determine the two AVEs by combining the theoretical gravity equation in Equation (5.2) with the empirical gravity equation in Equation (5.3). This gives:

$$\frac{d \ln V_{ij}}{d \ln NTM_{ij}^c} = \frac{d \ln V_{ij}}{d \ln \tau_{ij}} \frac{d \ln \tau_{ij}}{d \ln NTM_{ij}^c} \tag{5.6}$$

$$\frac{V_{ij}\big|NTM_{ij}^d = 1}{V_{ij}\big|NTM_{ij}^d = 0} - 1 = \left(\frac{\tau_{ij}\big|NTM_{ij}^d = 1}{\tau_{ij}\big|NTM_{ij}^d = 0} \right)^{-\theta} = \exp\left(\gamma_d\right) \tag{5.7}$$

The expressions for the AVEs as defined in Equations (5.4)–(5.5) can now easily be written as follows:

$$AVE_{ij}^{NTM^c} = -\frac{\gamma_c}{\theta} \tag{5.8}$$

$$AVE_{ij}^{NTM^d} = \exp\left(-\frac{\gamma_d}{\theta}\right) - 1 \tag{5.9}$$

Equation (5.3) shows that the coefficient on tariffs can be employed to identify the trade elasticity θ, used in the counterfactual experiments. This procedure is followed in some of the TTIP studies (Francois et al., 2013; Aichele, Felbermayr and Heiland, 2014; Egger et al., 2015).

Of course Equation (5.8) is an approximation which becomes increasingly poor when the change in the continuous NTM measure (entered in logs in the gravity equation) becomes large. In that case we can better use the exact expression for the change in the NTM measure of a continuous measure, from the old to the new level, so from $NTM_{ij}^{c,0}$ to $NTM_{ij}^{c,1}$ and denoted by $AVE_{ij}^{\Delta NTM^c}$. For completeness we also define the AVE associated with the change in a discrete variable (entered in levels in the gravity equation) from $NTM_{ij}^{d,0}$ to $NTM_{ij}^{d,1}$, $AVE_{ij}^{\Delta NTM^d}$:

$$AVE_{ij}^{\Delta NTM^c} = \frac{\tau_{ij}\Big|NTM_{ij}^c = NTM_{ij}^{c,1}}{\tau_{ij}\Big|NTM_{ij}^c = NTM_{ij}^{c,0}} - 1 = \exp\left(-\frac{\gamma^c \ln \dfrac{NTM_{ij}^{c,1}}{NTM_{ij}^{c,0}}}{\theta}\right) - 1$$
$$= \left(\frac{NTM_{ij}^{c,1}}{NTM_{ij}^{c,0}}\right)^{\frac{\gamma_c}{\theta}} - 1 \tag{5.10}$$

$$AVE_{ij}^{\Delta NTM^d} = \frac{\tau_{ij}\Big|NTM_{ij}^d = NTM_{ij}^{d,1}}{\tau_{ij}\Big|NTM_{ij}^d = NTM_{ij}^{d,0}} - 1 = \frac{\exp\left(-\dfrac{\gamma^d NTM_{ij}^{d,1}}{\theta}\right)}{\exp\left(-\dfrac{\gamma^d NTM_{ij}^{d,0}}{\theta}\right)} - 1 \tag{5.11}$$

Some studies calculate the percentage change in iceberg trade costs using an approximation. The relative change in the value of trade as a result of changing a zero/one variable like *NTM* is written as follows:[3]

$$\frac{\partial \ln V_{ij}}{\partial NTM_{ij}^d} = \frac{\partial \ln V_{ij}}{\partial \ln \tau_{ij}} \frac{\partial \ln \tau_{ij}}{\partial NTM_{ij}^d} \tag{5.12}$$

From the gravity equation in Equation (5.3) we have:

$$\frac{\partial \ln V_{ij}}{\partial NTM_{ij}} = \exp(\gamma_d) - 1 \tag{5.13}$$

Combining Equations (5.12)–(5.13) gives for the percentage change in iceberg trade costs:

$$\frac{\partial \ln \tau_{ij}}{\partial NTM_{ij}} = -\frac{\exp(\gamma_d) - 1}{\theta} \tag{5.14}$$

The exact change in iceberg trade costs instead is given in Equation (5.9). For larger values of γ, Equation (5.14) becomes an increasingly poor approximation of the exact expression in Equation (5.17). For example

[3] Our notation is somewhat loose here, since NTM_{ij}^d is a discrete variable. Formally, we should write $AVE_{ij}^{NTM^d,appr} = \frac{\tau_{ij}|NTM_{ij}^d=1 - \tau_{ij}|NTM_{ij}^d=0}{\tau_{ij}|NTM_{ij}^d=0}$.

with $\gamma = 1.21$ and $\theta = 7$, we would find a percentage change in τ_{ij} of -33.6% instead of the -15.9% based on Equation (5.9). Kee, Nicita and Olarreaga (2009) use Equation (5.14) to calculate the AVE of NTMs. The AVE of an NTM is defined as the percentage change in iceberg trade costs, thus implicitly assuming that iceberg trade costs without the NTMs are equal to one. Since the level of trade costs without NTMs is unknown, this is a natural normalisation. But, as we have shown with our numerical example, Equation (5.14) is an approximation and it seems better to use Equation (5.9) to calculate the gravity-inferred AVE.

5.2.2 *Two Approaches to Calculate NTM-Related Trade Cost Reductions*

The previous subsection has equipped us with the necessary tools to understand the differences between the two approaches to calculate the reduction in trade costs as a result of NTM provisions in FTAs: the bottom-up approach and top-down approach. To compare the expected trade cost reductions in the two approaches, we have to calculate the AVEs of the introduction of an FTA.

5.2.2.1 Bottom-Up Approach

The bottom-up approach first calculates the size of NTMs already in place between FTA partners and then makes assumptions, or specifies scenarios, to infer the potential reductions in NTMs that can be expected from the implementation of that particular FTA. So, these studies start with initial levels of AVEs associated with current NTMs in place, and then impose scenarios for the percentage reductions in these NTMs or the AVEs of the NTMs as a result of the conclusion of an FTA.

Oftentimes the size of NTMs is estimated at the sector level using detailed micro data – i.e. firm-level surveys and product-level data, and sometimes in combination with expert opinion. For instance, Francois et al. (2013) infer the size of NTMs based on business surveys with about 5,500 data points. These data are mapped into AVEs by estimating sector-level gravity equations. Fontagné, Gourdon and Jean (2013) estimate the size of NTMs in goods based on product-level data from the UNCTAD-TRAINS database for NTMs in goods, and estimate the size of NTMs in services at the sector level based on importer fixed effects in each country relative to a benchmark country with the lowest level of NTMs judged by the amount of trade (Fontagné, Guillin and Mitaritonna, 2011). In Section

5.3.2 we provide a detailed explanation of the specific estimations used in both papers.

To compare the bottom-up studies with the top-down studies we have to calculate the implied AVE of the FTA based on the AVEs of NTMs in place and scenarios for the reductions in these NTMs. We can do this in two ways, using either assumed percentage reductions in NTMs or assumed percentage reductions in the AVEs of NTMs. The first approach to calculate the AVEs of an FTA in bottom-up studies can be chosen when NTM levels have been calculated based on gravity estimation and all estimation details are available. We can then apply Equations (5.10)–(5.11) imposing a percentage reduction in the NTM from NTM_{ij}^{d0} to NTM_{ij}^{d1}. We see that for calculation of the associated AVE, $AVE_{ij}^{\Delta NTM^d}$ in case of a discrete NTM measure, we need the estimated coefficients and trade elasticities, respectively γ^d and θ.

The second approach to infer the AVEs of an FTA based on bottom-up studies can be followed when only initial AVEs of NTMs are available and by employing scenarios that assume the percentages by which these AVEs are reduced. Defining the initial level of AVE in the bottom-up studies as $AVE_{ij}^{NTM,NO-FTA}$ and a percentage change in these AVEs as $pc\_AVE_{ij}^{FTA} = \frac{AVE_{ij}^{NTM,FTA} - AVE_{ij}^{NTM,NO-FTA}}{AVE_{ij}^{NTM,NO-FTA}}$, (in the Centre for Economic Policy Research (CEPR) and CEPII studies for example typically 25%), we can calculate AVE of the FTA, AVE_{ij}^{FTA}, (so the percentage change in iceberg trade costs) as:

$$AVE_{ij}^{FTA} = \frac{\tau_{ij}^{FTA} - \tau_{ij}^{NO-FTA}}{\tau_{ij}^{NO-FTA}} = \frac{1 + AVE_{ij}^{NTM,FTA} - 1 + AVE_{ij}^{NTM,NO-FTA}}{1 + AVE_{ij}^{NTM,NO-FTA}}$$
$$= \frac{AVE_{ij}^{NTM,NO-FTA}}{1 + AVE_{ij}^{NTM,NO-FTA}} pc\_AVE_{ij}^{FTA} \tag{5.15}$$

For example, an initial AVE of 9.3% and a reduction by 25% as in the CEPR study for services in the EU leads to a percentage reduction in iceberg trade costs of 2.1%, (93/109.3)*25% = 2.1%.

A somewhat different version of the bottom-up approach can be found in the study on the effects of TPP by Ciuriak, Dadkhah and Xiao (2016). This is an ex ante study of the expected effects of TPP that is based on the negotiated treaty text to infer expected trade cost reductions.[4] In particular, this study maps the TPP treaty text into trade cost indicators such as the OECD's services trade restrictiveness index (STRI). Hence, they identify provisions in the text that lead to changes in trade cost indicators, controlling for what has been dubbed as 'legal inflation' – i.e. provisions in treaties that do not effectively reduce trade costs (Horn, Mavroidis and Sapir, 2010b). These changes in the trade cost indicators can then be mapped into associated AVEs (so percentage reductions in iceberg trade costs) based on gravity estimations with these trade cost indicators.

5.2.2.2 Top-Down Approach

The top-down approach infers the expected reductions in NTM trade costs exclusively based on gravity estimation. Therefore, this method does not calculate initial levels of NTMs but determines the trade cost reduction associated with an FTA directly from a similar specification as in Equation (5.3). In particular, calculating the iceberg trade costs reductions as a result of an FTA (τ_{ij}^{FTA}) using the top-down approach is straightforward: the variable NTM_{ij} has to be replaced by FTA_{ij} in Equation (5.3), to estimate:

$$V_{ij} = \exp\left(\beta' C_{ij} - \theta \ln\left(1 + t_{ij}\right) + \delta FTA_{ij} + \lambda T_{ij} + \eta_i + \nu_j\right)\varepsilon_{ij} \quad (5.16)$$

where FTA_{ij} can be either a dummy variable that indicates the presence of an FTA between i and j or an index that determines the 'depth' of the FTA between both countries. T_{ij} are other bilateral variables determining iceberg trade costs. Comparing Equations (5.2) and (5.16), we observe that iceberg trade costs can be written as $\tau_{ij} = \exp\left(-\frac{\beta' C_{ij} + \delta FTA_{ij}}{\theta}\right)$. The associateed AVE of an FTA can then be calculated based on the change of the FTA dummy, FTA_{ij}, from 0 to 1:[5]

$$AVE_{ij}^{FTA} = \frac{\tau_{ij}^{FTA} - \tau_{ij}^{NO-FTA}}{\tau_{ij}^{NO-FTA}} = \exp\left(-\frac{\delta}{\theta}\right) - 1 \quad (5.17)$$

The coefficient on the FTA variable (δ) assesses by how much FTAs have increased trade in the past and can thus be used to determine the

[4] In contrast, since negotiations are still ongoing on TTIP, there is still no final treaty text that can be used.

[5] Again, the importer and exporter specific terms will change with different FTA values, but this does not affect the iceberg trade costs estimations.

percentage change reduction in iceberg trade costs as a result of the FTA. Note that in this specification both the tariffs and non-tariff measures associated with an FTA are grouped. Some studies, on the other hand, explicitly include tariff levels in Equation (5.16), which allows to separately identify the NTM components associated with the implementation of the FTA. In this case, Equation (5.17) will estimate AVE_{ij}^{NTM} – i.e. the AVE reduction associated only with the NTM provisions in the FTA, independent of any tariff reductions in the agreement.

As discussed into detail in Section 5.3.2, the studies using the top-down approach differ with respect to the level of aggregation of trade data used (sectoral versus aggregate), whether endogeneity of FTAs is accounted for or not and whether the trade elasticities are estimated structurally (from the same gravity equation) or not. For instance, some studies (Felbermayr, Heid and Lehwald, 2013a; Felbermayr et al., 2015; Carrère, Grujovicz and Robert-Nicoud, 2015) employ a simple 0–1 FTA dummy, implying that TTIP would generate the same trade cost reduction between EU countries and the USA as FTAs have done on average in the past. On the other hand, Aichele et al. (2014) and Egger et al. (2015) instead consider the depth of an FTA and model TTIP as the move from no FTA to a deep FTA. Another important difference is that in the first set of studies the trade elasticity is taken from the literature, whereas in the studies employing the depth of FTAs the trade elasticities are estimated structurally with the gravity equation.

5.2.3 *Comparing Both Approaches*

When comparing both methodological approaches, there are advantages and drawbacks for each. On the one hand, the bottom-up approach requires a data-intensive process (i.e. the use of micro data and surveys) that provides detailed information on different trade costs associated with NTMs. This process also provides asymmetric bilateral trade cost data, which reflect initial country- and sector-specific trade cost levels, and, thus, the potential for reductions when negotiating FTAs.

On the other hand, the top-down approach can be applied using standard gravity datasets and econometric specifications, which makes it a less data- and analytical-intensive process. In addition, when properly specified, this approach can also inform about non-observable trade costs that are overlooked by the bottom-up approach. However, this more straightforward approach also comes at the cost of assuming symmetric trade cost reductions, which disregard different initial NTM values by country and sector.

5.3 Overview of Studies on TTIP

This section provides a brief introduction to the different studies that will be compared in this chapter. In general, the studies can be divided between computational general equilibrium (CGE)-based models and structural gravity (SG) models.[6] After this overview, we conduct a more systematic comparison of the way trade cost reductions are modelled in each TTIP study.

5.3.1 General Characteristics of the TTIP Studies

5.3.1.1 CEPR Study (Francois et al., 2013)

The most influential and mostly cited economic analysis of TTIP has been the CEPR study (Francois et al., 2013) using a CGE-based analysis.[7] This study employs a CGE model to simulate the expected economic impact of TTIP.[8] The model's main features are intermediate linkages, multiple sectors and production factors, endogenous capital accumulation, monopolistic competition and the inclusion of international transport margins, export subsidies, import tariffs and other taxes. The CEPR study uses the GTAP-8 database (base year 2007), with twenty sectors and eleven regions, where the EU is treated as a single region rather than twenty-eight disaggregated countries. A baseline scenario for 2027 is then projected by endogenising productivity growth such that macroeconomic aggregates in the baseline are equal to long-term GDP projections from the OECD and UN population projections.

The study explores the economy-wide impacts of several TTIP scenarios, of which reducing tariffs and NTMs are the most important. As an

[6] See Bekkers and Rojas-Romagosa (2019) for a detailed discussion of the differences between both modelling frameworks, and the related TTIP economic effects.

[7] This is the reference study by the European Commission and DG Trade (cf. European Commission, 2013) and the study discussed by most commentators (see for example The Economist, 2013; Mustilli, 2015; Rodrik, 2015; The Guardian, 2015; Wolf, 2015). The relevance of this study is highlighted by the request of the European Parliament to conduct an independent evaluation of this study, which was done by Pelkmans et al. (2014).

[8] The study uses a variant of the Global Trade Analysis Project (GTAP) CGE model. The main characteristics and references to the standard GTAP model are detailed in Hertel and Tsigas (1997) and Hertel (2013).

outcome of the CGE analysis, detailed simulation results are provided for expected changes in GDP, household disposable income, overall aggregate and bilateral export and import flows, trade diversion effects (from/to intra-EU, USA and third countries), terms-of-trade, tariff revenues, sectoral output and sectoral trade flows. The sustainability impact also includes detailed results on changes in wages for high- and low-skill workers, sectoral employment by skill level, labour displacement measures, changes in CO_2 emissions and land use. Finally, the study provides GDP and trade effects for third countries.

5.3.1.2 CEPII Study (Fontagné et al., 2013)

The CEPII study starts with a description of the current trade and investment relations between the EU and the USA. Given the limited average level of the import tariffs between both regions (2% in the USA and 3% in the EU), they predict that these tariffs will not be the most important topics in the TTIP negotiations.[9] As with the CEPR study, this study finds that the corresponding levels of protection provided by the non-tariff measures are much higher on average than those provided by the tariffs. The authors also find that these differ significantly across sectors. Thus, they state that the significant negotiation topics at the macroeconomic level are on non-tariff measures, regulation in services, public procurement, geographical indication of origin and investment. They argue that these topics are contentious and provide an overview of each topic. The sector-specific trade barriers, together with NTMs and other contentious topics explain the overall sensitivity of the TTIP negotiations.[10] Finally, to assess the macroeconomic effects of TTIP they use the MIRAGE CGE model (Bchir et al., 2002) that, similar to the CGE model in the CEPR study, provides a broad set of economic outputs.[11]

5.3.1.3 Egger et al. (2015)

Egger et al. (2015) examine the potential impact of TTIP with a hybrid approach that combines a CGE economic model with structural estimation of the trade elasticities and the expected trade cost reductions to

[9] However, they do acknowledge that tariffs will be important for some sensitive sectors: for both the EU and USA dairy products, clothing and footwear are sensitive. Furthermore, steel items are sensitive for the USA and meat products for the EU.

[10] As in other studies reviewed here, they acknowledge that not all of the different aspects of the negotiations can be incorporated into a model.

[11] This CGE model is also related to the GTAP-class models.

generate estimates of the welfare effects for the EU, USA and third countries. The study follows a two-step approach. In the first step a gravity model is employed to yield estimates of reductions in trade costs. These values are then used as inputs in the second step where a CGE model simulates the economy-wide effects. This study focuses on and reports largely the same outcome measures as Francois et al. (2013). The CGE model employed in Egger et al. (2015) is also very similar to the model in Francois et al. (2013). The main difference with respect to the CGE application is that Egger et al. (2015) use the more recent GTAP-9 database with base year 2011 instead of the older GTAP-8 database with base year 2007.

5.3.1.4 Felbermayr et al. (2015)

The study by Felbermayr et al. (2015) is a typical SG application based on a one-sector model with both a gravity equation to determine the trade costs associated with the TTIP experiment and a general equilibrium equation to calculate the welfare effects, where both equations follow directly from the theoretical gravity model. Baseline trade costs are calibrated to the fitted/predicted values of the estimated gravity equation. The paper does not follow the structural gravity literature in the determination of the parameters of the model, since the trade elasticity – a crucial parameter in the calculation of the welfare effects – is not estimated structurally, but is taken from the literature (i.e. Egger et al., 2011; Egger and Larch, 2011).

5.3.1.5 Felbermayr et al. (2013a)

Felbermayr et al. (2013a) explore the effects of TTIP on both trade and welfare and on the labour market. This is done with two distinct SG models. The first model explores the impact on trade, GDP and welfare for 126 countries, whereas the second model is limited to 28 countries due to the lack of available labour market data for more countries. The first model is identical to the model employed by Felbermayr et al. (2015) except for the variables included in the gravity equation.

5.3.1.6 Aichele et al. (2014)

To date, the study by Aichele et al. (2014) is the most sophisticated SG-based study on TTIP. These researchers use a multi-country and multi-sector Ricardian trade model with national and international input-output linkages identical to the model employed by Caliendo and Parro (2015) to study the impact of tariff reductions as a result of the

North American Free Trade Agreement (NAFTA). Counterfactual outcomes are calculated employing so-called exact hat algebra with baseline import shares calibrated to actual import shares as in the CGE approach.

5.3.1.7 Carrère et al. (2015)

Carrère et al. (2015) use a multi-sector SG approach to determine the real wage and unemployment effects of TTIP by including labour market frictions and equilibrium unemployment in an Eaton-Kortum-type trade framework. The authors also present welfare effects based on a weighted average of real wage and unemployment effects. A salient feature of this study is that the negative unemployment effects dominate the positive real wage effects in their set-up, which generate overall negative welfare effects in some countries. The negative unemployment effects stem from a reallocation of workers from sectors with fewer labour market frictions and smaller equilibrium unemployment to sectors with more labour market frictions and higher equilibrium unemployment.

5.3.2 NTM Reductions in Each TTIP Study

In this section we explain how each particular impact assessment study estimates the associated trade cost reductions from implementing TTIP.

5.3.2.1 Francois et al. (2013)

Francois et al. (2013) take into account the three types of trade cost reductions associated with FTAs: tariffs, NTMs and spillover effects. To determine the size of reductions in NTMs as a result of TTIP, this study follows a bottom-up approach, taking four steps. First, the size of NTMs is inferred from business surveys (with about 5,500 data points). Firms from a particular country *i* are asked to rank the overall restrictiveness of an export market *j* between 0 and 100. The bilateral indices are aggregated per sector to importer *j* specific indices. This aggregated number defines the size of NTMs for imports into country *j*. The import-specific indices are then included in a standard gravity regression – as in Equation (5.3) – by interacting the NTM measures with dummies for intra-EU, intra-NAFTA and transatlantic trade. Actionable NTMs between the EU and the USA are then defined as the difference in the ad valorem equivalent trade costs of the NTMs (using estimated tariff elasticities in goods, while for services a trade elasticity of 4 is used) for USA–EU trade, intra-EU trade (NTMs into the EU), for USA-EU trade and intra-NAFTA trade (NTMs into the USA). Comparing these trade cost estimates, the actionable NTMs to be negotiated in TTIP consist of the difference in costs perceived by businesses surveyed of importing into an EU country from the USA in comparison to importing into the same EU country from another EU country.

Second, NTMs are divided into two categories: cost-increasing barriers and rent-creating barriers.[12] On the basis of the ECORYS (2009) survey and expert judgement, on average (across sectors) 60% of the NTMs are cost-increasing. The other 40% of the claimed increase in prices as a result of NTMs, can be attributed to rents. The implication of these rents is that with existing NTMs firms have more market power and thus set higher prices.[13]

Third, the study assumes that only a fraction of NTMs can be reduced, as it is not possible to remove them because of legal, institutional or political constraints.[14] It is then assumed that 50% of the AVE of estimated NTMs can be reduced, or, as the authors term it, are actionable.[15]

Fourth, as part of the TTIP experiment only a fraction of the actionable share of NTMs is assumed to be lowered as a result of signing TTIP. Different scenarios are employed, but the baseline scenario has a 50% reduction in the actionable NTMs. The result of combining the actionability share with the share of actionable NTMs reduced (both 50%) is that NTMs are expected to fall by 25% with TTIP.

5.3.2.2 Fontagné et al. (2013)

The CEPII study uses the estimates for NTMs in goods from the study by Kee et al. (2009) and their own CEPII estimates (Fontagné et al., 2011) for NTM values in services. Kee et al. (2009) estimate AVE NTMs using a 0–1 dummy variable on NTMs at a very detailed product (tariff line) level (HS6) using the UNCTAD's TRAINS database. To consolidate this information, they then regress import values per country and tariff line

12 See Box 1 in Francois et al. (2013) for more details.

13 It is not clear from the description of the simulations whether prices are really reduced by 40% of the AVE of the actionable NTMs as a result of the TTIP experiment or whether the 60%/40% cut only serves to determine the share of NTMs that is cost-increasing.

14 These limitations in reducing NTMs stem from legal and even constitutional restrictions, political and consumer sensibilities and technical limitations, among others. See Egger et al. (2015) for a more detailed discussion on this topic.

15 The share is based on expert opinions, cross-checks with regulators, legislators and businesses opinions taken from the business survey in ECORYS (2009). More details are in Box 1 in Francois et al. (2013).

(corrected for endogenous tariffs) on the (instrumented) NTM dummies, constraining the coefficients to be positive. Thus, their calculations are based on product-level import equations that consolidate information from several sources, in particular, the NTMs already contained in the UNCTAD-TRAINS database. Finally, trade elasticities are estimated based on the Feenstra (1994) approach – using identification by heteroscedasticity – and these are then used to obtain the NTM AVE values.

Fontagné et al. (2011) estimate NTMs in services using a residuals method based on the importer fixed effect in each importer country relative to the importer fixed effect in a benchmark country with the highest value of predicted trade relative to actual trade. The importer fixed effect of the benchmark country defines trade costs in the most liberalised country and, thus, in the country with the largest scope for trade liberalisation. These estimates generate NTM AVEs of cross-border trade flows in services for nine services sectors and sixty-five countries from the GTAP database.

The CEPII study then employs a 25% reduction in the estimated NTM AVE values, based on the same arguments used in Francois et al. (2013) – i.e. the level of actionability (50%) times the expected level of NTMs that can be actually negotiated in TTIP (also 50%).

5.3.2.3 Felbermayr et al. (2013a) and Felbermayr et al. (2015)

Both these studies follow a top-down approach as in Equation (5.16), separately accounting for tariffs and using a dummy variable for FTAs. So instead of calculating the AVE TTIP with the depth of FTAs, they use a simple 0–1 dummy for all FTAs. The two studies only differ with respect to the number of countries included in the gravity estimation and the control variables employed.[16] The gravity equation is estimated with Poisson pseudo-maximum likelihood (PPML) accounting for endogeneity of FTAs, based on the approach in Egger et al. (2011). The two studies do not report the AVEs of their TTIP experiment, since they directly calculate the change in income, multilateral resistances and welfare as a result of the change in the FTA dummy from 0 to 1. However, the NTM AVE values can be easily obtained from Equation (5.17), using their estimated FTA coefficient (δ) and the employed trade elasticity (θ).

[16] The exact approach in Felbermayr et al. (2013a) can be found by consulting the companion study (Felbermayr et al., 2013b).

5.3.2.4 Egger et al. (2015)

This study calculates the reduction of NTMs in goods employing a top-down approach, while the reduction in NTMs in services is calculated with a bottom-up approach. To calculate the reductions in NTMs on manufacturing goods, a gravity equation as in Equation (5.16) is estimated including the depth of FTAs, while controlling for FTA endogeneity following the approach in Egger and Larch (2011). To measure the depth of FTAs the authors use the index of the FTA depth proposed by Dür et al. (2014) which ranges from 0 to 7, where TTIP is assumed to be a deep FTA with the maximum value of a FTA depth of 7.[17] Based on the estimated trade elasticities (δ), the NTM AVEs are calculated as moving from no FTA (index = 0) to a deep FTA (index = 7).

The AVEs of trade restrictions in services are taken from Jafari and Tarr (2015) based on the World Bank's STRI database (Borchert, Gootiiz and Mattoo, 2014). Both for manufacturing goods and services the remaining steps are the same as in Francois et al. (2013). Hence, NTMs are split up into cost-increasing and rent-generating NTMs and only the share of actionable NTMs is assumed to be reduced under TTIP. In this study the share of cost-increasing NTMs is again 50%, but in contrast to the CEPR study, the share of actionable NTMs is assumed to be now 100% (instead of 50%), which is consistent with the presumption that TTIP will be a deep FTA. On the other hand, the share of actionable NTMs in services varies by scenario. In one scenario there is no reduction in services NTMs and in the other scenario NTMs for non-financial services fall by 50%.

5.3.2.5 Aichele et al. (2014)

NTM reductions in this study are defined as a reduction in iceberg trade costs calculated using a top-down approach and separately accounting for tariff effects. A gravity model following Equation (5.16) is estimated including dummies for shallow and deep FTAs. A shallow FTAs is defined as an FTA with a score between 0 and 3 in the FTA depth index from Dür et al. (2014), and a deep FTA is defined as an FTA with an index between 4 and 7. The FTA dummies are instrumented by employing a measure for trade contagion proposed by Baldwin and Jaimovich (2012). To determine the reduction in overall iceberg trade costs for goods this study uses the estimated trade elasticities, whereas for

[17] In terms of the coding of FTA depth this means that the FTA should contain provisions on all seven topics identified by Dür, Baccini and Elsig. (2014).

services a trade elasticity of 5.9 is used, based on estimates from Egger, Larch and Staub (2012). Then the authors assume that the AVE NTM reductions associated with TTIP can be calculated by shifting their FTA-dummy definition from 0 (shallow FTA) to 1 (deep FTA).

5.3.2.6 Carrère et al. (2015)

This study accounts for reductions in NTMs following the top-down approach in Equation (5.16) with a 0–1 FTA dummy and separately estimating the effect of tariffs. Although the authors use data on thirty-five sectors for their SG model, the gravity equation is estimated by pooling all sectors. Thus, this study estimate a single trade elasticity of 3.17 and a coefficient on the FTA dummy of 0.52. Hence, despite having data at the sectoral level, only an aggregate NTM trade cost reduction is calculated.

5.4 Comparison of Trade Cost Reductions between Studies

In this section we do quantitative comparisons of the explicit and implicit trade cost values employed in each TTIP study and explain why there are significant differences in these estimations between studies. First, we explain differences in trade cost estimations when using the gravity model, and then we compare the iceberg trade cost reductions in each study.

5.4.1 Comparing Trade Cost Estimations Using the Gravity Estimations

The TTIP studies can be compared quantitatively based on the AVEs of the introduction of TTIP (or phrased differently the percentage reduction in iceberg trade costs as a result of implementing TTIP), $AVE_{ij}^{FTA} = \frac{\tau_{ij}^{FTA}}{\tau_{ij}^{NO-FTA}} - 1$. For example, from Felbermayr et al. (2013a) and Felbermayr et al. (2015) we can directly calculate the percentage change in iceberg trade costs using Equation (5.17) with δ the coefficient on the FTA dummy and θ the assumed trade elasticity. A trade elasticity of 7 in the baseline and estimates of δ of respectively 1.24 and 1.21 generate the numbers displayed in Table 5.1.[18] For the bottom-up studies we employ

[18] See Table 3 in Felbermayr et al. (2015) and Table II.2 in Felbermayr et al. (2013b). To calculate the average AVEs in Aichele et al. (2014) we can use the same methodology but we need to do some additional calculations, since the authors report different estimated trade elasticities and deep FTA dummies for more than thirty sectors. In particular, we

Table 5.1 *Trade-weighted average percentage iceberg trade cost reductions*

		AVE NTM initial levels			TTIP experiment: percentage change iceberg trade costs		
	Weighted averages	EU	USA	both regions	EU	USA	both regions
CEPR study	**Overall**	10.6	14.3	12.5	−2.3	−2.8	−2.5
	Agriculture/Primary	-	-	-	-	-	-
	Manufacturing	11.9	16.3	14.3	−2.5	−3.1	−2.8
	Services	9.3	10.0	9.7	−2.1	−2.1	−2.1
Egger et al. (2015)	**Overall**	16.5	16.5	16.5	−12.4	−13.6	−13.0
	Agriculture/Primary	15.9	15.9	15.9	−15.9	−15.9	−15.9
	Manufacturing	15.9	17.0	16.5	−15.9	−17.0	−16.5
	Services	17.6	15.4	16.6	−6.7	−6.0	−6.4
CEPII study	**Overall**	38.8	37.0	37.9	−6.5	−7.7	−7.1
	Agriculture/Primary	48.2	51.3	48.8	−8.1	−8.5	−8.3
	Manufacturing	42.8	32.3	37.0	−7.5	−6.1	−6.9
	Services	32.0	47.3	39.0	−6.1	−8.0	−7.1
Aichele et al. (2014)	**Overall**				−12.7	−13.8	−13.2
	Agriculture/Primary				−52.5	−52.5	−52.5
	Manufacturing				−16.5	−17.6	−17.1
	Services				−5.2	-4.6	−4.9
Felbermayr et al. (2013a)	**Overall**				−16.2	−16.2	−16.2
Felbermayr et al. (2015)	**Overall**				−15.9	−15.9	−15.9
Carrère et al. (2015)	**Overall**				−15.1	−15.1	−15.1

Sources: Own estimations based on NTMs and trade cost reductions estimates from referred studies and bilateral sector-specific USA–EU trade data from the GTAP-9 database.

the initial levels of AVEs of NTMs reported in the studies and apply percentage reductions in these AVEs. For services in the EU in the Egger et al. study, for example, we apply the formula in Equation (5.15) on an initial AVE of 17.6% and, thus, a 25% in the AVE (see Table 5.1) would lead to an AVE of TTIP of $AVE_{TTIP}^{ser,Egger} = \frac{0.176}{1.176} * -25\% = -7.5\%$.[19]

5.4.2 *Ad Valorem Equivalents of the Introduction of TTIP in Different Studies*

To make the TTIP experiment comparable across studies we report the AVE as a result of TTIP in Table 5.1. The bottom-up studies (Fontagné et al., 2013; Francois et al., 2013) report initial levels of NTMs and assume that the NTMs will be reduced by a fraction of the initial level. The top-down studies report the effect of (deep) FTAs on trade flows in gravity estimations. In Subsection 5.4.1 we discussed how the AVEs (percentage reductions in iceberg trade costs) of TTIP can be calculated with the two approaches. For the studies reporting trade cost reductions at sectoral levels, we calculate a weighted average for the three main sectors – agriculture, manufactures and services – based on more disaggregated subsectors. The weights are given by the amount of trade from the EU to the USA for US NTMs and from the USA to the EU for EU NTMs (using trade data from the GTAP-9 database).

The weighted iceberg trade cost reductions reported in Table 5.1 show that the differences are large, ranging from 2.5% reduction in trade costs in Francois et al. (2013) to 16.2% in Felbermayr et al. (2013a). In addition, Table 5.1 shows that services trade contributes relatively little to the overall reduction in trade costs. Given that services trade is only about 6% of total bilateral trade between the two regions, its contribution to the total trade cost reduction is also small. In general we find that the studies working with a bottom-up approach based on micro data on NTMs (Fontagné et al., 2013; Francois et al., 2013) estimate smaller trade cost reductions than the top-down approaches based on average FTA

first calculated the percentage changes in iceberg trade costs for the different sectors based on the estimated tariff elasticities and the coefficients for shallow and deep FTAs (in Tables 1 and 2 in Aichele et al. (2014)) and then calculated the weighted average AVEs for agriculture, manufacturing and services. We calculate AVEs per sector using the following formula, $\frac{\tau^{FTA}}{\tau^{NO-FTA}} - 1 = \exp\left(-\frac{\beta_{shallow}+\beta_{deep}}{\theta}\right) - 1$.

[19] 7.5% deviates from the 6.7% reported in Table 5.1 because the numbers in the table are based on trade-weighted average AVEs of TTIP.

effects (the rest of the studies). Both approaches are subject to criticism. In the bottom-up approach the share of NTMs that will be reduced as a result of TTIP is hard to motivate and a percentage like 25% or 50% always seems somewhat arbitrary. Furthermore, NTM data are often of poor quality with negative estimated AVEs for many products. The top-down approach, on the other hand, can be criticised for the fact that it is debatable whether TTIP will create similar NTM effects as in past deep FTAs. Moreover, modellers need to pay attention to estimation details of choosing the proper instrument, the correct FTA measure and the adequate functional form of the gravity equation (PPML).[20]

Comparing the studies within the two groups reveals that the CEPII study generates much larger NTM levels than the CEPR study. Furthermore, it is encouraging that the average trade cost reduction in the study by Aichele et al. (2014) is similar to the reduction in Egger et al. (2015), given that a similar methodology was used. Both studies calculate the impact of a move from no FTA to a deep FTA based on the same depth of FTA data. The difference is the operationalisation. Egger et al. (2015) maintain the 0–7 scale, whereas Aichele et al. (2014) convert this scale into two dummies, one for shallow FTAs and one for deep FTAs. For the agriculture sectors, nonetheless, there are notable differences, where Aichele et al. (2014) find much larger trade cost reductions than Egger et al. (2015). There are three important differences between the two gravity estimates. First, the instruments used are different. Second, the estimation method differs: PPML in Egger et al. (2015) versus IV in Aichele et al. (2014). Finally, Egger et al. (2015) include a separate dummy for trade between EU members, thereby driving down the coefficient on the FTA depth variable.

To summarise, it is difficult to give a value judgement on the expected trade cost reductions corresponding with TTIP. However, given the limitations on their estimation techniques, we consider that the approximately 16% NTM reductions reported in Felbermayr et al. (2013a) and Felbermayr et al. (2015) seem over-estimated. In particular, these studies do not account for the depth of FTAs and assume that TTIP will be similar to any average FTA in the past. This is an unrealistic assumption since most FTAs have strongly focused on relatively large tariff reductions in the past, but these are not possible within TTIP given the

[20] All studies using the top-down approach account for endogeneity of FTAs, although in a different way. All studies estimate the gravity equation using PPML, except for Aichele et al. (2014) who use Instrumental Variables (IV).

relatively low existing tariff levels. Furthermore, the effect of TTIP seems to rise significantly by not including a separate dummy for intra-EU trade. Carrère et al. (2015), moreover, do not account for the depth of FTAs and fail to correct for the endogeneity of FTAs. Therefore, we conclude that a reasonable lower bound for the average trade cost reduction as a result of TTIP is the 3% values in Francois et al. (2013) and a reasonable upper bound is the 13% values in Egger et al. (2015) and Aichele et al. (2014).

5.5 Relation between Trade Cost Reductions and the Expected Economic Effects of TTIP

In this section we first summarise the main economic effects from each study, using the welfare effects (i.e. real GDP and income changes) as our comparison variable.[21] We then relate the discrepancies in these overall economic effects to the trade cost reductions assumed in each study.

5.5.1 Expected Welfare Effects from TTIP

5.5.1.1 CEPR Study (Francois et al., 2013)

The main economic finding from the CEPR study is that an ambitious and comprehensive transatlantic trade and investment agreement could bring positive economic gains for both regions of 0.4% of real GDP for the USA and 0.5% for the EU, when comparing the baseline GDP level in 2027 with the simulated GDP level after TTIP. EU exports to the USA are expected to increase by 28%, while total exports increase 6% in the EU and 8% in the USA. Other scenarios are also evaluated, where results are expected to be lower than an ambitious TTIP agreement.

5.5.1.2 CEPII Study (Fontagné et al., 2013)

In general, the expected economic effects of TTIP in the CEPII study are similar to those of the CEPR study. As in the CEPR study, around 80% of the expected trade expansion would stem from lowered non-tariff measures. Overall, both regions will obtain non-negligible GDP and real income effects, in the long run, of around 0.3%. Results for alternative scenarios are presented as well, first distinguishing between the effects of

[21] See Bekkers and Rojas-Romagosa (2019) for a comprehensive analytical and quantitative comparison of these studies.

tariff elimination and NTM reductions, second using the ECORYS (2009) NTM levels as reference and third including third-country spill-over effects from regulatory harmonisation.

5.5.1.3 Egger et al. (2015)

The main economic result from the scenario that includes tariff elimination and reduction in NTMs in goods is that estimated gains in real income are situated between 1% and 2.25% for the USA and EU, respectively.

The bilateral trade growth in this paper (80%) is much higher than in the CEPR study (28%). Correspondingly, the real income effects are also higher now (about four times the results in the CEPR study). The main reason for the higher bilateral trade is that NTMs were estimated differently – as explained above.[22]

5.5.1.4 Felbermayr et al. (2015)

Felbermayr et al. (2015) estimate relatively large welfare effects of TTIP. They find that TTIP can yield real income gains for the EU of 3.9% and 4.9% for the USA.[23] They also report robustness checks, and, in particular, they calculate the welfare effects employing the average FTA coefficient of 0.36 reported in the literature survey by Head and Mayer (2010). As a result the welfare effects are much smaller. Switching off the extensive margin channel hardly changes the effects since the estimated coefficient of the FTA dummy in the selection equation (i.e. whether there is trade or not) is small. Finally, they also evaluate the effect of including the spillover effects, which magnifies the positive welfare effects as in other studies.

5.5.1.5 Felbermayr et al. (2013a)

This study finds the largest welfare effects of all the studies. For instance, for the USA and Great Britain this study estimates an increase in welfare (i.e. equivalent variation) of 13.4% and 9.7%, while the average welfare increase in the EU is about 8%. Also remarkable are the welfare losses of third countries (9.5% in Canada, 7.2% in Mexico and 7.4% in Australia).[24]

[22] Egger et al. (2015) also have more recent data on NTMs in services and have a pessimistic (no real changes in trade in services) and optimistic (real changes in all services sectors but finance) perspective.

[23] This study does not report changes in trade flows and focuses exclusively on welfare effects.

[24] It is unclear, however, why the welfare effects are so large in comparison to the CGE studies, but also in comparison to similar studies (i.e. Felbermayr et al., 2015). Bekkers

5.5.1.6 Aichele et al. (2014)

This paper finds that TTIP will generate real per capita income changes of 2.1% for the EU and 2.7% for the USA. These gains are achieved through strong bilateral trade increases of 171% (from the USA to the EU) and 216% (from the EU to the USA), spurred mainly by NTM reductions. Interestingly, the real income effects from this study are somewhat larger – and the trade flows more than double – than those in Egger et al. (2015) even though the trade cost reductions are similar in both studies.

5.5.1.7 Carrère et al. (2015)

This study report effects of TTIP on real wages, unemployment and welfare. Welfare is a weighted average of the real wage and unemployment. Since we only use real income as our comparison variable, we do not take into account the authors' unemployment effects.[25] In particular, we use their real wage effects as the main welfare variable from this study. The authors find positive but relatively small real wage effects of 0.3% in the USA and on average 0.2% in the EU.

5.5.2 Impact of Estimated Trade Cost Reductions on Predicted Welfare Effects

The different studies discussed in this chapter all map the estimated trade cost reductions as a result of TTIP into projected welfare effects. This is done employing either CGE models or structural gravity models. In Bekkers and Rojas-Romagosa (2019) we compare these two approaches and also evaluate the impact of differences in model structure on predicted welfare effects. Here we limit ourselves to evaluating the impact of variation in trade cost reductions on predicted welfare effects with a flexible CGE model, also evaluating the impact of variation in trade elasticities.[26]

Figure 5.1 displays the percentage change in welfare in the EU as a function of percentage changes in iceberg trade costs between the EU and the USA for three values of the trade elasticity, $\theta = 3$, $\theta = 5$ and $\theta = 7$. The figure shows that for the intermediate value of the trade elasticity

and Rojas-Romagosa (2019) presents an extensive comparison of TTIP, which can explain these discrepancies.

25 These are analysed in detail in Bekkers and Rojas-Romagosa (2019).

26 The specific model employed is a simplified CGE version that is closer to the structural gravity models. For a detailed description see Bekkers and Rojas-Romagosa (2019).

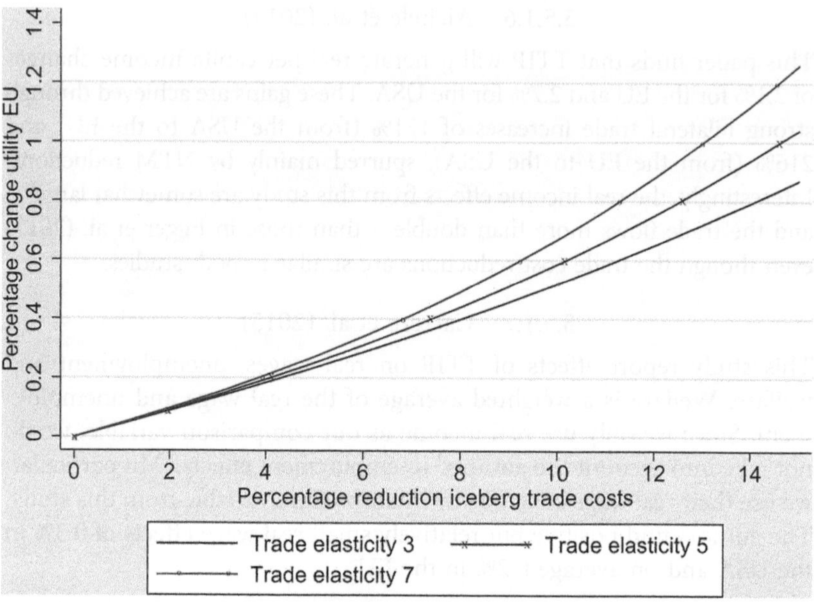

Figure 5.1 Welfare changes in the EU as a function of changes in iceberg trade costs τ_{ij}^{NTM} for various values of the trade elasticity.
Source: Own calculations with flexible CGE model as described in Hertel and Tsigas (1997), Hertel (2013), and Bekkers, Francois and Rojas-Romagosa (2018)

of 5, reported as the median value in Head and Mayer (2014), welfare gains from reductions in iceberg trade costs rise more than proportionally with the reduction in iceberg trade costs. For example, a doubling of the reduction in trade costs from 4% to 8% raises the welfare gains from 0.2% to more than 0.4%. The figure shows furthermore that the relation is convex, i.e. at larger trade costs the impact of a change in iceberg trade costs becomes larger.

From the figure we can also draw clear conclusions on the impact of the size of the trade elasticity on the welfare effects of reductions in iceberg trade costs between FTA partners. At larger trade elasticities the effect of reductions in trade costs becomes larger and the difference rises with the size of the trade cost shock. For example, for a trade cost reduction of 14%, the predicted welfare gain for the EU is only about 0.8% with a trade elasticity of 3 and about 1.2% with a trade elasticity of 7. These findings seem at odds with the result in the literature (Arkolakis, Costinot and Rodríguez-Clare, 2012) that the welfare gains from trade are larger at a smaller trade elasticity, corresponding with the intuition that love-of-variety forces are stronger at a lower trade elasticity, making it more valuable to be able to import. Their result, however, is about the welfare gains from trade and not from trade liberalisation. We have seen in Figure 5.1 that a larger trade elasticity raises the gains from trade liberalisation, because trade responses are bigger in this case.

However, since the top-down AVE trade cost reduction estimation requires the specification of a trade elasticity (see Equation (5.1), then the overall estimated iceberg trade costs are conditional on the trade elasticity. In particular, a higher trade elasticity results in lower iceberg trade costs. Therefore, the relation between welfare effects, trade cost reductions and trade elasticities is conditional on how the trade costs are associated (or not) with particular trade elasticity values.

5.5.3 *Spillover Effects*

Another importance source of divergencies in estimated trade cost reductions comes from the so-called spillover effects – i.e. changes in trade costs in third countries that are related to the NTM reductions between the TTIP partners. These spillover effects were first introduced in the discussion on TTIP by Francois et al. (2013), distinguishing between direct and indirect spillovers. Direct spillovers occur when third countries find it less costly to export to the EU and the USA as a result of TTIP. Indirect spillovers take place when third countries partially take over the harmonised standards in the EU and USA, resulting in lower trade costs between third countries and for exports from the EU and USA to third countries. The spillover effects stem from the expectation that TTIP will lead to improved regulatory cooperation between the EU and the USA and that this new regulatory framework will become a global standard. Harmonisation of regulations will make it less costly to comply with the fixed costs of exporting to the EU and US market: these costs have to be incurred only once if regulations are harmonised.

The obvious effect of modelling spillovers is that negative trade diversion effects on third countries become smaller. The assumption of positive spillover effects is not uncontroversial. When two countries harmonise standards, they will also replace old standards, possibly agreed upon with third countries. This might make it more difficult for third countries to comply with the new standards, thus generating cost increases instead of cost reductions. The empirical literature on the scope for spillover effects is summarised in Baldwin (2014), although he organises the discussion around the concept of 'negative trade diversion'. When a country signs a deep FTA it might improve the functioning of its services sector, implement stricter rules on competition policy and streamline its government procurement, for example. To a large extent these measures are non-discriminatory in nature, thus also generating benefits for non-members. The studies cited in Baldwin (2014) indicate that the scope for negative trade diversion is very limited: in most cases trade with non-FTA partners also increases when an FTA is signed. This does not provide, however, conclusive evidence for the presence of direct spillover effects: trade with non-FTA partners might also increase after an FTA has been signed because countries signing an FTA might be implementing other types of reforms together with signing an FTA.

Only Francois et al. (2013) works with direct and indirect spillover effects in the authors' main simulations, whereas most other studies report the effects of spillovers in the robustness checks. All studies, however, follow Francois et al. (2013) by assuming that direct spillovers (third countries exporting to the EU) are 20% of the trade cost reductions between the EU and the USA and indirect spillovers are 10% (third countries exporting to each other).[27]

When we analyse the spillover effects, Table 5.2 shows that the economic effects of including spillovers vary considerably within studies. Whereas Fontagné et al. (2013) and Felbermayr et al. (2015) find that the spillover effects raise welfare by about two-thirds, the other studies find effects in the range of 20% to 25%.[28] We can explain the large effect in Felbermayr et al. (2015) by the way baseline trade costs are modelled in their single-sector model. As discussed below, this approach biases the effects of trade cost reductions upwards and, thus, also the effect of spillovers. Thus, by excluding both these studies as outliers, we conclude that including 20% direct and 10% indirect spillovers is expected to have additional welfare increases on the TTIP partners of about 25%.

27 For example, if there is a 5% total trade cost reduction between the EU and USA, the direct spillover (i.e. 20% over total trade costs) will represent an additional 1% total trade cost decrease for third countries exporting to the USA or EU and an additional 0.5% indirect spillover reduction (i.e. half the size of the direct spillover decrease) for EU and US export costs to third countries and for trade between third countries.

28 The large effects in Fontagné et al. (2013), however, could be explained from the fact that this study only reports effects rounded to one decimal, while the absolute differences are less significant.

Table 5.2 *Estimated TTIP welfare effects, with and without spillover effects*

	Without spillovers		With spillovers		Relative difference
	EU	USA	EU	USA	
CEPR study	0.4	0.3	0.5	0.4	20.8%
CEPII study	0.3	0.3	0.5	0.5	66.7%
Egger et al. (2015)	2.3	1.0	3.0	1.1	26.5%
Aichele et al. (2014)	2.1	2.7	2.7	3.4	25.4%
Felbermayr et al. (2015)	3.9	4.9	7.8	7.1	67.7%

Source: Own estimations based on reported results from cited studies.

5.6 Summary and Conclusions

Average tariff levels have been decreasing steadily since the Second World War. As a consequence, the relative importance of non-tariff measures has been rising, and in the latest deep FTAs there has been an special emphasis on how trade facilitation mechanisms, behind-the-border measures and the harmonisation and mutual recognition of regulations can yield substantial decreases in NTMs. As such, the estimation of these potential NTM reductions has become a key variable to properly estimate the expected economic effects of these deep FTAs.

In this chapter we detailed how NTMs can be calculated using two different estimation techniques: bottom-up or top-down. In particular, we detail and compare how seven different impact assessments of TTIP have estimated the potential trade cost reductions from this agreement, why there are some significant discrepancies in the cost reduction values, and how these differences can explain the different expected welfare effects that come out of these studies.

The main finding of this chapter is that a reliable and transparent estimation of the NTM trade cost reductions associated with FTAs, is indeed a key issue to ultimately evaluate these agreements and yield reliable economic impacts. We find that accounting for differences in the expected NTM reductions can explain a large share of the discrepancies regarding the overall potential economic effects of TTIP.

6

Gauging Procurement Policy Change during the Crisis Era

Evidence from the Global Trade Alert*

SIMON J. EVENETT AND ANIRUDH SHINGAL

6.1 Introduction and Motivation

The contribution of fiscal policy to restoring economic growth has waxed and waned since the onset of the global economic growth. After an initial burst of fiscal stimulus in 2008 and 2009, many governments retrenched, turning to austerity policies from 2010. While some detect a revival of fiscal activism during the past year (Davies, 2016; Ip, 2016), monetary policy has been the principal tool of macroeconomic policy in many G20 nations.

If fiscal policy has been so muted – at least in terms of spending levels and contribution to national income growth – then is there little to say about the impact of public procurement policies during the crisis era? Not necessarily. By altering the relative treatment of domestic bidders for state contacts vis-à-vis their foreign rivals, changes in public procurement policy can shift expenditures across borders.

Given that many governments' expenditures on goods and services amount to large shares of national income, the potential redirection of demand could have significant implications for the fortunes of internationally active firms, the employment prospects of their staff, the value

* This chapter was produced as part of the project 'Productivity, Non-tariff Measures and Openness' (PRONTO) funded by the European Commission under the Seventh Framework Programme, Theme SSH.2013.4.3-3 'Untapped Potential for Growth and Employment Reducing the Cost of Non-tariff Measures in Goods, Services and Investment', grant agreement no. 613504. A presentation on the data referred to in this chapter was made at the European University Institute in Florence, Italy, in September 2016. We thank Patrick Messerlin and Julien Gourdon for comments on that presentation. The Global Trade Alert (GTA) is an independent research initiative and received no financial support from the European Commission for generation of original GTA data used in this chapter.

for money in state contracting, international trade and investment flows and, should matters become contentious, for trade disputes.

Even in countries where fiscal policy has not been expansionary, changes in public procurement policies can have important implications for cross-border commerce and therefore become a legitimate area for commercial policy discussions. The criticism – and latter copy-catting – by foreign governments of early crisis-era policies to impose stringent 'Buy America' provisions in the US fiscal stimulus policies speaks about the potency of this matter.

From an economic point of view, public procurement policies can distort the allocation of resources and alter conditions of competition in bidding for state contracts. Arguably, there is also a legitimate societal concern that in the desire to favour one group of bidders over another the total cost of state purchases increases. In this manner, public procurement policies may act as a largely hidden form of redistribution from current and future taxpayers to narrow sectoral interests.

But what changes have governments made in public procurement policies during the crisis era? Apart from members of the Agreement on Government Procurement (GPA) of the World Trade Organization (WTO), whose public procurement policies are briefly summarised in that organisation's Trade Policy Reviews, there are few sources on changes in regulations and laws governing public purchasing. For sure, since 2014 a number of data collection efforts have begun and these are to be welcomed.

So as to ground deliberations to the greatest extent possible in facts, the proximate purpose of this chapter is to summarise the contents of the independent Global Trade Alert (GTA)'s initiative to collect data on government procurement policy changes since November 2008. This effort sought to identify policy changes that improved as well as worsened the treatment of foreign commercial interests in state purchasing policy. In total, 507 announced changes to public procurement policies have been identified by the GTA team.[1]

[1] Consistent with the goal of promoting evidence-based deliberations on public policy-making, the GTA provides this data free of charge to third parties. Please contact Simon Evenett at simon.evenett@unisg.ch for this data. As the description of the GTA's data collection efforts makes clear, the number of procurement measures documented rises over time and the GTA is happy to share updates of this data as well. If it is not apparent already – after all, the title page of this chapter indicates Evenett's links to the GTA – it should be stated that one of the authors of this chapter has been heavily involved in the design, execution, dissemination and financing of this initiative.

The ultimate purpose of this chapter is to inform other, ongoing data collection efforts, public policy deliberations on crisis-era policy response as it relates to fiscal policy and public procurement policy in particular, and discussions on the relative merits of strengthening disciplines on public procurement matters in trade agreements.

Although an accord on government procurement matters was first agreed at the multilateral level in the 1970s, compared to other areas of international trade policy, negotiations and international obligations on public procurement matters remain a relatively nascent area. Notwithstanding the adoption of government procurement obligations in many regional trade agreements during the past twenty years, some levels of government (in particular subnational levels) and certain areas of expenditure tend not to be covered by such disciplines.

The implication is that there is plenty of room for expanding trade disciplines in this area of public policy. Whether governments are minded to do so is a separate matter. All of these matters, including assessments of the likely economic and commercial impact of potential disciplines, can surely be constructively informed by information on what steps governments have actually taken during an era of acute economic pain followed by growth underperformance.

No doubt some are eager to learn about the trade impact of crisis-era public procurement measures. Notwithstanding certain economic models showing that under specific circumstances government procurement discrimination against foreign bidders has no effect on aggregate trade flows (see Evenett and Hoekman, 2005 for an account of the relevant issues), it would seem from the reaction of business people and policymakers that foreign changes in state purchasing policy can have significant cross-border implications.

We too are keen to learn what those effects may have been, but note that to the best of our knowledge we know of no empirical paper that separately identifies the effects of government procurement policy changes since the onset of the global economic crisis.[2] Analysts cannot run before they can walk. Data must be collected before econometric

[2] Evenett and Fritz (2015a) did include public procurement policy changes into one of the categories of potential trade distortions that could affect the exports of the Least Developed Countries (LDCs). As of this writing, there are nineteen entries in the GTA database whereby a harmful public procurement policy change has been implemented since November 2008 that affects products exported by the LDCs. It may be useful to note at this point that over the same time horizon, 925 government policies harmful to the commercial interests of the LDCs have been implemented. It is for this type of reason, and

analysis is possible. Some may find the delays frustrating – but in our opinion this reflects the parlous state of data collection on non-tariff measures when the global economic crisis hit.

Worse, we fear that the near empirical vacuum on high-quality data on non-tariff measures at the beginning of the global economic crisis may have been exploited by some analysts, interest groups and public officials to dismiss outright the subsequent importance of crisis-era non-tariff measures in general and, in this case, changes in public procurement law and regulations.

Instead, here we report statistics on the amount of exports by the Group of Twenty leading economies (G20 nations) that are in product categories where adverse foreign public procurement policy changes have been implemented since November 2008. These statistics provide some sense of the scale of this public policy 'problem' across countries and over time. Researchers may find these numbers of use in identifying the bilateral trade flows where public procurement policy changes might have had the largest effect. Inevitably, progress in this area on data, empirical analysis and implications for policymaking is incremental. Still, in this chapter we hope to contribute to a better understanding of crisis-era policy response in state purchasing.

The remainder of this chapter is organised as follows. In Section 6.2 the GTA data collection initiative is described and discussed in a manner that facilitates a better understanding of the statistics reported in later sections. Those engaged in data collection efforts on procurement policy may find the observations in this section of interest. Section 6.3 summarises the evidence in the GTA database on the resort to government procurement discrimination and liberalisation since November 2008. Implications for policy deliberation, data collection efforts and research are drawn in Section 6.4.

6.2 Data Collection on Public Procurement Measures by the Global Trade Alert

When the extent of what was to become known as the global financial crisis became clearer in late 2008 and early 2009 concerns grew that governments might resort to beggar-thy-neighbour activities, just as they did after the onset of the Great Depression in the 1930s. G20 Leaders, at

others, that Evenett and Fritz did not emphasise the role of foreign public procurement policy changes as a major factor holding back LDC exports during the crisis era.

their first crisis-era summit in November 2008 in Washington, DC, vowed they had learnt the lessons of history and declared they would eschew protectionism.[3] Several international organisations were tasked by G20 Leaders with monitoring trade- and investment-related policy decisions and periodic reports were produced. For our purposes, it is worth noting that none of these international monitoring reports gives public procurement measures much prominence.[4]

One concern that arose immediately was that no organisation was collecting data on the wide range of policy measures that governments could use in the twenty-first century to discriminate against foreign commercial interests, taken to be not just traders but also investors, foreign workers and foreign owners of intellectual property rights. Given that protectionism has a bad name and that governments face substantial pressures to protect domestic commercial interests during sharp global downturns, the possibility that governments would 'innovate' and deploy less well-known tools of discrimination against foreign commercial interests could not be discounted.[5] Concerns compounded when it became apparent that the WTO secretariat had adopted a particularly narrow, historically motivated view of its monitoring mandate. That United Nations (UN) agencies had made so little progress in nearly fifty years in defining, classifying and collecting data on non-tariff measures – initiatives that many involved contended were stymied by national governments – reinforced fears that if times were tough the public international organisations would not be able to effectively monitor their own members.

Such concerns led to the creation of the GTA, which is based at the University of St. Gallen, Switzerland, and was launched under the aegis of the Centre for Economic Policy Research (CEPR), the Europe-wide

[3] In fact, the relevant summit communiqué was more specific, identifying certain trade policies governments would eschew. Since this communiqué statement was non-binding and given the possibility that governments might have meant something different from this statement than what could be inferred by third parties, there is little to be gained by declaring whether or not eschewing discrimination in public procurement fell within the spirit or the letter of this communiqué's statements on protectionism.

[4] Having said this, the latest report by the WTO Director-General on developments in the world trading systems refers specifically to six government procurement-related policy changes undertaken by G20 governments from mid-October 2015 to mid-May 2016. See WTO (2016b).

[5] Indeed the experience of the 1980s – when a sharp global economic downturn was followed by substantial resort to voluntary export restraints rather than the import quotas and tariffs of the 1930s – was disquieting.

network of researchers whose headquarters is in London, United Kingdom. A major objective of the GTA is to document and make available information on changes in government policy that are likely to have altered the relative treatment of domestic vis-à-vis foreign commercial interests since 1 November 2008, the month that the G20 Leaders first met in crisis mode.

That information has been made available on a searchable public website, which itself adds to the transparency of the world trading system.[6] Such information has been used to evaluate government – in particular G20 government – policy stance. Increasingly, the data collected in this initiative are being used in analyses of trade policy development and international commercial flows.[7] Given the focus of this chapter on public procurement matters it is important to state that the range of policies reported in the GTA database is wider.

To better understand the GTA database it helps to differentiate between four matters: policy scope, unit of analysis, data collection and classification of reported measures. Each is addressed in turn below.

6.2.1 Policy Scope

An important point of differentiation between the GTA and the official reports on protectionism is that – at least as far as their headline numbers are concerned – the latter confine themselves to a specific set of policy instruments. This has, as implied above, the disadvantage that governments may deliberately choose policy instruments that fall outside the scope of official monitoring. To avoid this problem, the GTA has always focused on likely changes in the *relative treatment* and not on specific policy instruments.[8]

Specifically, the GTA will include information on any policy change – no matter the instrument used – that alters the *relative treatment* of domestic firms vis-à-vis foreign rivals. The changes could in principle favour as well as harm foreign commercial interests – hence the GTA is not only looking for examples of 'bad news' (that is, looking for harmful

6 www.globaltradealert.org.

7 As of this writing, the term 'Global Trade Alert' is mentioned in 1,010 distinct entries in the Google Scholar database.

8 In a recent evaluation of different methods of tracking crisis-era protectionism, the Swedish Board of Trade endorsed the relative treatment – or discrimination-based – approach to identifying relevant policy variables (Swedish Board of Trade, 2016).

measures.) Moreover, the GTA considers policy changes at all levels of government, although the focus in reality has tended to be more on central and first subnational tiers of government.

Given that the GTA's monitoring relates to policy announcements made since 1 November 2008, the information in the GTA database can then best be thought of as capturing the unanticipated changes in policy stance since 1 November 2008. Policy changes that were announced before 1 November 2008 but were implemented afterwards are not included in the GTA database because an informed private sector party could have anticipated the policy change.

In the language of economists, the GTA tries to capture the 'flow' of policy change rather than the 'stock' of policies in force on 31 October 2008. This is important for interpretational reasons – it may be that two governments implemented identical public procurement measures, but one did so after 1 November 2008 and one just before1 November 2008. Only the former measure would be recorded in the GTA database, yet given the extraneous information mentioned directly above, in the policy context in question it might be unwise to condemn the former and praise the latter.

Despite the relative treatment standard, with the goal of monitoring as best as possible policy intervention motivated by liberalisation or strategic advantage, early on the GTA team decided not to report the

- negotiation or formal implementation of regional trade agreements;[9]
- implementation measures following the timetable established in a WTO accession;
- implementation of technical barriers to trade and sanitary and phytosanitary standards;[10]
- foreign policy-induced sanctions;[11]
- measures associated with free trade zones;
- measures involving international commerce below *de minimum* levels.

[9] Suspension of regional trade agreement provisions or attempts to manage trade between members of a regional trade agreement are included if it can be argued that the private sector was genuinely surprised by the announcement.

[10] Cases where it can be demonstrated on the basis of the available public record that a government has misused these measures to favour domestic firms are included in the GTA database.

[11] Counter-sanctions are included on the grounds that the sanctioned country chose to hit back with a commercial policy measure.

Some have contended that, as a result of its broader coverage of policy instruments, it is no wonder that the GTA finds more harmful measures than in official reports. Since the policy instruments covered by the latter are also covered by the GTA, it is possible to undertake apples-for-apples comparisons between different data sources. The last such comparison was undertaken in November 2015 and published in the Eighteenth GTA report (Evenett and Fritz, 2015b, chapter 12). Depending on the metric used the GTA finds between 57 per cent and 250 per cent more instances of protectionism than the WTO secretariat over the same time frame.

Although in principle the GTA includes information on any government policy affecting the relative treatment of domestic firms, policy instruments are grouped together into over twenty categories in the database (which helps to sort the database, allows for targeted searches of the database and computation of specific summary statistics.) Given the focus of this chapter, it is worth noting that public procurement measures are separated into three categories: measures that require a certain level of local sourcing or hiring, measures conferring price preferences or other preferences on domestic bidders and other (not otherwise specified, n.e.s.) public procurement measures.

6.2.2 *Unit of Analysis: An Announcement of Government Intervention*

Governments often include information on multiple policy interventions in a given announcement, such as a state budget speech before a legislature. This poses a problem for those monitoring changes in policy stance. If one chopped up each such announcement and made the unit of account in the database a single government intervention, then the database would be swamped by a small number of announcements of multiple interventions.

Alternatively, if the unit of analysis is an announcement then in some circumstances it will make sense to distinguish between the announcement itself and the different policy instruments associated with the announcement. This alternative approach was taken by the GTA team – a point worth bearing in mind as some public procurement measures have been announced at the same time as other government measures.

Given that the products and sectors of the economy implicated by each government intervention may differ, when using the GTA database it is important to remember that counts of the total number of announcements need not correspond to total number of government policy interventions, total number of products implicated and total number of times a sector has been affected, etc.[12]

It is for this reason that some users have not been keen on statistics based on the total number of announced measures – and why the GTA team reports different summary statistics extracted from their database and why ultimately the GTA team began computing the share of national exports likely to be facing foreign policy instruments of different types. Obviously the summary statistic used should reflect the research or policy question at hand. The view taken by the GTA team has to been to generate the richer data set possible that enables analysts to extract the underlying data or summary statistic that best suits their current purpose.

6.2.3 *Data Collection*

An important operational principle for the GTA team is to support, as far as is possible, each report on a government announcement with information from official sources, taken to include sources published by the government in question (which may be online) or information published by international organisations. Other sources of information may be considered but as many facts as possible are to be taken from official sources.

For each potential entry in the GTA database, information is collected on:

- the identity of the government making the announcement;
- the date of the announcement and any dates when announced measures come into effect or lapse;
- the policy instrument referred to in the announcement;
- the stated rationale for the policy change.

From this information, the following are obtained:

- whether the measures in the announcement have an inception date (date when it was first implemented);
- whether each measure's duration is finite;
- whether each measure is still in force;
- when the measure involves trade in goods, which four-digit product categories in the UN COMTRADE database are implicated;

[12] The relevance of this observation will become apparent in the next section of the chapter.

- which sectors in the UN two-digit Central Product Classification (CPC) classification are implicated by the measure.
- with data on the relevant commercial flows (UN COMTRADE for trade in goods, for example) what trading partners are likely to be affected by the implementation of the measure.

All of this information is written up in a pre-specified format and submitted for evaluation. Each submission is reviewed twice by senior members of the GTA team. A submitted measure may be rejected outright, revisions may be asked for, or accepted. Only accepted measures are then published.

The GTA team regularly tracks dozens of government websites across the world – the goal is to have the best possible worldwide coverage. In addition, the reports of leading public international organisations are monitored as well. Certain international law firms and national and international business organisations publish information on public policies of interest to them and these are consulted for promising leads. Lastly, key phrase searches are conducted on Twitter every week and libraries of commercial policy-related terms are used to identify other leads. Whenever a lead is investigated the primary goal is to find an official source that relates to the matter in question and then an independent assessment is made of any related policy announcement. In this way, private sector sources are employed without unduly influencing the research and evaluation process used by the GTA team.

Some measures – such as the implementation of an anti-dumping investigation – pass through several stages and the reported GTA measure is updated after every stage. Periodic checks of earlier reported measures are undertaken to ensure information is as up-to-date as possible.

These data collection methods have yielded information on literally thousands of government policy interventions since November 2008 and the GTA database has, at this writing, nearly 10,000 entries. Still, there is no guarantee that every relevant measure has been documented. Moreover, the extensive use of the Internet to search for government announcements begs questions about coverage. Could some governments be less transparent than others, especially when they are undertaking controversial policies such as protectionism? Are the public sector governance norms in some countries more transparent than in others?

Could countries whose official languages are less well known be underreported? Do some countries make a small number of government announcements involving multiple policy interventions or do others make an announcement for almost every state intervention?

These are fair questions to ask and should certainly be borne in mind when interpreting summary statistics from the GTA database and for conducting empirical analysis generally.[13]

Another important point to bear in mind is that it may take time to successfully complete a report on government policy intervention. Moreover, governments may take time to report or acknowledge previous state intervention. An important feature of the GTA's methods is to keep looking for government intervention implemented since 1 November 2008. In contrast, the monitoring by international organisations focuses only on the most recent six-month interval and does not update its earlier published totals in light of evidence found at a later date. As the most recent report of the GTA has shown, the protectionist record of the G20 countries is much worse once updating is allowed.

Another key implication is that very recent totals of instances of government protectionism and liberalisation tend to be sharply revised up over time – therefore, falling totals of recorded protectionism in the most recent quarters or years should not be read as indicating necessarily less resort to beggar-thy-neighbour activity. Anyone seeking to report on government procurement policy changes in 'real time' ought to bear this observation in mind.

6.2.4 *Classification of Reported Measures*

As the relative treatment standard is used to determine whether an announcement should be included in the GTA database, given that treatment of foreign rivals can worsen or improve, it makes sense to classify government announcements depending on their likely effect on foreign commercial interests.

For the sake of the following argument, assume that a government announcement refers to a single state intervention. If the implementation of that measure would benefit foreign commercial interests then the measure is classified green (as in a traffic light system). If a measure is implemented and almost certainly harms foreign rivals then it is classified red. If a measure is implemented and likely harms foreign commercial interests then it is classified amber. The introduction of the amber

[13] If an analyst suspects that the GTA's coverage of policy intervention varies across countries, then one might consider weighting observations by the total number of interventions (of all types) in the GTA database.

classification allows for some doubt about a measure's effects or about the sources supporting a reported measure.

Perhaps confusingly the GTA team also reports measures that have yet to be implemented and are likely to be harmful (or worse) as amber.[14] Therefore, users of the GTA database should distinguish between amber measures where the state intervention in question has been implemented (in which case there is an inception date in the published report on the measure) and where the intervention has not been implemented. This distinction is easy to make in the Excel spreadsheets that the GTA team sends to users requesting data.

When the GTA reports refer to protectionism they refer to implemented amber and red measures. When the GTA reports refer to liberalising measures this refers to implemented and green measures.

When a government announcement involves more than one instance of state intervention then it is possible that some interventions are liberalising and others protectionist. How to colour code these measures? In cases where each intervention has the same effect on the relative treatment of foreign commercial interests, then the overall colour code reflects that. However, in cases where the relative treatment is mixed across interventions, the measure is classified amber.[15]

One implication is that users of the database should pay particular attention when using information on measures involving multiple state interventions that are coded amber and implemented. It may be that the state intervention that a researcher is particularly interested in has a different impact on the relative treatment of foreign commercial interests than the overall colour coding forms the measure suggests.

The purpose of this section has been to describe the construction and implementation of the GTA database. That database now includes 9,741 published reports on government announcements. As of this writing, 150 more measures are in the review process. Since 2013, approximately 2,000 new reports have been published each year. In contrast, the WTO's Trade Monitoring Database contains a total of 3,831 measures of government interventions taken during the global economic crisis.[16]

[14] These measures are included in the GTA database as some users want an 'early warning' system, that is, what policy intervention has been announced yet whose implementation is still to come.

[15] The GTA will soon have a new website where each policy intervention is colour coded.

[16] This WTO database can be accessed at http://tmdb.wto.org/searchmeasures.aspx?lang=en-US.

Given the focus in this chapter on public procurement-related measures, it is worth noting that at the time of this writing the GTA database contains 548 reports on government announcements that involve some measure relating to state purchasing. In contrast, the WTO's Trade Monitoring Database includes fifty-one entries which refer to 'procurement'. As will become clear later, twelve of those fifty-one entries refer to public procurement-related initiatives undertaken by the United States.

6.3 Public Procurement Policy Change during the Crisis Era: Evidence from the Global Trade Alert Database

The GTA database includes reports on 507 public procurement-related measures that were implemented from November 2008, though not all of these measures are currently in force.

Figure 6.1 shows the imposition of public procurement-related measures over time and suggests a constant, though somewhat declining trend, with a peak in 2009. This said, the GTA database reports these measures with a lag, so the fairly high numbers reported in 2014–16 are a worrying sign, especially given that the 'red' discriminatory measures constitute the overwhelming majority of all reported measures in any given year since 2009 (see Figure 6.2).

The United States is responsible for 351 of the 507 measures (69.2 per cent share of the total) that were imposed since November 2008. The distribution of the remaining 30.8 per cent of all measures, shown in

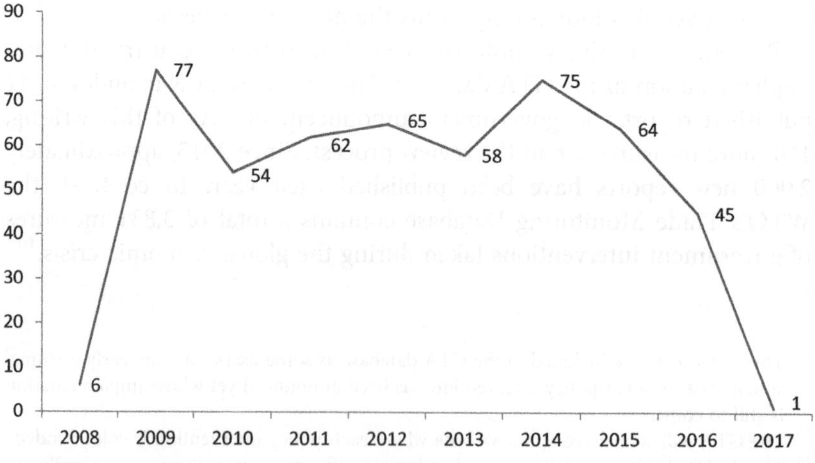

Figure 6.1 Evolution of all public procurement-related measures over time.

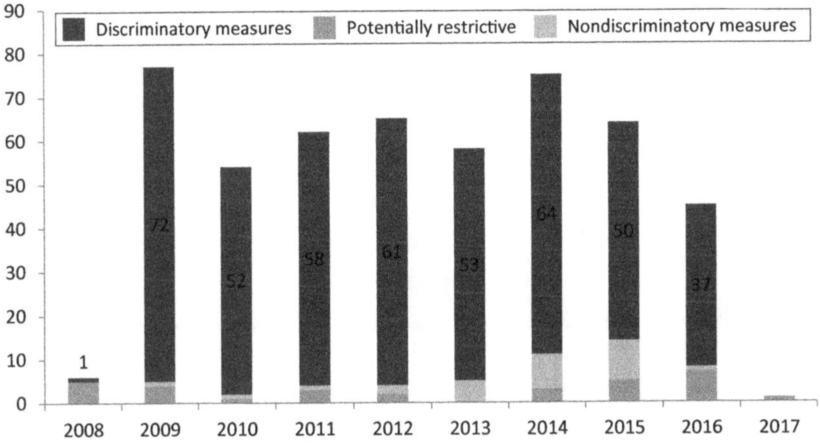

Figure 6.2 Evolution of all public procurement-related measures over time by GTA classification.

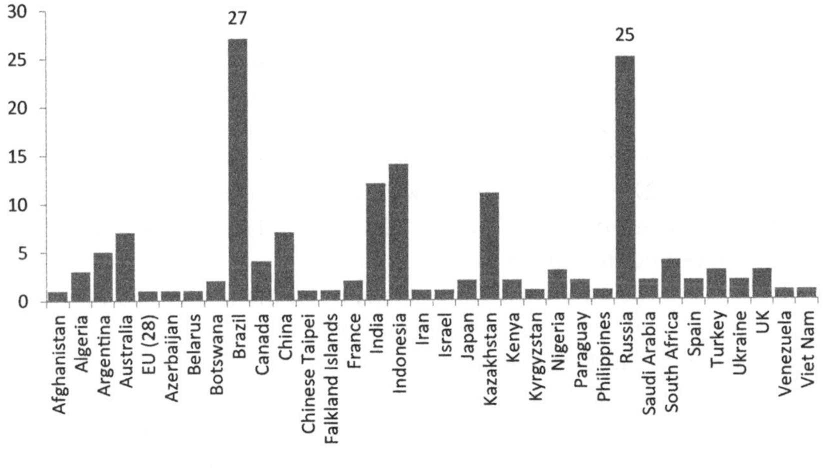

Figure 6.3 Public-procurement related measures imposed in non-US countries.

Figure 6.3, reveals that Brazil, Russia, Indonesia, India and Kazakhstan have also used these measures extensively. Eight countries' governments have implemented five or more public procurement measures since the global economic crisis. All but one of these eight countries are G20 members.

The distribution of the discriminatory (i.e. red and amber colour coded) procurement measures also reveals the dominance of the

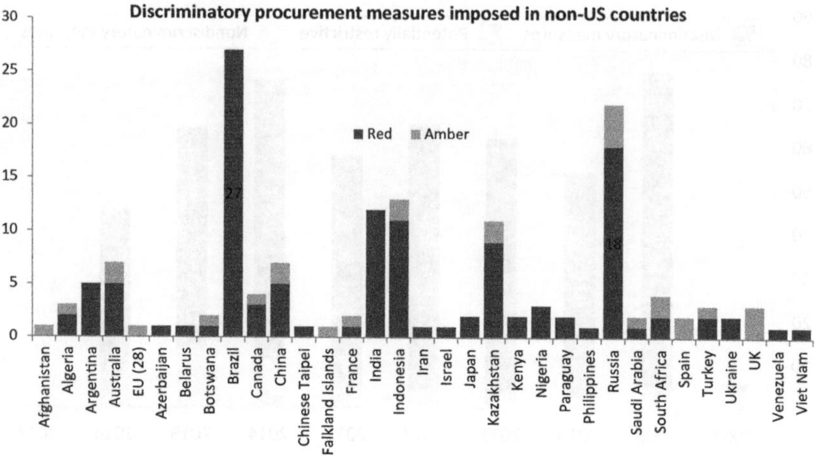

Figure 6.4 Discriminatory procurement measures imposed in non-US countries.

USA – of all discriminatory procurement measures (n = 479), most (n = 328, of which 'red' = 325) have been imposed in the USA. The distribution of the remaining 151 measures imposed in the non-US countries, shown in Figure 6.4, mirrors that shown in Figure 6.3.

By measure type, public procurement localisation measures account for the majority of discriminatory procurement measures imposed both in the USA (277 out of 328, of which 'red' = 276) and in non-US countries (84 out of 151, of which 'red' = 66). The distribution of the latter is reported in Table 6.1.

In terms of the implementation status, more than half (51.8 per cent) of US discriminatory procurement measures (n = 328) that had been imposed are *not* in force. In contrast, 126/151 of non-US discriminatory procurement measures are currently in force. These distributions, by GTA classification, are shown in Figures 6.5 and 6.6, respectively. In both cases, there is plenty of crisis-era procurement discrimination to be unwound.

Looking next at liberalising (or 'green' colour-coded) measures (n = 28), the majority of these (82 per cent) have also been implemented in the USA and the overwhelming majority (89.3 per cent) are still in force. The majority (64.3 per cent) of 'green' procurement measures are also public procurement localisation measures and most took effect in 2014–15 (see Table 6.2).

The UN CPC sectors affected most often by procurement measures in the GTA database are 41–42 (basic metals and fabricated metal

Table 6.1 *Discriminatory procurement measures imposed by countries other than USA, by type of measure*

Type of measure	Amber	Share (%)	Red	Share (%)
Bailout/state aid measure, Export incentive, Public procurement localisation			1	0.8
Bailout/state aid measure, Public procurement localisation	1	3.6	2	1.6
Bailout/state aid measure, Public procurement localisation, State trading enterprise			1	0.8
Bailout/state aid measure, Public procurement preference, Trade defence measure (AD, CVD, safeguard)			1	0.8
Export incentive, Investment measure, Localisation requirement, Migration measure, Public procurement localisation	1	3.6		0.0
Import tariff, Investment measure, Non-tariff barrier (not otherwise specified), Public procurement localisation			1	0.8
Import tariff, Public procurement localisation			1	0.8
Investment measure, Localisation requirement, Public procurement localisation			1	0.8
Investment measure, Public procurement, n.e.s.				0.0
Non-tariff barrier (not otherwise specified), Other service sector measure, Public procurement localisation			1	0.8
Non-tariff barrier (not otherwise specified), Public procurement localisation			1	0.8
Public procurement localisation	18	64.3	66	53.7
Public procurement localisation, Public procurement preference			2	1.6
Public procurement localisation, State-controlled company			2	1.6
Public procurement localisation, Subnational government measure	1	3.6	1	0.8
Public procurement preference	4	14.3	35	28.5
Public procurement preference, State-controlled company			5	4.1
Public procurement, n.e.s.	3	10.7	2	1.6
Total	**28**	**100.0**	**123**	**100.0**

Note: AD = anti-dumping; CVD = counter-vailing duties.

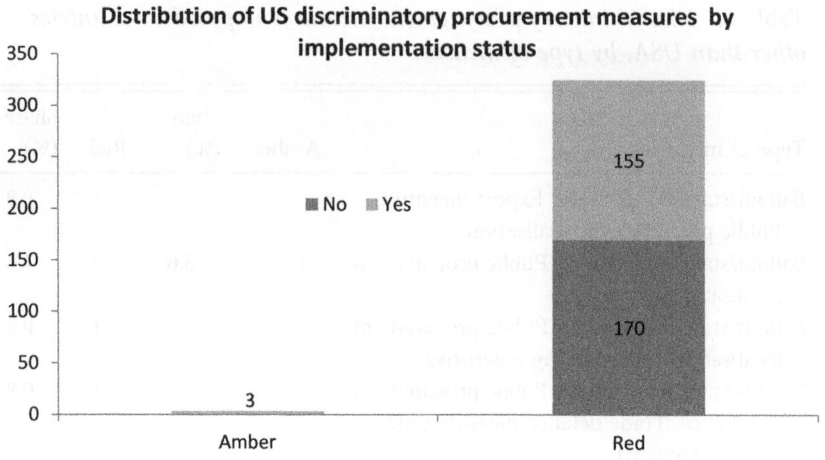

Figure 6.5 Distribution of US discriminatory procurement measures by implementation status.

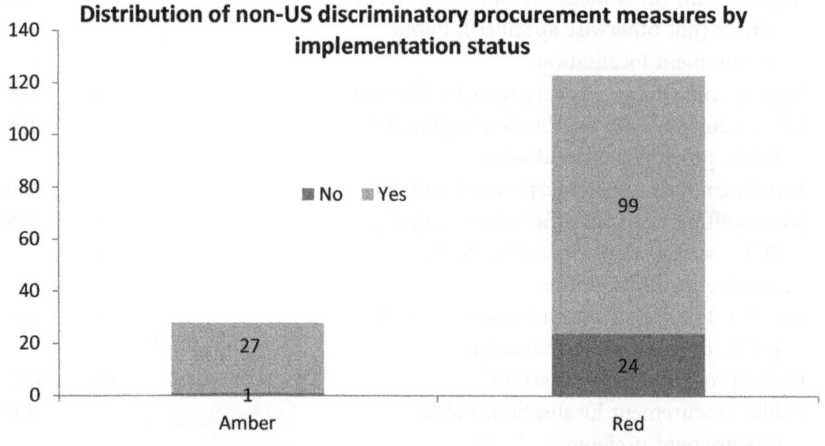

Figure 6.6 Distribution of non-US discriminatory procurement measures by implementation status.

products). These sectors have been affected by 123 implemented public procurement-related measures (Figure 6.7).

Of the measures affecting these sectors:

- Nearly all (122 measures) have been imposed by the USA.
- Nearly all (120 measures) are public procurement localisation measures.

Table 6.2 *Distribution of 'green' procurement measures by type of measure and evolution over time*

Type of measure	2009	2010	2011	2012	2013	2014	2015	2016
Investment measure, Public procurement, n.e.s.	1					1		
NTB (n.e.s.), Public procurement localisation, TBT							1	
Public procurement localisation		1		1	4	7	4	1
Public procurement localisation, Subnational government measure				1			3	
Public procurement, n.e.s.			1		1		1	
Total	**1**	**1**	**1**	**2**	**5**	**8**	**9**	**1**

Note: TBT = technical barriers to trade; NTB = non-tariff barriers.

- All (123 measures) are classified as discriminatory by the GTA.
- Less than half (56 measures) are currently in force.
- Nearly a quarter (30 measures) were imposed in 2016; 17 were imposed in 2009.
- Nearly three-quarters (88 measures) were in stay for two years.
- More than 90 per cent (111 measures) affected Brazil, Canada, China, France, Germany, India, Italy, Japan, Mexico, South Korea, Russia, Sweden and the United Kingdom.

The countries most frequently affected (n = 156) by procurement measures in the GTA database are Brazil, Canada, China, France,

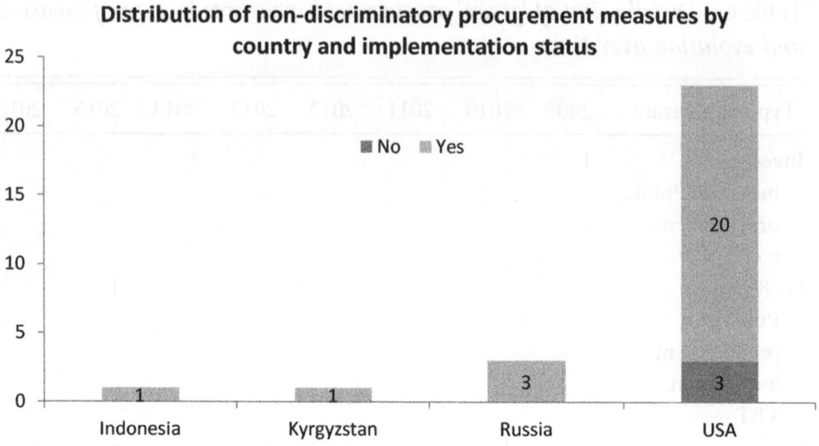

Figure 6.7 Distribution of non-discriminatory procurement measures by country and implementation status.

Germany, India, Italy, Japan, Mexico, South Korea, Russia, Sweden and the United Kingdom.

Of all measures affecting these countries:

- All (156 measures) have been imposed by the USA.
- All (156 measures) are public procurement localisation measures.
- All (156 measures) are classified as discriminatory by the GTA.
- Less than half (66 measures) are currently in force.
- Nearly a fifth (30 measures) were imposed in 2016; whereas 23 measures were imposed in 2009.
- More than 80 per cent (125 measures) were in force for two years.

Counts of measures give a sense of the frequency of resort to discrimination in public procurement, but not to the scale of the trade affected. To precisely identify the latter, one needs information on state purchases from foreign suppliers at detailed product level. Unfortunately, such data are not available. However, data on a nation's total purchases across foreign sources at the product level are available and, carefully interpreted, might be useful.

Some products are only bought by state bodies, especially in sectors where there are large government monopolies. For example, if the sole supplier of railway services in a country is the national rail company, then it is quite likely – if not almost certain – that the state is responsible for the total national imports of locomotives.

Moreover, if the state expands markedly the number of products covered by a restrictive procurement regulation then at a time when global trade is growing very slowly – if not stagnant as the global trade volume numbers since January 2015 suggest – then the expansion in the total amount of imports in products affected by procurement discrimination is more likely to be due to the policy change than to changes in private sector sourcing patterns.

It is for these reasons that we took advantage of calculations made during the preparation of the Twentieth Global Trade Alert report (Evenett and Fritz, 2016) that reveal the exposure of each G20 country's exports to foreign public procurement discrimination. For that report, at the four-digit product level every bilateral trade relation where a discriminatory public procurement measure was in effect in a given year was identified. The trade associated with each of these bilateral product-level trade flows was identified and the date a measure came into effect used to weight each trade flow (such that, if a measure was only in effect in December 2012 then only a twelfth of the annual trade flow data for 2012 was used in the subsequent calculations).

For each year between 2009 and 2015, considering when discriminatory public procurement measures came into effect, in the calculations for that report the percentage of each G20 nation's exports in products where procurement discrimination is in effect (taking account of the fact that only some trading partners implement such discrimination) was calculated. These calculations are based only on discriminatory public procurement policy measures implemented since November 2008. Therefore, any legacy of pre-crisis procurement discrimination would add further to these numbers.

These numbers are reported in Figure 6.8, which shows the percentage share of G20 exports potentially at risk through discriminatory public procurement policies in 2009 (dark shaded bars) and the change in these exposure shares between 2009 and 2015 (light shaded bars).

Figure 6.8 suggests that Mexico, South Korea, Japan and China had the highest shares of their total exports potentially affected by discriminatory procurement policies in 2009. In the case of Mexico and South Korea, the exposure shares were above 10 per cent. In contrast, Saudi Arabia had almost none of its exports potentially at risk through discriminatory public procurement policies, which may not be terribly surprising given its export mix. Argentina, Russia, Italy and Australia also reported low exposure shares (less than 1 per cent) in 2009.

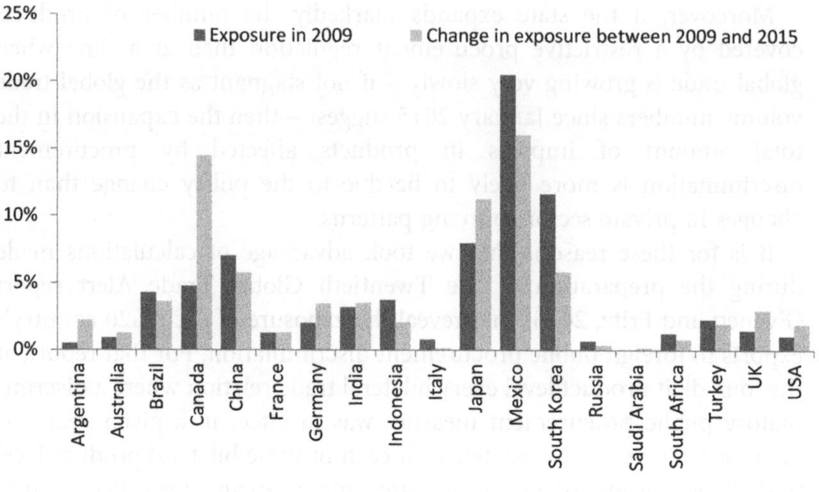

Figure 6.8 G20 exports (% share, 2009 and change over 2009–15) potentially at risk through discriminatory public procurement policies.

Interestingly, Mexico, Canada, Japan, South Korea and China reported the largest increases in their respective exposure shares from 2009 to 2015. Significantly, Argentina, Australia, the UK and the USA, all of which had low exposure shares in 2009, had a lot more of their exports potentially affected by discriminatory procurement policies in 2015.

6.4 Concluding Remarks

This chapter has shed light on the resort to public procurement policy change since the onset of the global economic crisis. Particular use was made of the GTA database, which contains over 500 entries relating to changes in state purchasing. Having described how this database was constructed and indicated where analysts and users need to use the database with particular care, a summary of the principal procurement-related findings was presented.

Some may have been struck by the frequency with which the United States has resorted to public procurement discrimination. While it is certainly the case that the United States expanded such discrimination at the beginning of the crisis, it should be recalled that that country has by international standards a very transparent system of government and that it tends to report each public offering of state largesse. These two factors probably account for the large number of American entries in the GTA database.

Still, the GTA database contains plenty of information on procurement discrimination by other nations. Compared to the WTO's database on crisis-era policy response, the GTA database contains information on three times as much non-US procurement discrimination. Eight non-US nations have implemented five or more discriminatory public procurement measures since the crisis began. 'Buy America' cannot be blamed for all of the procurement discrimination of recent years. Addressing such discrimination is a global challenge, especially when one realises that seven of the eight of these nations are G20 members.

That conclusion is reinforced by the growing shares of national exports in product lines and to trading partners where public procurement discrimination has been imposed. For sure, such data have their flaws and, after all, export exposure is not the same as export losses. Still, the fact that the percentages of exports exposed to such discrimination are rising quickly suggests that either the number of larger nations using such discriminatory tools is growing or that the products implicated by such expansion are rising too. Either way, export interests are potentially compromised and this may generate a vocal constituency in favour of further trade disciplines on state purchasing.

There is a long way to go, however, between identifying a potential interest and the successful negotiation and implementation of trade disciplines. With better – but certainly not perfect – data available, analysis of the impact on trade and investment flows can begin. Should detailed price data ever become available, then the impact of crisis-era procurement discrimination on the value-for-money that states are getting from public purchases can be estimated as well. All in all, the prospects are brighter for more evidence-driven deliberation on public procurement matters in the years ahead.

7

Preferences, Income Distribution, and the Burden of Non-tariff Measures*

IGOR BAGAYEV AND RONALD B. DAVIES

7.1 Introduction

The link between trade and inequality has been of central importance in analysing international trade since the seminal work of Stolper and Samuelson (1941). While early work on the topic was primarily theoretic, with improved data availability more recent contributions have examined it empirically, with examples using aggregate data including Bergh and Nilsson (2010) and those with micro data including Cosar, Guner, and Tybout (2016).[1] Some studies, such as Jaumotte, Lall, and Papageorgiou (2013), find that the inequality impact of trade is secondary when compared to factors such as technological change while others such as Lim and McNelis (2014) find that the impact is conditional on other factors. In any case, the evidence consistently points to a significant potential for increased trade to exacerbate inequality. More recent contributions, however, discuss the role in inequality itself in determining trade when preferences are non-homothetic. In particular, a growing literature has replaced homothetic preferences with Stone-Geary preferences. Examples include Francois and Kaplan (1996), Bekkers, Francois, and Manchin (2012), Markusen (2013), Caron, Fally, and Markusen (2014), and Bertoletti and Etro (2016). In particular, Bekkers et al. (2012) find evidence in the data on prices of tradeables and inequality that is consistent with the hierarchical demand patterns predicted by the

* We thank Mahdi Ghodsi, Oliver Rieter, and Robert Stehrer for kindly providing the NTM data. We also thank participants of the 2016 World Trade Forum in Florence, Italy for useful comments. This chapter was produced as part of the project 'Productivity, Non-Tariff Measures and Openness' (PRONTO) funded by the European Commission under the Seventh Framework Programme, Theme SSH.2013.4.3-3 'Untapped Potential for Growth and Employment Reducing the Cost of Non-tariff Measures in Goods, Services and Investment', grant agreement no. 613504.

[1] Goldberg and Pavncik (2007) provide an overview of the literature, with Turnovsky and Rojas-Vallejos (2016) providing a recent theory contribution and an updated review.

Stone-Geary approach to incorporating non-homothetic preferences in a trade model.[2] Within these models, the key is that the consumption of certain goods (luxuries) only begins when a given consumer reaches a minimum income level. The empirical work also finds that income distribution within a country can be a driving force in trade patterns (e.g. Francois and Kaplan, 1996; Hummels and Klenow, 2005; Dalgin, Trindade, and Mitra, 2008; Fieler, 2011; and Tasarov, 2012).

This chapter contributes to this discussion by pointing out that when preferences are non-homothetic, income distribution can have an influence on the measurement of trade policies. We do so by presenting a simple trade model with modified Stone-Geary preferences in the presence of non-tariff measures (NTMs). In the empirical literature, where the researcher is often forced to work with aggregated rather than product-level data, NTMs are commonly measured by coverage ratios.[3] These can be simple coverages, i.e. the share of products within a sector that face an NTM, or trade-weighted coverages where the measure factors in the share of imports within the sector made up of products facing an NTM.[4] The first is problematic because it misses the fact that some products are more important than others. The second is troublesome because trade values, and thus the trade shares, are determined by the NTMs, introducing endogeneity. Furthermore, as is the focus of our discussion, the trade shares can depend on other country characteristics driving the trade shares, including income inequality.

Because of this, trade-weighted coverage ratios will have variation driven, not by policy, but by country characteristics. As an example, consider Figures 7.1 and 7.2 which illustrate the country average coverage ratios for technical barriers to trade (TBTs) and sanitary and phytosanitary regulations (SPSs) across the EU. As can be seen, there is marked variation in each NTM measure despite the fact that the NTMs underlying them are the same across all these countries. While there can certainly be price variation across destinations due to, for example, heterogenous shipping costs, here, we demonstrate that such variation can also be driven by variations in income inequality in the presence of

[2] Choi, Hummels, and Xiang (2009) find a comparable result using income inequality measures.

[3] Examples include Trefler (1993), Goldberg and Maggi (1999), Lee and Swagel (2000), Disdier, Fontagne, and Mimouni (2008), and Bao and Qiu (2010).

[4] See Deardorff and Stern (1997) for discussion of various NTM measurements.

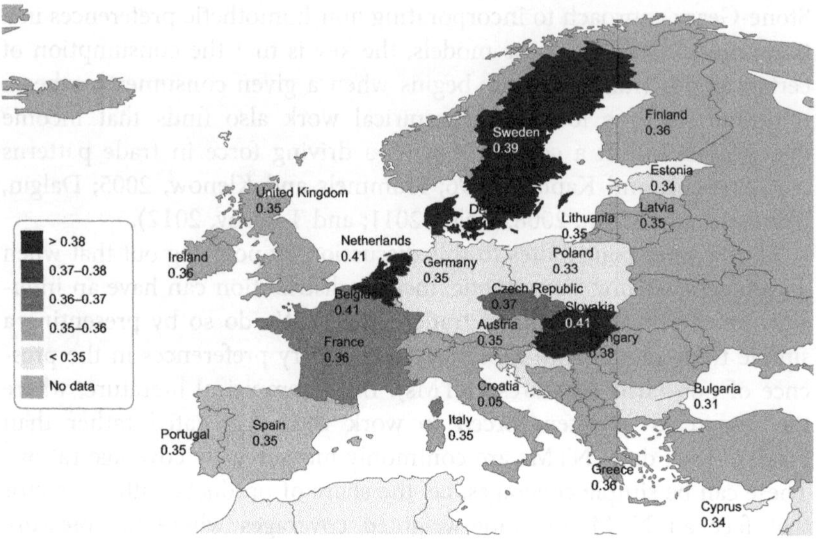

Figure 7.1 Average TBT coverage ratio.

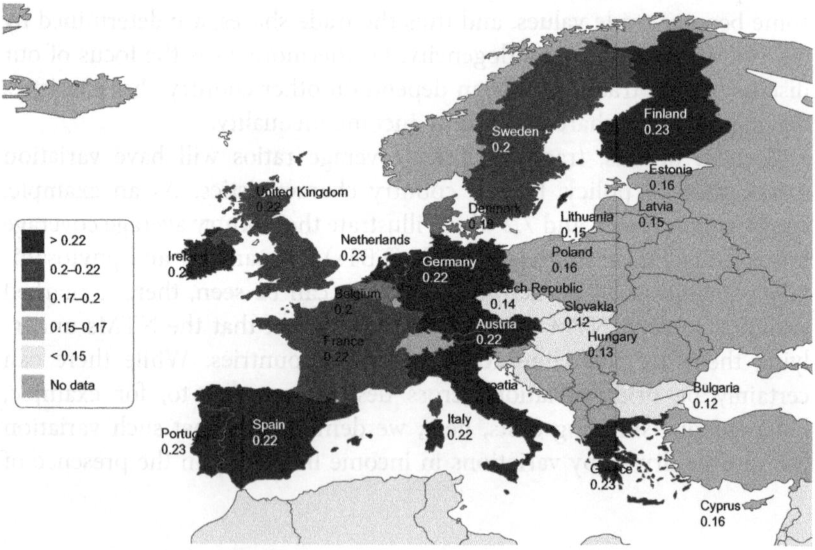

Figure 7.2 Average SPS coverage ratio.

non-homothetic preferences. We then confirm this using data on TBTs and SPSs in the EU for 2008–14.

In particular, our estimates suggest two things. First, given the predictions of our model, the estimates suggest that within the EU NTMs are tilted towards luxuries, i.e. those products purchased primarily by wealthier consumers, rather than necessities (products purchased by all). This is worth recognizing because understanding which consumers bear the burden of NTMs is important when considering the distribution of those costs across consumers of different income levels.[5] Second, given that the coverage ratio is correlated with inequality, something that itself affects trade volumes, our results suggest that failing to control for the direct impact of income inequality on trade has the potential to bias the estimated effects of NTMs.[6] Our estimates suggest that this may be a larger issue when using disaggregated data than in national-level import regressions.

In the next section, we introduce a stylized model of trade with non-homothetic preferences intended to illustrate the link between income inequality and the coverage ratio. In Section 7.3, we introduce the data we use. Section 7.4 explores the linkage between income inequality and the coverage ratio. Section 7.5 concludes.

7.2 NTMs and the Coverage Ratio with Non-homothetic Preferences

In this section, we introduce a very simplified model of trade under non-homothetic preferences. The rationale for this is that it illustrates a link between income distribution and NTM coverage ratios which depends on whether NTMs fall on necessities, i.e. they impact all consumers, or on luxuries, meaning that they affect primarily high-income individuals.

[5] For example, if wealthier individuals are more able to carry the burden of NTMs leading to higher prices than are the poor, this may increase governmental willingness to introduce NTMs.

[6] Examples of analyses using NTM coverage ratios are Trefler (1993), Goldberg and Maggi (1999), Lee and Swagel (2000), Disdier et al. (2008), and Bao and Qiu (2010). Note that this is not restricted to NTMs; trade-weighted tariff measures which are used by many of those suffer a similar problem. Further, this is simply one type of endogeniety of the coverage ratio; there is obviously the issue of how trade volumes and thus shares depend on the NTMs. This latter issue, however, is not relevant to our current discussion where we look, not on how trade depends on NTMs, but on how NTM measures depend on other variables.

To this end, consider a small open economy with N consumers, all of whom have identical preferences and all of whom face identical prices (which depend on, among other factors, whether or not a given product has an NTM). Each individual has an income $w_i > 0$ where aggregate income is $W = \sum_i \omega_i$. Preferences are across two goods, Y which is the numeraire with unit price and X which is a differentiated product sector. For simplicity, assume that all varieties of X are imported. Preferences are described by:

$$u_i(x_{1,i}, x_{2,i}, Y_i) = x^{\alpha} Y^{1-\alpha} = (x_{1,i} + \gamma)^{\alpha\beta} x_{2,i}^{\alpha(1-\beta)} Y_i^{1-\alpha} \qquad (7.1)$$

with $\gamma_s > 0$ and α, $\beta \in (0, 1)$. In words, preferences are Cobb-Douglas across sectors, and, within the X industry, preferences across varieties are modified Stone-Geary preferences. We will refer to x_1 as a 'luxury' good since, as is shown momentarily, consumption is positive only when minimum levels of consumption for the 'necessities' x_2 and Y are reached.

Whether or not x_1 is consumed by consumer i depends on her income level. Specifically, demands for the two X varieties are:

$$x_{1,i}(p_1, p_2, \omega_i) = \begin{cases} \dfrac{\alpha\beta\omega_i}{p_1} - (1-\alpha\beta)\gamma \text{ if } \omega_i > p_1 \dfrac{(1-\alpha\beta)}{\alpha\beta}\gamma \\ 0 \qquad \text{otherwise} \end{cases} \qquad (7.2)$$

and

$$x_{2,i}(p_1, p_2, \omega_i) = \begin{cases} \dfrac{\alpha(1-\beta)\omega_i}{p_2} - \dfrac{p_1}{p_2}\alpha(1-\alpha\beta)\gamma \text{ if } \omega_i > p_1 \dfrac{(1-\alpha\beta)}{\alpha\beta}\gamma \\ \dfrac{\alpha(1-\beta)}{(1-\alpha\beta)} \dfrac{\omega_i}{p_2} \qquad \text{otherwise} \end{cases} \qquad (7.3)$$

In words, the consumer purchases the luxury only when her income exceeds $p_1 \frac{(1-\alpha\beta)}{\alpha\beta}\gamma$. Let the set of consumers for whom ω_i exceeds this level be denoted by Δ, a group we refer to as the 'rich' with consumers not in this group referred to as 'poor'. Define $\omega_\Delta = W^{-1}\sum_{i\in\Delta}\omega_i$, $i\in\Delta$, i.e. the share of income held by the rich and n_Δ as the share of the population that is rich. Since demands for the commodities are linear in income within each group, aggregate demands for the two X varieties are:

$$x_1(p_1, p_2, W, N, \Delta) = \frac{\alpha\beta}{p_1}\omega_\Delta W - (1-\alpha\beta)\gamma n_\Delta N \qquad (7.4)$$

and

$$x_2\left(p_1,p_2,W,N,\Delta\right)=\left(1-\alpha\beta\omega_\Delta\right)\frac{\alpha(1-\beta)}{(1-\alpha\beta)}\frac{W}{p_2}+\frac{p_1}{p_2}(1-\beta)\gamma n_\Delta N. \tag{7.5}$$

From these, it is clear that aggregate demand, and therefore imports, is a function of the income distribution. For future use, the import share in X for the luxury x_1 is:

$$S_1\left(p_1,p_2,\frac{W}{N},\Delta\right)=\frac{\alpha\beta\omega_\Delta\frac{W}{N}-p_1(1-\alpha\beta)\gamma n_\Delta}{\left(\frac{\alpha\beta(1-\beta)}{(1-\alpha\beta)}\omega_\Delta+\frac{\alpha(1-\beta)}{(1-\alpha\beta)}\right)\frac{W}{N}-p_1(1-\alpha)\gamma n_\Delta} \tag{7.6}$$

Thus the trade share depends on prices, per capita GDP $\left(\frac{W}{N}\right)$, and the distribution of income across the two consumer types (Δ).

7.2.1 *The Coverage Ratio*

The coverage ratio, C, is calculated as the trade-weighted sum of indicator variables, NTM_i, that equal 1 when a variety faces an NTM, i.e. $C = S_1 NTM_1 + (1 - S_1)\, NTM_2$. Note that from this, holding policy constant but changing a variable z (such as per capita income),

$\frac{dc}{dz}=(NTM_1-NTM_2)\frac{dS_1}{dz}$. Thus, if the NTM is only on the luxury, i.e. $NTM_1=1$ and $NTM_2=0$, the impact of z on the coverage ratio will equal the impact of z on the luxury's share of imports. With this in mind, consider a rise in income inequality. This can be generated in three ways. First, suppose that the number of consumers in each group is constant, but income shifts from the poor to the rich, i.e. a rise in ω_Δ.[7] When this happens, we see that:

$$\frac{dS_1\left(p_1,p_2,\frac{W}{N},\Delta\right)}{d\omega_\Delta}=\frac{\alpha^2\beta(1-\beta)W^2}{(1-\alpha\beta)\left(\left(\frac{\alpha\beta(1-\beta)}{(1-\alpha\beta)}\omega_\Delta W+\frac{\alpha(1-\beta)}{(1-\alpha\beta)}\right)W-p_1(1-\alpha)\gamma n_\Delta N\right)^2}>0 \tag{7.7}$$

7 Recall that shifts in income within groups do not affect aggregated demand, therefore we only examine shifts across groups.

i.e. the luxury's share in imports rises. If there is an NTM on the luxury (necessity) only, then the coverage ratio rises (falls).[8] Similarly, we see that if we hold the income of the two groups constant but increase the percentage of the population qualifying as rich:

$$\frac{dS_1\left(p_1, p_2, \frac{W}{N}, \Delta\right)}{dn_\Delta} = \frac{-\alpha\beta(1-\beta)\gamma N}{\left(\left(\frac{\alpha\beta(1-\beta)}{(1-\alpha\beta)}\omega_\Delta W + \frac{\alpha(1-\beta)}{(1-\alpha\beta)}\right) W - p_1(1-\alpha)\gamma n_\Delta N\right)^2} < 0 \tag{7.8}$$

The intuition is the following. Any poor individual purchases only the necessity with that amount depending on their individual income; all rich individuals on the other hand purchase an amount of the necessity that is independent of their income. Conversely, all poor buy an amount of the luxury that is independent of their income, i.e. 0; all rich use the income left over after buying the fixed amount of the necessity to purchase the luxury. Increasing the share of income held by the rich increases per capita income of the rich and therefore the total amount of income remaining after the rich buy their necessities. Increasing the share of population that is rich lowers that group's per capita income and has the opposite effect. Both of these predictions are consistent with the estimates of Francois and Kaplan (1996) and Dalgin et al. (2008), who delineate products into luxuries and necessities and find that, as importer inequality rises, imports shift towards luxuries. Note that an outcome of this prediction is that, if the NTM is only on the luxury (necessity), the coverage ratio falls (rises) as the share of the population that is rich increases (decreases).

In the data, we do not know precisely how income and population are distributed across the two groups. However, when there are two groups, the Gini coefficient, which is observed, is $G = \omega_\Delta - n_\Delta$. As such, if the NTM is on the luxury good, an increase in the Gini coefficient (from either a rise in ω_Δ or a fall in n_Δ) should increase the coverage ratio. If the NTM is on the necessity, the coverage ratio falls as the Gini coefficient rises. Alternatively, we have access to income shares by quantiles. Since quantiles hold the share of consumers in a given group constant (i.e. n_Δ does not change), then an

[8] Note that if NTMs apply to both or neither, the coverage ratio is 1 or 0, regardless of the income distribution.

increase in the share of income held by the top quantile would be equivalent to an increase in ω_Δ, with predictions for trade shares and the coverage ratio the same as a rise in the Gini coefficient.

In addition to income distribution, an increase in average income would increase the trade share of the luxury:

$$\frac{dS_1\left(p_1,p_2,\frac{W}{N},\Delta\right)}{d\frac{W}{N}} = \frac{\alpha(1-\beta)p_1\gamma n_\Delta}{(1-\alpha\beta)\left(\left(\frac{\alpha\beta(1-\beta)}{(1-\alpha\beta)}\omega_\Delta\frac{W}{N}+\frac{\alpha(1-\beta)}{(1-\alpha\beta)}\right)\frac{W}{N}-p_1(1-\alpha)\gamma n_\Delta\right)^2} > 0 \tag{7.9}$$

Thus, as per capita GDP rises (i.e. GDP rises and/or population falls) the coverage ratio rises (falls) if the NTM is only on the luxury (necessity).

As a final note, recognize that, defining the value of imports M as

$$M\left(p_1,p_2,\frac{W}{N},\Delta\right) = \frac{\alpha(1-\beta)+(1-\alpha)\alpha\beta\omega_\Delta}{(1-\alpha\beta)}W - p_1(1-\alpha)\gamma n_\Delta N \tag{7.10}$$

we have the following:

$$\frac{dM(p_1,p_2,W,N,\Delta)}{d\omega_\Delta} = \frac{(1-\alpha)\alpha\beta}{(1-\alpha\beta)}W > 0 \tag{7.11}$$

$$\frac{dM(p_1,p_2,W,N,\Delta)}{dn_\Delta} = -p_1(1-\alpha)\gamma N < 0 \tag{7.12}$$

i.e. the value of imports is increasing in the Gini coefficient. Dalgin et al. (2008) estimate the effect of importer income inequality on total imports, finding that the effect varies according to the importer and exporter income level. In particular, as the importer becomes richer (increasing relative demand for luxuries) and the exporter becomes richer (increasing the production of luxuries), total imports increase as inequality rises. That said, as their data work on a bilateral basis and here we do not distinguish across origin of the imported products, there is not a clear mapping between their results and our theory.

As the coverage ratio is correlated with the Gini coefficient, this suggests that failure to control directly for the Gini coefficient will bias the estimated impact of the NTM on trade values upwards if the NTM is on the luxury only or downwards if it is only on the necessity. Since

Dalgin et al. (2008) find that the impact of inequality on trade is sizable, there is a potential for such biases to be economically meaningful.

7.3 Empirical Specification and Data

In the above stylized model, we show that the relationship between income distribution and coverage ratios depends on whether the NTMs are on luxuries (where rises in per capita income and/or the Gini coefficient increase the coverage ratio), necessities (where the opposite occurs), or neither/both (where the coverage ratio is 0 or 1 accordingly). We take this prediction to data on the coverage ratio across EU countries from 2008 to 2014 where, since policies are the same, variation in the coverage ratio for a given sector s across countries c in year t is driven only by variation in the trade shares of products within the sector.[9] We use trade-weighted coverage ratios for two different types of NTMs: TBTs and SPSs. Both are obtained from data compiled by Ghodsi, Reiter, and Stehrer (2015).[10] These measures are on the unit interval. The initial data are a dummy variable equal to 1 if there is an NTM of the relevant type on a six-digit product. Note that this information indicates whether or not there is *any* SPS/TBT on this product which applies to all imports, i.e. we do not consider exporter-specific NTMs. These are then aggregated up to coverage ratios for four-digit sectors in our baseline results (with two-digit sectors and national coverage ratios being used in alternative specifications). Note that when all six-digit products are covered (or not) by an NTM, the coverage ratio is 1 (or 0) regardless of the trade shares. Even when this is not the case, the coverage ratio can be 1 or 0 because, within the four-digit sector, only products with/without NTMs are imported. Our trade data used for aggregating come from the BACI data set which is based on the COMPTRADE data.[11]

In the data, 84 of the 1,194 four-digit sectors we use have no variation in the TBT coverage ratios across countries. Of these, 14 (16 per cent of this group) fall in HS sector 26 (ores, slag, and ash) with no other discernible pattern. In comparison 647 have no variation in SPS coverage

[9] Note that our data are an unbalanced panel across sector-countries. In particular, there is a drop-off in observations after 2012, with roughly 19 per cent of observations coming from each of the prior years. If we omit the 2013–14 observations, results are essentially unchanged.

[10] See Ghodsi, Gruebler, and Stehrer (2016a) and Ghodsi, Gruebler, and Stehrer (2016b) for examples working with such data.

[11] These can be found at www.cepii.fr/.

across countries (with 8 of the 84 sectors without variation in TBTs also without variation in SPSs). Here, there is no clear pattern across sectors with the largest percentage (6 per cent) in HS sector 84 (nuclear reactors, boilers, machinery, and mechanical appliances). Setting sectors without variation aside, in Table 7.1, we list the ten four-digit sectors with the largest standard deviation for the TBT and SPS coverage ratios, i.e. those with the most variation across EU countries (relative to the average size of the coverage ratio).[12] Looking at these, certain products such as paper products for TBTs and minerals for SPSs do not immediately come across as consumer products at all and read more as intermediate inputs (and as such may not be good candidates for applying our theory). Others, such as 'base metals clad with silver', 'perfumes', and 'candles' are arguably more in line with items consumed directly; further, one could make a case that such products are luxuries rather than necessities.[13] In any case, the theory does not make predictions about which products do or do not have NTMs applied to them, but that there is a relation between the coverage ratio and income distribution, with the direction of the correlation dependent on the nature of the sector.

With that in mind, following on from the theory, the baseline specification is:

$$\ln\left(CR_{c,s,t}\right) = \beta_c + \beta_s + \beta_t + \beta_1 \ln\left(\text{GDP per capita}_{c,t}\right) + \beta_2 \text{Inequality}_{c,t} + \varepsilon_{c,s,t} \tag{7.13}$$

i.e. we regress the coverage ratio (for TBTs or SPSs) on log of per capita income and a measure of income inequality. We use two measures of inequality: the log of the Gini coefficient (*Gini*) and the log of the share of income held by the richest quintile (*Quintile*). If the NTM in question falls primarily on luxuries, we expect positive coefficients for β_1 and β_2. We alter this specification in two ways. First, rather than using logged GDP per capita, we instead use logged GDP and logged population separately. Although the theory indicates that only per capita income matters, this alternative specification relaxes the assumption that the coefficients are equal yet opposite. Second, although the theory predicts that country size is unimportant for trade *shares* and thus the coverage

[12] We use the standard deviation here as the small average for some sectors created large coefficients of variation although the coverage ratios all fell within a fairly narrow band.

[13] Others, such as 'hydraulic brake fluids' seem much more like a necessity.

Table 7.1 *Top fifteen sectors ranked by cross-country variance in coverage ratio*

TBT	HS sector code	Average	Std. dev
Balloons and dirigibles	8801	0.487	0.502
Parachutes	8804	0.487	0.502
Tugs and pusher craft	8904	0.4722	0.5016
Fishing vessels	8902	0.4615	0.5013
Vessels and other floating structures	8908	0.4554	0.5005
Containers for compressed or liquefied gas	7311	0.4508	0.4996
Aluminium containers for compressed or liquefied gas	7613	0.4508	0.4996
Base metals clad with silver	7107	0.6667	0.488
Coins	7118	0.6667	0.488
Refractory cements	3816	0.3647	0.4842
Tar distilled from coal	2706	0.6449	0.4808
Newsprint, in rolls or sheets	4801	0.3478	0.4784
Tissue, towel, napkin stock or similar	4803	0.3478	0.4784
Composite paper and paperboard	4807	0.3478	0.4784
SPS	**HS sector code**	**Average**	**Std. dev**
Sulphur of all kinds	2503	0.5574	0.4987
Chalk	2509	0.5574	0.4987
Siliceous fossil meals	2512	0.5574	0.4987
Slate	2514	0.5574	0.4987
Limestone flux	2521	0.5641	0.498
Casks, barrels, vats, tubs	4416	0.5667	0.4976
Wood tar	3807	0.5785	0.4959
Asbestos	2524	0.5761	0.494
Phosphides	2853	0.5906	0.4937
Hydraulic brake fluids	3819	0.5906	0.4937
Reagents	3822	0.5906	0.4937
Colour lakes	3205	0.5984	0.4922
Organic compounds	2942	0.5984	0.4922
Perfumes and toilet waters	3303	0.5984	0.4922
Candles, tapers and the like	3406	0.5984	0.4922

Note: Average and standard deviation are calculated by four-digit sector across countries.

ratio, we consider a specification using both logged GDP and logged GDP per capita to examine this further. Our non-NTM data are all obtained from the World Development Indicators (World Bank, 2016).[14]

Table 7.2 indicates the average four-digit coverage ratio for each NTM, the coefficient of variation in this, and the averages for our two inequality measures for each of the countries in our sample.[15] As can be seen, there is significant variation in average coverage ratios both across countries and across four-digit sectors within a country. For TBTs, Denmark has the highest average coverage ratio across four-digit sectors (0.4208) and Croatia has the lowest (0.0497). Since the average of this across countries is 0.35, this indicates significant differences across nations. Turning to SPSs, Croatia again has the lowest average whereas Slovenia now has the highest at 0.29, 50 per cent higher than the average across countries. Note that Croatia has a much lower average NTM coverage than the other countries for both measures; we therefore test the robustness of our results to its exclusion below. Likewise, we find differences in inequality across countries. In terms of the Gini, the average across nations is 32.3, ranging from a high of 46.65 for Slovenia to a low of 26.08 in Slovakia. *Quintile* shows a similar variation, with a high of 52.2 in Slovenia to a low of 35.58 in Slovakia (and an average across countries of 40.2). Finally, it is worth recognizing that there are differences across countries in terms of how much the coverage ratios vary across products within a country.

Table 7.3 reports the summary statistics for the sample. In our estimations, errors are clustered at the country-year level (excepting when using country-wide coverage ratios; there we cluster only at the country level).

7.4 Results

In Table 7.4 we present our baseline results using the four-digit coverage ratios. Columns (1)–(4) use TBT coverages whereas (5)–(8) use SPS coverages. Even numbered columns utilize per capita GDP; odd numbered ones split it into GDP and population. Finally, columns (1), (2), (5), and (6) use *Gini* as the measure of inequality with the remainder using *Quintile* instead. Next to each variable name, in parenthesis, is the predicted coefficient sign presuming that the NTMs are on the luxuries. As discussed above, this suggests that a rise in inequality (Equations (7.7)

[14] These data are at http://databank.worldbank.org/.

[15] The averages in this table are those used to construct Figures 7.1 and 7.2.

Table 7.2 *Coverage rates across and within countries*

		TBT		SPS			
Country	Obs.	Average	Coeff. variation	Average	Coeff. variation	Gini	Quintile
Austria	4,675	0.3517	0.9527	0.2247	1.4778	30.45	38.61
Belgium	5,349	0.4116	0.8283	0.1961	1.6290	29.00	37.38
Bulgaria	3,833	0.3142	1.0664	0.1181	2.2270	33.57	41.01
Cyprus	3,708	0.3401	1.0021	0.1617	1.8642	31.71	40.60
Czech Republic	4,290	0.3659	0.8958	0.1402	2.0176	26.29	36.50
Germany	3,766	0.345	0.9744	0.2233	1.4872	31.29	39.60
Denmark	5,635	0.4208	0.8036	0.1874	1.6827	28.89	36.28
Spain	4,709	0.3522	0.9541	0.2238	1.4851	34.80	41.19
Estonia	3,710	0.3363	1.0027	0.157	1.9055	32.00	40.09
Finland	4,656	0.3589	0.9383	0.2261	1.4812	27.85	37.24
France	3,848	0.3637	0.9235	0.2188	1.5100	33.08	41.22
UK	4,780	0.3541	0.9481	0.2199	1.5040	34.37	41.71
Greece	4,662	0.3552	0.948	0.2278	1.4744	34.22	41.16
Croatia	2,335	0.0497	3.3668	0.0057	8.3339	33.71	42.25

Hungary	4,624	0.3821	0.89	0.1315	2.0924	27.53	36.44
Ireland	4,682	0.3578	0.9489	0.2286	1.4785	30.91	39.28
Italy	4,704	0.3519	0.9544	0.2228	1.4875	33.74	40.73
Lithuania	3,810	0.3525	0.9664	0.1534	1.9170	35.77	42.86
Latvia	3,756	0.3544	0.9643	0.1513	1.9259	37.41	43.60
Netherlands	5,461	0.4144	0.8159	0.2267	1.4400	29.93	38.34
Poland	5,463	0.331	0.9901	0.156	1.8816	33.72	41.75
Portugal	4,675	0.3533	0.9519	0.2253	1.4800	36.63	44.12
Slovenia	4,430	0.2818	1.2156	0.29	1.2524	46.65	52.20
Slovakia	5,079	0.4089	0.8199	0.1151	2.2827	26.08	35.58
Sweden	5,364	0.3864	0.8733	0.1974	1.6303	27.13	36.07

Notes: Average is the average of the coverage ratio across four-digit sectors within the country.
Coeff. variation is the coefficient of variation in the coverage ratio across four-digit sectors within the country. Gini and Quintile are the non-logged averages of a given country over the sample period.

Table 7.3 *Summary statistics*

	Obs.	Mean	Std. deviation	Minimum	Maximum
TBT coverage ratio	112,004	0.3560937	0.3387033	0	1
SPS coverage ratio	112,004	0.1897906	0.316561	0	1
GDP	112,004	26.46304	1.308321	24.03815	28.86857
GDP per capita	112,004	10.30581	0.4080621	8.905566	10.77051
Population	112,004	16.16675	1.128554	13.8897	18.22357
Gini coefficient	112,004	3.455952	0.1221655	3.258865	3.842673
Quintile	112,004	3.68207	0.0758006	3.55134	3.955082

Note: GDP, GDP per capita, Population, Gini coefficient, and Quintile are all measured as natural logs.

and (7.8)) would increase the coverage ratio. Similarly, an increase in per capita income would increase the coverage ratio (Equation (7.9)); this would also occur from a rise in GDP or a fall in population.

As can be seen, our results are broadly in line with our predictions when the NTM is on the luxury good. Beginning with the inequality measures, in all but one case we find that more inequality is correlated with a higher coverage ratio. Further, these coefficients are economically meaningful, with column (1) suggesting a 1 per cent rise in the Gini coefficient would be associated with a coverage ratio 0.1 higher, an increase of 27.5 per cent relative to the sample mean. The results are even larger for the *Quintile* measure of inequality where the estimated effect would be nearly twice as large. As inequality has been shown by others to have a meaningful predictive power for trade levels, this suggests that including TBT coverage ratios but not inequality has the potential to bias the estimated effect of TBTs (with the direction of the bias depending on whether inequality increases or decreases imports, something which Dalgin et al. (2008) show is a complicated relationship). Compared to TBTs, the estimated change in the SPS coverage ratio is smaller, roughly half the size when using the Gini coefficient and one-third as large when using *Quintile.* That said, because the average SPS coverage ratio is smaller (0.190 as compared to 0.356 for TBTs), the percentage change relative to the mean is only slightly smaller, estimated at 22.1 per cent.

Turning to the income measures, although in each case the estimated coefficient has a sign in line with NTMs on luxuries, the coefficients are

Table 7.4 *Baseline results: four-digit level*

	(1)	(2)	(3)	(4)	(5)	(6)	(7)	(8)
	TBT	TBT	TBT	TBT	SPS	SPS	SPS	SPS
GDP (+)	0.0231		0.0185		0.0229*		0.0194	
Population (−)	(0.0300)	0.0184	(0.0289)	0.0143	(0.0131)	0.0274*	(0.0126)	0.0231*
GDP per	−0.257**		−0.281**		−0.228***		−0.234***	
capita (+)	(0.116)		(0.114)		(0.0532)		(0.0548)	
Gini (+)	0.0981**	(0.0341)		(0.0328)	0.0419**	(0.0146)		(0.0139)
		0.0949**				0.0417**		
Quintile (+)	(0.0445)	(0.0435)	0.174**	0.155**	(0.0171)	(0.0197)	0.0536**	0.0405
			(0.0670)	(0.0652)			(0.0260)	(0.0287)
Observations	112,004	112,004	112,004	112,004	112,004	112,004	112,004	112,004
Adjusted R-squared	0.801	0.801	0.801	0.801	0.808	0.808	0.808	0.808

Notes: ***, **, and * on coefficients denote significance at the 1 per cent, 5 per cent, and 10 per cent levels respectively. Robust standard errors clustered by country-year in parentheses. All specifications include country, year, and four-digit sector dummies.

less precisely estimated. When using GDP per capita, we only find significance for this variable when using *Quintile* as the inequality measure. When relaxing the assumption that the GDP and population coefficients are proportional but opposite, we find a significant population coefficient in each case, where again it points towards NTMs on luxuries. The GDP coefficient, however, is only significant once (where as predicted it is positive). One noticeable difference between the GDP and population coefficients is their point estimates; the estimated coefficients for GDP are about 10 per cent as large as those for population (in absolute value). In unreported results, since Table 7.2 indicated that Croatia has very low coverage ratios relative to the other countries, we omitted this nation and repeated our estimation. When doing so, we found comparable results to the full sample estimates, and, if anything, slightly higher point estimates.[16]

In Tables 7.5 and 7.6, we repeat this exercise but use coverage ratios at the two-digit and country-wide levels. Our expectation is that when sectors are more aggregated this increases the likelihood of NTMs applying to both necessities and luxuries within the increasingly broad category. This could potentially weaken the links between income distribution and changes in the coverage shares in our estimates. Starting with the two-digit results, we find that the coefficient signs on inequality again point towards NTMs on the luxuries. Now, however, we find far less significance than in the four-digit results. In part, this is to be expected given the fall in the number of observations when we aggregate. Alternatively, as just mentioned, this may result from four-digit sectors where the NTMs are relatively clearly on luxuries or necessities, but when aggregated to a two-digit sector, this broader classification is less clearly delineated. Turning to the other variables, we find that when using SPS NTMs, the coefficients are also in line with NTMs on the luxury. In addition, we find somewhat more significance for GDP and per capita GDP than we did in the four-digit results. In contrast, when using TBTs, although the population coefficients point towards NTMs on the luxuries, the GDP and GDP per capita coefficients suggest the opposite. Beyond these differences, when using the two-digit data the point estimates for all the coefficients fall in size. When using the country-level data in Table 7.6, we again see a decline in significance and the magnitude of the point estimates. That said, our inequality measures are still significant when using the SPS coverages where they continue to point towards NTMs on the luxuries. Taken

[16] These are available on request.

Table 7.5 *Baseline results: two-digit level*

	(1)	(2)	(3)	(4)	(5)	(6)	(7)	(8)
	TBT	TBT	TBT	TBT	SPS	SPS	SPS	SPS
GDP (+)	−0.00513*	−0.00471*	−0.00520**	−0.00480*	0.00443**	0.00466*	0.00391*	0.00403*
Population (−)	(0.00260)		(0.00256)		(0.00211)		(0.00202)	
GDP per capita (+)	−0.0179**		−0.0194**		−0.0339***		−0.0343***	
	(0.00826)		(0.00821)		(0.00792)		(0.00802)	
		(0.00281)		(0.00274)		(0.00237)		(0.00225)
Gini (−)	0.00433	0.00409			0.00531*	0.00513		
Quintile (−)	(0.00311)	(0.00337)	0.00941*	0.00757	(0.00318)	(0.00331)	0.00581	0.00378
			(0.00495)	(0.00535)			(0.00472)	(0.00499)
Observations	8,604	8,604	8,604	8,604	8,604	8,604	8,604	8,604
Adjusted R-squared	0.897	0.897	0.897	0.897	0.780	0.780	0.780	0.780

Notes: ***, **, and * on coefficients denote significance at the 1 per cent, 5 per cent, and 10 per cent levels respectively. Robust standard errors clustered by country-year in parentheses. All specifications include country, year, and two-digit sector dummies.

Table 7.6 *Baseline results: country level*

	(1)	(2)	(3)	(4)	(5)	(6)	(7)	(8)
	TBT	TBT	TBT	TBT	SPS	SPS	SPS	SPS
GDP (+)	−3.57e-05		−4.44e-05		−3.64e-06		−6.52e-06	
Population (−)	(5.47e-05)		(4.86e-05)		(1.36e-05)		(1.29e-05)	
	−0.000171		−0.000197		−2.74e-05		−3.06e-05	
GDP per capita (+)	(0.000196)	−5.28e-05	(0.000186)	−6.31e-05	(4.42e-05)	−7.51e-06	(4.44e-05)	−1.06e-05
Gini (+)	0.000140	(6.13e-05)		(5.53e-05)	3.29e-05**	(1.48e-05)		(1.42e-05)
		0.000124				2.98e-05**		
Quintile (+)	(9.12e-05)	(0.000104)	0.000211	0.000173	(1.22e-05)	(1.22e-05)	4.42e-05**	3.78e-05**
			(0.000140)	(0.000158)			(1.69e-05)	(1.80e-05)
Constant	0.00330	0.000250	0.00366	0.000150	0.000457	1.43e-05	0.000535	1.14e-05
	(0.00327)	(0.000947)	(0.00318)	(0.00106)	(0.000704)	(0.000176)	(0.000700)	(0.000182)
Observations	101	101	101	101	101	101	101	101
Adjusted R-squared	0.896	0.892	0.897	0.892	0.971	0.971	0.971	0.971

Notes: ***, **, and * on coefficients denote significance at the 1 per cent, 5 per cent, and 10 per cent levels respectively. Robust standard errors clustered by country in parentheses. All specifications include country and year dummies.

together, the results of Tables 7.5 and 7.6 show two things. First, even at higher levels of product aggregation, we find evidence suggesting that NTMs are geared towards luxuries (although the results are less robust). Second, since the link between the coverage ratio and inequality grows smaller as the level of aggregation rises, the potential for bias when using NTM coverage ratios but not inequality may be more severe when using disaggregated data than, say, total trade levels.

In the theory, the trade shares and therefore the coverage ratio, were independent of country size.[17] As such, in the baseline estimates, we used either per capita GDP or its decomposition into GDP and population as controls. In Table 7.7, we use the four-digit data in an extended specification where we control for inequality, per capita GDP, and GDP, i.e. controlling for the distribution of income, average income, and total income.[18] When compared to the corresponding columns in Table 7.4, the only change we find is that the point estimates for per capita GDP increase by an order of magnitude. In addition, we find that, holding the average income and inequality constant, larger countries have lower coverage ratios with this estimate significant in the SPS regressions. Although we do not have a prior expectation for this coefficient, this suggests that even when controlling for country size, the other coefficients are suggestive of NTMs on luxuries.

In Tables 7.8 and 7.9 we repeat our Table 7.4 specification but split our four-digit data into manufacturing and non-manufacturing samples respectively.[19] Beginning with the manufacturing results in Table 7.8, for TBTs we find results comparable to the whole sample estimates in Table 7.4, i.e. TBTs on luxuries. For SPSs, on the other hand, although the sign pattern is consistent with SPSs on luxuries, we find no significant estimates. One possible reason for this is the relative infrequence of SPSs on manufactured goods; the average TBT coverage ratio for manufactures is 0.329 while the average SPS coverage ratio is only 0.114. Non-manufactures, on the other hand, exhibit significant coefficients only for SPSs as reported in Table 7.9. Here, as in the full sample results, the

[17] Note that we are discussing trade shares, as in Francois and Kaplan (1996), and not values such as in Dalgin et al. (2008) or prices as was done in Bekkers et al. (2012). In those specifications, theory indicated a role for market size. Were we to estimate import values (as in Equation (7.11)), we would need to do so as well.

[18] In unreported results, we also did so for the two-digit and country-level data. When doing so, we found results comparable to Table 7.7 but, as in the baseline, significance and point estimates decline as aggregation increases.

[19] Specifically, manufacturing includes four-digit sectors in two-digit codes 25 and higher.

Table 7.7 *Extended results: four-digit level*

	(1) TBT	(2) TBT	(3) SPS	(4) SPS
GDP (?)	−0.0877	−0.113	−0.140**	−0.148***
	(0.134)	(0.132)	(0.0554)	(0.0563)
GDP per capita (+)	0.101	0.121	0.159***	0.163***
Gini (+)	(0.140)	(0.139)	(0.0583)	(0.0598)
Quintile (+)	0.0958**	0.165**	0.0432**	0.0532**
	(0.0435)		(0.0178)	
		(0.0650)		(0.0268)
Observations	112,004	112,004	112,004	112,004
Adjusted R-squared	0.801	0.801	0.808	0.808

Notes: ***, **, and * on coefficients denote significance at the 1 per cent, 5 per cent, and 10 per cent levels respectively. Robust standard errors clustered by country-year in parentheses. All specifications include country, year, and 4-digit sector dummies.

estimates are consistent with SPSs on luxuries and the significance of the coefficients is quite strong. TBTs, on the other hand, display no significance and the sign pattern suggests TBTs on necessary non-manufactures. It is worth noting that for non-manufactures, NTM coverages are higher than in manufactures, with an average coverage ratio of 0.454 for TBTs and 0.463 for SPSs. In Table 7.10 we instead use our extended specification using both GDP and GDP per capita. When doing so, we find significant coefficients for manufacturing TBTs and non-manufacturing SPSs where the estimates suggest the NTMs are tilted towards luxuries.

Finally, one feature of the coverage ratio data is that there is a sizable share of observations where the coverage ratio is either zero or one. A zero occurs when there are no NTMs on imported six-digit products or are simply no NTMs (and thus the coverage ratio is independent of trade shares). Similarly, a coverage ratio of one means that NTMs apply to all imported products or all of them face NTMs. For TBTs, 17 per cent of the sample has a zero coverage and 26 percent has a coverage of one. For SPSs, the coverage ratio equals zero 61 per cent of the time (again, recall the relative infrequency of SPSs compared to TBTs) and one in 15 per cent of the cases. With this in mind, we re-estimate our baseline results two final times, using a Tobit estimator in Table 7.11 and a Poisson estimator in Table 7.12.[20]

[20] Results using Poisson Pseudo Maximum Likelihood (PPML) are available on request. These yield similar results.

Table 7.8 *Manufacturing results: four-digit level*

	(1)	(2)	(3)	(4)	(5)	(6)	(7)	(8)
	TBT	TBT	TBT	TBT	SPS	SPS	SPS	SPS
GDP (+)	0.0355		0.0291		0.00262		0.00190	
	(0.0393)		(0.0377)		(0.00564)		(0.00548)	
Population (−)	−0.405**		−0.434***		−0.0122		−0.0136	
GDP per capita (+)	(0.156)	0.0305	(0.153)	0.0242	(0.0164)	0.00276	(0.0169)	0.00207
		(0.0458)		(0.0441)		(0.00576)		(0.00562)
Gini (+)	0.134**	0.130**			0.00972	0.00974		
Quintile (+)	(0.0586)	(0.0585)	0.230**	0.203**	(0.00610)	(0.00618)	0.0135	0.0129
			(0.0889)	(0.0885)			(0.00988)	(0.00986)
Observations	87,641	87,641	87,641	87,641	87,641	87,641	87,641	87,641
Adjusted R-squared	0.770	0.770	0.770	0.770	0.718	0.718	0.718	0.718

Notes: ***, **, and * on coefficients denote significance at the 1 per cent, 5 per cent, and 10 per cent levels respectively. Robust standard errors clustered by country-year in parentheses. All specifications include country, year, and four-digit sector dummies.

Table 7.9 *Non-manufacturing results: four-digit level*

	(1)	(2)	(3)	(4)	(5)	(6)	(7)	(8)
	TBT	TBT	TBT	TBT	SPS	SPS	SPS	SPS
GDP (+)	−0.0106		−0.0104		0.0908**		0.0793*	
	(0.00849)		(0.00848)		(0.0451)		(0.0438)	
Population (−)	0.0420		0.0449		−0.818***		−0.849***	
GDP per capita (+)	(0.0275)	−0.0112	(0.0277)	−0.0110	(0.189)	0.108**	(0.193)	0.0956**
		(0.00875)		(0.00872)		(0.0494)		(0.0469)
Gini (+)	−0.00732	−0.00722			0.146**	0.141**		
Quintile (+)	(0.0137)	(0.0137)	−0.0156	−0.0131	(0.0636)	(0.0675)	0.211**	0.152
			(0.0217)	(0.0209)			(0.0937)	(0.0972)
Observations	24,363	24,363	24,363	24,363	24,363	24,363	24,363	24,363
Adjusted R-squared	0.923	0.923	0.923	0.923	0.882	0.881	0.882	0.881

Notes: ***, **, and * on coefficients denote significance at the 1 per cent, 5 per cent, and 10 per cent levels respectively. Robust standard errors clustered by country-year in parentheses. All specifications include country, year, and four-digit sector dummies.

Table 7.10 *Manufacturing and non-manufacturing extended results: four-digit level*

	Manufacturing				Non-manufacturing			
	(1)	(2)	(3)	(4)	(5)	(2)	(3)	(4)
	TBT	TBT	SPS	SPS	TBT	TBT	SPS	SPS
GDP (?)	−0.157	−0.188	−0.00608	−0.00792	0.0197	0.0227	−0.489**	−0.524**
	(0.188)	(0.185)	(0.0116)	(0.0118)	(0.0224)	(0.0229)	(0.203)	(0.206)
GDP per capita (+)	0.178	0.202	0.00847	0.00956	−0.0296	−0.0322	0.563***	0.586***
	(0.197)	(0.195)	(0.0138)	(0.0142)	(0.0234)	(0.0238)	(0.211)	(0.216)
Gini (+)	0.131**		0.00979		−0.00756		0.150**	
	(0.0578)		(0.00618)		(0.0138)		(0.0646)	0.207**
Quintile (+)		0.218**		0.0135		−0.0155		
		(0.0867)		(0.00999)		(0.0219)		(0.0947)
Observations	87,641	87,641	87,641	87,641	24,363	24,363	24,363	24,363
Adjusted R-squared	0.770	0.770	0.718	0.718	0.923	0.923	0.881	0.881

Notes: ***, **, and * on coefficients denote significance at the 1 per cent, 5 per cent, and 10 per cent levels respectively. Robust standard errors clustered by country-year in parentheses. All specifications include country, year, and four-digit sector dummies.

Table 7.11 *Tobit estimation: four-digit level*

	(1)	(2)	(3)	(4)	(5)	(6)	(7)	(8)
	TBT	TBT	TBT	TBT	SPS	SPS	SPS	SPS
GDP (+)	0.0389		0.0293		0.0915**		0.0734*	
Population (–)	(0.0469)	0.038	(0.0451)	0.0284	(0.0463)	0.114**	(0.0434)	0.0940*
GDP per	−0.521***		−0.547***		−0.902***		−0.903***	
capita (+)	(0.181)		(0.181)		(0.206)		(0.210)	
Gini (+)	0.177**	(0.0546)		(0.0524)	0.177**	(0.0531)		(0.0489)
		0.171****				0.174**		
Quintile (+)	(0.0704)	(0.0721)	0.283***	0.251**	(0.0692)	(0.0835)	0.200*	0.162
			(0.109)	(0.110)			(0.102)	(0.118)
Constant	7.163***	−0.495	7.396***	−0.726	11.83***	−1.309*	12.22***	−1.089
	(2.621)	0.7081	(2.589)	(0.747)	(2.697)	(0.792)	(2.731)	(0.846)
Sigma	0.202***	0.202***	0.202***	0.202***	0.259***	0.260***	0.259***	0.260***
	(0.00821)	0.0082	(0.00821)	(0.00821)	(0.0105)	(0.0105)	(0.0105)	(0.0105)
Observations	112,004		112,004	112,004	112,004	112,004	112,004	112,004
Pseudo R-squared	0.9119	0.9117	0.9120	0.9119	0.8370	0.8367	0.8369	0.8367

Notes: ***, **, and * on coefficients denote significance at the 1 per cent, 5 per cent, and 10 per cent levels respectively. Robust standard errors clustered by country-year in parentheses. All specifications include country, year, and four-digit sector dummies.

Table 7.12 *Poisson estimation: four-digit level*

	(1)	(2)	(3)	(4)	(5)	(6)	(7)	(8)
	TBT	TBT	TBT	TBT	SPS	SPS	SPS	SPS
GDP (+)	0.0534		0.0333		0.186**		0.145*	
Population (−)	(0.0914)		(0.0874)		(0.0903)		(0.0825)	
	−0.992***		−1.020***		−1.781***		−1.780***	
	(0.344)		(0.345)		(0.418)		(0.421)	
GDP per capita (+)		0.0547	0.0341			0.215**		0.168*
Gini (+)	0.318**	(0.106)	(0.101)		0.327**	(0.102)		(0.0923)
		0.311**				0.332**		
Quintile (+)	(0.138)	(0.143)	0.464**	0.416*	(0.131)	(0.159)	0.346*	0.296
Constant	12.59**	−2.357*	(0.218)	(0.221)	21.62***	−4.139***	(0.190)	(0.220)
			12.96***	−2.594*			22.52***	−3.588**
	(4.927)	(1.387)	(4.944)	(1.472)	(5.518)	(1.537)	(5.524)	(1.599)
Observations	112,004	112,004	112,004	112,004	112,004	112,004	112,004	112,004

Notes: ***, **, and * on coefficients denote significance at the 1 per cent, 5 per cent, and 10 per cent levels respectively. Robust standard errors clustered by country-year in parentheses. All specifications include country, year, and four-digit sector dummies.

As those tables show, the results tell the same story as the original estimates: NTMs seem to be applied mostly to luxuries.

7.5 Conclusion

With declining tariffs, the impact of NTMs has risen in importance when discussing trade policy. As the literature on NTMs continues to grow, it is important for researchers to be aware of how these measures are constructed. Here, we discuss one feature of this – the impact of trade shares on NTM coverage ratios. In particular, we show how even among a group of countries where NTMs are the same, coverage ratios can vary considerably. Here, we link this variation to income distribution, a trade determinant receiving a resurgence in attention. When import demand is driven by Stone-Geary preferences where some goods are luxuries consumed only by the rich and others necessities consumed by all, we show that the correlation between the coverage ratio and income distribution measures can suggest whether NTMs are on average applied to luxuries or necessities. Using data on the EU for 2008–14, we find that the estimates point towards NTMs on luxuries. Since this would imply that the NTM burden would fall relatively on the wealthy, recognizing this may be of use in debating the impact, merits, and political economy of NTM liberalization.

PART III

Dealing with Non-tariff Measures: Legal and Institutional Contexts

8

Nontariff Measures Reforms

A Practitioner's Perspective*

FABIO ARTUSO

8.1 Nontariff Measures and Trade Facilitation

Nontariff measures (NTMs) are regulatory instruments and policies that apply to traded products. Insofar as NTMs address a market failure and improve the business environment they are fully justified on welfare grounds. A badly designed or implemented NTM, however, could unnecessarily restrict trade and work against the realization of trade facilitation objectives. A common feature of efforts to reduce the trade-impeding effects of NTMs and improve the business environment is to increase the transparency of prevailing NTMs and to ensure that such measures are not more trade restrictive than necessary to achieve the legitimate policy objective of each specific regulation, such as protecting the environment, human health, animal well-being, etc.

From a trader's perspective, a well-functioning NTM regime would include the following:

1. A codified system to consider traders' perspectives when a regulation is being considered and to include them in the drafting process. This would ensure a better definition of the market failure and it would improve the regulatory response, in the attempt to balance the interests of the different stakeholders involved.
2. A systematic publication of the NTMs' text on a trade portal, freely available online. The portal's usability could be greatly improved if regulations are coded with the United Nations Conference on Trade

* The author has been working extensively as Senior Trade and Regional Integration Specialist for the World Bank Group in several Association of Southeast Asian Nations (ASEAN) countries, including Cambodia, Laos PDR, Indonesia, Myanmar, Thailand, Vietnam. The views expressed are personal and do not necessary reflect the official position of the World Bank Group.

and Development (UNCTAD) Multi-Agency Support Team (MAST) methodology and if they are indexed by Harmonized System (HS) code. Ideally regulations should also be linked to forms and procedures to obtain licenses, permits, etc.

3. A transparent methodology to launch complaints against an NTM that creates unnecessary effects on the market, such as distorting competition or penalizing a category of traders. Governments' accountability improves greatly where clear rules are established to regulate how complaints are to be treated, maximum time to provide an answer, and transparency requirements.

These objectives and expectations regarding NTMs can be realized only if the relevant government has established the necessary administrative mechanisms and institutional structures to serve the private sector. Allocating sufficient financial and human resources to enable public institutions to implement these mechanisms is critical.

Central elements of well-designed support programs that seek to address the specific challenges of individual countries in drafting and enforcing NTMs include the following focal issues:

1. Accountability
2. Transparency
3. Technical Capacity
4. Impact Assessment

Successful experiences in supporting countries to deal with NTMs have shown that positive results can be sustained over time only where comprehensive institutions are established with a strong legal mandate emanating from a high authority in the country. Where the mandate is informal or where this is too narrow, efforts in improving human and institutional capacity are very likely to result in poor achievements.

Typically, competence over NTMs is fragmented across several ministries and governmental agencies, which have responsibility for developing regulations in their mandate area, such as health, agriculture, environment, industry, etc. Their primary interest is to address specific market failure. De facto, they often fail to consider the trade implications of their regulations, because of their poor understanding of how the stratification of bureaucratic requirements contributes to deteriorate the business environment. In developing countries this phenomenon is particularly acute, as the practice of performing ex ante costs and benefits analysis of a proposed regulation is not yet commonly used.

In practice, however, regulatory decisions have spillover effects across different areas. Regulations on consumers or occupational health can have implications for domestic producer competitiveness. Conversely, reductions in trade barriers and improvements in trade facilitation can have implications for consumer safety. For example, it is hard for a poorly developed administration to establish how reliable exporters should be considered before being granted the green channel by Customs. Moreover, agricultural regulatory decisions can have implications for the environment and for public health. Here, specialized skills are necessary to determine, for example, which pesticides should be authorized in a country.

Eventually, a government is called to perform a very delicate balancing exercise where it should consider, on the one side, the need to fulfill a legitimate policy objective typically originating in a market failure and, on the other side, to do so in the least trade-restrictive modality. This balancing exercise should be optimized both during the regulatory drafting process and when the regulation is implemented. In fact, nicely written NTMs could result in an unnecessary market distortion because of the way they are enacted, for example, by imposing to the traders the need to visit several offices and submit the same information multiple times to obtain a license or permit. Reengineering and automating procedures could then represent an important opportunity to review inter-agency processes and consider the inclusion of costs and benefits assessment methodologies.

8.2 National Coordination Mechanisms

A central theme in supporting countries to improve their NTMs management is the development of customized interministerial institutional structures that can fit the specific administrative and political needs of each country. The emerging trend in developing countries, in fact, is that it is unpractical to develop a costs and benefits assessment capacity in each ministry designing and enacting NTMs. In fact, NTMs are typically under the responsibility of two or three dozen institutions and any effort to create capacity within the issuing agency has led to poor results, including because of high staff turnover. The support to establish an NTM Committee, then, appears as the most cost-effective investment as it charges one central agency, typically the Ministry of Commerce, with the technical mandate to analyze and review NTMs issued by line ministries. Often officials from the Ministry of Commerce staff an NTM

Secretariat in charge of completing analytical work that forms the base for recommendations to be taken by the NTM Committee.

It is important to outline, however, that recommendations of the Committee are not binding for the NTM issuing agency that shall retain the final responsibility for the NTM formulation and implementation modality. A comprehensive legal mandate would then empower the Committee to invoke the intervention of a higher authority to take a decision if the line ministry disagrees with the recommendation issued by the Committee. A critical feature of well-functioning NTM Committees is a codified process to consult the private sector on new regulations and to deal with their complaints on existing regulations. Automating this consultative function can contribute considerably to increase transparency and accountability.

Best practices from other countries are of little use in this exercise because local variables in each country are very diverse, including with reference to the legal context, the political cross-ministerial dynamism, and the availability of human and financial resources. However, it is possible to identify critical conditions that have occurred in some countries that have succeeded to some extent to establish functioning institutional mechanisms.

In Brazil, the process showed the importance of establishing a clear mandate and to give sufficient power and resources to the leading institution. It showed the importance of having a sufficient number of skilled staff bound to perform specific tasks in a given time frame. Moreover, the importance of providing sufficient financial resources to the lead institution was apparent, together with the practice to seek cooperation with research institutions, private sector organizations, and pools of experts in specific technical areas.

In Mexico, experience shows that institutional arrangement to conduct the NTM review has better chances of succeeding if:

1. It is driven by a high level of the administration with the appropriate mandate: The Federal Commission on Regulatory Improvement (COFEMER) was created by amendments to the Federal Administrative Procedure Act (LFPA).
2. The guillotine's framework and the institutions are formally established and credible.[1] This can be achieved through a government

[1] In the guillotine method, the review process consists of counting and then reviewing a large number of regulations against specified criteria. This tool is based on the principle of

BOX 8.1 THE STANDARD COST MODEL (SCM)

The SCM was first adopted by the Dutch government in the 1990s and it is now widely used in several OECD countries. It is used to prioritize reform programs aimed at simplifying regulatory burden to business. It measures the regulatory administrative compliance costs on traders. It consists of calculating, over a period of time, the total compliance cost of an NTM by multiplying:

- The number of businesses subject to a regulation;
- The frequency of filing;
- The estimated time to comply with the administrative requirement by different categories of employees;
- The salary-cost of employees tasked with completing and supervising the paperwork originated by the NTM.

decision, like that made in Mexico through the LFPA that established processes, institutions, objectives, and the deadlines for completion.

3. The institution or institutions that perform the regulatory simplification process are supported by experts that manage its application and carry out a thorough review process that is independent from each of the provisions in the guillotine.

The government of Mexico decided to adopt the Standard Cost Model (SCM) methodology to quantify the benefits of the improvements implemented in the federal proceedings (Box 8.1). This methodology helps to focus efforts and to consider proposals with the most impact and provide measurable results regarding the liberation of resources. The SCM is a data-intensive streamlining methodology but a simpler version of the model used in Organisation for Economic Co-operation and Development (OECD) countries can also be considered by countries with weaker analytical capacity.

South Korea tried to include good regulatory practices into legal drafting by establishing a ten-year reform program with the Basic Act on Administrative Regulations, which mandated the regulatory reform and review processes. South Korea established an independent central agency charged with controlling the regulatory quality. A Regulatory Reform Committee, a presidential commission chaired by the prime

the "reversal of burden of proof," whereby the regulators must justify why a regulation is needed or else remove it (Cadot, Malouche, and Sáez, 2012).

minister, was also set up with the mandate to decrease the overall compliance costs, rather than focusing simply on reducing the number of regulations.

More developed economies can rely on broader capacity across the agencies involved with issuing NTMs. These countries tend to delegate to each agency the regulatory impact assessment. This is the case of Australia, for example, which – in 2015 – enacted the Regulatory Burden Measurement Framework, whereby the "cost burden of new regulation must be fully offset by reductions in existing regulatory burden." The Australian government has decided to put onto the issuing agency the burden of calculating the compliance cost of each new regulation, including NTMs. The compliance cost includes administrative costs, i.e., costs incurred by regulated entities primarily to demonstrate compliance with the regulation (usually record keeping and reporting costs) and substantive compliance costs, i.e., costs incurred to deliver the regulated outcomes being sought (usually purchase and maintenance costs). Moreover, agencies have to calculate the delay costs, i.e., expenses and loss of income incurred by a regulated entity through an application delay or an approval delay. Agencies are required to present the average annual impact of the regulatory change in all costings. An estimation over a ten-year default duration of the regulation should be prepared. This methodology is more comprehensive and complex than the SCM as it requires greater capacity in the administration to manage a significant amount of data. It is apparent that a developing country could hardly aim at achieving this level of complexity in assessing the impact of new regulations. Moreover, the Regulatory Burden Measurement Framework imposes that the overall burden on business cannot be increased with the introduction of new regulations. If this is the case, the administration should offset it by reducing requirements in existing regulations. This is an indication that the Australian system has achieved a level of maturity that cannot be assimilated to the dynamism characterizing all developing economies.

8.3 International Disciplines and Principles on Establishing NTMs Committees

The World Trade Organization (WTO) does not provide a comprehensive NTM discipline in a single text. This is spread across several agreements, including the General Agreement on Tariffs and Trade (GATT); the Sanitary and Phytosanitary (SPS) Measures Agreement; the Technical

Barriers to Trade (TBT) Agreement; the Import Licensing Procedures (ILP) Agreement; and the Trade Facilitation Agreement (TFA).

The overarching principle governing NTMs, i.e., the National Treatment, is encapsulated in Article III of the GATT, imposing that "like products be treated alike" or that no distinction of treatment can be made between imported and domestically produced products. This principle is complemented by Article XX of the GATT that enables WTO members to restrict importation of hazardous products. The SPS, TBT, and ILP agreements specify the way Article XX can be used in practice, while the TFA focuses on the procedural implementation of NTMs.

The SPS Agreement encourages member countries to pattern their SPS regulations on international standards (i.e., the *Codex Alimentarius* for food products). In order to adapt regulations to local conditions, countries "must establish SPS measures on the basis of an appropriate assessment of the actual risks involved, and, if requested, make known what factors they took into consideration, the assessment procedures they used and the level of risk they determined to be acceptable."

Article 2.2 of the TBT Agreement establishes that

> [m]embers shall ensure that technical regulations are not prepared, adopted or applied with a view to or with the effect of creating unnecessary obstacles to international trade. For this purpose, technical regulations shall not be more trade-restrictive than necessary to fulfil a legitimate objective, taking account of the risks non-fulfilment would create. Such legitimate objectives are, inter alia: national security requirements; the prevention of deceptive practices; protection of human health or safety, animal or plant life or health, or the environment. In assessing such risks, relevant elements of consideration are, inter alia: available scientific and technical information, related processing technology or intended end-uses of products.

The ILP Agreement imposes the principle of transparency, establishing that "the rules and all information concerning procedures for the submission of applications, including the eligibility of persons, firms and institutions to make such applications, the administrative body(ies) to be approached, and the lists of products subject to the licensing requirement shall be published ... in such a manner as to enable governments and traders to become acquainted with them" (article 1.4(a)). The ILP Agreement imposes also the principle of fairness and simplicity (articles 1.3; 1.5; 1.6; 1.7; 1.8).

The TFA lists the information that shall be published "in a non-discriminatory and easily accessible manner in order to enable governments, traders, and other interested parties to become acquainted with them" (paragraph 1.1). It also imposes an obligation on Member States to publish on the Internet procedures, forms, and documents required for import, export, and transit (paragraph 2.1) and an obligation to establish Enquiry Points (paragraph 3.1). Under the TFA, Member Countries are also expected to establish a National TFA Committee. The composition and the mandate of this Committee overlaps substantially with the NTM Committee mentioned above. There is therefore significant scope to either merge the two institutions into one single Committee or to establish a hierarchical relationship between them, depending on the local conditions in each country.

The ASEAN Trade in Goods Agreement (ATIGA) provides a WTO-compatible NTMs' discipline, anticipating also the obligation to publish trade information online in National Trade Repositories (NTRs) that have subsequently been described in the TFA as Trade Portals. In 2014, the ASEAN Economic Ministers endorsed the Regional and National NTMs Works Programs, which include a set of detailed prescriptions for ASEAN Member States, including:

1. To establish a National NTM Committee;
2. To collect and classify all national NTMs;
3. To develop guidelines on operating procedures for each NTM;
4. To notify the NTMs inventory to the ASEAN Secretariat;
5. To publish NTMs in a web portal (NTR) to be connected with the ASEAN Trade Repository;
6. To review the stock of NTMs, establishing criteria to assess the impact or undertake a cost-benefit analysis;
7. To establish criteria for streamlining NTMs;
8. To enforce and monitor the modification of NTMs according to the recommendations of the NTMs Secretariat.

8.4 World Bank Support and Experience in ASEAN Countries

The World Bank Group (WBG) has been active in providing support to ASEAN governments to reduce the trade-impeding effects of NTMs and to improve the operation of associated institutional bodies and agencies. In Cambodia, the main counterpart for the NTM support program is the Ministry of Economy and Finance. Support started in 2012 with assistance to collect and analyze some 120 laws and regulations, from which about 400 measures were extracted and classified following the MAST system. NTMs were subsequently published in the Cambodian National Trade Repository[2] that complies substantially with the requirements listed in the TFA.

The Repository is managed by a team of officials from the Ministry of Economy and Finance, which is also responsible for the maintenance and updating of the portal. The portal has subsequently been upgraded with the inclusion of regulations related to services and investment that are pending publication. NTMs have been published in the local language. Translation in English has been partially completed, with the support of the Royal University of Law and Economy.

Conscious that interministerial coordination is facilitated by a comprehensive legal mandate, the Ministry of Economy and Finance promoted the adoption of two Sub-Decrees focusing on the Committee's tasks and responsibilities as regards NTMs and the NTR, respectively. Compliance with the ASEAN Work Program on NTMs triggered the adoption of these regulations. Both Committees are supported by a Secretariat, hosted in the Ministry of Economy and Finance and they include a Focal Point for each of the ministries and agencies responsible for developing and enforcing NTMs.

The Committees' mandates mirror the contents of the ASEAN Work Program, listing in detail tasks and responsibilities that enable them and their Secretariats to seek cooperation from line ministries and agencies on all NTM-related issues, including collection, classification, publication, review, and streamlining. An example of the activities undertaken by the Committees is provided in Box 8.2.

Thanks to its expanding mandate, the department of the Ministry of Economy and Finance serving as the Committees' Secretariats obtained approval to hire about ten additional staff who benefited from substantial training on NTM classification, analysis, and streamlining provided by the World Bank. A comprehensive logical framework for the Secretariat's work was developed at the end of 2016, setting out a set of smart indicators linked to clear results to be obtained over the next five years. The achievement of those results is highly dependent on the provision of financial and technical support by Development Partners, since the Ministry of Economy and Finance can only support a portion of the total costs to run the Secretariats professionally.

[2] www.cambodiantr.gov.kh/.

BOX 8.2 REVIEWING EXPORT COSTS IN CAMBODIA

In 2013, a study was promoted by the Secretariat to the Cambodian National NTM Committee to assess the impact on export competitiveness of current export measures. The study focused on the requirement for exporters to be annually registered and the obligation to obtain a certificate of origin regardless of the preferential nature of the export transaction. The study exemplified ways to approximate the impact of high export costs on the competitiveness of the private sector, indicating that high costs (40 percent higher than the ASEAN average) have a strong impact on the possibility for small and medium-sized enterprises (SMEs) to reach (and survive in) export markets.

In November 2013, the Royal Government of Cambodia decided to remove the annual registration and to issue Certificates of Origin only when needed by traders. These reforms, together with improvements in trade facilitation and logistics, contributed to expand trade flows and supported export differentiation away from garments and apparels.

In Laos PDR, the Ministry of Commerce launched in 2012 the National Trade Repository[3] addressing all requirements foreseen in the ATIGA. The WBG provided technical support to the Department of Import and Export of the Ministry of Commerce, which is currently managing the trade portal, substantially compliant also with the TFA. The portal currently lists about 300 legal documents and about 400 NTMs. The work to collect and classify regulations to be listed in the portal triggered coordination around NTMs under the guidance of the Ministry of Commerce. Differently from Cambodia, however, a comprehensive legal mandate listing all tasks and responsibilities of a national NTM Committee is still pending. The government of Laos PDR, in fact, reputed that the existing Trade Facilitation coordinating structure could cover also the mandate of the NTM Committee described in the ASEAN Work Program. However, it became apparent soon after that cooperation from line ministries was not forthcoming in the absence of an explicit legal mandate. The Ministry of Commerce has currently developed a proposal to include the NTM responsibility under the National Trade Facilitation Committee to be established under the TFA and a final cabinet decision on this subject is pending.

[3] www.laotradeportal.gov.la.

Despite this legal uncertainty, however, Laos PDR was the first country in ASEAN to achieve ATIGA compliance on the National Trade Repository, contributing to increase transparency of NTMs and their practical application, by providing a schematic description of the procedural steps necessary to obtain the main licenses and permits. Information on NTMs was collected and classified according to the UNCTAD MAST system. A review of these NTMs was initiated by the Ministry of Commerce, starting from regulations directly under its purview. Unfortunately, though, the lack of a clear mandate prevented the Ministry of Commerce from getting sufficient cooperation from the other line ministries and agencies that did not succeed in reviewing effectively their measures.

Given the limitation in financial and human resources, the Laos government could consider adopting a simplified methodology to analyze and review NTMs. Probably an SCM approach could be appropriate in the current local context, where a full-fledged Regulatory Impact Assessment could be hardly sustained over time.

In Myanmar, work on NTMs started with the provision of technical support to identify and collect measures for publication in the National Trade Portal. About 120 laws and regulations were collected and their analysis and classification was completed with support from UNCTAD, with Economic Research Institute for ASEAN and East Asia (ERIA) funding. The portal was eventually launched in 2016 with support from the United States Agency for International Development (USAID).[4] However, only a portion of the NTMs that were collected in 2014–15 were published.

A series of training workshops were delivered to the Ministry of Commerce between 2012 and 2016, involving also line ministries and agencies and research institutes, such as the Economic Research Institute of Yangon and Myanmar Development Research Institute. Awareness and understanding of NTMs was greatly improved as a result of this training, but limited progress was achieved in analyzing and streamlining NTMs, in the absence of a clear legal mandate to the Ministry of Commerce to carry out this work across different agencies.

Nevertheless, important results were achieved in reviewing licensing requirements on imported goods. In fact, up to 2012, a license was required to import any type of goods. A negative list was developed in 2015, based on the recommendations developed in a methodological note

[4] www.myanmartradeportal.gov.mm.

prepared by the Ministry of Commerce in cooperation with the WBG. The Ministry of Commerce is aware that more licensing requirements could be abolished, but additional technical inputs are necessary to appreciate the implications of removing licenses in sensitive areas such as food and chemical products. A similar effort is undergoing also to review licenses for exports, whereby unnecessary requirements are intended to be removed.

The Ministry of Commerce is also engaged in an important effort to review its legal mandate within the overall structure of the government. This process is informed by a series of workshops, including to review how different countries have regulated governmental responsibility to collect, classify, publish, analyze, and review NTMs. A law that would explicitly transpose into directly enforceable national legislation multilateral and regional principles on NTMs could provide the Ministry of Commerce with an effective tool to reach out to line ministries and agencies and obtain their cooperation, addressing the constraints identified in Section 8.2 above. This could be an interesting innovative approach that could be replicated elsewhere, depending on favorable local conditions.

Turning to Viet Nam, work has focused on completing preparation of its ATIGA-compliant National Trade Repository. Here also a major focus has been on collecting, classifying, and publishing data on NTMs, together with the other information expected that will be included in a trade portal. To date, some 300 measures have been collected and classified using the MAST system. Support is also being provided to the government to improve the interministerial structure and to enhance the capacity to review and streamline NTMs.

8.5 Lessons Learned and Conclusions

The WBG's support to selected ASEAN countries over a five-year period (2012–16) consolidated into a solid program supporting governments in achieving their objective in a difficult policy area. The following lessons learned have emerged from this experience:

1. It is important to define two separate levels to deal effectively with NTMs:
   a. At the **political level** it is important to establish an interministerial structure involving high-level representatives of all ministries and agencies issuing NTMs. A legal mandate detailing tasks and responsibilities of the interministerial committee should be issued by the highest authority in the government. The committee should

be charged with formulating overall recommendations on streamlining NTMs and with stimulating its members to cooperate on the collection and notification of new measures. The committee should be given the opportunity to invoke the intervention of a high authority (Prime Minister or Deputy Prime Minister), in case this proves to be necessary. It is important for the committee's members to have a basic understanding of the political implications of NTMs, but it is not essential that they master them technically.

b. At the **technical level**, a permanent Secretariat should prepare and support the deliberations of the Committee. The Secretariat should have clear terms of reference, listing its tasks and responsibilities, and it should report regularly to the Committee, based on annual and multi-annual work-plans. The Secretariat should be staffed with professional staff with both legal and economic expertise, in order to advise on all aspects of NTMs. Over time, the capacity of the staff should be enhanced, particularly on cost-benefit analysis methodologies and on econometrics. This is a critical area to provide quality inputs for the recommendations to be taken by the Committee. The Secretariat should be hosted in a central agency, which could be the Ministry of Commerce/Trade or the Ministry of Finance, depending on the local conditions in the beneficiary government.

2. Developing countries should consider approaching NTMs by initially focusing their efforts on collection, classification, and publication of prevailing measures. This requires a robust national coordinating structure, with a focus on improving transparency and accountability. Such an initial mapping effort can then evolve into a process of analysis of NTMs and streamlining. The latter activities require strengthened capacity and additional resources over a sustained period of time.
3. Governments should select one standard analytical tool to review the impact of NTMs on the country's competitiveness or on the population's welfare. The complexity of the cost-benefit methodology should be commensurate with the level of analytical capacity in the government. For example, it would be prudent for countries with low capacity to standardize the use of an SCM methodology for all new regulations. With the improvement of the administration's capacity, this can evolve into more accurate regulatory impact assessment methodologies.
4. The effective management of NTMs can contribute significantly to improve the business environment. It is also an important component of any trade policy, but it is largely developed with little involvement

of the institutions with a trade mandate. The legal mandate of the Ministry of Commerce, or any other central agency entrusted with developing and implementing the trade policy, should explicitly mention the role it should play in NTMs, including vis-à-vis the line ministries and agencies. It is also important that the principles and obligations originating in multilateral agreements and free trade agreements (FTAs) are explicitly transposed into national legislation, so that specific NTMs would have to be drafted consequently.

5. The collection, classification, and publication of NTMs should become an embedded task of a central agency, possibly the same agency hosting the Secretariat mentioned above. This would ensure ongoing sustainability beyond the ad hoc support provided by development partners. Capacity development efforts should focus on using the MAST classification system and to ensure that NTMs are linked to HS codes, in order to facilitate traders' searches.
6. The process to draft new NTMs should be codified, ensuring the consultation of the main stakeholders, including private sector associations and consumers' organizations. Policy makers could greatly benefit from different stakeholders' inputs, but the consultation has more chances of succeeding if it takes place in a structured format that improves accountability and transparency of the whole process. Similarly, clear procedures should also be established to enable private sector operators to lodge complaints against existing NTMs, providing clear details on the problems raised by the regulations.

Aid for Trade resources can be made available to developing countries to address NTM issues, but the chances to obtain a higher return on investment are greater if the following preconditions are met:

1. There is a clear understanding of the importance of this policy agenda at the highest level in the country. Specific policy notes could be drafted to simulate the effects on consumer products' prices or on competitiveness of a specific measure.
2. There is a solid interest to develop institutions entrusted to dealing with NTMs with a clear legal mandate. This should translate into a multi-annual capacity development program that supports the implementation of a predefined work-plan, establishing desired outcomes and listing detailed activities.
3. Development partners align their support to a clear strategy to be developed by the government. This would ensure better aid effectiveness.

9

Good Regulatory Practices and International Trade

ROBERT BASEDOW

9.1 Introduction

Regulatory divergences are perceived as the most important trade barriers today (Hoekman, 2015; Hoekman and Mavroidis, 2015a). Over the last decades, countries have significantly lowered classic trade barriers such as tariffs and quotas. In many sectors and trade relationships, diverging regulatory requirements across countries are the main source of trade costs. Diverging regulatory requirements require businesses to get informed about regulatory requirements in other markets, to accordingly specify products and services and ultimately to proof regulatory compliance to local authorities (OECD, 2015a). These information, specification and compliance costs are often sizeable and avoidable. Regulatory divergences in many cases do not reflect diverging public policy objectives. They result from a lack of awareness and information among regulators for the international regulatory environment.

Trade policymakers have turned to Good Regulatory Practice(s) (GRP (s)) as a promising approach to limit unnecessary regulatory divergences and trade costs. The planned Transatlantic Trade and Investment Partnership (TTIP) and the Transpacific Partnership (TPP) for instance foresaw that the contracting parties adhere to and systematically use GRP to limit unnecessary regulatory divergence. GRPs refer to the use of three public management tools: (1) ex ante regulatory impact assessment(s) (RIA(s)) for planned regulation; (2) ex post evaluation of existing regulation; and (3) stakeholder engagement through public consultations (OECD, 2012). GRPs allow states to become aware and to balance the manifold desired and undesired effects of new and existing regulation across public policy domains including on international trade relations (OECD, 2012, 2015b; Basedow and Kauffmann, 2016).

This chapter assesses the theoretical potential and actual use of GRP to limit regulatory divergence and trade costs. It raises four questions. First, what is in theory the contribution of GRP to limiting regulatory divergence across jurisdictions? Second, how do countries in practice use GRP to limit unnecessary regulatory divergence? Third, how could countries enhance their use of GRP to limit regulatory divergence and trade barriers? And finally, what is the potential contribution of the World Trade Organization (WTO) and preferential trade agreements (PTAs) in enhancing the use of GRP? The chapter builds on Organisation for Economic Co-operation and Development (OECD) data (OECD, 2015b, 2015c) and OECD research (Basedow and Kauffmann, 2016). Its empirical section focuses on the experience of OECD countries. It is structured as following. The first section offers a conceptual introduction. It defines in detail GRPs and discusses their theoretical potential to limit regulatory divergence. The second section discusses the use of OECD countries of GRP. It evaluates whether, when and how countries seek to assess trade impacts of new and existing regulation through GRP. The third and last section summarises the findings and discusses how countries could enhance their use of GRP. Special attention is afforded to the potential contributions of the WTO and PTAs in this enterprise.

9.2 Good Regulatory Practices in Theory

9.2.1 The Rise of the Regulatory State and Good Regulatory Practices

The role of the state and regulation significantly evolved in Western countries since the 1980s. After the Second World War, the state directly intervened in the economy and society as an omnipresent and powerful economic agent (Ayres and Braithwaite, 1992; Majone, 1994, 1997; Braithwaite and Drahos, 2000). State-owned enterprises – often monopolies – dominated many sectors. They served economic and social-political objectives. They ensured for instance supply with electricity and water, and offered postal, telecommunication, air and rail transport services. On the other hand, state-owned enterprises also sought to promote full employment, social security, labour and environmental protection. The central role of the state in the economy and society reflected the prevailing Keynesian macroeconomic paradigm.

Regulation transformed into the key public policy tool with the rise of the neo-liberal paradigm in Western countries during the 1970s and 1980s (Ayres and Braithwaite, 1992; Majone, 1994, 1997; Braithwaite and Drahos, 2000). In the light of the stagflation crises of the 1970s and the inability of Keynesian policies to resolve them, Western policy-makers gradually endorsed the neo-liberal macroeconomic paradigm.

The neo-liberal macroeconomic paradigm stipulates that states should avoid heavy-handed intervention and instead strengthen markets to ensure an efficient allocation of resources. Western states thus partially withdrew as direct economic actors, privatised many state-owned enterprises and promoted competition in previously monopolistic sectors. States turned toward regulation – as a less intrusive instrument – to pursue their public policy objectives. The 1980s and 1990s thus saw a significant increase in regulatory activity notably in Western Europe. While often described as an era of 'deregulation', it is more accurate to describe the 1980s and 1990s as an era of 'reregulation'.

The rise of the so-called regulatory state (Majone, 1994) triggered a democratic legitimacy and accountability challenge. Western states had legitimation and accountability mechanisms in place to check on the activities of state-owned enterprises and such like. While these mechanisms were not widely seen as being effective, they ensured a minimum degree of democratic legitimacy and accountability. In many countries regulatory activity, however, at first developed unchecked despite its important effects on citizens, society and the economy. The legitimacy and accountability challenge was particularly acute in the European Union (EU), which drew even more on regulation than nation states and was even further removed from its demos (Majone, 1994; Scharpf, 1999, 2003).

GRP – and more generally regulatory policy – emerged as a response to these legitimacy and accountability challenges. GRPs comprise ex ante RIAs of planned regulation, ex post evaluations of existing regulation and stakeholder consultations on planned and existing regulation. Regulatory policy, in turn, is a meta-policy structuring states' regulatory systems and overall approach to regulation. GRP and regulatory policy seek to enhance the input legitimacy ('government by the people') and output legitimacy ('government for the people') of regulatory activity (Scharpf, 2003). GRPs increase transparency and inclusiveness in norm development and implementation in order to ensure legitimacy. They also subject planned and existing regulations to systematic assessments of their costs and benefits in order to evaluate whether and how to enhance efficiency and effectiveness of regulation. They seek to ensure a high quality of regulation. High quality regulation is defined as a norm, which is effective while imposing minimal costs on society. GRP may thereby help to minimise inter alia unnecessary trade costs for society. It is, however, important to note that GRPs are not a 'trade policy tool'.

9.2.2 *Regulatory Impact Assessment and Trade Considerations*

RIA is the most prominent element of GRP. RIA is a systematic approach to ex ante assess potential positive and negative effects of planned regulation and potential non-regulatory alternatives (OECD, 2005a; Renda, 2015; Dunlop and Radaelli, 2016). It normally takes the form of a cost-benefit analysis of various regulatory and non-regulatory options. RIA does not seek to replace political decisions, but to inform policymakers of the implications of policy options under consideration. RIA, moreover, plays an important role in the dissemination of information about regulatory initiatives within public administrations and society. Lead services in charge of a public policy domain typically prepare RIAs. Special oversight bodies at the centre of government should ensure that RIAs are of high quality. In many cases, RIAs are then discussed at political cabinet level as part of the decision-making process. Stakeholder consultations often form an integral part of the drafting process of RIAs.

RIA can play an important role in limiting regulatory divergence and trade costs. By asking lead services to take the international regulatory landscape into account, RIAs may increase awareness of administrations for foreign and international regulatory approaches, potentially arising regulatory frictions and trade costs (OECD, 2005a; Renda, 2015). Trade impacts, moreover, are of an economic nature. They lend themselves to quantification and monetisation, which is often a standard approach in cost-benefit analyses of RIAs. RIAs, however, also face generic and trade-specific challenges. RIAs aim at national welfare maximisation. Even when using RIAs, regulators may disregard unnecessary regulatory divergence and trade costs, if costs primarily affect and fall on foreigners. What is more, traders are normally preoccupied with the regulatory environment at large rather than a single norm. RIAs, however, typically assess only a single regulation. The implementation and enforcement stage is also an important source of regulatory and trade frictions. RIAs normally do not assess the implementation and enforcement but only the design of regulations. Finally, RIAs in general are often used as a legitimation rather than analytical tool. Policymakers often decide on a regulation and subsequently draft RIAs to justify their choice. RIAs thus cannot inform rule-making and enhance regulatory quality.

9.2.3 *Ex Post Evaluations and Trade Considerations*

Ex post evaluations of existing regulations constitute an important yet less frequently used public management tool (Allio, 2015). Ex post evaluations inform policymakers of direct and indirect, intended and unintended effects of existing regulations. They provide feedback about the effectiveness and efficiency of regulations; and thereby point to options for improving individual regulations and sectorial regulatory frameworks at large (Allio, 2015). Unlike RIA, ex post evaluations adopt broad analytical focus and assess the joint impacts of sectorial regulations on society. Ex post evaluations often take the form of a cost-benefit analysis and are combined with stakeholder consultations. They form part of regulatory stock management programmes (red tape reduction), may be programmed (periodic review clauses in regulation) or come about on an ad hoc basis.

Ex post evaluations have an important role to play in attempts to limit regulatory divergence. Adverse trade impacts of regulation are often unintended and unexpected. Regulators may overlook negative trade impacts in ex ante RIAs. Ex post evaluations enable regulators to identify unanticipated effects. As discussed above, adverse trade impacts of regulation often stem from the regulatory environment at large. Unlike RIAs, ex post evaluations enable regulators to evaluate the impacts of a regulatory environment at large. Ex post evaluations, nonetheless, have limitations. First, they are less frequently used and thus less developed (Metzenbaum, 1998; Allio, 2015). The processes and methodologies for ex post evaluations are still at a formative stage in many OECD countries. Second, ex post evaluations face cognitive and hierarchical challenges (Bennard and Dickinson, 2011). Ex post evaluations require bureaucrats to critically evaluate their own or the work of colleagues and eventually to break with institutional regulatory paradigms. Bureaucrats may find it difficult to perform this task.

9.2.4 Stakeholder Consultations and Trade Considerations

Stakeholder consultations have become a central element of high quality regulatory systems (OECD, 2005a). Regulators ask stakeholders through consultations to provide input in the norm development, implementation and review phase. Consultation may take the form of online platforms or public meetings. Consultations provide regulators with crucial information about societal demands, impacts and technical information of planned and existing regulation. By increasing inclusiveness and transparency, they support legitimacy and ownership of regulation and policies among the regulated.

Stakeholder consultations play a crucial role in identifying and limiting unnecessary regulatory divergence and trade costs as part of ex ante RIA and ex post evaluations. Stakeholder consultations are particularly useful to identify unforeseen effects of regulations. In international settings, the quality of consultations may however suffer from linguistic barriers. More generally, consultations risk strengthening the voice of powerful stakeholders, while further marginalising weak constituencies. Multinational corporations for instance may find it easy to take part in consultation processes, while citizens, non-governmental organisations (NGOs) or small business may struggle to take part (Mendes, 2015). It may be necessary to combine consultations with outreach efforts to involve weak constituencies.

9.2.5 *A Note of Caution: The Inherent Limitations of GRP and Regulatory Convergence*

To summarise, GRPs have the potential to make an important contribution to limit unnecessary regulatory divergence and adverse trade impacts in domains where states share public policy objectives. The discussion showed that each element of GRP – RIA, ex post evaluations and stakeholder consultations – has specific advantages and disadvantages. The different elements complement each other. The joint use of RIA, ex post evaluations and consultations should deliver the best overall results.

GRP cannot, however, bring about regulatory convergence in all circumstances. First, states may pursue diverging public policy objectives translating into diverging regulations. In line with democratic demands, the EU and the USA for instance deal very differently with genetically modified organisms (GMOs). GRP cannot and must not aim at limiting such regulatory divergence. Second, regulatory divergence may not stem from diverging public policy objectives but reflect regulatory path dependence. Regulatory traditions and systems vary, which may translate into different regulatory designs, implementation and enforcement strategies. Despite the fact that states may ultimately pursue the same objectives through regulation, GRP cannot ensure regulatory convergence in these cases. States may have to use more activist tools such as mutual recognition agreements to facilitate trade. Finally, regulation often serves protectionist purposes. Regulations of service sectors often have the explicit purpose of keeping foreign competitors out of markets. It is manifest that GRP cannot bring about regulatory convergence and facilitate trade relations, if regulation was indeed designed and implemented to achieve the opposite.

9.3 Good Regulatory Practices in Practice

All OECD countries have formally committed to GRP (OECD, 2012). But to what extent do states use GRP to identify and to limit unnecessary regulatory divergence and trade costs? The following section builds on the OECD Regulatory Indicators Survey (OECD, 2015c) and evaluations of national GRP guidelines (see the Appendix) to clarify the use of GRP to assess trade impacts. It focuses in particular on the RIA guidelines of Australia, Austria, Canada, Germany, Switzerland, the United Kingdom and the EU. These jurisdictions reported the most frequent use of GRP to assess the trade impacts of regulation. It is therefore reasonable to assume that these countries have the most refined approaches and methods to assess the trade impacts of regulation. The main emphasis in this section lies on the use of RIAs, as they are the most frequently used and refined GRP element.

9.3.1 RIA: How Systematically Do Countries Assess Trade Impacts?

RIAs typically focus on budgetary, public sector or environmental impacts (OECD, 2015b). OECD research, nonetheless, shows that the assessment of trade impacts of regulation is part of national RIA procedures in a majority of OECD countries (OECD, 2015c; Basedow and Kauffmann, 2016). Twenty-four out of thirty-four countries report to evaluate trade impacts of some, major or all regulations as part of their national RIA procedures. Ten countries, on the other hand, report that they never assess trade impacts of their regulation as part of RIAs. If one unpacks these numbers it becomes clear that the trade impacts of primary laws are more systematically assessed than the trade impacts of subordinate regulations. Twenty-four countries assess the trade impacts of all, major or some primary laws, whereas twenty-two countries assess the trade impacts of all, major or some subordinate regulations. In short, there is leeway for OECD countries to intensify the use of RIA for the assessment of trade impacts.

Regulators use threshold and proportionality rules to determine when and to what degree to assess various potential impacts listed in RIA guidelines (Basedow and Kauffmann, 2016). Threshold and proportionality rules are important due to the limited resources of public administrations. It is impossible and indeed superfluous for regulators to assess all potential impacts in detail. A review of the RIA guidelines of Australia, Austria, Canada, the EU, Germany, Switzerland and the USA shows that threshold rules are vague. Most countries ask regulators to complete a checklist – often by ticking boxes – to determine potentially important impacts in need of detailed assessment. The vagueness is necessary to leave regulators the discretion to deal with and to assess the manifold potential trade impacts of regulation. The inherent risk, however, is that regulators ignore potentially important impacts. Proportionality is ensured through different types of RIA reports. In many countries, checklists or inter-service consultations help regulators to assess the amplitude of expected impacts. Depending on the expected impacts, regulators may complete low, medium or high impact assessments. These types of RIA typically differ in length, analytical depth and methodology.

In many countries, the preparation of RIAs is a highly centralised exercise (Basedow and Kauffmann, 2016). The lead regulator or service assesses the various potential impacts of regulation. In most jurisdictions, RIA reports are submitted only late to inter-service consultations and quality checks before going to the political cabinet level. The high degree of centralisation may limit the flow of information and involvement of experts. Taking into consideration the breadth of potential impacts, limited expert involvement may negatively affect the quality of RIAs. It is indeed questionable whether for instance a health regulator may easily identify and evaluate the likely effects of a regulation on global value chains (GVCs) in the concerned sector. In practice, the risk of insufficient expert involvement is reduced through the desire of lead regulators to avoid public critique at the final stages of the RIA endorsement. Lead regulators and services in practice often talk informally to experts in other parts of government to ensure that their views are taken on board. Only the EU, Germany and New Zealand have more formalised inter-service collaboration during the RIA drafting process to ensure expert involvement. Other countries may reflect on the benefits of formalising such collaboration in view of enhancing RIA quality.

9.3.2 *RIA: What Type of Trade Impacts Do Countries Assess?*

What exactly are trade impacts of regulation? The national RIA guidelines of OECD countries (see the Appendix) mention four types of potential impacts subject to assessment as part of the RIA process: (1) general macroeconomic effects; (2) specific impacts on economic openness, imports, exports, international investment flows and international competitiveness; (3) interactions between proposed domestic regulation and the international regulatory environment; and (4) other impacts on third countries.

Australia, Austria, Canada, Switzerland, the United Kingdom and the European Commission assess trade impacts of regulation inter alia through assessments of the likely macroeconomic impacts of regulation. Macroeconomic assessments cover for instance effects on labour markets and product markets, GDP growth and such like. They may or may not contain effects on countries' foreign economic and trade relations. Austria for instance requires lead regulators and services to econometrically model the impact of regulations with major expected impacts on the demand and supply side of the economy. The standard model requires an assessment of impacts on exports and imports. The British RIA guidelines hardly specify the content of the macroeconomic assessment and leave great discretion to lead regulators and services.

Australia, Austria, Canada, Germany, Switzerland and the European Commission assess trade impacts through an evaluation of the effects of regulation on exports, imports and foreign direct investment (FDI). Austria and Switzerland also ask regulators and services to evaluate effects of regulation on the 'international competitiveness' and openness of their economy. It is noteworthy that all RIA guidelines and reviewed RIA reports implicitly adopt an export-oriented perspective. Lead regulators and services seem to aim at minimising detrimental effects on national exports. This implicit bias towards exports is problematic. The bulk of trade of OECD economies is part of global value chains. Production takes place in highly complex, internationally fragmented production chains. The international competitiveness of OECD-based companies critically hinges not only on low costs of exporting but also of importing.

Austria, Canada and the European Commission assess interactions between proposed national regulation and the international regulatory context. Lead regulators and services need to evaluate whether proposed measures are compatible with international legal commitments inter alia under PTAs, international investment agreements or WTO law. The RIA guidelines of these jurisdictions, moreover, require lead regulators and services to consider international and foreign regulations and standards and to justify any deviation from international regulation or approaches taken in major trading partners. It needs to be emphasised that even though the assessment of legal interactions between domestic and international norms is a straightforward cost-effective strategy to limit unnecessary regulatory divergence, remarkably few OECD countries seem to use it.

Finally, the European Commission and Switzerland assess impacts of proposed regulation on third countries. In the EU, the focus lies in particular on impacts of proposed regulation on developing and least developed countries. It forms part of the EU's agenda on 'policy coherence for development'. In the Swiss context, the aim is primarily to give sufficient weight to potential regulatory impacts on the intricate legal relationship with the EU's Single Market.

9.3.3 *RIA: How Do Countries Assess Trade Impacts?*

The reviewed RIA guidelines (see the Appendix) clearly favour the quantification and monetisation of trade impacts. They discuss in varying detail the econometric and monetisation methods, which lead regulators and services should use. Austria, Australia and Canada for instance offer fairly precise guidance and an institutional infrastructure to support lead regulators and services in quantitative assessments. Other countries leave considerable leeway to lead regulators and services to determine the assessment method. Some impacts – such as legal interactions between proposed domestic, foreign and international norms – require qualitative legal analysis rather than quantitative and monetised assessments.

An important insight from the review of substantive assessment foci and recommended methods is that states assess and model domestic impacts as part of RIA. They do not try to capture regulatory divergence per se or to model the costs and benefits of varying degrees of regulatory divergence. Taking into consideration that GRP and RIA are tools to maximise domestic welfare, the finding is not particularly striking. It underlines, however, that RIA does not or only very partially provides information on the cross-border impacts on GVCs.

9.3.4 *Ex Post Evaluation: A Promising but Underused Instrument*

OECD countries use ex post evaluation only sporadically (OECD, 2015b, 2015c). If countries use ex post evaluation to scrutinise existing laws and regulations, the focus lies on financial and administrative burdens for the public sector rather than the effectiveness and efficiency of norms. Not even half of respondent countries – sixteen out of thirty-five jurisdictions – reported that their guidelines asked regulators and services to assess as part of ex post evaluations whether existing laws and regulations duplicated or contradict international norms (OECD, 2015c). In a similar vein, even fewer countries – thirteen out of thirty-five jurisdictions – formally evaluate in ex post evaluations whether existing laws and regulations comply with international commitments such as trade agreements. When asked how often countries had in practice evaluated compliance of domestic with international norms as part of ex post evaluations over 2003–15, thirty-two jurisdictions reported to have actually never done so (OECD, 2015c). In short, even OECD countries with highly developed regulatory systems barely use ex post evaluation in general and for the assessment of trade impacts in particular.

9.3.5 Stakeholder Engagement: Realising Its Full Potential

All OECD countries have formally endorsed stakeholder consultations. OECD research shows that stakeholder consultations are a legal requirement as part of the norm development process in all OECD countries (OECD, 2015c). Stakeholder consultations are not normally targeted at a specific group or the assessment of specific impacts, but give opportunity to interested parties to raise their concerns and to share relevant information with policymakers. As such there is limited scope in 'designing' consultation processes to enhance awareness for trade impacts. To use the full potential of stakeholder consultations for the identification of trade impacts, the *APEC–OECD Integrated Checklist on Regulatory Reform* (OECD, 2005b) nonetheless recommends allowing foreign stakeholders to participate in consultation processes. Only the EU and the USA currently allow foreigners to take part in stakeholder consultations. Canada grants foreign governments – but not business or NGOs – the right to voice their views as part of consultations. Australia and New Zealand only allow stakeholders from the respective other jurisdiction to take part in consultations.

The limited access of foreign stakeholders to consultations in most OECD countries reflects concerns over regulatory sovereignty. The public debate on the planned transnational stakeholder consultations under the TTIP illustrates these concerns. NGOs, academics and citizens worry that foreign businesses may capture lead regulators and services and promote the adoption of laws and regulations tailored to the needs of foreigners rather than nationals (Corporate Europe Observatory, 2015, 2016; Mendes, 2015). One way to deal with such concerns might be to limit access of foreigners to consultations relating to laws and regulations of major importance, which determine the grand orientation of public policies; while granting access to consultations regarding subordinate technical regulations. Finally, it needs to be mentioned that such concerns partly disregard the realities of today's world economy. Many businesses have affiliated companies abroad and may through them have the right to participate in local consultations.

9.4 Conclusion and Outlook

GRPs have important potential to limit unnecessary regulatory divergence and trade costs. They raise awareness for trade impacts and related costs. They thereby promote the development of more trade-friendly regulation for instance through recourse to international regulation and standards where possible. GRP, however, also faces limitations. At times policymakers may need to use more activist tools – such as mutual recognition agreements – to limit regulatory divergence and trade costs. Where regulatory divergence for instance reflects differences in national regulatory systems and regulatory path dependency, GRPs are unlikely to deliver. What is more, GRP cannot and must not limit regulatory divergence, which reflects diverging public policy objectives. Finally, GRP cannot do away with regulations with outright protectionist objectives.

The evaluation of OECD countries' actual use of GRP – namely RIAs, ex post evaluations and stakeholder consultations – shows that there is significant scope to improve the contribution of GRP to reducing unnecessary regulatory divergence and trade costs. First, even within the OECD many countries do not systematically assess trade impacts of planned regulation. The review of national RIA guidelines suggests that countries' assess fairly different things when it comes to trade impacts. Some countries model macroeconomic effects of planned regulation, whereas others model effects on exports, imports and FDI flows. Only a handful of countries look at legal interactions between proposed domestic regulation and the international regulatory landscape. The methodologies also vary. Some RIA guidelines call for a far-ranging quantification and monetisation of expected effects, whereas other guidelines hardly discuss and guide lead regulators and services with regard to assessment methods. An important observation from the review of RIA guidelines is that countries do not assess 'regulatory divergence' vis-à-vis other jurisdictions per se but focus on domestic impacts.

OECD countries, moreover, hardly use ex post evaluations in general and even less for the identification of trade impacts. Between 2003 and 2015, for instance, only two out of thirty-four respondent jurisdictions reported to have used ex post evaluation to scrutinise whether their domestic measures duplicated, complied with or contradicted international measures and commitments. Trade impacts of regulation are, however, likely to accrue from exactly such interactions between domestic and international measures. Taking into consideration that many trade impacts of regulations are unanticipated, the rare use of ex post evaluations is a significant shortcoming.

Finally, all OECD countries use stakeholder consultations in the process of norm development. Consultations provide a platform for stakeholders to share their manifold – including trade-related – concerns with policymakers. It is important to note though that most OECD countries restrict access of foreign stakeholders to consultations. The limited access of foreigners to consultations reflects concerns over regulatory sovereignty. Foreigners, however, may hold important pieces of information with regard to the trade impacts of regulation.

To conclude, OECD countries' use of GRP may be enhanced in two regards. First, no OECD country systematically uses all elements of GRP. A more systematic and frequent use of GRP is thus a first important step to use the full potential of GRP to identify regulatory divergence and trade costs. Second, the methods and processes of RIA, ex post evaluations and stakeholder consultation may need improvement. Many countries seem to struggle to identify and to assess trade impacts of regulation.

9.4.1 The Role of the WTO and PTAs in the Promotion of GRP

The chapter focused on the experiences of OECD countries. In global comparison, OECD countries have highly developed regulatory systems in place. The finding that OECD countries pay only limited attention and have not fully defined approaches to assessing trade impacts of regulation implies that the situation is similar or worse in most other countries. There remains significant room for a more systematic, refined and better integrated application of each GRP to identify trade impacts and unnecessary trade costs.

The WTO may play an important role in promoting and enhancing the use of GRP. The WTO's Technical Barriers to Trade (TBT) and Sanitary and Phytosanitary (SPS) Committees already use GRP – notably stakeholder consultations – to limit the trade-adverse effects of domestic regulation. Under the TBT and SPS Agreements, WTO members must notify relevant domestic regulations to the Committee. Other WTO members may then consult with stakeholders at home and eventually raise concerns over the unnecessary trade-restricting effects of regulations (Hoekman and Kostecki, 2009; Narlikar, Daunton and Stern, 2012). The WTO has thereby been playing a role in the promotion of GRP for more than two decades. As such, it has also undertaken attempts to compare and benchmark relevant national GRP strategies (WTO, 2011a).

It has been suggested that the role of the WTO in the promotion of GRP could be strengthened (Arvíus and Jachia, 2015; Malyshev and Kauffmann, 2015; Wijkström, 2015; Mavroidis, 2016a). On the one hand, the WTO could step up its use of GRP, and extend the notification and comments process to other types of trade-related regulation as well as private standards and regulations. It could also start using impact assessments to evaluate the impacts of PTAs and plurilateral agreements on the multilateral trade regime (Lawrence, 2013). The WTO could thereby set precedence and encourage WTO members to start systematically using GRP. The WTO might also establish itself as a platform for peer learning on GRP. The discussion of GRP approaches and methods shows that the assessment of trade impacts is complex. The WTO might create a dedicated working group to benchmark countries' approaches, to facilitate peer discussion and learning and to develop trade-focused GRP guidelines. Such a working group should not only involve national trade policymakers but equally involve regulators and meta-regulators. After all, regulators and meta-regulators – not trade policymakers – conduct RIAs, ex post evaluations and stakeholder consultations.

In a similar vein, PTAs may be a valuable tool to promote GRP. In particular the TPP – now known as the Comprehensive and Progressive Agreement on Transpacific Partnership (CPTPP) – called on signatory parties to adopt GRP and to modernise their regulatory systems. It reflects the rationale that more ambitious and activist regulatory cooperation – for instance through norm harmonisation or mutual recognition – can only succeed if countries have effective, transparent, high quality regulatory institutions and processes in place. The TPP was designed as a capacity-building platform to allow parties with less developed regulatory systems to use the experience of parties with highly developed regulatory systems. PTAs in general may serve this purpose and complement WTO-based efforts to strengthen and enhance the use of GRP.

Last but not least, it needs to be recalled that GRPs are not and must not be considered as trade policy tools. GRPs are an approach to ensure high quality and legitimate regulation. They seek to identify and to balance the manifold complex impacts of regulation across public policy domains in order to maximise social welfare. Trade impacts are one element in this assessment and balancing exercise. Efforts to promote GRP through the WTO and PTAs must not limit and degrade GRP to a one-dimensional trade policy tool.

Appendix: National RIA and GRP Guidelines

Australia: *Best Practice Regulation: A Guide for Ministerial Councils and National Standard Setting Bodies*, available at: www.pmc.gov.au/resource-centre/regulation/best-practice-regulation-guide-ministerial-councils-and-national-standard-setting-bodies.

Australia: *The Australian Government Guide to Regulation*, available at: https://cuttingredtape.gov.au/handbook/australian-government-guide-regulation.

Australia: *Trade Impact Assessments*, available at: www.dpmc.gov.au/sites/default/files/publications/014_Trade_Impact_Assessments.docx.

Austria: *Handbuch Wirkungsorientierte Folgenabschaetzung*, available in German at: www.bka.gv.at/DocView.axd?CobId=49873.

Canada: *Triage Statement Guide*, available at: www.canada.ca/en/treasury-board-secretariat/services/federal-regulatory-management/guidelines-tools/triage-statement-form.html.

Canada: *Medium/High Impact Regulatory Impact Analysis Statement Template*, available at: www.canada.ca/en/treasury-board-secretariat/services/federal-regulatory-management/guidelines-tools/regulatory-impact-analysis-statement-medium-high-impact-template.html.

Canada: *Guidelines on International Regulatory Obligations and Cooperation*, available at: www.tbssct.gc.ca/rtrap-parfa/iroc-cori/iroc-cori-eng.pdf.

Canada: *Canadian Cost-Benefit Analysis Guide*, available at: www.tbssct.gc.ca/rtrapparfa/analys/analys-eng.pdf.

Germany: *Arbeitshilfe zur Gesetzesfolgenabschaetzung*, available at: www.bmi.bund.de/SharedDocs/downloads/DE/veroeffentlichungen/themen/verfassung/arbeitshilfe-gesetzesfolgenabschaetzung.html.

New Zealand: *Regulatory Impact Analysis Handbook*, available at: www.treasury.govt.nz/regulation/regulatoryproposal/ria/handbook.

Switzerland: *Handbuch RFA*, available at: www.seco.admin.ch/themen/00374/00459/00465/04053/index.html?lang=de.

Switzerland: *Checkliste RFA*, available at: www.seco.admin.ch/themen/00374/00459/00465/04053/index.html?lang=de.

United Kingdom: *Better Regulation Framework Manual: Practical Guidance for Government Officials*, available at: www.gov.uk/government/uploads/system/

uploads/attachment_data/file/421078/bis-13-1038-Better-regulation-framework-manual.pdf.

United Kingdom: *Green Book: Appraisal and Evaluation in Central Government*, available at: www.gov.uk/government/publications/the-green-book-appraisal-and-evaluation-in-central-government.

European Union: Better Regulation Guidelines, available at: http://ec.europa.eu/smartregulation/guidelines/toc_guide_en.htm.

10

Rules of Origin as Non-tariff Measures

Towards Greater Regulatory Convergence*

BERNARD HOEKMAN AND STEFANO INAMA

10.1 Introduction

Trade agreements require the parties to agree on the rules (regulations) that will determine whether a product is eligible to benefit from whatever provisions are embodied in the agreement. Thus, to be eligible for preferential market access benefits an exporter will need to document that the product has been produced in an eligible country. Such *preferential* rules of origin (RoO) have been the focus of much research, lobbying and policy debate. To a significant extent the more difficult it is for exporters to satisfy RoO – the more restrictive or stringent the RoO are – the less valuable preferential access will be. Less well-known and studied are *non-preferential* RoO. These are needed to determine whether a product is subject to a nation's trade policy. For example, if the EU imposes an anti-dumping measure on imports of a product originating in China, there is need to determine the origin of that product to avoid possible circumvention.[1] The same is true when it comes to access to government procurement markets: if India opens up access to public procurement contracts to firms from China, it will be necessary to determine whether goods are eligible – i.e. what constitutes a Chinese product. More generally, all countries regulate what constitutes the origin of a product (so-called marks of origin or country of origin labelling) for consumer information reasons, to be able to implement health and safety-related regulations, for statistical purposes, and so forth.

* The chapter represents the personal opinions of the authors and in no way reflects the official opinions or positions of any organization or its employees with which the authors are or have been affiliated.

[1] In practice the link with trade defence mechanisms like anti-dumping is addressed in major jurisdictions such as the USA and EU through special anti-circumvention measures. See Inama, Vermulst and Eeckhout (2009).

RoO differ across countries and products. The most commonly used approaches are based on whether a manufacturing or other processing operation results in: (i) an ad valorem percentage calculated according to different approaches;[2] (ii) a change in tariff heading (how a product is classified in the Harmonized Commodity Description and Coding System (the Harmonized System or HS), the World Customs Organization (WCO) tariff classification nomenclature used by World Trade Organization (WTO) members; or (iii) involves a specific technology, method or process. A recent trend is the adoption of an upper bound on the amount or share of imported (non-originating) physical materials that may be embodied in a product. The latter is easier for firms to understand and to comply with than value added based criteria, and has been advocated by low-income countries in the context of non-reciprocal preferential market access programmes implemented by Organisation for Economic Co-operation and Development (OECD) nations and emerging economies.

Differences in specific RoO *across* products that are applied by importing countries increase the complexity of trade policy for businesses, generate trade costs and affect investment and sourcing decisions in ways that can reduce efficiency. In addition, differences between countries in the RoO for the *same* product further increase complexity for traders that sell to multiple markets. Differences across RoO regimes maintained by importing countries create costs for firms as they imply that firms seeking to benefit from preferential access regimes will need to ensure that production processes are tailored so as to satisfy each RoO regime that prevails in each market they sell to. Such effects also arise in the case for non-preferential RoO: differences across countries, both in terms of substantive requirements and in terms of labelling, will imply specific fixed costs of exporting to different markets. Thus, RoO act as NTMs for any given market, and differences in RoO across markets have analogous effects as difference in regulatory requirements for the same product in different countries. Reducing this heterogeneity is an obvious way to reduce the costs that are associated with RoO. As discussed below, this has long been on the multilateral trade policy agenda, but only for non-preferential RoO. The reason is that preferential RoO have long

[2] Such approaches may be summarized as (i) whether a minimum share of the value added embodied in a product was the result of activities in the last country in which the product was processed/produced according to different calculation techniques or (ii) a given percentage of non-originating materials has not been exceeded or a minimum percentage of originating inputs has been used in the manufacturing of the finished product.

been held to fall outside the ambit of the WTO because (i) non-reciprocal trade preferences are granted at the discretion of importing countries and (ii) in the case of reciprocal trade agreements (free trade agreements, or FTAs) there has been a tacit consensus that each WTO member would be better off to have free hands in this area, i.e. acceptance of policy space.

Economic research on RoO has largely been focused on estimating their trade-distorting effects, often using methodologies that are centred on determining the ad valorem tariff equivalents of RoO[3] or classifying RoO into types and constructing indexes in order to assess patterns of convergence or divergence across countries and trade agreements.[4] While such efforts are useful in determining how RoO can (and do) act as non-tariff barriers to trade, this type of research is not particularly useful in informing efforts by governments to cooperate on RoO with a view to facilitate trade. This requires detailed analysis of the specific RoO adopted by different countries and trade blocs and their evolution, and an understanding of where governments have been able to adopt rules that are similar. Such analysis has been lacking as an input into the WTO Harmonization Work Programme (HWP) for non-preferential RoO. Recent preferential trade agreements (PTAs) provide important information on this question.

In what follows we first briefly review the state of play in the WTO and private sector perspectives on RoO (Section 10.2). In Section 10.3 we discuss evidence for a reduction in regulatory heterogeneity in the area of preferential RoO as a result of recent PTAs. Ongoing research suggests that many of the preferential RoO adopted in recent PTAs are not very different from the draft harmonized non-preferential RoO that emerged from WTO deliberations in some sectors. While there are still significant differences in RoO across products and countries, there is also a trend towards a greater degree of convergence. Section 10.4 discusses approaches towards developing a taxonomy for codifying RoO as non-tariff measures (NTMs) as opposed to efforts to measure trends in convergence and divergence in the RoO used by major trading powers. Section 10.5 concludes.

10.2 WTO Rules and Negotiations on Harmonization of Non-preferential RoO

The General Agreement on Tariffs and Trade (GATT) left importing nations free to define what criteria or conditions they apply to determine

3 See, e.g., Cadot et al. (2006), Cadot and Ing (2016) and Conconi et al. (2018).

4 Estevadeordal, Harris and Suominen (2009).

the origin of a product as long as this applies on a most-favoured-nation (MFN) basis. The same applies to preferential access programmes for developing countries: these may not discriminate across eligible developing exporting countries.[5] However, there have been efforts over time to establish greater multilateral discipline on RoO. During the Uruguay Round these culminated with adoption of the WTO Agreement on Rules of Origin (ARO). In the case of implementation of unilateral preferential programmes, starting in 2005 developed countries committed to facilitate exports of the least-developed countries (LDCs) by providing these nations with duty-free, quota-free (DFQF) access for at least 97 per cent of product lines. A number of OECD countries, including the EU member states, have implemented programmes that provide DFQF access to all products except arms. This gave rise to discussion in the WTO on RoO as the LDCs argued that strict RoO substantially reduced the value of DFQF access. As a result, there have been deliberations and some progress in agreeing to adopt RoO that are simpler and easier to satisfy.

The pursuit of incremental convergence in the RoO that apply for LDCs has complemented the long-running effort to agree to harmonize RoO for non-preferential trade policy purposes. Talks on harmonizing non-preferential RoO have long been deadlocked because of differences between the EU and the USA, in part because of concerns relating to the implications of harmonization for the use of trade policy instruments such as anti-dumping. Although a deal in the WTO proved elusive, the EU and the USA have in recent years engaged in the negotiation of

[5] RoO are an important dimension of FTAs, but the GATT/WTO does not impose any rules on the RoO that signatories of such agreements apply notwithstanding the general recognition that such RoO are not just a matter of concern to participating countries but can affect third parties. For example, in the context of the 1972 FTA between the European Economic Community (EEC) and European Free Trade Association (EFTA) States, the USA argued that the rules of origin would generate

> trade diversion by raising barriers to third countries' exports of intermediate manufactured products and raw materials. This resulted from unnecessarily high requirements for value originating within the area. In certain cases the rules disqualify goods with value originating within the area as high as 96 percent. The rules of origin limited non-originating components to just five percent of the value of a finished product of the same tariff heading [for] nearly one-fifth of all industrial tariff headings. In many other cases a 20 percent rule applied.
>
> (GATT, 1974, pp. 152–3, cited in Hoekman and Kostecki, 2009, p. 487)

For further discussion of WTO rules on PTAs and RoO, see Mavroidis (2016c).

reciprocal PTAs that require agreement on the RoO that will apply. A number of 'mega-regional' trade initiatives, most notably the Comprehensive Economic and Trade Agreement (CETA) (Canada–EU), bilateral agreements between South Korea and the EU and the USA, respectively, and the Comprehensive and Progressive Agreement on Transpacific Partnership (CPTPP) are cases in point. These agreements have required deals to be struck on RoO.

The WTO ARO requires that non-preferential RoO be applied in a non-discriminatory manner, are transparent, are not designed to be a barrier to trade and are administered in a consistent, uniform, impartial and reasonable manner. It does not impose substantive obligations on the content or design of RoO during the transitional period. The ARO set the ambitious objective of the adoption of a single set of non-preferential RoO 'equally for all purposes'[6] to avoid a situation where RoO may vary across products and may even vary for a given product depending on the type of trade policy instrument they apply to. In practice, a country may use more restrictive RoO for anti-dumping actions than it does, for example, to trade in the same product(s) that occurs under the umbrella of a mutual recognition agreement pertaining to applicable technical standards.

Besides the goal of using the same RoO for all purposes (which does not require harmonization across countries), the most important objective of the ARO is to work towards the harmonization of non-preferential RoO (Art. 9) across countries. This has been pursued through a HWP managed by the WTO Committee on Rules of Origin, and primarily executed by a Technical Committee that involves the active participation of the WCO. The ARO provides for the development of a harmonized set of non-preferential RoO based on the change of tariff classification (using the HS) as the preferred method to define substantial transformation.[7] In cases where the HS nomenclature does not allow substantial transformation to be determined by a change in tariff classification test, the Technical Committee will consider the use of supplementary tests such as value added criteria or to agree on 'specific manufacturing processes' that if used will confer origin (imply sufficient transformation of a product).

The HWP was to be completed in July 1998. Results of the technical review undertaken by the WCO were submitted to the WTO by a revised deadline of November 1999. As of today, however, the HWP and the associated draft text have yet to be completed by the Committee on Rules

6 See article 9 (1) (a) of the WTO ARO.

7 See article 9 (1) (c) ii of the WTO ARO.

of Origin. Despite considerable progress, as witnessed by the development of a draft text, a final consensus could not be obtained. This reflects opposition of some WTO members, including the United States, to the implications of the results of the HWP on different WTO agreements. That is, there is resistance to adoption of a set of RoO that would harmonize RoO across trade policy instruments – e.g. anti-dumping vs health and safety standards vs labelling – and the associated reduction in discretion for the implementation of the associated policies. This so-called implications issue led to the cessation of formal negotiations in the mid-2000s. Discussions since 2007 have been limited to updating the draft text to reflect a new version of the HS and informal workshops on the implications of the absence of harmonized RoO for business.

10.3 RoO in Recent PTAs

Despite the stalemate on non-preferential RoO, negotiations on preferential RoO have thrived as a result of PTAs and efforts by developing countries to enhance the economic salience of non-reciprocal preferential market access programmes. A basic tenet (the conventional wisdom) of most RoO experts and trade officials is that there are no possible spillovers among preferential and non-preferential RoO, since they serve different trade policy objectives. Preferential RoO serve to determine whether a preferential tariff is applicable under a regional trade agreement (RTA) or a unilateral arrangement, while non-preferential RoO serve to determine the application of an MFN tariff or specific WTO agreements.

Recent research on private industry views and experience and views on dealing with RoO reveals that this distinction is not very important for firms. For many firms compliance with RoO is a normal part of a business transaction that has a cost. The main difference between preferential and non-preferential RoO is that the former are associated with an expected benefit of reduced duty or duty-free entry in the export market, but in many cases companies are obliged to comply with RoO in any event. A recent survey (Anliker, 2016) revealed 100 per cent awareness by respondent companies of non-preferential RoO, with some 55 per cent of firms perceiving non-preferential rules to be relevant to their daily operations. Reasons for this included such RoO being demanded by clients, by importing country Customs authorities and/or financial service providers (e.g. for letters of credit). This helps to explain why large companies are prepared to incur the cost of buying and maintaining sophisticated IT systems and related personnel to be able to more efficiently assure compliance with RoO – both preferential and non-preferential. Smaller companies are generally less aware and less able to assess the importance of RoO in their day-to-day business. Most companies favour harmonizing RoO as a measure to facilitate trade and bring down cost of compliance, with a clear preference for greater acceptance and use of self-declaration of origin by firms as opposed to having to use certificates of origin issued by certifying authorities or Chambers of Commerce (the latter generally give rise to fees associated with obtaining such certification).

There has been considerable evolution in the technique and content of drafting RoO in PTAs. South–South agreements – e.g. the Southern African Development Community (SADC); the Common Market for Eastern and Southern Africa (COMESA); Southern Common Market (MERCOSUR) and the Association of Southeast Asian Nations (ASEAN) – traditionally adopted a simple formula, such as an across-the-board percentage criterion mirroring the percentage rules in the US Generalized System of Preferences (GSP) scheme. In addition they often adopted as an alternative a change of tariff heading criterion following the EU model. In short, these PTAs have not developed their own RoO model. Over time they started to develop product-specific rules of origin (PSROs), but again borrowing the drafting techniques from the existing US and EU models. Indeed, there have been cases where following negotiation of a PTA with the EU or USA countries have imposed the associated RoO on their regional partners in the South.

Despite the claimed rigid separation between non-preferential and preferential RoO, the border between the two regimes has always been porous. The North American Free Trade Agreement (NAFTA) had a major influence on the ARO. It was US insistence that resulted in the ARO making the change of tariff classification (CTC) the preferred methodology for drafting rules for non-preferential RoO – as opposed to the EU approach of using a combination of criteria – the CTC, percentage criterion and specific working and processing requirements. By itself this could be interpreted as a first sign of convergence, even though there are different modalities across PTAs in drafting RoO according to the CTC criterion. This primacy of the CTC over other methodologies for determining substantial transformation gave rise to some differences in view during the initial phases of the HWP negotiations among the EU and NAFTA partners in the Technical Committee on Rules of Origin (TCRO) and later in the WTO Committee on Rules of Origin (CRO). In fact, the 1996–9 TCRO negotiations on non-preferential RoO was the first time the EU and the USA had confronted each other. Until then the EU had for some twenty-plus years been dealing with RoO in the context of its PTAs with European Free Trade Association (EFTA) members and the African, Caribbean and Pacific (ACP) countries. These countries were confronted with the then newly matured experience of the USA and its partners obtained in negotiating the Canada–USA Trade Agreement (CUSTA) and the NAFTA.

While none of the negotiators in the TCRO at that time would have admitted that preferential RoO had a bearing on the HWP, it was clear, as demonstrated by the dynamic of the negotiations, that the discussions on non-preferential RoO started from the respective preferential RoO backgrounds, at least at the technical level. In other words, each 'bloc' proposed and defended its own model of RoO. The eventual draft text that emerged from the HWP was therefore the result of a compromise between the EU and NAFTA models, with a number of innovations and some disagreement on specific sectors, like machinery.[8] In retrospect, the 1999 draft harmonized rules of origin (HRO) text represents a tangible sign of convergence that, even if not agreed, influenced the way RoO were negotiated in subsequent PTAs. An example is the progressive acceptance of the use of the wholly obtained criterion as a requirement for the list of product-specific rules (a typical EU feature) included in the EU–Mexico agreement and later in the Canada–EU CETA. Another example is the use of chemical reaction, a concept inherited from the HWP work, as a specific requirement for some chemical products given the inherent technical difficulty of determining the corresponding CTC for chemical products.

Despite the HWP coming to a standstill in 2007, the many PTAs that have been negotiated since then have implied that RoO are front and centre in the negotiating agenda of the majority of WTO members. The EU in particular has made substantial changes to its RoO model starting in the early 2000s. First, it progressively abandoned the 'straightjacket' model that it imposed on itself as a result of its Pan-European RoO that were adopted in the early 1990s. According to the Pan-European RoO model each EU partner in an FTA had to adopt an almost identical set of RoO set by the EU including the PSROs to allow cumulation among different FTAs and avoid a proliferation of divergent RoO across FTAs.

[8] The 'machinery package' allowed each member to choose either a 'change of tariff classification rule' (the preferred US method for origin determination) or a 'value added rule' (the preferred EU method for determining origin in this specific sector and circumstance. This is the so-called dual-rule approach. See WTO document JOB(07)/73).

While strictly adhered to for more than a decade this approach was revealed to be excessively rigid when the EU was negotiating with significant trading partners because it did not allow concessions to be made on PSROs. Second, it introduced a sweeping and unprecedented reform of unilateral RoO, especially for the LDCs. While limited to this set of countries, this reform provides a potential base on which to build in further reforms of EU RoO.

The developments in preferential RoO in PTAs have led to some simplification and streamlining of the RoO, informed by lessons learned over more than twenty years of operation of major PTAs. Progressively, the EU and the USA, as well as counterpart OECD nations (e.g. Japan, South Korea, Australia and New Zealand) have abandoned methodologies based on calculations of value added in favour of a value of materials used ad valorem percentage calculation. Some innovations have also been introduced, such as the deduction of cost of freight and insurance in recent US PTAs and in the CPTPP. There are, of course, differences in the arithmetical calculations and definitions of what goes into the numerator and denominator, but there is convergence towards determining ad valorem percentages based on a value of materials calculation rather than a value added or net cost approach, as used in NAFTA for automotive products. This tendency is confirmed by the evolution of the use of the net cost method in US PTAs that has been gradually introduced in subsequent agreements, and the introduction of the build-up and build-down method that has replaced the transaction value used in NAFTA – see Table 10.1.

Thus, developments regarding preferential RoO in the PTAs that include the major players are pointing towards simplification and

Table 10.1 *Evolution of the NAFTA percentage-calculation-based RoO*

Regional value content criterion	NAFTA	CHL–USA	CAFTA	USA–SIN	USA–AUS	USA–KOR	TPP
No. of PSROs	1,125	1,043	1,017	2,974	965	758	1,245
of which:							
Net cost	323	0	6	0	0	6	22
Transaction	248	0	0	0	0	0	0
Build-up	0	164	146	239	148	147	398
Build-down	0	157	147	213	144	152	457

Source: Own calculations.

streamlining. This has supported greater trade as shown by the relatively high utilization rate of major PTAs, which range from 80 per cent to 90 per cent (Swedish Board of Trade and UNCTAD, 2018). In a nutshell, there has been a lot of work on RoO that has had a pay-off.

The reforms of the Canadian GSP RoO for LDCs (in 2003) and the Everything But Arms (EBA) RoO (redefined in 2011) have contributed to the debate over simplification and relaxation of preferential RoO for LDC DFQF programmes and brought new life to the discussions in the CRO. This has led to two Ministerial Decisions on preferential RoO for LDCs and is a tangible sign that progress can be made at the multilateral level as well. The challenge now is to build on this progress to resume work at the multilateral level on RoO.

10.4 Determining Convergence in RoO and Codifying RoO as NTMs

10.4.1 A Taxonomy to Identify Convergence in RoO

The lack of progress and meaningful discussions on RoO at the multilateral level since 2007 contrasts with the gradual movement towards de facto and de jure convergence across both preferential and non-preferential RoO in major jurisdictions. Divergence certainly continues to exist for some sectors, but it is important to recognize that the situation on the ground has been changing. This suggests that multilateral discussions can build on this and focus on the reasons for continued divergence in specific sectors.

In pursuing reforms and better understanding RoO regimes it is necessary to distinguish between the policy-objectives that underpin a given set of RoO (the 'substance') from the specific criteria used and how they are administered, i.e. the 'format' of a RoO. The substantive dimension of a RoO is the degree of restrictiveness it implies as regards the value chain it impacts on. It is the substance that matters. If countries have common objectives as to what RoO are supposed to do, it is much more straightforward to achieve convergence, since the form a RoO takes is mostly a matter of drafting methodology.

Although blocked for almost a decade at the time of writing, the mandate of the CRO to pursue harmonization of RoO provides a continuing opportunity to revitalize multilateral discussion on RoO at the WTO by drawing on and building on PTA experiences as well as unilateral reforms. Making progress in the CRO – or for that matter in developing the RoO associated with new PTAs – requires a better understanding of how different RoO evolved in international trade.

As discussed above the traditional type of research carried out on RoO has not been particularly conducive to lead governments towards a simplification of RoO. A new stream of research[9] aims at showing to governments the progress that they have been able to make through progressive rounds of negotiations with their partners in different PTAs, through consultations with their civil society, and practice. This research shows, at product-specific level, where governments have adopted RoO that are similar, either as a result of natural evolution of the international trading system (presumably lowering of MFN tariffs and related trade barriers) and/or technological progress. A product-specific comparison of the WTO HWP for non-preferential RoO with recent PTAs provides important and factual information on how governments may simplify RoO. (For each agreement there are around 6,000 product-specific RoO observations).

One possible advantage of this approach is that simplification may be undertaken at sectoral level, if governments are not willing to embrace encompassing reforms. This à la carte approach may provide the kind of 'comfort level' that may generate reflections in Government and movement in WTO circles. In fact hundreds of PTAs have been negotiated and progressively implemented since NAFTA. Each of these PTAs contain a set of RoO. While the negotiations on the HWP have stagnated since 2007 thousands of PSROs have been negotiated and put to a test during PTAs implementation. The scope of the research is to revisit the overall 'state of the art' of RoO by drawing a detailed comparison as follows:

- A subheading by subheading (6,366 subheadings) analysis of PSROs to identify where there is convergence, partial convergence or divergence among:
  - (a) The results of the HWP process as last updated;
  - (b) TPP and US–Korea FTA as examples of the North American Model mainly based on CTC and regional value content (RVC); and
  - (c) CETA – the first instance of the European model and the North American model coming to confront each other – and the EU–South Korea FTA.

In order to draw such a comparison a taxonomy has been developed to compare each of the PSROs contained in the above-mentioned PTA according to the following categories:

[9] For a preliminary view of the results of this research in progress, see Crivelli and Inama (2018).

A. Totally or partial convergent
   1. All RoO (the four FTAs and the HW) are identical or similar in terms of stringency and drafting form.
   2. The majority of the RoO are identical or similar in terms of stringency and drafting form.
   3. RoO are identical or similar in terms of stringency but have a different drafting form.

B. Divergent
   4 Ai) Different in terms of stringency and drafting form being more stringent compared with the harmonized rules (4Ai).
   4 Bii) Different in terms of stringency and drafting form being less stringent compared with the harmonized rules (4Bii).

The preliminary results of this research (Crivelli and Inama, 2018) reveal that there is a predominant tendency towards convergence and simplification: 53 per cent of the total tariff lines at the six-digit level show a degree of convergence (Table 10.2). If the percentage of tariff lines where the PSRO was found to be more liberal in the PTAs examined than with the HWP[10] (33 per cent) is added we reach a total percentage of 85 per cent where the PSROs taken together are either convergent and/or liberal.

A number of caveats should be made. The first is that these preliminary results need to be further refined and validated. Second, the details matter a lot for PSROs. Third, the degree of convergence may be assessed differently in a negotiating context. Fourth, the convergence covers PSROs and does not deal with other ancillary concepts of RoO such as cumulation and de minimis thresholds. That said, the numbers reveal some clear messages to those who may be ready to listen. These can be summarized as follows:

- There are sectors where there is significant convergence. Chemicals is an example, which was also one of the sectors where there was an early harvest in the TTIP negotiations.
- The differences relate more on the 'form': i.e. the way in which the RoO are drafted than on substance, i.e. the leniency/stringency of the RoO.
- For some sensitive sectors, e.g. clothing and fisheries, there is a substantial divergence.

The extent to which these PSRO are convergent/divergent is illustrated further in Tables 10.3 and 10.4. These tables provide examples of cases of

[10] The results of the HWP in terms of PSROs are widely considered to be more liberal since it involves a set of non-preferential RoO.

Table 10.2 *Comparison of six-digit PSRO: HWP, CETA, USA–Korea, EU–Korea and CPTPP*

Convergence/ divergence categories	Category description	No. of tariff lines	Share (%)	Average MFN	Total QUAD imports from the world (US$ million)
1	Totally convergent	135	2	1.52	641,546
2	Partially convergent	1,287	20	2.76	2,298,623
3	Partially convergent in stringency and different drafting form	1,994	31	3.15	1,648,448
4Ai	Divergent, more stringent compared with harmonized rules	823	13	5.49	960,754
4Bii	Divergent, less stringent compared with harmonized rules	2,127	33	6.00	1,321,871
Total		6,366	100		

Source: Crivelli and Inama (2018).

Table 10.3 *HRO, CETA, TPP, EU and US PTAs with South Korea: signs of convergence*

Example 1

HS code	HRO	CETA	TPP	EU–KOR	USA–KOR
28.50 Hydrides, nitrides, azides, silicides and borides, whether or not chemically defined, other than compounds which are also carbides of heading 28.49.	*CTH*	*A change from any other subheading*, or: A change from within any one of these subheadings, whether or not there is also a change from any other subheading, provided that the value of non-originating materials classified in the same subheading as the final product does not exceed 20 per cent of the transaction value or ex-works price of the product.	*A change to a good of heading 28.50 from any other heading.*	*Manufacture from materials of any heading, except that of the product.* However, materials of the same heading as the product may be used, provided that their total value does not exceed 20 per cent of the ex-works price of the product.	*A change to heading 28.10 through 28.53 from any other heading.*

Example 2

HS code	HRO	CETA	TPP	EU–KOR	USA–KOR
87.12 Bicycles and other cycles (including delivery tricycles), not motorized	*CTH, except from heading 87.14*; or 35 per cent value added rule	*A change from any other heading, except from 87.14*; or A change from heading 87.14, whether or not there is also a change from any other heading, provided that the value of non-originating materials of heading 87.14 does not exceed 50 per cent of the transaction value or ex-works price of the product.	*A change to a good of heading 87.12 from any other heading, except from heading 87.14*; or No change in tariff classification required for a good of heading 87.12, provided there is a regional value content of not less than: a) 35 per cent under the build-up method; or b) 45 per cent under the build-down method; or	Manufacture in which the value of all the materials used does not exceed 45 per cent of the ex-works price of the product.	*A change to headings 87.12 through 87.13 from any other heading, except from heading 87.14*; or, provided that there is a regional value content of not less than: (a) 35 per cent under the build-up method, or (b) 45 per cent under the build-down method.

Table 10.3 (*cont.*)

HS code	HRO	CETA	TPP	EU–KOR	USA–KOR
			60 per cent under the focused value method taking into account only the non- originating materials of headings 87.12 and 87.14.		

Note: Text in italics indicates significant convergence across different agreements.

Table 10.4 *HRO, CETA, TPP, EU and US PTAs with South Korea: signs of divergence*

Example 1

HS code	HRO	CETA	TPP	EU–KOR	USA–KOR
16.04 Prepared or preserved fish; caviar and caviar substitutes prepared from fish eggs.	CTH	A change from any other chapter, except from Chapter 3.	A change to a good of heading 16.05 from any other chapter.	Manufacture: - for animals of Chapter 1, and/or - in which all the materials of Chapter 3 used are wholly obtained.	A change to heading 16.05 from any other chapter.

Example 2

HS code	HRO	CETA	TPP	EU–KOR	USA–KOR
6203.42 Men's Cotton Pants	Change to goods of this split chapter provided that the goods are assembled in a single country in accordance with Chapter Note.	Weaving accompanied by making up (including cutting); **or** Making up preceded by printing accompanied by at least two preparatory or finishing operations (such as scouring, bleaching, mercerizing, heat setting, raising, calendaring, shrink resistance processing, permanent finishing, decatizing, impregnating, mending and hurling), provided that the value of the unprinted fabric	A change to a good of headings 62.01 through 62.08 from any other chapter, except from headings 51.06 through 51.13, 52.04 through 52.12 **or** 54.01 through 54.02, subheadings 5403.33 through 5403.39 **or** 5403.42 through 5403.49, **or** headings 54.04 through 54.08, 55.08 through 55.16, 58.01 through 58.02 **or** 60.01 through 60.06, provided the good is cut or knit to shape, or both, and sewn or otherwise	Weaving accompanied by making up (including cutting) **or** Embroidering accompanied by making up (including cutting), provided that the value of the unembroidered fabric used does not exceed 40 per cent of the ex-works price of the product **or** Coating accompanied by making up (including cutting), provided that the value of the uncoated fabric used does not exceed 40 per cent of the ex- works	A change to subheadings 6203.41 through 6203.49 from any other 4-20 chapter, except from headings 51.06 through 51.13, 52.04 through 52.12, 53.07 through 53.08, **or** 53.10 through 53.11, 54.01 through 54.02, subheadings 5403.33 through 5403.39, 5403.42 through heading 54.08, **or** headings 55.08 through 55.16, 58.01 through 58.02, **or** 60.01 through 60.06, provided that the

		used does not exceed 47.5 per cent of the transaction value or ex-works price of the product.	assembled in the territory of one or more of the Parties.	price of the product **or** Making up preceded by printing accompanied by at least two preparatory finishing operations (such as scouring, bleaching, mercerizing, heat setting, raising, calendaring, shrink resistance processing, permanent finishing, decatizing, impregnating, mending and hurling), provided that the value of the unprinted fabric used does not exceed 47.5 per cent of the ex-works price of the product.	good is both cut and sewn or otherwise assembled in the territory of one or both of the Parties.

convergence for some sectors, as well as continued areas of divergence. The text in italics in Table 10.3 shows where there is significant convergence or equivalence among the agreements. To some extent recent progress towards convergence between preferential and non-preferential RoO and more generally simplification of RoO has been facilitated by the removal of MFN tariffs for products – e.g. because of the Information Technology Agreement (ITA) and analogous zero-for-zero sectoral agreements for chemical products. However, there are also other sectors with positive MFN duties where convergence has been occurring. What is needed is further research to validate the initial findings and narrow down the results and most of all a political momentum to trigger the change. The results presented here suggest that there is value in seeking to identify emerging 'best practices' for sectors where there is convergence and to identify sectors where there is continued divergence.

10.4.2 RoO as NTMs

Developing a taxonomy of RoO as constituting different types of NTMs may serve a number of purposes. One is simply to map the universe of RoO – to document the RoO used by different countries. Another is to characterize RoO regimes depending on qualitative dimensions – e.g. their complexity, stability over time, etc. Researchers frequently are interested in determining the trade restrictiveness of different RoO, and a taxonomy of RoO can be useful as an input into empirical analysis. In terms of quantification of RoO, a taxonomy should codify RoO at the product-specific level. To ensure this is comparable across countries and preferential trade regimes, such an effort needs to be undertaken at the six-digit level of the HS (i.e. the subheading level). This spans over 5,000 categories, implying an upper bound for the total number of PSROs to be codified of 200,000 given there are some 400 PTAs in force. Concording different sets of RoO and PSROs to each other and automating the codification of PSROs using algorithms to classify different RoO into 'types' is a major challenge and in practice may not be a realistic option given the variation in the 'format' and textual language used to define PSRO across different PTAs and non-reciprocal PTAs.

Efforts have been made to classify RoO by type and to factor in an ex ante assessment of the restrictiveness of different types of RoO on the basis of a mix of judgement and econometric estimation. Estevadeordal (1999) pioneered such analysis, focusing on NAFTA RoO with the aim to assess the possible impact of extending the NAFTA model to other PTAs in the Americas. An important contribution of this research and subsequent efforts to assess the economic effects of RoO is a methodology for measuring the restrictiveness of RoO in relation to a tariff phase-out schedule negotiated under a PTA. The approach was applied to a potential EU–MERCOSUR PTA using the framework of the Pan-European RoO (Estevadeordal and Suominen, 2004, 2006). The index of restrictiveness developed by Estevadeordal and subsequent analysts that have built on his approach has been mostly used for econometric analyses of the impact of RoO.

NAFTA RoO were negotiated at the product level (mostly at the six-digit tariff line level) and were defined using three methods: (1) a tariff shift, (2) a RVC, or (3) a technical requirement. The first criterion can be specified as requiring a change at the section level (two-digit HS), heading level (four-digit HS), subheading level (six-digit HS) or item level (higher than six-digit HS), with the possibility of including specific exceptions. The three methods could also be combined, for example, a change of subheading plus a specific RVC and a technical requirement. Moreover, there are many cases in which the agreement defines alternative RoO for the same product.

To obtain the restrictiveness index, each rule or set of rules is codified according to different criteria and a qualitatively ordered index is constructed based on a set of assumptions. First, a CTC at the chapter level is assumed to be more stringent than at the heading level, a change at the heading level more than at the subheading level, and so on. Second, an RVC requirement increases the restrictiveness of a given rule, as do technical requirements. For each pair (or sometimes trio) of alternative rules being applied to the same product, Estevadeordal selects the one with the higher restrictiveness index. A categorical RoO variable is then constructed ranging from 1 (the most lenient) to 7 (the most restrictive). Level 1 occurs when the rule requires a change of tariff item or less. At level 2 the rule requires more than a change of tariff item but is equal to or less than a change of tariff subheading (CTSH). At level 3 the rule requires more than a CTSH but is equal to or less than a CTSH and RVC. At level 4 the rule requires more than a CTSH and RVC but is equal to or less than a change of tariff heading (CTH). At level 5 the rule requires more than a change of tariff level but is equal to or less than CTH and RVC. At level 6 the rule requires more than a change of tariff level and an RVC but is equal to or less than a change of chapter (CC). Finally, at level 7 the rule requires more than a CC but is equal to or less than a CC or technical requirement.

Although the HS increasingly is used for drafting RoO, it was conceived for tariff classification purposes and not for drafting RoO. It follows that assuming that a change of tariff classification at the eight-digit level is more lenient than a CTSH is rather arbitrary. As demonstrated in the WTO negotiations on non-preferential RoO, there are entire chapters of the HS in which a CTSH may be extremely restrictive. This is the case for chemical products, for example, where important chemical reactions that change the nature of a product may not be reflected in a change of subheading. It is quite difficult therefore to determine the level of restrictiveness of different RoO using criteria and classification of the type just discussed. To illustrate the problem, assume we want to classify the restrictiveness of the rules using the Estevadeordal index in the following cases (using NAFTA RoO):

Rule 1 *'A change to heading 6205.90 from any other chapter, except from heading Nos. 51.06 through 51.13, 52.04 through 52.12 . . . provided that the good is both cut and sewn or otherwise assembled in the territory of one or more of the NAFTA parties.'*

Rule 2 *'A change to heading 62.06 through 62.10 from any other chapter, except from headings Nos. 51.06 through 51.13 . . . provided that the good is both cut and sewn or otherwise assembled in the territory of one or more of the NAFTA countries.'*

Rule 3 *'A change to heading 61.05 through 61.06 from any other chapter, except from headings Nos. 51.06 through 51.13, 52.04 through 52.12 . . . provided that the good is both cut (or knit to shape) and sewn or otherwise assembled in the territory of one or more of the NAFTA parties.'*

Rule 4 *'A change to heading 63.02 from any other chapter, except from headings Nos. 51.06 through 51.13, 52.04 through 52.12, 53.07 through 53.08 or 53.10 through 53.11, Chapters 54 through 55, or heading Nos. 58.01 through 58.02 or 60.01 through 60.02 provided that the good is both cut (or knit to shape) and sewn or otherwise assembled in the territory of one or more of the NAFTA parties.'*

Because none of these rules includes an RVC, the choice in terms of the level of restrictiveness according to the Estevadeordal index is either level 1 or level 2. Because the rules require more than a change of tariff item, one may classify all the rules under one level. Alternatively, if one considers that requirements for cutting and sewing are technical requirements, they would fall under level 7.

A closer look at rules 1–4 indicates that they are very different in terms of 'real world' restrictiveness. **Rule 1** depicts a single transformation requirement from woven silk to a silk shirt. **Rule 2** requires a double transformation: (1) the processing of the fabric and (2) the production of the apparel. **Rule 3** requires a triple transformation or yarn forward: from the manufacturing of the yarn to men's shorts. **Rule 4** provides for an extremely stringent rule requiring a quadruple transformation. Thus the example shows that even if the drafting style of rules in this case, '*A change to heading ... from any other chapter, except from headings ...*' is similar and maps the rules to similar levels of restrictiveness, the actual level of restrictiveness implied by the different rules may vary considerably.

These considerations have implications for the development of a taxonomy for codifying RoO for NTM classification purposes. They imply that any such classification should not incorporate a typology that maps RoO into different degrees of (presumptive) trade restrictiveness and builds this into the classification. The extent to which different RoO regimes – and differences in RoO regimes – impede trade should be left to empirical analysis. The key challenge in developing a classification for NTM purposes is to characterize and 'map' different approaches and requirements into common and comparable categories at a useful level of disaggregation – what is denoted in this chapter as the 'form' taken by PSROs. If the classification is designed at too broad a level, limiting the coding to the main principles used to define origin, there is little value added since this will result in different sets of RoO being compared or lumped together on the basis of oversimplified assumptions that do not reflect the complexity and diversity of RoO. On the other hand, if the taxonomy is designed in a very detailed manner, the task of codification becomes very difficult to operationalize in a way that is useful.

A possible way to proceed in designing a taxonomy that reflects the reality of RoO that vary substantially is to use a limited set of codes to characterize the major existing RoO models. Such a compromise approach brings the number of codes down to a manageable level while providing sufficient detail on the nature and criteria used in different RoO without implying (imposing) a value judgement as regards levels of implied restrictiveness. The Appendix illustrates what such an approach could look like, using examples taken from different RoO regimes to inform a codification exercise especially in the case of preferential RoO.[11]

[11] A version of this taxonomy was developed as a contribution to the Multi-Agency Support Team (MAST) established in 2006 to work on the taxonomy of NTMs. Discussions are

The task is considerably easier in the case of drafting a taxonomy for codifying the administrative part of RoO, i.e. related to the documentary evidence required to demonstrate compliance with RoO. This is because the administrative dimensions of RoO mostly apply across all products – there are seldom product-specific administrative requirements. When there are, they mostly apply at broad category levels (an example is textiles and apparel in certain US PTAs). There are only a limited number of ways of administering RoO. The most used methodologies are: (i) certificate of origin on paper issued by certifying authorities with use of stamps and/or signatures; (ii) certificate or statement of origin issued by the exporter (with or without registration with certifying authorities); and (iii) a statement of origin issued by the importer.

Overreliance by some Customs administrations on archaic forms of administering RoO based on documentary evidence, i.e. a certificate of origin, the exchange of seals and signatures of certifying officers or non-manipulation certificates issued in the country of transit, has made administration of RoO into a non-tariff barrier. Shifting to a Customs-authorised exporter declaration of origin with retroactive checks and post-clearance recovery offers one model for reducing RoO-related administrative costs. The 2017 reform of EU RoO for its GSP regime provides for listing registered exporters in a database administered by national customs agencies. Registered exporters will be given a number and may issue a declaration of origin. When this self-declaration is presented at an EU port of entry, customs will consult the joint database to ascertain whether the exporter has been registered and, if so, will grant preferential tariff rates. Verification of an exporter's declaration and post-clearance recovery are part of this administrative method. This is an example of a reform in the administration of RoO that may facilitate trade. There are other options as well, such as the method employed by US Customs and Border Protection, which is based on importer declarations and disregards evidence provided by exporters or certificates of origin issued by third parties. Whatever method is used, reliance on certificates of origin and the exchange of seals and signatures should be a thing of the past.

still ongoing among the members of MAST (which comprises eight international organizations) and the approach in the Appendix is simply a proposal that we consider to be informative and operational but that may not be adopted by the group. This proposal includes preferential and non-preferential RoO with the caveat that the section on non-preferential rules requires further study to fine tune and better reflect existing practices.

10.5 Concluding Remarks

The subject of RoO and especially non-preferential RoO has been contested for decades. The nature of RoO – a technical and tedious subject – is not one that attracts the interest of trade policy officials and Ministers. Yet these same actors are prone to use RoO when convenient, to please or displease lobbies and trading partners. Business has been ambivalent on the issue of RoO. On the one hand businesses often complain about the complexity of RoO but on the other hand they do not push governments to make the extra effort required to seek a multilateral solution. The focus instead has been on 'easy fixes' in bilateral deals (PTAs), which are seen as more appealing and less costly. A focus on PTAs may also reflect the evolving nature of international (regional) trade – e.g. the rise in the intensity of regional value or supply chains – which has led businesses to push negotiators and governments to simplify the RoO applying to PTAs.

The preliminary results of ongoing research outlined in this chapter shows that the two large players, the EU and USA, have made progress towards simplification of RoO in their PTAs. There have been some positive spillovers, as demonstrated by the high utilization rates recorded in some US and EU PTAs. The issue at stake for the trading system is how to leverage these various positive developments and to cross-fertilize (multilateralize) the simplifications introduced on both sides of the Atlantic to span trade arrangements involving the rest of the world. One path to do so is to break the wall that has separated preferential and non-preferential RoO. In a number of sectors like chemicals both business and the existing RoO have already built a bridge across the preferential and non-preferential RoO divide. Discussions in the CRO and elsewhere that are aimed at greater harmonization and simplification of RoO would be facilitated by further development and use of the type of taxonomy proposed in this chapter to measure convergence in PSRO. This would demonstrate to the sceptics that progress and simplification is possible and has already taken place.

Single transformation is a good rule of thumb for drafting RoO in a world characterized by global value chain–based production. Given that this type of production involves firms specializing in specific tasks or activities, RoO that entail a need for more extensive value addition or transformation will undercut the ability of countries to engage in this type of production and trade unless they are part of larger regional integration arrangements that permit cumulation for RoO purposes. This is not the case for many developing nations and the design of RoO therefore should reflect this reality. Traditional protectionist double or triple transformation requirements greatly impede participation in value chains. While it will be difficult to abolish such RoO for 'sensitive sectors' – e.g. textiles and clothing for the USA, certain processed agricultural products in the EU and Japan – the fact that progress on this front has proved possible in the context of implementing DFQF market access programmes for LDCs and that for many products PTAs have been moving to greater use of single transformation–based RoO criteria are positive signs. Sceptics may continue to argue that such a simple rule of thumb is unthinkable but the evidence from recent PTAs and developments in the administration of non-reciprocal preferences schemes suggest that efforts to bring together the relevant actors (firms, Customs and trade officials) can allow reforms to be agreed and implemented.

Such a process is distinct from efforts to categorize RoO as NTMs. Developing a taxonomy to codify RoO for NTM classification purposes is important to be able to determine the effects of RoO – i.e. as an input into empirical analysis. The aim here in our view should be simply to classify RoO regimes and approaches so as to provide a better sense of how RoO are defined and thus the degree to which they are similar or different. RoO have characteristics that distinguish them from other regulatory policies that can be characterized as NTMs such as product standards. In the case of sanitary and phyto-sanitary (SPS) and technical barriers to trade (TBT) measures, compliance with a regulation is a necessary condition for being able to export (sell) a product – e.g. a TBT labelling requirement to show the quantity of sulphites in a bottle of wine. In the case of RoO the NTM-effect takes the form of a conditional tax: if the RoO is not satisfied an importer must pay the relevant MFN tariff, the applicable anti-dumping duty, etc. It is never the case that a product would be prohibited from entering the market as would be the case when binding quotas are in place or specific SPS or TBT measures must be met. That said, clearly different types of RoO and the specific criteria that apply will have a differential impact on the cost of production and thus the probability that an exporter will choose (or be forced) to pay the applicable MFN tariff.

The technicalities of RoO and the heterogeneity in how they are worded makes this instrument of trade policy a difficult subject for any NTM taxonomy. The approach presented in the Appendix for grouping and classifying RoO that is based on the main models used in PTAs may be useful as one input into a typology of RoO that in turn could be used as the basis for empirical assessments of the effects of RoO. Such an effort could also be useful in identifying where RoO have largely converged and where they differ.

Appendix: A Draft Taxonomy of RoO for NTM Purposes

O1 – Preferential ROO

Paragraph 2 of Annex 2 of the WTO Agreement on Rules of Origin defines preferential RoO as follows: '*Preferential rules of origin shall be defined as those laws, regulations and administrative determinations of general application applied by any Member to determine whether goods qualify for preferential treatment under contractual or autonomous trade regimes leading to the granting of tariff preferences going beyond the application of paragraph 1 of Article I of GATT 1994.*'

Preferential RoO are those RoO generally contained in autonomous arrangements such as those called for by the GSP, EBA or the African Growth and Opportunities Act (AGOA) and reciprocal trade preferences negotiated in FTAs.

O11 – Origin Criterion

This criterion determines the origin of a good. A good is either originating in a country since (i) it is wholly obtained in a country, i.e. it does not contain any non-originating material and (ii) it has undergone substantial transformation in that country.

The category of wholly obtained products is often a general standard list of products, albeit with notable differences, that is contained in every set of RoO.

Substantial transformation may be defined by (i) ad valorem percentage criterion, (ii) change of tariff classification and (iii) specific working or processing requirement.

O111 – Wholly Obtained

The origin status is conferred to a good that is entirely produced or manufactured in a country without using non-originating materials.

> ***Example***: live animals born and raised in a country; vegetables that have been grown and harvested in a country.

O112 – Substantial Transformation: Ad Valorem Percentage Criterion for Value Addition

The originating status is conferred to a good that has complied with a given percentage of value added. The calculation of such value added results from adding the cost of originating materials used in its production plus the direct cost of processing as a percentage of a given finished price of the good, normally ex-factory price.

The formula is normally made of the following components: Cost of originating materials + direct cost of processing $\times$ 100 $\geq$ than a given value added/appraised value (ex-factory price).

> ***Example***: 'For an imported article to be GSP-eligible, it must be the growth, product, or manufacture of a beneficiary developing country (BDC), and the sum of the cost or value of materials produced in the BDC plus the direct costs of processing must equal at least 35 percent of the appraised value of the article at the time of entry into the United States.'[12]

O113 – Substantial Transformation: Ad Valorem Percentage Criterion as Value of Materials

The originating status is conferred to a good that does not exceed a given amount of non-originating material out of a given finished price of the good, normally ex-works price or free-on-board (FOB) price or achieve a minimum content of originating materials. The value of material can be calculated by subtraction.

> ***Example of a rule*** providing not to exceed a given percentage of non-originating materials: Manufacture in which the value of all the (non-originating) material used does not exceed 70 percent of the ex-works price of the product.[13]
>
> ***Example of a rule*** providing to comply with a value of materials calculated by subtraction:
>
> Build-down Method:[14] Based on the Value of Non-Originating Materials.

[12] See US GSP Guidebook 2015, available at https://ustr.gov/sites/default/files/GSP%20Guidebook%20October%202015%20Final.pdf.

[13] See list of product-specific rules in COMMISSION REGULATION (EU) No. 1063/2010 of 18 November 2010 amending Regulation (EEC) No. 2454/93 laying down provisions for the implementation of Council Regulation (EEC) No. 2913/92 establishing the Community Customs Code.

[14] Example excerpted from TPP text available at https://ustr.gov/sites/default/files/TPP-Final-Text-Rules-of-Origin-and-Origin-Procedures.pdf.

$$\text{RVC}(X\text{per}\quad\text{cent}) = \frac{\text{Value}\quad\text{of}\quad\text{the}\quad\text{Good} - \text{VNM}}{\text{Value}\quad\text{of}\quad\text{the}\quad\text{Good}} \times 100$$

Example of rule providing to comply with a minimum value of originating materials:

Build-up Method:[15] Based on the Value of Originating Materials:

$$\text{RVC}(X\text{per}\quad\text{cent}) = \frac{\text{VOM}}{\text{Value}\quad\text{of}\quad\text{the}\quad\text{Good}} \times 100$$

where:

- RVC is the regional value content of a good, expressed as a percentage;
- VNM is the value of non-originating materials, including materials of undetermined origin, used in the production of the good;
- VOM is the value of originating materials used in the production of the good in the territory of one or more of the Parties.

O114 – Substantial Transformation: CTC with PSROs at HS Chapter and HS Heading Level and Exceptions at HS Four Digits

The originating status is conferred to a good that is classified in a different tariff classification of the non-originating materials used and the PSROs are set at chapter and heading level. The CTC exceptions are usually contained in an additional annex or protocol attached to the tariff preferences or the trade agreement. The CTC exceptions are expressed in the form of CTC at HS chapter level or heading level but not at subheading level (six digits of the HS).

Example of a general rule. Working or processing operations will be considered sufficient when the resulting goods are classified under an HS tariff heading (four digits) other than that covering each of the non-originating materials or parts used in the production.[16]

Example of an exception to the general CTC rule using HS chapter exclusion: heading 17.01 – Cane or beet sugar and chemically pure

[15] Example excerpted from TPP text available at https://ustr.gov/sites/default/files/TPP-Final-Text-Rules-of-Origin-and-Origin-Procedures.pdf.

[16] See Japan GSP scheme general rule at www.mofa.go.jp/policy/economy/gsp/explain.html#section8.

sucrose, in solid form – Manufactured from products other than those of Chapter 12 or 17.[17]

Example of a PSRO exception to the general CTC rule using HS heading exclusion (a): heading 72.29 – Wire of other alloy steel – Manufactured from products other than those of heading 72.27 to 72.29.[18]

Example of a PSRO using HS heading exclusion (b): heading 7217 – Wire of iron or non-alloy steel – Manufacture from semi-finished materials of heading 7207.[19]

O115 – Substantial Transformation: Change in Tariff Classification: With PSROs at HS Heading Level and Subheading Level with Single or Multiple Exceptions of CTC, Including Change of Tariff Subheading at Six-Digit Level

The originating status is conferred to a good that is classified in a different tariff classification of the non-originating materials used and the PSROs may be set at chapter level, heading level or subheading level.[20] The CTC exceptions are expressed at HS chapter level (HS two digits), heading level (HS four digits), at subheading level (six digits of the HS) or a combination thereof.

Example of a PSRO set at tariff item level using exception at chapter level. A change to tariff items 1901.20.02, 1901.20.05, 1901.20.15, 1901.20.20, 1901.20.25, 1901.20.30, 1901.20.35 or 1901.20.40 from any other chapter, except from chapter 4.[21]

Example of a PSRO set at tariff item level using exceptions at heading levels. A change to tariff items 2106.90.12, 2106.90.15 or 2106.90.18 from any other tariff item, except from headings 2203 through 2209.[22]

Example of a PSRO set at subheading level using exceptions at heading levels. A change to a good of subheading 2008.11 from any other chapter, except from heading 12.02.[23]

Example of a PSRO set at subheading level using multiple exceptions at heading level. 6110.12 to 6110.19: A change to a good of subheading 6110.12 through 6110.19 from any other chapter, except from heading 51.06 through 51.13, 52.04 through 52.12 or 54.01 through 54.02,

[17] See list of PSROs in the GSP scheme of Japan at www.mofa.go.jp/files/000077857.pdf.

[18] See list of PSROs in the GSP scheme of Japan at www.mofa.go.jp/files/000077857.pdf.

[19] See EU list of PSROs of EBA at http://eur-lex.europa.eu/LexUriServ/LexUriServ.do?uri=OJ:L:2010:307:0001:0081:EN:PDF.

[20] In the case of NAFTA it may be set at the eight-digit level of the tariff classification.

[21] See NAFTA list of PSROs at https://hts.usitc.gov/currentfile.

[22] See NAFTA list of PSROs at https://hts.usitc.gov/currentfile.

[23] See TPP PSROs at https://ustr.gov/sites/default/files/TPP-Final-Text-Annex-3-A-Product-Specific-Rules.pdf.

subheading 5403.33 through 5403.39 or 5403.42 through 5403.49, or heading 54.04 through 54.08, 55.08 through 55.16, 56.06 or 60.01 through 60.06, provided the good is cut or knit to shape, or both, and sewn or otherwise assembled in the territory of one or more of the Parties.[24]

Example of a PSRO set at heading level using exceptions at heading levels and chapter level. Heading 38.25 A change to heading 38.25 from any other chapter, except from Chapters 28 through 37, 40, or 90.[25]

Example of a PSRO set at subheading level using exceptions at subheading level. 2008.99 – Other – Change of HS chapter except from subheading 0810.90 and 0812.90, or subheading 0714.90.[26]

O116 – Substantial Transformation: Working of Processing Requirement

The originating status is conferred to a good that has undergone a specific working or processing requirement.

Example. Articles of apparel and clothing accessories, not knitted or crocheted: Manufacture from fabric.[27]

O117 – Alternative Requirements

The originating status may be conferred to a good that has fulfilled one of two alternative requirements.

Example (a). Electrical machinery and equipment and parts thereof; sound recorders and reproducers, television image and sound recorders and reproducers, and parts and accessories of such articles; except for: Manufacture from materials of any heading, except that of the product or Manufacture in which the value of all the materials used does not exceed 70 per cent of the ex-works price of the product.[28]

[24] See TPP PSROs at https://ustr.gov/sites/default/files/TPP-Final-Text-Annex-3-A-Product-Specific-Rules.pdf.

[25] See PSROs for USA–Korea at https://ustr.gov/sites/default/files/Annex_6-A_SPECIFIC_RULES_OF_ORIGIN.pdf.

[26] See text of ASEAN–Japan Economic Partnership Agreement (EPA) PSROs at www.mofa.go.jp/policy/economy/fta/asean/annex2.pdf.

[27] COMMISSION REGULATION (EU) No. 1063/2010 of 18 November 2010 amending Regulation (EEC) No. 2454/93 laying down provisions for the implementation of Council Regulation (EEC) No. 2913/92 establishing the Community Customs Code.

[28] COMMISSION REGULATION (EU) No. 1063/2010 of 18 November 2010 amending Regulation (EEC) No. 2454/93 laying down provisions for the implementation of Council Regulation (EEC) No. 2913/92 establishing the Community Customs Code.

Example (b). 8411.22 Turbo-propellers: of a power exceeding 1,100 kW: Regional Value content of (40) or CTSH, except from sub-headings 8411.11 through 8411.82.

O12 – Cumulation

O121 – Bilateral

This cumulation is granted as donor country content rules in the context of the GSP and is also common in bilateral FTAs.

Example. In addition, a total of up to 15 per cent of the 35 per cent local content value (as appraised at the US port of entry) may consist of US-originating parts and materials. This concept is called 'bilateral cumulation of origin'.[29]

O122 – Diagonal

This cumulation is usually granted on a regional basis under autonomous preferential arrangements like the GSP or in the context of the FTAs. It allows to consider as originating all materials that originate in other member states of the regional grouping.

Example. 'Originating in a country of one regional group shall be considered as materials originating in a country of the other regional group when incorporated in a product obtained there, provided that the working or processing carried out in the latter beneficiary country goes beyond the operations described in Article 78(1) and, in the case of textile products, also beyond the operations set out in Annex 16.'[30]

O1123 – Full This cumulation is usually granted in the context of the FTAs. It allows to consider working and processing carried out in the other partner(s) as being carried out in the country where the last transformation takes place.

Example. 'Working or processing carried out in the EU, in the other East African Community (EAC) Partner States, in the other ACP States or in the overseas countries and territories (OCTs) shall be considered as

[29] https://agoa.info/about-agoa/rules-of-origin.html.

[30] See EU regulation COMMISSION REGULATION (EU) No. 1063/2010 of 18 November 2010 amending Regulation (EEC) No. 2454/93 laying down provisions for the implementation of Council Regulation (EEC) No. 2913/92 establishing the Community Customs Code.

having been carried out in an EAC Partner State when the products produced undergo subsequent working or processing in this EAC Partner State.'[31]

O1124 – n.e.s. This cumulation is provided for in some EU FTAs agreement and in the EBA as well as in Canada–Peru FTAs Agreement usually defined as cross-cumulation. It allows cumulation among different kind of agreements or preferential arrangements.

> ***Example.*** *Extended cumulation.* At the request of any beneficiary country's authorities, extended cumulation between a beneficiary country and a country with which the EU has an FTA in accordance with Article XXIV of the GATT in force, may be granted by the Commission, provided that each of the following conditions is met: (a) the countries involved in the cumulation have undertaken to comply or ensure compliance with this Section and to provide the administrative cooperation necessary to ensure the correct implementation of this Section both with regard to the European Union and also between themselves. (b) the undertaking referred to in point (a) has been notified to the Commission by the beneficiary country concerned.[32]

O13 – Proof of Origin

A proof of origin is a document or statement which serves as a documentary evidence of the originating status of the goods to which it relates. Proofs of origin include certificates of origin issued by certifying authorities, a self-declaration of origin by exporters or a declaration of origin made by the importer.

O131 – A Certificate of Origin Issued by a Certifying Authority

A document where a government authority or body empowered to issue proofs of origin expressly certifies that the good is considered originating according to the applicable RoO.

> ***Example.*** RULE 1. The Certificate of Origin shall be issued by the Government authorities of the exporting Party. RULE 2 (a) The Party

[31] See Paragraph 3 of article 4 of Protocol 1 of the EU–EAC EPA available at http://trade.ec.europa.eu/doclib/docs/2015/october/tradoc_153845.pdf.

[32] See paragraph 7 of article 86 of EU Regulation No. 1063/2010 of 18 November 2010 amending Regulation (EEC) No. 2454/93 laying down provisions for the implementation of Council Regulation (EEC) No. 2913/92 establishing the Community Customs Code.

shall inform all the other Parties of the names and addresses of their respective Government authorities issuing the Certificate of Origin and shall provide specimen signatures and specimen of official seals used by their said Government authorities. (b) The above information and specimens shall be provided to every Party to the Agreement and a copy furnished to the ASEAN Secretariat. Any change in names, addresses or official seals shall be promptly informed in the same manner.[33]

O132 – A Certificate of Origin Issued by Exporter

A document where the exporter certifies that the good is considered originating according to the applicable RoO either by delegated authority of by registration.

Example. The Registered Exporter system (the REX system) is the system of certification of origin of goods that will be applied in the GSP of the European Union as from 1 January 2017. It is based on a principle of self-certification by economic operators who will make out themselves so-called statements on origin. To be entitled to make out a statement on origin, an economic operator will have to be registered in a database by his competent authorities. The economic operator will become a 'registered exporter'[34]

O133 – Importer Declaration

A document where the importer expressly certifies that the good is considered originating according to the applicable RoO.

Example. Whenever articles are entered with a claim for the duty exemption provided in this paragraph: (1) the importer shall be deemed to certify that such articles meet all of the conditions for duty exemption.[35]

O14 – Proof of Direct Shipment

A proof of direct shipment is required.

Example. The goods must be shipped directly on a Through Bill of Lading (TBL) to a consignee in Canada from the beneficiary or LDC in which the

[33] See ASEAN China FTA at www.asean.org/wp-content/uploads/images/2013/economic/afta/ACFTA/3- percent20ACFTA percent20TIG percent20Annex percent203.pdf.

[34] See https://ec.europa.eu/taxation_customs/business/calculation-customs-duties/rules-origin/general-aspects-preferential-origin/arrangements-list/generalised-system-preferences/the_register_exporter_system_en.

[35] See general notes to the US harmonized tariff schedule at file:///Users/stefanoinama/Downloads/General percent20Notes percent20(4).pdf.

goods were certified. Evidence in the form of a TBL (or a copy) showing that the goods have been shipped directly to a consignee in Canada must be presented to the Canada Border Services Agency (CBSA) upon request. An importer may be requested to submit further documentation to substantiate the TBL, such as sales order, report of entry documents and cargo control documents.[36]

O2 – Non-preferential RoO[37]

Article 1 of part 1 of the WTO Agreement on Rules of Origin defines non-preferential RoO as follows:

> For the purposes of Parts I to IV of this Agreement, rules of origin shall be defined as those laws, regulations and administrative determinations of general application applied by any Member to determine the country of origin of goods provided such rules of origin are not related to contractual or autonomous trade regimes leading to the granting of tariff preferences going beyond the application of paragraph 1 of Article I of GATT 1994.

Non-preferential RoO are normally used to apply MFN rates of duty and other WTO agreements. Non-preferential rules are distinct from preferential RoO since compliance does not provide for preferential tariffs.

O21 – Origin Criterion

O211 – Wholly Obtained

The origin status is conferred to a good that is entirely produced or manufactured in a country without using non-originating materials.

> ***Example.*** Live animals born and raised in one country; vegetables that have been grown and harvested in one country.

O212 – Substantial Transformation: Ad Valorem Percentage Criterion as Value Addition

The originating status is conferred to a good that has complied with a given percentage of value added. The calculation of such value added results from adding the cost of originating materials used in its production plus the direct cost of processing as a percentage of a given finished price of the good, normally ex-factory price.

[36] See Canadian rules at www.cbsa-asfc.gc.ca/publications/dm-md/d11/d11-4-4-eng.html.
[37] This part of the taxonomy on non-preferential RoO requires further study and validation.

Example. 84.40 – Book-binding machinery, including book sewing machines – CTH; or 45 per cent value added rule.[38]

O213 – Substantial Transformation: Ad Valorem Percentage Criterion as Value of Materials

The originating status is conferred to a good that does not exceed a given amount of non-originating material out of a given finished price of the good, normally ex-works price or FOB price or achieve a minimum content of originating materials. The value of material can be calculated by subtraction.

O214 – Substantial Transformation: Change in Tariff Classification: Without Exception

The originating status is conferred to a good that is classified in a different tariff classification of the non-originating materials used and the PSROs are set at chapter and heading level. The CTC exceptions are usually contained in an additional annex or protocol attached to the tariff preferences or the trade agreement. The CTC exceptions are expressed in the form of CTC at HS chapter level or heading level but not at subheading level (six digits of the HS).

O215 – Substantial Transformation: Change in Tariff Classification: With Exception

The originating status is conferred to a good that is classified in a different tariff classification of the non-originating materials used and the PSROs may be set at chapter level, heading level or subheading level. The CTC exceptions are expressed at HS chapter level (HS two digits), heading level (HS four digits), at subheading level (six digits of the HS) or a combination thereof.

O216 – Substantial Transformation: Technical Requirement

Example. Certain apparel exports receive originating status in the country where they are both cut and sewn.

O217 – Alternative Requirements (in the Explanatory Text: This Refers to 'or')

A good's origin can be determined by using one of two or more criteria available to prove a substantial transformation.

[38] See EU common customs code at: http://ec.europa.eu/taxation_customs/sites/taxation/files/resources/documents/roo_chap_84-85_en.pdf.

O22 – Proof of Origin

A proof of origin is a document or statement which serves as a prima facie evidence to support that the goods to which it relates satisfy the origin criteria under applicable RoO. Proofs of origin include certificates of origin, a self-issued certificate of origin or a declaration of origin.

Example.

O221 – issued by authority

A document where a government authority or body empowered to issue proofs of origin expressly certifies that the good is considered originating according to the applicable RoO.

Example.

O222 – issued by exporter

A document where the exporter expressly certifies that the good is considered originating according to the applicable RoO.

Example.

O223 – self-declaration

O224 – importer declaration

A document where the importer expressly certifies that the good is considered originating according to the applicable RoO.

Example.

O229 – Proof of origin: n.e.s.

11

Behind-the-Border Measures and the New Generation of Trade Agreements

Technical Barriers to Trade and Sanitary and Phytosanitary Measures Compared

MANFRED ELSIG AND SEBASTIAN KLOTZ

11.1 Introduction

The last couple of years have been an eventful time for trade policy and in particular for major preferential trade agreements (PTAs), such as the so-called mega-regionals. Early 2016, twelve Pacific Rim countries, including Canada and the United States (USA), signed the Trans-Pacific Partnership (TPP) agreement. Around the same time, Canada and the European Union (EU) agreed at the level of negotiators to conclude the Comprehensive Economic and Trade Agreement (CETA). Finally, the USA and the EU continued their efforts to find common ground in the negotiations towards the proposed Transatlantic Trade and Investment Partnership (TTIP) treaty.

At the end of 2016, however, the USA elected a new president who had campaigned actively against trade agreements. In his first video address he announced that he would stop the ratification procedures for TPP, a threat he later followed up on his first day in office in early 2017 through issuing a presidential order (The New York Times, 2017). The US president was equally critical towards the North American Free Trade Agreement (NAFTA), an agreement signed with Canada and Mexico in 1994. After intense negotiations, the three countries signed a replacement NAFTA deal, the USA–Mexico–Canada Agreement (USMCA), during a G20 summit in late 2018. The dynamics around TTIP also changed over time. After the US elections, a transatlantic trade deal seemed to be off the table. As trade tensions between the EU and USA increased in 2017, however, talks on some type of a transatlantic trade deal reconvened.

The process of drafting, signing and ratifying mega-regional agreements has been politicized for some time. The new generation of PTAs has faced public scrutiny in many European countries, in particular in some of the most trade-dependent nations, such as Germany, France, Belgium and Austria. Thousands of people have taken to the streets to protest against CETA and TTIP in the past few years (Reuters, 2016). An important area of contestation relates to new rules behind-the-border measures, so-called non-tariff measures (NTMs), many of which touch on standards and regulations. Trade sceptics lament that agreements that foresee increased 'regulatory cooperation' would in reality lead to a loss of national sovereignty in regulating one's own health, social and environmental laws, as illustrated by the infamous chlorinated chicken episode or concerns about investors suing domestic environmental policies through investor–state arbitration. These concerns were echoed by national and regional governments. Only after some concessions vis-à-vis the Belgian government of Wallonia could EU Member States proceed to sign CETA (The Guardian, 2016). Anti-PTA sentiments also arose in the USA in the context of the 2016 presidential campaign. The criticism focused on job losses in manufacturing industries and, in this context, trade agreements were quickly identified as the main culprit for de-industrialization.

11.1.1 TBT and SPS at the World Trade Organization

This chapter takes a close look at the core of behind-the-border regulations, namely provisions related to technical barriers to trade (TBT) and sanitary and phytosanitary measures (SPS) in the aforementioned trade agreements (CETA, TPP, USMCA and TTIP). The TBT and SPS Agreements, to which all of the four PTAs refer, were the result of the Uruguay Round trade talks and entered into force with the creation of the World Trade Organization (WTO) in 1995.

The SPS Agreement covers all measures whose purpose it is to protect human or animal health from food-borne risks, human health from animal- or plant-carried diseases and animals and plants from pests or diseases. The TBT Agreement, in contrast, covers all technical regulations, voluntary standards and conformity assessment procedures to ensure that these are non-discriminatory and do not create unnecessary obstacles to trade, except when these are sanitary or phytosanitary measures as defined by the SPS Agreement.

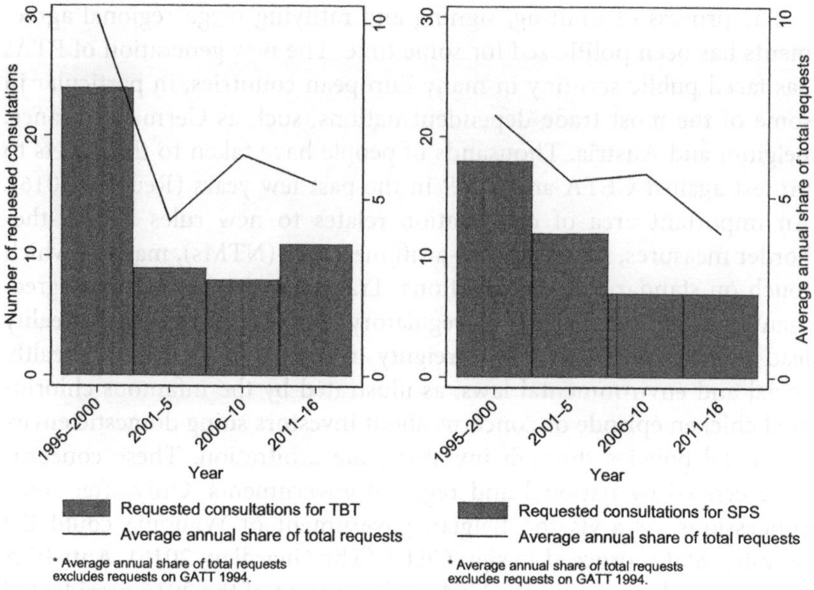

Figure 11.1 Requests for consultations referring to the WTO TBT and SPS Agreements, 1995–2016.
Source: Authors' illustration based on WTO (2016c)

Between 1995 and 2016, a total of fifty-two and forty-four requests for consultations cited the TBT and SPS Agreement, respectively.[1] In particular in the first few years, both Agreements accounted for a significant share of total consultation requests at the WTO (Figure 11.1). On average, the TBT and SPS Agreements accounted for 7 per cent and 6 per cent of annual consultation requests between 1995 and 2016, respectively. The only WTO Agreements that have been cited more frequently are the Anti-Dumping Agreement, the Agreement on Subsidies and Countervailing Measures and the Agreement on Agriculture.

Given the different foci and scope of the two agreements, TBT- and SPS-related measures draw attention from different economic sectors. Figure 11.2 shows, for instance, that TBT measures are particularly relevant for the chemicals, plastics and machinery sectors. SPS measures,

[1] There were two more requests for consultations that cited the TBT Agreement in 2017. In 2017 and 2018, there were two and one requests for consultations that cited the SPS Agreement, respectively.

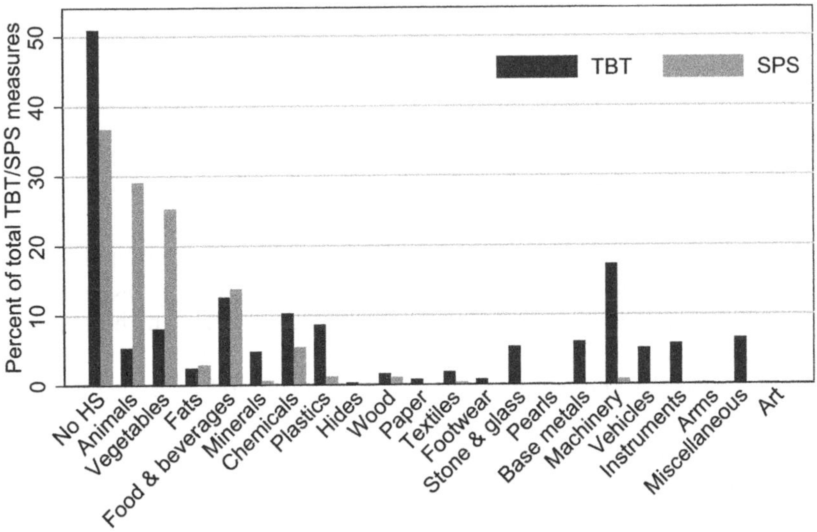

Figure 11.2 TBT and SPS measures by sector.
Source: Authors' illustration based on WTO (2016d)

in contrast, are common for live animal and vegetable products. TBT and SPS are also almost equally present in the food and beverages sector. Even though TBT and SPS measures vary by industry, Figure 11.2 also illustrates that many TBT and SPS measures cannot be allocated to a certain industry, one reason being that these measures often include non-product-specific requirements on, for example, packaging, marking or labelling.

In the next section, we briefly discuss the existing literature on NTMs and PTAs with a special focus on TBT and SPS. This is followed by providing some descriptive empirical evidence on how TBT and SPS obligations have evolved over time. Then we address three key questions related to the new generation of large PTAs: first, how much innovation versus imitation characterizes the TBT and SPS chapters in mega-regionals such as CETA, TPP and USMCA? Tackling this question will allow us to better understand the degree to which new templates have been agreed as well as the source and extent of obligations that may have been copy-pasted from past agreements. Second, to what extent may CETA, TPP and USMCA meet their objectives to become design blueprints for future (transatlantic) trade agreements? To answer this question, we investigate the degree to which EU and US negotiators, respectively relied on CETA and TPP texts to draft their proposals for the TBT and SPS chapter negotiations in the context of the TTIP talks. We first focus on TPP because the USA was still a TPP member at the time at which it drafted its TTIP proposals. Since then, however, the USA has pulled out of TPP. We therefore also compare its TTIP draft proposals to the latest US agreement – the USMCA. Third, we take a closer look at the EU and US TTIP draft proposals to understand where the parties converge and where they diverge. Understanding how compatible or not these draft proposals are will give us an idea on how likely it will be to find agreement on NTM-related obligations between the transatlantic partners.

In answering these questions, we principally rely on text-as-data approaches. We find that in all four agreements negotiators draw relatively more on TBT than SPS legal texts from previous PTAs. When focusing on TPP and USMCA, we observe a significant import of legal texts from past US trade deals. By contrast, CETA's negotiators relied less on previous PTAs and appear to have developed a more innovative approach on TBT and SPS matters. We further find evidence suggesting that EU negotiators attempted to implement these innovations in TTIP. Indeed, the European draft proposals for the TBT and SPS chapters of TTIP rely heavily on CETA texts, speaking to a prominent role CETA could play long-term. Interestingly, TPP plays a fairly limited role in the US draft proposal for TTIP, even though it is an agreement largely written by the USA. Similarly, we find little textual overlap between the US TTIP proposal and its latest trade agreement – the USMCA. Finally, when focusing on specific treaty language, we find that the EU and USA converge on general topics such as the objective, scope and coverage of TBT and SPS in TTIP, but do diverge in more detailed items such as standard-setting processes and conformity assessment procedures. This reflects differences in regulatory philosophies that will be hard to bridge. In the concluding section we point towards future research directions.

11.2 Literature Review

The proliferating number of PTAs has been the focus of a growing body of literature in law, economics and international relations. Whereas the economics literature primarily concentrates on quantifying the effect of NTMs on trade flows (for a comprehensive overview, see Ederington and Ruta, 2016), a variety of contributions have focused on mapping and assessing the design of NTMs. Early studies focused on the relationship between plurilateralism and multilateralism, in other words, between PTAs and the WTO. Piermartini and Budetta (2006, 2009) and Lesser (2007) provide selective insights into NTMs, with a focus on TBT, across large numbers of PTAs.[2] More recently, Molina and Khoroshavina (2015) expanded the sample size to include 238 trade agreements. The mentioned studies find that the majority of PTAs do refer to the WTO TBT Agreement and only partially go beyond it. Indeed, the most recent contribution by Molina and Khoroshavina (2015) finds that 85 per cent of PTAs refer to the WTO TBT Agreement – in one form or another. In one-third of the surveyed agreements, the parties affirm their rights and obligations under the TBT Agreement. In one-quarter of these agreements, the parties indicate specifically that TBT issues are to be governed by the WTO TBT Agreement. Most of this work has focused exclusively on technical standards and regulations.

Allee, Elsig and Lugg (2017a) extend the analysis beyond TBT issues and investigate the importance of WTO rules for PTA provisions on anti-dumping, services, SPS, intellectual property, safeguards, procurement, dispute settlement and investment. The authors find considerable differences across the issue areas. While anti-dumping sections in over 90 per cent of the surveyed PTAs refer to WTO rules, less than 5 per cent of the investment provisions do so. The numbers for TBT and SPS measures confirm previous research: around three-quarters of PTAs that include TBT and/or SPS provisions, also include a reference to the WTO. Allee et al. (2017a) go one step further. In addition to identifying WTO references, the authors also calculate the amount of WTO language that is directly incorporated into PTAs. Their text-as-data approach yields interesting results. On average, around 11 per cent of the TBT and SPS chapters in the almost 300 surveyed PTAs are copied in verbatim from the respective WTO agreements. Some TBT and SPS chapters copy up to 60 per cent and 51 per cent from the relevant WTO agreement, respectively.

Why do parties that are engaged in preferential trade negotiations rely so heavily on the existing multilateral rules? The reasons for this are manifold. Allee et al. (2017a), for instance, point to a number of explanations why WTO treaties are attractive. First, the WTO regime is well established and some areas, such as TBT-related rights and obligations, have been developed in Geneva over many decades. Second, the WTO

[2] Piermartini and Budetta (2006, 2009) assess seventy-three agreements, Lesser (2007) eighty-two agreements.

dispute settlement system has interpreted these rules over time providing clarity and predictability. Third, almost all PTA signatories are WTO members and therefore attempt to build strong ties between the PTAs and the WTO laws. And finally, most trade negotiations are well trained and informed about WTO law.

The recent contributions by Baccini, Dür and Haftel (2014) and Allee and Elsig (2019) provide additional systematic evidence by expanding the analyses on the import from other PTAs either in terms of the amount of text or closeness to certain templates. Indeed, Allee and Elsig (2019) find that, when considering the closest match between two PTAs, the TBT and SPS chapters between PTAs overlap on average around a striking 70 per cent. Baccini et al. (2014) corroborate the view that negotiators do not 'reinvent the wheel' but rather choose from a limited menu of principal models or templates. The authors find that most PTAs draw heavily from existing templates of at least three competing models: the Southern model, the EU model and the NAFTA model. In a nutshell, the Southern model includes primarily narrow and shallow agreements in which member states agree on the (often partial) reduction of tariffs on a selected number of goods. Provisions on trade in services, foreign direct investment (FDI) or other non-trade issues are very limited, if not absent. The EU model presents the institutions-based integration type in which powerful bodies and institutions are created to reinforce the integration process. These agreements cover non-trade issues but the legal language is kept relatively vague and leaves it to the created institutions to enforce the commitments. The NAFTA model, by contrast, promotes rules-based integration. Trade and non-trade commitments as well as their enforcement are more precisely formulated which limits the need to create further institutions.

To what extent the EU and the NAFTA models influenced the design of the latest mega-regionals, CETA and TPP, is the focus of two other studies by Allee, Elsig and Lugg (2017b) and Allee and Lugg (2016), respectively. The former study suggests that the EU and Canada brought distinct ideas about what they wanted to the negotiation table, as indicated by their previous PTAs, and ended up writing a mostly unique agreement. Indeed, not only is the overall share of text copied from previous PTAs into CETA relatively moderate, there also appear few agreement(s) that served as a clear or dominant template for the negotiations. Based on the text analyses, both sides were able or willing to import roughly similar amounts of texts from their past PTAs. This stands in contrast to the findings of Allee and Lugg (2016) who conduct a similar analysis of TPP. The language of previous US PTAs is disproportionally prominent in TPP compared to other TPP drafters' past PTAs. Ten of the PTAs that match TPP most closely are previous US PTAs. Some bilateral PTAs such as, for instance, with Bahrain, Oman and South Korea have almost half of their contents copied into TPP.

In this chapter, we follow the above work and study in more detail the TBT and SPS chapters of CETA, TPP, USMCA and TTIP. Before doing so, we provide an overview of the evolution of TBT and SPS in PTAs over the past decades.

11.3 Evolution of TBT and SPS in PTAs

TBT and SPS play a particularly important role in trade negotiations because they regulate politically sensitive areas and can present a balancing act between pursuing legitimate domestic policy objectives and taming protectionist agendas that negatively affect international trade.

On the one hand, the WTO recognizes each member's right to adopt the standards and regulations they consider appropriate – for example, for human, animal or plant life and health, for the protection of the environment or to meet consumer and/or security objectives. On the other hand, it is a key concern enshrined in WTO treaties to ensure that these measures are non-discriminatory and do not create unnecessary obstacles to trade. To prevent potential protectionism in disguise and tack of transparency, the WTO encourages its members to apply international standards, guides or recommendations, except when such international standards are ineffective or inappropriate to achieve their legitimate goals (Articles 2.4, 5.4 and Annex 3 of the WTO TBT Agreement). To reduce the burden of cross-country differences in standards and regulations further, countries may decide to cooperate on or even harmonize TBT- and SPS-related standards.

While it is beyond the scope of this chapter to assess the depth of TBT and SPS provisions in detail, we focus below on four broad areas that show how the structure and content of TBT and SPS provisions has evolved over time:[3] the presence of TBT/SPS provisions, the reference to the respective WTO Agreement, cooperation features and, finally, attempts towards mutual recognition and harmonization.

[3] For a more detailed analysis of TBT provisions in PTAs, see Molina and Khoroshavina (2015).

The presence of TBT/SPS chapters and provisions in PTAs is an obvious prerequisite for the discussion. The variable indicates whether or not the parties consider TBT- and SPS-related issues to be crucial in defining the rules of preferential trade between them. A second important variable is the reference to the respective WTO Agreements. As previously outlined, PTA partners refer to WTO rules for a number of reasons. These references can come in different forms and shapes. In the US draft proposal for TTIP, for instance, it reads that:

> *The Parties affirm their rights and obligations with respect to each other under the TBT Agreement.*

The EU draft proposal, for instance, states that:

> *The WTO Agreement on Technical Barriers to Trade (hereinafter referred to as 'the TBT Agreement') is hereby incorporated into and made part of this Agreement.*

For the purpose of this chapter, we do not differentiate between the different phrasings and restrict ourselves to capture whether or not there is a TBT/SPS chapter/provision in the PTA.[4] Our third indicator of the importance and scope of TBT and SPS in PTAs is concerned with the cooperation and information exchange that the parties envisage. While recent PTAs often include separate chapters on regulatory cooperation, this was not always the case. In modern agreements, such as TTIP, the obligation to cooperate in this area may read as follows

> *The Parties shall strengthen their co-operation in the areas of technical regulations, standards, metrology, conformity assessment procedures, accreditation, market surveillance and monitoring and enforcement activities in order to facilitate the conduct of trade between the Parties, as laid down in Chapter [. . .] (Regulatory Cooperation).*[5]

A significantly deeper commitment than cooperation on TBT and SPS matters, is the harmonization of such. Harmonization presupposes a common legislative framework which, in reality, may not be achievable or desirable for a number of reasons. In this case, PTA parties may resort to equivalence as a complementary approach. The parties would accept as equivalent the technical regulation and/or conformity assessment

[4] For a more detailed analysis of references to the WTO TBT Agreement in PTAs, see Molina and Khoroshavina (2015).

[5] EU draft proposal for the TTIP TBT chapter.

procedures of each other. Using TTIP as an example again, the text may read as follows:

> *The Parties undertake to co-operate towards global harmonization of technical requirements in the framework of existing or planned international agreements or organizations in which the US and the EU or its Member States participate.*[6]

As a final variable, we consider whether or not the use of international standards, guidelines or recommendations is explicitly encouraged in the PTA. In the context of the WTO SPS Agreement, the development of international standards is a prerogative of various standardization bodies, such as the Codex Alimentarius Commission, the International Office of Epizootics and the Secretariat of the International Plant Protection Convention. As we discuss below, the definition of an international standard as well as its development is more disputed in the TBT context. For the purpose of this chapter, we limit ourselves to whether or not the use of international standards is encouraged in the TBT chapter of a PTA. Above variables are taken from the Design of Trade Agreements (DESTA; Dür, Baccini and Elsig 2014) database which has manually coded a number of TBT and SPS features.

Figure 11.3 illustrates that, even though the numbers of PTAs (including TBT and SPS chapters and provisions) countries sign varies considerably by year, the relative share of PTAs including TBT and SPS matters in total PTAs has steadily increased. To show this overall trend graphically, we computed the annual average shares of the TBT and SPS variables in total PTAs as illustrated by the bold line.

Figure 11.3 graphically shows what can also be seen in Tables 11.1 and 11.2 – namely, the extent to which parties harmonize TBT and SPS measures is much less prominent than the extent to which they commit to cooperation or refer to the respective WTO Agreement.

Tables 11.1 and 11.2 provide more fine-grained information for PTAs with different groups of countries and over time. Until recently, TBT-related provisions were predominantly found in trade agreements between developed and developing countries, so-called North–South PTAs. Indeed, the share of total PTAs that included such provisions was considerably higher in North–South (N–S) PTAs than in North–North (N–N) and South–South (S–S) PTAs. Over time, the vast majority

[6] EU draft proposal for the TTIP TBT chapter.

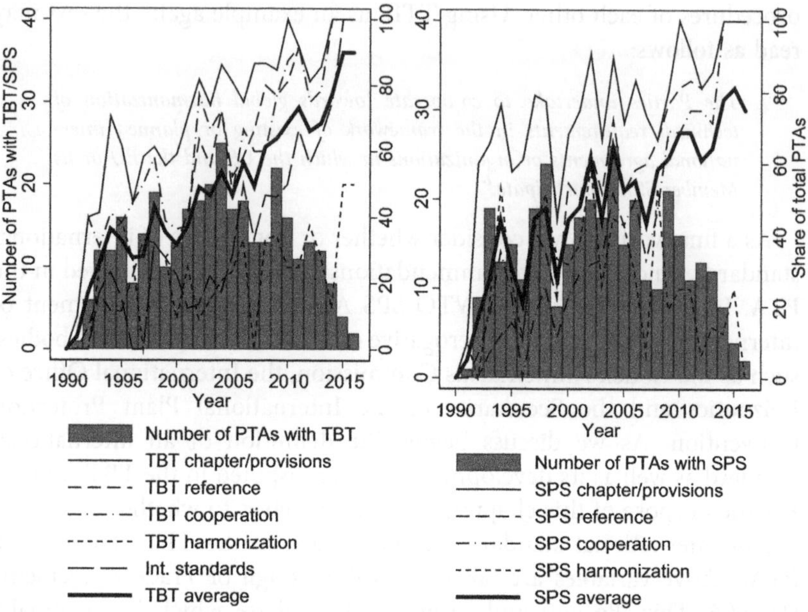

Figure 11.3 Evolution of TBT and SPS in PTAs, 1990–2016.
Source: Authors' illustration based on DESTA

of PTAs have significantly incorporated TBT- and SPS-related rules, regardless of the level of the parties' development.

11.4 TBT and SPS in the New Generation of Mega-regionals

Having briefly illustrated the evolution of TBT and SPS in PTAs over time, we take a closer look at the new generation of mega-regional trade agreements: CETA, TPP, USMCA and TTIP. Whereas the final treaty texts are available for CETA, TPP and USMCA, the analysis of TTIP is based on the drafts that were published by the EU Commission, in the case of the EU proposal, and leaked by Greenpeace in the case of the US proposal (Greenpeace, 2016).

The analysis relies on the text-as-data methodology that has been employed by Allee et al. (2017b) and Allee and Lugg (2016). First, all prior PTAs of CETA, TPP, USMCA and TTIP signatories are identified in DESTA. The relevant PTAs (are all available in English), and in the case of TTIP PTA draft texts, are then transformed from .pdf into .txt

Table 11.1 *Evolution of TBT in PTAs by development group, 1990–2016*

Years	Group (Number of total PTAs)	Per cent of PTAs with a TBT chapter/ provision	Per cent of PTAs with a reference to the WTO	Per cent of PTAs encouraging cooperation on TBT matters	Per cent of PTAs encouraging harmonization on TBT matters	Per cent of PTAs encouraging the use of international standards
1991–5	N–N (9)	13	0	0	0	0
	N–S (35)	60	14	46	14	17
	S–S (60)	46	11	31	9	13
1996–2000	N-N (1)	0	0	0	0	0
	N–S (20)	85	40	70	30	40
	S–S (104)	51	28	42	3	13
2001–5	N–N (7)	67	33	67	17	17
	N–S (27)	96	74	74	48	37
	S–S (100)	74	54	57	6	13
2006–10	N–N (3)	67	67	67	33	33
	N–S (32)	88	78	69	34	53
	S–S (69)	85	69	72	28	43
2011–15	N–N (1)	100	100	100	100	100
	N–S (33)	90	90	86	66	69
	S–S (28)	88	88	83	58	63

Source: Authors' illustration based on DESTA.

Table 11.2 *Evolution of SPS in PTAs by development group, 1990–2016*

Years	Group (number of PTAs)	Per cent of PTAs with an SPS chapter/ provision	Per cent of PTAs with a reference to the WTO	Per cent of PTAs encouraging cooperation on SPS matters	Per cent of PTAs encouraging harmonization on SPS matters
1991–5	N–N (9)	63	0	0	0
	N–S (35)	66	0	20	34
	S–S (60)	54	15	20	20
1996–2000	N–N (1)	0	0	0	0
	N–S (20)	95	25	35	50
	S–S (104)	63	37	13	34
2001–5	N–N (7)	67	67	33	17
	N–S (27)	93	63	52	30
	S–S (100)	76	57	34	47
2006–10	N–N (3)	67	67	33	0
	N–S (32)	78	69	63	6
	S–S (69)	84	69	52	38
2011–15	N–N (1)	100	100	100	0
	N–S (33)	90	86	86	7
	S–S (28)	88	88	71	25

Source: Authors' illustration based on DESTA.

files. These files are analysed using WCopyfind (version 4.1.5), an open source windows-based program that compares documents on the similarities in their words and phrases. The program allows for a number of refinements. Similar to the previously mentioned authors, the present analysis follows the convention to use a minimum of six consecutive identical words for a match. All punctuation, outer punctuation, numbers, letter case and non-words are ignored. Finally, it should be pointed out that WCopyfind only reports the PTAs that have a minimum of matches between the PTA and the mega-regional PTAs. If a PTA is not included in the following figures, this indicates that the PTA did not have any matches with the mega-regional PTA of interest.

11.4.1 The Comprehensive Economic and Trade Agreement

In order to study the design of CETA's TBT chapter, we build and expand on Allee et al. (2017b) and compare CETA to the forty-one PTAs the EU and Canada signed previously as well as to the two WTO TBT Agreements from 1979 (Tokyo Code) and 1994 (Uruguay Round). A relatively small number of eleven treaties (27 per cent) appear to have influenced the design of the CETA chapter on TBT (Figure 11.4). We find that, on average, 16 per cent of these chapters were copied into CETA and that considerably more text was copied from Canadian PTAs. Out of the six most relevant previous PTAs, Canadian negotiators copied an average of 25 per cent into the CETA TBT chapter. The most important agreement is the bilateral PTA with Jordan out of which a striking 50 per cent was copied into CETA (Figure 11.4). The EU only copied text from its bilateral PTAs with Singapore (10 per cent) and Korea (9 per cent). Overall, Canada did not only copy a larger share of text from its previous PTAs, it also used a higher share of PTAs available than the EU. Out of the twelve PTAs Canada already has, six were influential to the design of CETA's TBT chapter. In contrast, the text of only two out of twenty-eight EU PTAs appears to have had an influence on CETA.

The WTO TBT Agreement does not appear influential at first. However, a qualitative assessment of the text shows that the Agreement actually forms the foundation of the CETA TBT chapter. Indeed, Canada and the EU refer to the TBT Agreement seven times and explicitly incorporate Articles 2–9 as well as Annex 1 and 3.

Canada's influence in the design of CETA is also reflected in its SPS chapter, if less pronounced (Figure 11.5). Out of the twenty-five PTAs

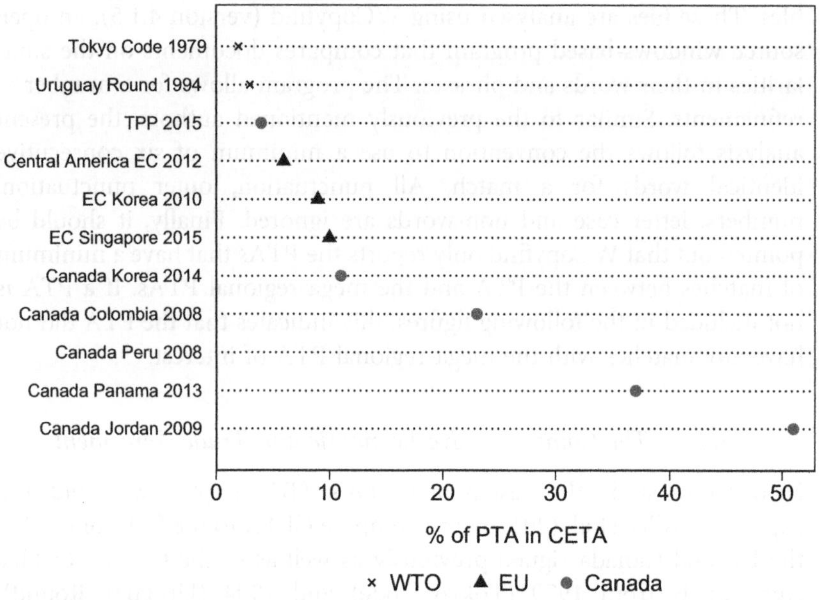

Figure 11.4 TBT in CETA.
Source: Authors' illustration based on text-as-data analysis

that Canada and the EU previously signed and which included a SPS chapter, only eight appear to have been influential in the design of the CETA SPS chapter. On average, 7 per cent of these agreements were incorporated into the chapter. Canada's PTAs with Colombia (17 per cent) and Peru (16 per cent) were copied most significantly. Interestingly, we find that the relatively low average share of Canadian PTAs copied into CETA's SPS chapter is pulled down by the very limited influence of TPP (3 per cent). On average, Canadian negotiators managed to copy an average of 12 per cent from previous PTAs whereas EU negotiators only included 4 per cent of their five most influential PTAs.

Similarly to the TBT chapter, the WTO rules form an integral part of CETA's SPS chapter as

'The parties affirm their rights and obligations under the SPS Agreement.'

Overall, we find that more text was copied from previous TBT than SPS chapters. Canadian negotiators also drew considerably more text from previous PTAs than EU negotiators did. Still, compared to TPP discussed below, CETA appears more innovative as the average shares of texts copied from previous PTAs are lower than in TPP's case.

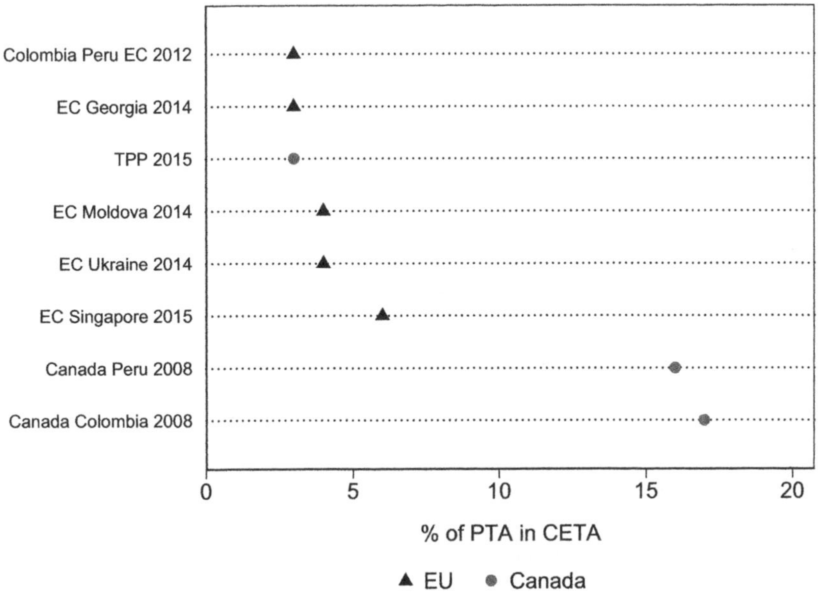

Figure 11.5 SPS in CETA.
Source: Authors' illustration based on text-as-data analysis

11.4.2 The Trans-Pacific Partnership Agreement

In order to assess the extent to which the TBT chapter in TPP is novel or imitated from past agreements, we compare the chapter to the seventy-one TBT chapters that TPP members signed in their previous trade agreements since 1995 as well as to the TBT Agreements from 1979 (Tokyo Code) and 1994 (Uruguay Round). A significant amount of texts from fifty-two of these agreements (73 per cent) have made their way into TPP (Figure 11.6).

We observe that, on average, 21 per cent of the previous TBT chapters are copied into TPP. In line with Allee and Lugg (2016), our analysis finds that the USA has by far had the most influence on the design of TPP's TBT chapter compared to other TPP parties. Eight out of the ten most influential PTAs are US agreements. More than 35 per cent of the TBT provisions from bilateral US PTAs such as with Bahrain, Oman and Morocco were copied into TPP. On average, US negotiators managed to incorporate 30 per cent of previous TBT provisions into TPP (Table 11.3). Interestingly, US negotiators copied on average considerably more from

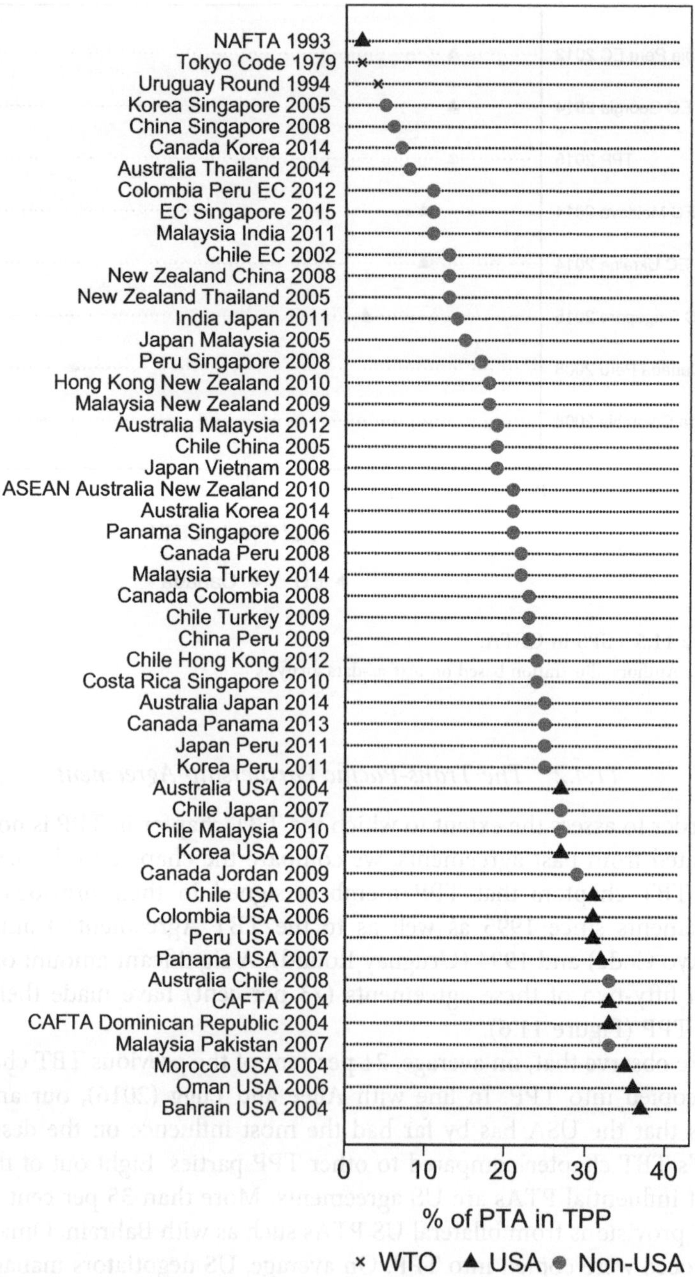

Figure 11.6 TBT in TPP.
Source: Authors' illustration based on text-as-data analysis

Table 11.3 *Text-as-data results by TPP country*

Country	Average per cent copied from previous PTA TBT (number of influential PTAs*)	Average per cent copied from previous PTA TBT with TPP partners (number of influential PTAs)	Average per cent copied from previous PTA TBT with non-TPP partners (number of influential PTAs)	Average per cent copied from previous PTA SPS (number of influential PTAs)	Average per cent copied from previous PTA SPS with TPP partners (number of influential PTAs)	Average per cent copied from previous PTA SPS with non-TPP partners (Number of influential PTAs)
Australia	22.0 (7)	25.0 (5)	14.5 (2)	16.3 (4)	20.0 (3)	5.0 (1)
Brunei	0.0 (0)	0.0 (0)	0.0 (0)	0.0 (0)	0.0 (0)	0.0 (0)
Canada	21.2 (5)	22.0 (1)	21.0 (4)	15.3 (4)	10.5 (2)	20.0 (2)
Chile	24.6 (8)	29.5 (4)	19.8 (4)	15.6 (5)	19.5 (2)	13.0 (3)
Japan	20.0 (5)	21.5 (4)	14 (1)	0.0 (0)	0.0 (0)	0.0 (0)
Malaysia	20.7 (7)	19.8 (4)	22.0 (3)	16.6 (5)	18.3 (3)	14.0 (2)
Mexico	2.0 (1)	2.0 (1)	0.0 (0)	5.0 (1)	5.0 (1)	0.0 (0)
New Zealand	16.0 (6)	19.5 (2)	14.3 (4)	11.5 (6)	12.3 (3)	10.7 (3)
Peru	23.8 (6)	23.8 (4)	24.0 (2)	13.4 (5)	15.0 (2)	12.3 (3)
Singapore	14.0 (6)	17.0 (1)	13.4 (5)	7.7 (3)	8.0 (1)	7.5 (2)
USA	29.6 (12)	22.8 (4)	33.0 (8)	19.8 (9)	18.3 (4)	21.0 (5)
Vietnam	0.0 (0)	0.0 (0)	0.0 (0)	0.0 (0)	0.0 (0)	0.0 (0)

* The number of influential PTAs is the number of PTAs for which WCopyfind identified a minimum of matches between the PTA and the mega-regional PTAs.

Source: Authors' illustration based on text-as-data analysis.

PTAs with non-TPP countries (33 per cent) than from PTAs with TPP countries (23 per cent).

The dominant position of the USA is followed by Chile and Peru which both managed to integrate an average of almost a quarter of their previous TBT provisions into TPP (Table 11.3). To a certain extent, this dominance is driven by the partners with which Chile and Peru have signed previous PTAs. Indeed, Chile's impact on TPP is mainly driven by its PTAs with other large TPP economies such as Australia (33 per cent) and the USA (31 per cent) (Figure 11.6). On average, 30 per cent of text from Chile's previous PTAs with TPP countries was copied into TPP, and only 20 per cent from PTAs with non-TPP countries.

PTAs with large economies, which are likely to have significant negotiation power, are also important for Peru. The most influential PTAs with other TPP countries include the bilateral treaties with the USA (31 per cent) and Canada (22 per cent). Interestingly, however, there is also a large part of 23 per cent of text copied from the PTA with the non-TPP country China. On average, similar shares of text were copied from TPP and non-TPP PTAs: 23 per cent and 24 per cent, respectively.

At first sight, both NAFTA and the WTO TBT Agreements appear to have had a rather limited impact on TPP's TBT chapter. However, with regards to the WTO Agreements their presence is more substantial as the employed text-as-data methodology tends to underestimate the importance of WTO rules. PTA parties adopt (parts of) the WTO Agreements through referencing rather than replicating the text (Allee et al. 2017a). Only 4 per cent of the Uruguay WTO TBT Agreement was copied into TPP. However, the TBT chapter actually explicitly incorporates large, yet selected, parts of the WTO Agreement.[7]

Turning to SPS, we compare the TPP SPS chapter to sixty-nine SPS chapters that TPP members signed previously as well as to the WTO SPS Agreement. The texts of thirty-three out of these sixty-nine agreements (48 per cent) appear to have significantly been incorporated into TPP (Figure 11.7). However, the share of influential agreements is lower compared to TBT (73 per cent); the amount copied from previous agreements is also lower. On average, we find that 15 per cent of previous SPS chapters were copied into TPP.

Figure 11.7 shows that the USA has had the biggest influence on the SPS chapter, however, its dominance is less pronounced than in the TBT

[7] The TPP TBT chapter incorporates Articles 2.1, 2.2, 2.4, 2.5, 2.9, 2.10, 2.11, 2.12; Articles 5.1, 5.2, 5.3, 5.4, 5.6, 5.7, 5.8, 5.9; Paragraphs D, E and F of Annex 3.

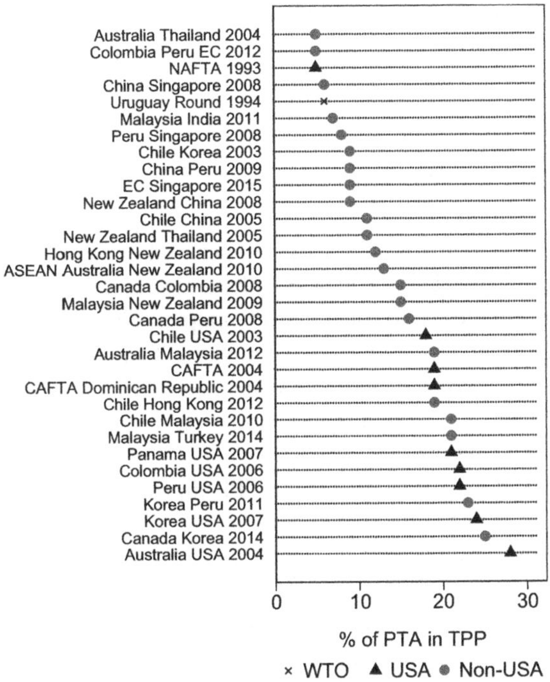

Figure 11.7 SPS in TPP.
Source: Authors' illustration based on text-as-data analysis

context. Still, five out of the ten most influential SPS chapters have been concluded by the USA. The largest shares of text were copied from bilateral PTAs with Australia (28 per cent), Korea (24 per cent), Peru (22 per cent), Columbia (22 per cent) and Panama (21 per cent). On average, US negotiators managed to copy 20 per cent from previous US PTAs into the SPS chapter of TPP. As in the case of TBT, US negotiators actually drew more text from previous PTAs with non-TPP partners than TPP partners (Table 11.3).

The influence of the WTO SPS Agreement appears limited with 6 per cent. However, the TPP countries explicitly state in Article 7.4 that '*The Parties affirm their rights and obligations under the SPS Agreement*' and that '*Nothing in this Agreement shall limit the rights and obligations that each Party has under the SPS Agreement.*' Overall, references to the WTO SPS Agreement are less frequent than to the TBT Agreement and appear mainly in the articles on Definitions, Objective, Cooperation, SPS Committee, Equivalence, Science and Risk Analysis and Transparency.

In summary, we find that the TBT chapter of TPP is not only influenced by a larger number of previous PTAs but also incorporates more text from previous PTAs than the SPS chapter. US treaty language dominates both chapters. US negotiators used a large range of previous TBT chapters to influence the TPP TBT chapter. Interestingly, the USA is the only country that copied a considerably higher share of text from previous TBT chapters with non-TPP countries than from TBT chapters signed with TPP countries. On average, the USA managed to copy 30 per cent of previous TBT chapters into TPP. In contrast, US negotiators only copied an average of 20 per cent from previous chapters into the TPP SPS chapter. Nonetheless, in comparison to the influence of the other TPP countries, it can be said that TPP, to a large extent, is 'Made in America', as was proclaimed by US authorities at the time (Office of the United States Trade Representative, 2017).

This did not prevent the newly elected US president, however, from stopping the ratification procedures for TPP through a presidential order on his first day in office. The remaining eleven TPP countries reopened the negotiation process and eventually signed the Comprehensive and Progressive Agreement for Trans-Pacific Partnership (CPTPP) in March 2018. Having retreated from TPP, the USA focused on the renegotiation of NAFTA, its trade agreement with Canada and Mexico which came into force in 1994.

11.4.3 The United States–Mexico–Canada Agreement

NAFTA was by far the most comprehensive trade agreement to date and subsequently became an important template for future trade deals (Baccini et al., 2014). Its effects on the US, Canadian and Mexican economies, however, were always disputed and public opinion divided. The critique culminated in the 2016 US presidential campaign when the presidential candidate Donald Trump called NAFTA 'the single worst trade deal ever approved in [the United States]' (Politico, 2016). Between 2017 and 2018, the three countries renegotiated NAFTA. Its replacement, the USA–Mexico–Canada Agreement (USMCA), was announced during a G20 summit in late 2018.

In this section, we take a closer look at the TBT and SPS chapters of USMCA. We are primarily interested in two questions. First, is the USMCA an innovative agreement or is it mainly based on provisions from past agreements? Second, is the USMCA closely related to the US TTIP drafts that had been published two years before or does it follow a new approach? Figures 11.8 and 11.9 suggests that the TBT chapter is certainly inspired by TPP. More than a third of TPP's TBT chapter is copy-pasted into USMCA. On average, 21 per cent of text from previous PTAs

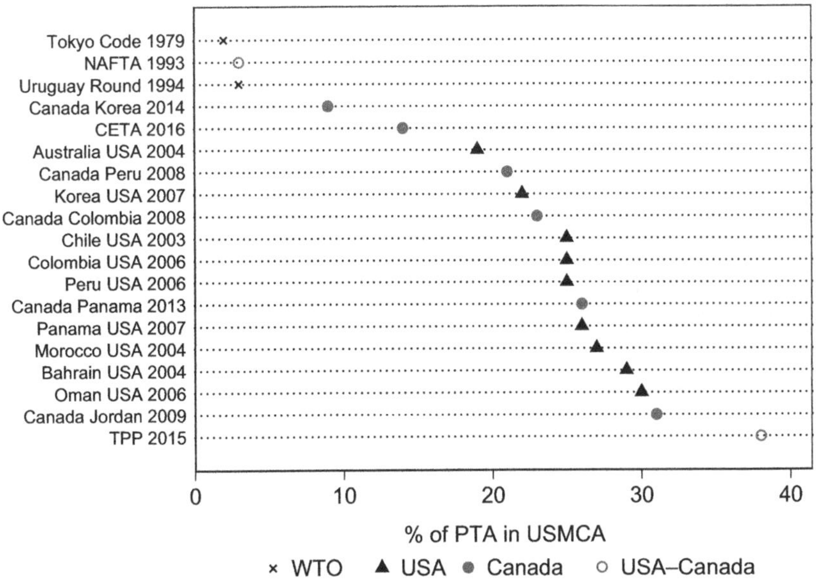

Figure 11.8 TBT in USMCA.
Source: Authors' illustration based on text-as-data analysis

was incorporated into the USMCA TBT chapter. Most of the other PTAs that influenced the USMCA TBT chapter are also previous US agreements. Our analysis suggests that Canadian negotiators were able to include some text from previous agreements, particularly from PTAs with Jordan, Panama, Colombia and Peru. Compared to the other agreements, however, there is relatively little text taken from CETA. The small textual overlap between the CETA and USMCA chapters on TBT may provide a first indication of the different approaches of the USA and the EU. Interestingly, none of the trade agreements that Mexico had previously signed are heavily featured in USMCA. From the TBT chapter of the original NAFTA, only 3 per cent of text was incorporated in USMCA. Article 11.3 of the USMCA TBT chapter incorporates most of the WTO TBT Agreement.[8]

The analysis of the USMCA chapter on SPS shows a similar pattern. On average, 23 per cent of text from previous PTAs was copy-pasted into USMCA. TPP is by far the most influential trade agreement – a striking

[8] The USMCA TBT chapter incorporates Articles 2.1, 2.2, 2.3, 2.4, 2.5, 2.9, 2.10, 2.11 and 2.12; Articles 3.1, 4.1 and 7.1; Articles 5.1, 5.2, 5.3, 5.4, 5.6, 5.7, 5.8 and 5.9; and Paragraphs D, E, F and J of Annex 3.

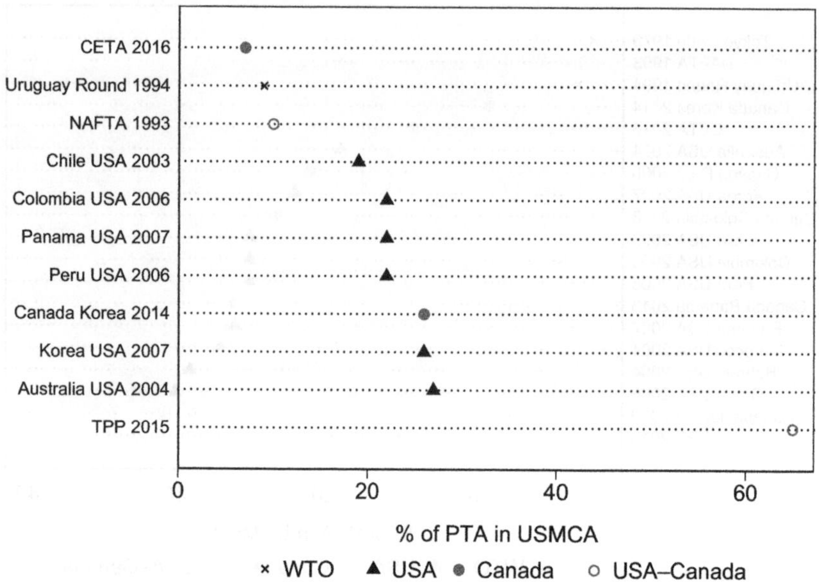

Figure 11.9 SPS in USMCA.
Source: Authors' illustration based on text-as-data analysis

65 per cent of its SPS chapter is transferred to USMCA. With the exception of Canada's agreements with Korea and the EU, it is again US PTAs from which most text is replicated in USMCA. As is the case for TBT, the overlap between CETA and USMCA is relatively small.

In summary, we find that around 20 per cent of the USMCA chapters on TBT and SPS is incorporated from previous agreements – in particular from previous US and Canadian agreements. We find that TPP served as a major source of text for both chapters but particularly for the SPS chapter. While there is some overlap with CETA, our analysis suggests that Canadian negotiators did not (manage to) incorporate significant amounts of its text into USMCA. Since CETA is the latest EU agreement with a North American country, this may also have an impact on future negotiations of a transatlantic deal between the EU and the USA.

11.4.4 The Transatlantic Trade and Investment Partnership

In this section, we focus on the TTIP draft proposals (published in 2016) of the EU and USA and contrast them in Figures 11.10 and 11.11. In order to understand which, if any, previous EU PTAs may have

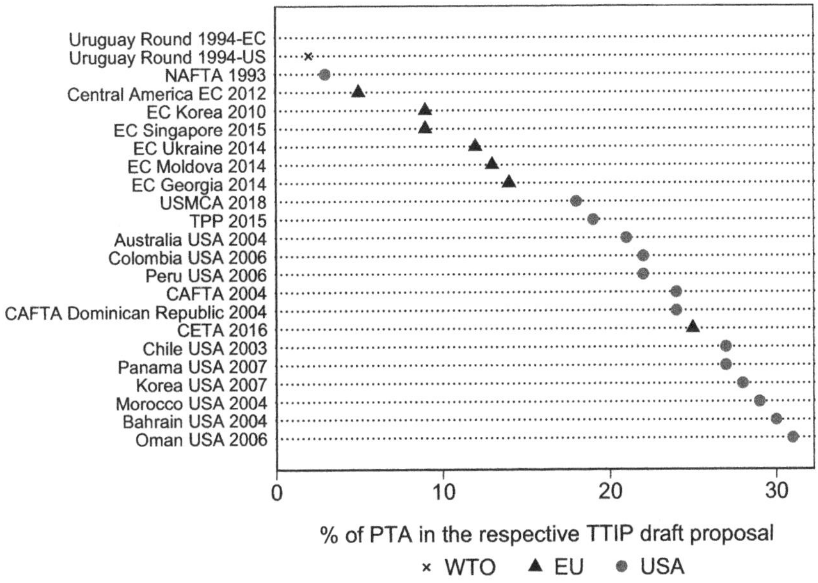

Figure 11.10 TBT in EU and US TTIP draft proposals.
Source: Authors' illustration based on text-as-data analysis

influenced the design of the EU's draft proposals for TTIP's TBT chapter, we compare the draft to twenty-eight previous EU PTAs as well as the two WTO TBT Agreements from 1979 (Tokyo Code) and 1994 (Uruguay Round). We find that only eight (27 per cent) of these texts had an impact and that, on average, only 11 per cent of their texts was incorporated into the EU's TBT draft for TTIP. By far the most significant share was copied from CETA – 26 per cent (Figure 11.10). A side-to-side comparison between CETA's chapter and the EU's TTIP TBT draft suggests that the largest parts were drawn from CETA's articles on Scope and Definitions, Cooperation, Technical Regulations and Transparency.

The US negotiators appear to have drawn more heavily from previous US PTAs when designing the TBT draft proposal. On average, 22 per cent of the most influential US TBT chapters was copied into the draft (Figure 11.10). They also seem to have used the full range of previous PTAs – out of the fifteen previous PTAs and the two TBT Agreements, only two treaties did not have an impact on the US TBT draft for TTIP.

The top three PTAs with Oman, Bahrain and Morocco, which also heavily influenced TPP, are found to be important text sources for American negotiators. Most text drawn from the USA–Bahrain PTA originated from its articles on Scope and Coverage, International Standards, Conformity Assessment Procedures and Transparency. An interesting observation is that the USA's most recently negotiated PTAs, the TPP and the USMCA, did not have significantly more overlap with the TTIP draft proposal than other, older, PTAs.

Whereas the share of text copied from the WTO TBT Agreement is small, the Agreement does present an important building block for the EU as it explicitly incorporates the TBT Agreement and makes it part of the TTIP draft as well as refers to it seven times. The US TBT draft proposal refers ten times to the WTO TBT Agreement with explicit references such as '*The Parties affirm their rights and obligations with respect to each other under the TBT Agreement.*'

CETA is also found to be the, by far, most important source of treaty text for the EU's SPS draft. Around a third of CETA's SPS chapter was copied into the TTIP draft proposal, mainly taken from its articles on Trade Conditions, Import Checks and Fees and the Joint Management Committee. Out of the fifteen available previous PTAs and the two TBT Agreements, EU negotiators only used eight texts (47 per cent) and copied an average of 10 per cent (Figure 11.11).

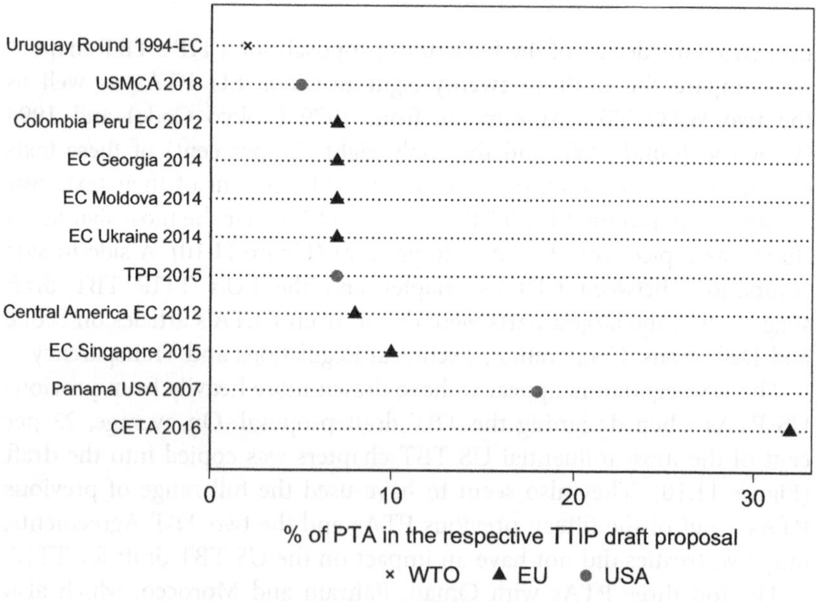

Figure 11.11 SPS in EU and US TTIP draft proposals.
Source: Authors' illustration based on text-as-data analysis

On the US side, we find again that text from TPP and USMCA is not heavily featured in the TTIP SPS proposal. Instead, the draft relies more on the 2007 agreement with Panama. Most text from the USA–Panama agreement was drawn from its article on the Committee on Sanitary and Phytosanitary Matters.

The EU and the USA both refer nine times to the WTO SPS Agreement with references such that they '. . . *affirm their rights and obligations [USA: with respect to each other] under the [USA: WTO] SPS Agreement*'.

In summary, we find a pattern that is similar to the previously discussed mega-regionals CETA, TPP and USMCA. Both EU and US negotiators drew less text from previous PTAs when drafting their SPS proposal than they did when drafting the TBT proposal. Furthermore, we find that the US TTIP proposals only overlap to a limited extent with TPP and USMCA. This is surprising since our previous analysis indicates that it was the USA who had the most influence on the text of these two agreements. In contrast, the EU TTIP proposals rely heavily on CETA – an agreement on which, according to our analysis, the EU managed to only include relatively little text from its previous agreements.

11.4.5 Comparing US and EU Draft Proposals for TTIP

The previous discussion indicates that the USA was particularly influential in designing the TBT and SPS chapters of TPP and USMCA while Canada managed to replicate considerable shares of its previous PTAs in CETA. It appears somewhat puzzling that the USA did not use much of the TPP template to draft the TBT and SPS chapters for TTIP, while the EU did rely heavily on CETA. This could be interpreted as the USA looking for a new approach going into the negotiations, with the EU having elaborated together with Canada some important design elements for its future approach. The final question we focus on is how compatible are the EU and US TTIP drafts and in which areas do they converge or diverge?

We offer below a side-by-side comparison for two selected areas. We have chosen two different design features, namely scope and coverage (capturing the ambitions and objectives) and standard-setting processes (capturing the regulatory philosophy). In relation to the article of the Scope and Coverage (USA) and the Objective and Scope (EU) (Table 11.4), we observe substantial convergence. The text in bold shows the text overlaps that the text-as-data analysis using WCopyfind identifies. The underlined passages show the text that we regard as de facto

Table 11.4 *US vs EU TTIP TBT: objective, scope and coverage*

Scope and coverage (USA)	Objective and scope (EU)
This Chapter applies to the preparation, adoption, and application of standards, technical regulations, and conformity assessment procedures of covered bodies that may, directly or indirectly, **affect trade in goods between the Parties**, including **any amendments thereto and any additions to** their rules or product coverage, except amendments and additions of an insignificant nature. Notwithstanding paragraph 1, **this chapter does not apply to: (a) purchasing specifications prepared** by governmental bodies **for production or consumption requirements of** such **bodies; or (b) sanitary and phytosanitary measures as defined in Annex A of the Agreement on the Application of Sanitary and Phytosanitary Measures.**	The objective of this Chapter is to promote convergence in regulatory approaches by reducing or eliminating conflicting technical requirements as well as redundant and burdensome conformity assessment requirements. **This Chapter applies to the preparation, adoption and application of** technical regulations, standards and conformity assessment procedures that may **affect trade in goods between the Parties.** **This chapter does not apply to:** **(a) purchasing specifications prepared by** a governmental body **for production or consumption requirements** of governmental bodies; or **(b) sanitary and phytosanitary measures as defined in Annex A of the** WTO **Agreement on the Application of Sanitary and Phytosanitary Measures.** All references in this Chapter to technical regulations, standards and conformity assessment procedures shall be construed to include **any amendments thereto and any additions to** the rules or the product coverage thereof.

Source: Respective TTIP draft proposals.

matches but that the software did not identify because the word strings did not meet the requirement of six identical consecutive words. Both parties use similar language, the EU explicitly stating the objective of the TBT chapter being the only significant difference.

Arguably, this presents more of a difference in the mode of expression and linguistic style than a difference in substance. Below we focus on standard-setting processes – an area in which long-standing divergences exist in terms of the regulatory approach.

As outlined in detail by Büthe and Mattli (2011), the TBT-related standard-setting processes between the USA and the EU are for historical reasons systematically different. While the US American system is characterized by fragmentation, overlap and competition among multiple standard-setters, the standard-setting processes in the EU are hierarchical and coordinated by the European Committee for Standardization (CEN) and the European Committee for Electrotechnical Standardization (CENELEC). Both organizations have cooperation agreements with the International Organization for Standardization (ISO) and the International Electrotechnical Commission (IEC), resulting in a considerable overlap of standards. The overlap between US standards and ISO/IEC standards, in stark contrast, is estimated to be below 1 per cent (Egan and Pelkmans, 2015). While the WTO TBT Agreement does not define international standards exclusively as the products of ISO and IEC, Annex 1 and 3 of the WTO TBT Agreement do assign them a prominent role and a certain degree of regulatory authority.

The differences in interest are evident. While the USA has an incentive to either limit the prominence of ISO/IEC standards as international standards or strengthen its influence in the standard development at ISO and IEC, the EU has an incentive to find ways for the USA to begin adopting more systematically ISO and IEC standards (Egan and Pelkmans, 2015). Following this logic, we find some nuanced indications of these opposing positions in the respective TTIP drafts. For instance, while the European draft includes – already ambitious – provisions on the cooperation between standardization bodies, the USA seems to go beyond this as it is very much concerned about '*allow[ing] persons of the other Party to participate on terms no less favorable than persons of the Party*' in standard-setting processes (Table 11.5).

While a detailed discussion is beyond the scope of this chapter, we also find evidence of diverging views on the definition of international standards as well as on different aspects of conformity assessment procedures.[9]

Overall, we find that the EU and USA use similar language for horizontal articles such as on the scope and coverage as well as general

[9] For a related discussion on this topic, see Egan and Pelkmans (2015).

Table 11.5 *US vs EU TTIP TBT: standards and standardization*

Standards (US)	Standardization (EU)
Where a Party requests a body to develop a standard that may be used for purposes of complying in whole or part with technical regulation or conformity assessment procedure, the Party shall specify in the request that the body shall: (a) allow **persons of the other Party** with relevant technical expertise to participate in any of its technical bodies, including by accessing working documents, attending meetings, submitting technical proposals and advice concerning development of the standard, and ensuring prompt consideration of any such proposals and advice; (b) not impose conditions on such participation that impede **persons of the other Party** with relevant technical expertise from participating, such as obligations to adopt or implement the standard, to withdraw an existing standard, to be affiliated with a national standards body or other entity that includes persons of the Party, or represent a national position or view; . . .	The Parties shall promote closer cooperation between the standardization bodies located within their respective territories with a view to facilitating, inter alia: (a) the exchange of information about their respective activities, (b) the harmonization of standards based on mutual interest and reciprocity, according to modalities to be agreed directly by the standardization bodies concerned, (c) the development of common standards, and (d) the identification of suitable areas for such co-operation, in particular in new technologies.

Source: Respective TTIP draft proposals.

cooperation. The more detailed articles, in contrast, do include some nuanced differences that reflect long-standing and partly conflicting views on issues such as standardization and conformity assessment. The brief analysis of TTIP suggests that the political power of countries in standard-setting organizations and conformity assessment bodies is reflected in their approach to designing corresponding chapters in trade agreements – a topic which needs further exploration.

11.5 Conclusions

Trade agreements have always been somewhat contested; however, the criticism that the new generation of mega-regional agreements (CETA, TPP and TTIP) has received is unprecedented. An important area of contestation relates to the envisaged cooperation on behind-the-border issues, so-called non-tariff measures (NTMs).

In this chapter, we took a close look at the core of NTMs, namely technical barriers to trade (TBT) and sanitary and phytosanitary measures (SPS) in the afore-mentioned trade agreements to address three questions. First, how much innovation versus imitation characterizes CETA, TPP and USMCA? Second, to which extent do CETA and TPP present templates for TTIP? Third, in which areas do the EU and USA converge and diverge?

Using a text-as-data approach, we find that in all four agreements negotiators rely more heavily on texts from previous PTAs when designing the TBT chapter than the SPS chapter. In both chapters in the TPP and USMCA treaties, we identify a considerable prominence of legal texts from existing trade deals, predominantly from US agreements. By contrast, CETA negotiators relied less on previous PTAs and appear to have developed a more innovative approach to TBT and SPS matters. We also find evidence suggesting that EU negotiators attempt to implement these innovations in TTIP. Indeed, the European draft proposals for the TBT and SPS chapters of TTIP rely heavily on CETA text. Interestingly, TPP plays a fairly limited role in the US draft proposal for TTIP, even though it is an agreement largely written by the USA and most recent. Similarly, we find relatively little overlap between the US TTIP proposal and the USMCA. Finally, we find that the EU and USA converge on general topics such as the objective, scope and coverage of TBT and SPS in TTIP but do diverge in more detailed items such as standard-setting processes and conformity assessment procedures.

The findings of this chapter open up multiple avenues for future research. In particular, we intend to further explore the possibilities that text-as-data methodologies offer. While the quantification of text overlaps between agreements provides us with a first indication of the distribution of negotiation power, we would like to learn more about the content that is actually being copied from one agreement to the next. Are the copied text passages merely standard provisions or do they contain substantial concessions that define the trade relations between the PTA signatories? A second avenue we intend to explore further is the nexus between the processes at standard-setting organizations and the design of related PTA chapters. More precisely, we would like to build on the above TTIP discussion and address the question as to whether, and if so how, countries' political power at standard-setting organizations such as ISO and the Codex Alimentarius affects the design of the TBT and SPS chapters in trade agreements.

12

Nontariff Responses to China's Development Strategy

The WTO's Interface Challenge*

CHAD P. BOWN

12.1 Introduction

China's accession to the World Trade Organization (WTO) in 2001 came after lengthy negotiations. China's exporters were granted nondiscriminatory tariff treatment by what are now more than 160 other WTO member countries. For its part, China agreed to carry out numerous steps to open itself to global trade and investment markets. In return for its agreement to abide by certain rules that normally govern a market economy, China was led to believe that trading partners like the United States would officially revoke its nonmarket economy (NME) status in December 2016.[1] For China, the practical consideration of such a step was that its exporters would stop facing a special type of trade restriction.

* Bown thanks Junie Joseph for outstanding research assistance and Caroline Freund, Joseph Gagnon, Gary Hufbauer, Nicholas Lardy, Rory MacFarquhar, Jeff Schott, and Nicolas Veron for useful comments. Madona Devasahayam, Barbara Karni, and Steve Weisman provided invaluable editorial assistance. An earlier version of this chapter was circulated as Bown (2016a).

[1] In February 2000, for example, then-US Trade Representative Charlene Barshefsky told the House of Representatives' Ways and Means Committee that "China's WTO entry will guarantee our right to continue using our current 'non-market economy' methodology in anti-dumping cases for fifteen years after China's accession to the WTO" (Charlene Barshefsky, testimony during the hearing on the US–China bilateral trade agreement and accession of China to the WTO, Committee on Ways and Means, House of Representatives, 106th Congress, Second Session, February 16, 2000, www.gpo.gov/fdsys/pkg/CHRG-106hhrg67129/html/CHRG-106hhrg67129.htm). See also Gary Clyde Hufbauer and Cathleen Cimino-Isaacs, "The Outlook for Market Economy Status for China," Trade and Investment Policy Watch blog, April 11, 2016, Peterson Institute for International Economics, Washington, DC.

The milestone of December 2016 has focused attention on both short- and long-run issues confronting the international trading system. The first and immediate concern for countries like the United States is whether a sudden requirement to begin treating China as a market economy makes it too difficult to stem the flow of low-priced imports. But the second and more complex issue involves how to address the fact that China, while making tremendous strides over its first fifteen years in the WTO, has nevertheless not completely transformed into a transparent, market-oriented economy. In fact, China's subsequent domestic transformation introduced new and unexpected challenges to international cooperation over trade policy that may pose a systemic threat to the WTO.

The longer-run issue is not a new theoretical concern. The legal scholar John H. Jackson referred to it as the "interface question"; even during the period of the General Agreement on Tariffs and Trade (GATT), and more than a decade before China was granted entry into the WTO, he described it as

> Many of the unfair trading practices ... have been considered unfair because they interfere with or distort free-market-economy principles. GATT, of course, was largely based on such principles. It is not surprising, therefore, that it is often difficult to apply GATT's trading rules to nonmarket economies.
>
> (Jackson, 1989, p. 218)

What is new is the magnitude and the immediacy of the modern interface challenge. This is due to the combined size of China's nonmarket economy, the depth of its integration into the international system, and the implication that its policy choices may impose considerable externalities on trading partners. This is important, given that the economics literature indicates a key role for agreements like the WTO is to coordinate national policies so as to neutralize international externalities (Bagwell, Bown, and Staiger, 2016).

This chapter begins by introducing the terms of China's protocol of WTO accession (Section 12.2), before then turning to a description of how the United States has chosen to apply its antidumping and countervailing duty laws toward China during the first fifteen years of China's WTO membership (Section 12.3). There I also describe some of the elements behind China's incomplete transformation to a market economy that have given rise to these short- and long-run dilemmas confronting the international system.

Then, in Section 12.4, I examine data to assess whether a potential change in China's NME status reduces the United States' access to special trade policies in a way that might result in a sudden surge in imports from China. For the United States – the case study under examination – I conclude that the answer is likely no, but this is primarily due to a recent US policy decision to begin use of countervailing duties (CVDs) against China. Most US antidumping duties applied against China between 2007 and 2015 were accompanied by a simultaneous CVD. A change in China's NME status that reduced the size of US applied antidumping duties – further described in Section 12.5 – may thus result in only a modest increase in imports.

Nevertheless, in Section 12.6, I turn to the potential consequences of a failure by the United States and the existing WTO membership to negotiate a solution to the NME issue with China. The most benign outcome has China pursuing a formal grievance with the WTO, which, after two or three years of litigation, a country like the United States could lose. At that point, a continued failure to resolve China's NME status could result in China being legally authorized to retaliate by raising its tariffs on US exports. More immediately, China could impose costs on the United States and other WTO members by retaliating outside of the rules. China first engaged in such behavior vis-à-vis the United States in 2009 by repeatedly imposing WTO-inconsistent antidumping duties against US exporters in response to its discontent over US trade policy decisions. At its peak in 2011, China's antidumping covered 8 percent of total US goods exports to China, adversely affecting billions of dollars of US auto, poultry, specialty steel, and agricultural products.

Section 12.7 then concludes by returning to long-term and systemic concerns. There I provide a more normative discussion of considerations needed when applying Jackson's interface question to China's integration into the WTO system.

12.2 China's 2001 WTO Accession Protocol

China's protocol of accession included a specific provision allowing existing WTO members to treat China as an NME in antidumping investigations. The legal question (not addressed here) is whether this provision expired automatically after fifteen years (as of December 11, 2016). Article 15(a)(ii) of China's accession protocol (WTO, 2001) contains the language explicitly permitting other WTO members to treat China as an NME in their antidumping investigations. The controversy arises in part because Article 15(d) then indicates that "the provisions of subparagraph (a)(ii) shall expire 15 years after the date of accession."

The unsettled legal question is how to interpret the remaining elements of Article 15 if Article 15(a)(ii) is removed. Are WTO members permitted to continue to treat China as an NME in antidumping investigations as before, or must they stop? Do the remaining provisions somehow create an intermediate scenario, in which a country can still use NME techniques in dealing with China, but the burden of proof for justifying China as an NME shifts to the country affected by China's actions? The focus of this chapter is on the implications of different potential policy decisions the United States and China might undertake; I will not attempt to address the legal issue potentially confronting the WTO's Dispute Settlement Body.

Under US law, the Department of Commerce must take various factors into consideration in determining whether a trading partner is an NME (Table 12.1). Based on its assessment of these factors, the United States through 2016 continued to treat China as an NME.[2]

While the formal analysis below is limited to the United States, the United States is not the only country for which the China NME issue has been important. The European Union and Japan have similarly treated China as an NME under their antidumping laws, just like several major emerging economies. Many of the same import-competing manufacturing sectors in these countries, for example, faced the same concerns as the US industries described below.[3]

12.3 US Law on Antidumping and Countervailing Duties

The WTO Agreement on Antidumping and Agreement on Subsidies and Countervailing Measures detail the basic provisions that members must follow when implementing their antidumping and CVD procedures. The

[2] In December 2005, Chinese respondent firms in a US antidumping investigation asked the Department of Commerce to reevaluate China's NME status. The department accommodated the request, issuing memos in May and August 2006 updating its rationale for continuing to apply NME methodologies to China. The first memo (Department of Commerce, 2006a) focused on distortions in China's banking sector; the second (Department of Commerce, 2006b) provided a more comprehensive explanation of each of the US statutory factors for NME designation listed in Table 12.1.

[3] For a discussion of non-US use of antidumping against China and the NME issue, see Chad P. Bown, "China's Market Economy Status and Antidumping: A $100 Billion, $10 Billion, or $1 Billion Dispute?" Trade and Investment Policy Watch blog, June 8, 2016, Peterson Institute for International Economics, Washington, DC.

Table 12.1 *Factors the US Department of Commerce must consider in identifying a country as a nonmarket economy*

Factor	Legal language
Currency	(i) the extent to which the currency of the foreign country is convertible into the currency of other countries
Wages	(ii) the extent to which wage rates in the foreign country are determined by free bargaining between labor and management
Inbound foreign direct investment	(iii) the extent to which joint ventures or other investments by firms of other foreign countries are permitted in the foreign country
Other inputs	(iv) the extent of government ownership or control of the means of production
Price controls and output	(v) the extent of government control over the allocation of resources and over the price and output decisions of enterprises
Anything else	(vi) such other factors as the administering authority considers appropriate

Source: Omnibus Trade and Competitiveness Act of 1988, from which the legal language quotes directly. The "administering authority" in factor (vi) is currently the Department of Commerce.

next two sections describe how the United States applies those laws, including how they are applied to imports from an NME.

12.3.1 How Does the United States Apply Its Antidumping Law?

Under US antidumping law, the government investigates whether a foreign firm is selling its product in the United States at a price that is less than fair value (LTFV) and whether those imported sales injure the import-competing US industry.[4] The US International Trade

[4] This chapter does not address the fact that some types of normal, profit-maximizing behavior (without predatory intent or effect) can satisfy the legal definition of dumping described below. Examples include international price discrimination and behavior by large fixed-cost industries whose short-run production decision involves whether the market price covers average variable (not total) costs. Blonigen and Prusa (2016) survey the economics literature on dumping and antidumping. Bown and Crowley (2013a) present evidence that some US antidumping use can be understood as a short-run

Commission conducts the injury investigation; its process is largely unaffected by the NME issue described here and is therefore not examined below. The Department of Commerce conducts the separate and independent dumping investigation. The trading partner's NME status directly affect its procedures.

In general, Commerce's dumping determination relies on one of three methods to establish the fair value benchmark: (a) the price in the exporter's home market for the foreign firm's sales of the same good, (b) the price in a third-country market in which that exporter sells the same good, or (c) a constructed value of the exporting firm's costs.

Commerce's historical concern for exporters from NMEs like China is that the data used to construct the fair value benchmark could be misleading where supply and demand forces are not at work. That is, observed NME "prices" of final goods under methods (a) or (b) or of factor inputs like labor or capital under method (c) may not be reliable indicators, because they could lead to a downward bias in the fair value benchmark, which could make it less likely to find evidence of dumping. To address this concern, a new approach was developed that provided Commerce with flexibility to rely on price data from "surrogate" countries to construct an LTFV benchmark in investigations involving exporting firms from NMEs.

Consider an example. Suppose Commerce was asked to investigate whether imports from a Chinese company that produces steel pipes were dumped into the US market.[5] Because China is an NME, Commerce needs to identify a surrogate country. The surrogate must be a market economy (so that information from input and output prices are meaningful), be at a comparable level of economic development as China, have domestic production in the industry being investigated, and have data that are relatively accessible, so that proxy measures of the Chinese firm's costs under method (c) can be developed.

Suppose India is selected as the surrogate country. To perform the calculation, Commerce would take the quantities of the inputs used to make the pipe (hours of labor, units of raw material, etc.) provided by the Chinese company and multiply them by the prices of the inputs using

"escape" – from otherwise low levels of US import tariff protection – in the face of bilateral import volume surges.

5 This example is loosely based on a 2007 antidumping and countervailing duty investigation of circular welded pipe from China, described in the panel report of the US antidumping and countervailing duties dispute with China (WTO, 2010).

Indian data.[6] If the price of the Chinese pipe sold in the US market is less than the constructed measure of the Chinese steel pipe firm's cost (the fair value benchmark), Commerce would find that the Chinese firm had dumped. The size of the applied antidumping duty (the "dumping margin") is the difference between the constructed fair value benchmark and the US import sales price.

If China is not an NME, Commerce would have to rely on data provided by the Chinese steel pipe firm on its actual costs, the price of the good sold in China, or the price of good sold in a third market. From China's perspective, NME status provides Commerce with excessive discretion, making it more likely to find evidence of dumping and higher dumping margins than if China were treated as a market economy.

12.3.2 How Does the United States Apply Its Countervailing Duty Law on Imports from China?

US law allows the government to investigate whether a foreign firm that is selling its product in the United States has been subsidized, and whether those subsidized imports are injuring import-competing US producers. In broad terms, a subsidy is defined as a financial contribution from the government (or any public body) of a trading partner to a foreign firm that confers a benefit to that firm. If the US industry is injured and there is evidence that the injury was caused by subsidized imports, the United States can impose a CVD equal to the subsidy rate.

The Department of Commerce conducts CVD investigations. In the mid-1980s, it made the decision not to conduct CVD investigations on imports from NMEs. In 2006 it reversed that decision with respect to China and began investigating petitions alleging subsidized imports from China.[7] Beginning in 2007 the USA argued that it could apply its CVD

[6] Commerce would also add in profit, factory overhead, as well as selling, general, and administrative (SG&A) expenses, constructed based on the ratio of these components of costs to the costs of the other inputs in India.

[7] In November 2006, the department initiated its first CVD investigation on imports from China, deviating from a long-held practice of not considering NMEs under CVD law, its practice since a 1984 decision (*Georgetown Steel*). The 2006 investigation involved imports of coated free sheet paper from China. It was conducted in parallel with an antidumping investigation. This investigation is important historically because it was the first US CVD investigation of China that found subsidies. No CVDs were applied, however, because the International Trade Commission did not find evidence of injury in the final determination.

law because it was possible for Chinese firms to receive the equivalent of government subsidies.

The United States' argument for the reversal was that although China had made steps toward becoming more market oriented overall, important nonmarket economic forces remained.[8] In some areas of the economy, for example, the Chinese government or Chinese Communist Party continued to interfere. Government officials or party members were taking leadership positions on company boards; this allowed them to implement industrial policy set out at the national or regional level, including through holding companies such as the State-Owned Assets Supervision and Administration Commission of the State Council (SASAC). The United States also alleged that state-owned enterprises (SOEs) had not been fully phased out of certain sectors in China, including banking and hot-rolled steel, a key input for many downstream steel products, as well as petrochemicals. It also alleged that China underpriced some commercial rents.

To see how a CVD investigation works, consider a Chinese steel pipe manufacturer alleged to have had access to implicitly subsidized inputs. The pipe is a downstream steel product made from cheap hot-rolled steel bought from a Chinese SOE, the loans to finance the operation were provided by a Chinese state-owned commercial bank at below-market interest rates, and the pipe factory was constructed on land that did not require market-based rents. The US government argued that these implicitly subsidized inputs conferred a benefit to the Chinese firm in its pipe production.

To determine the size of the subsidy, the Department of Commerce developed methods analogous to the surrogate country approach it used in antidumping determinations. However, instead of drawing the proxy information from a single surrogate country, it used multiple techniques. As a surrogate for the Chinese price for the hot-rolled steel input, Commerce relied on the world market price for hot-rolled steel. Instead of actual land rents paid by the Chinese firm, it turned to land prices from Bangkok, Thailand. Instead of interest rates at Chinese state-owned

[8] The Department of Commerce's arguments are developed in a series of public memos (Department of Commerce, 2006a, 2006b, 2007); see also Smith (2013). Lardy (2014) provides empirical evidence of the declining role of the state in the Chinese economy during the 2000s. Wu (2016) provides an insightful analysis of the conflicts between the evolution of the Chinese economy over this period and the legal disciplines under the WTO.

commercial banks, Commerce used a regression analysis of inflation-adjusted interest rates in thirty-three lower-middle-income countries to construct a benchmark interest rate for the firm's costs of borrowing. This approach allowed Commerce to construct a measure of the Chinese firm's costs to reveal the size of the implicit subsidy, which would determine the CVD it could apply if the International Trade Commission also found evidence of injury caused by the subsidy.[9]

Commerce began to use such an approach in CVD investigations of imports from China in 2006, with the first CVDs applied in 2007. China has subsequently challenged certain procedural elements of the new US approach through formal WTO dispute settlement, with mixed legal decisions.

Commerce has continued to use these methods to investigate whether imports from China are unfairly subsidized. It received more than fifty petitions between 2006 and 2015, imposing CVDs in roughly 75 percent of the completed investigations. Investigations have covered steel products, chemicals, tires, wood products, and even solar panels and wind towers. Almost all CVD investigations involving imports from China during this period have been conducted simultaneously with antidumping investigations.

12.4 US Imports from China and Imports Affected by Antidumping and Countervailing Duties

China's exports to the United States stood at roughly $500 billion in 2015. They were almost four times higher than they were immediately before China joined the WTO, in 2001 (Figure 12.1).

At the same time as China's exports to the United States were growing rapidly, the United States was imposing antidumping import restrictions on an increasingly large share of those imports. On a trade-weighted basis, less than 1.5 percent of China's total goods exports to the USA were subject to a US-imposed antidumping import restriction in 2000. By 2015 US-imposed antidumping import restrictions affected roughly 7 percent (about $35 billion) of China's annual exports to the United

[9] Where both dumping and subsidies are found, so that the Department of Commerce can simultaneously apply an antidumping duty and a CVD on the same product, the size of the duties must be adjusted to avoid double-counting of, say, the subsidy in the amount by which the firm was found to have priced below LTFV. See Prusa and Vermulst (2013) for a discussion of this issue.

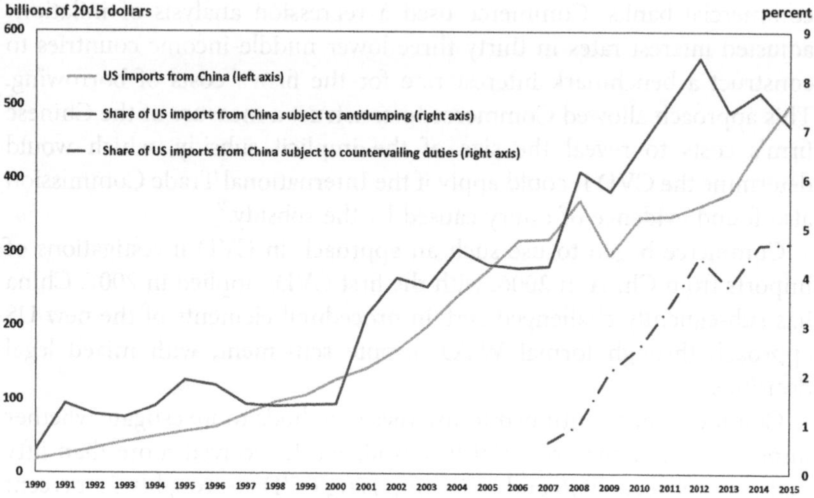

Figure 12.1 US goods imports from China and bilateral import share subject to antidumping and countervailing duties, 1990–2015.

Note: Shares are trade-weighted import coverage ratios, following the methodology in Bown (2011). The United States first applied a countervailing duty to imports from China in 2007

Source: Data in Bown (2016b) and six-digit Harmonized System trade data from UN Comtrade, made available through World Integrated Trade Solution (WITS)

States.[10] The significant uptick after 2007 is consistent with research indicating that import restrictions tend to increase during macroeconomic slowdowns – e.g., the Great Recession – and periods of sharp appreciation of the real exchange rate.[11] Yet, to the extent that China believes that its exports to the United States have been limited because of its treatment under NME status, it is clear why China is concerned about its NME status.

[10] This estimate is an import coverage ratio and is based on the methodology first developed by Bown (2011). This $35 billion is not an estimate of how much China's exports decreased because of US-imposed antidumping import restrictions. Such an estimate requires information on product-level elasticities of the import-responsiveness to import duties and is beyond the scope of this chapter.

[11] See, for example, the analysis by Bown and Crowley (2013b) of the United States' use of antidumping, CVD, and safeguard measures use 1988–2010, including during the Great Recession.

An alternative interpretation of China's NME status is that it was the price to be paid for the overall benefits of WTO accession. Put differently, roughly 93 percent of China's annual exports of $500 billion to the United States were not subject to antidumping or countervailing duties in 2015. In exchange for NME status, China received nondiscriminatory tariff treatment—and relatively low duties and secure access—to the US import market for roughly $465 billion in annual trade.[12]

Figure 12.1 also shows the share of US imports from China that is subject to US-imposed CVDs. Between 2007 and 2015, when the United States imposed its first CVD on Chinese imports, most new US antidumping investigations involving imported products from China have been accompanied by a CVD investigation. The shares of US imports from China that are subject to antidumping *and to* CVDs increased between 2007 and 2015. In addition, there is evidence of a significant reduction in the difference between the two series. In 2007 there was a 3.6 percentage-point gap between the level of US imports from China covered by antidumping and the level of US imports covered by CVDs. By 2015 that gap had narrowed to 2.4 percent.[13] The implication is that by 2015 more than two-thirds of US imports from China covered by antidumping duties were also covered by CVDs.

US imports from China vary widely by sector (Figure 12.2). The largest import sector in 2015 was electronics and electronic machinery ($136 billion). Figure 12.2 also documents heterogeneity in the share of bilateral industry-level imports subject to special trade protection. Roughly 31 percent of US imports from China in the metals sector in 2015 were covered by a US antidumping duty, compared to only 5 percent of textiles and

[12] Compare, for example, China's choice of accepting NME treatment in exchange for being granted most favored nation (MFN) tariff treatment with the choice that Japan accepted when it joined the multilateral trading system in 1955. At the time of Japan's entry into the GATT, more than fifty countries invoked a general GATT exception that allowed them not to apply the same MFN tariff on Japanese imports that they applied to imports from all other GATT members (Bown and Crowley, 2016). Many countries continued to discriminate against imports from Japan in this manner until the early 1970s. The United States was an exception; it applied MFN tariffs on Japanese imports, addressing trade frictions with Japan primarily through antidumping and negotiated voluntary export restraints (Bown and McCulloch, 2009).

[13] Most of the post-2007 applications of new antidumping have been accompanied by new CVDs, but the post-2007 removals of the US antidumping duties on China imposed before 2007 were not accompanied by any removals of CVDs. Recall that a 1984 policy decision (*Georgetown Steel*) meant that the United States did not impose CVDs on imports from China prior to 2007.

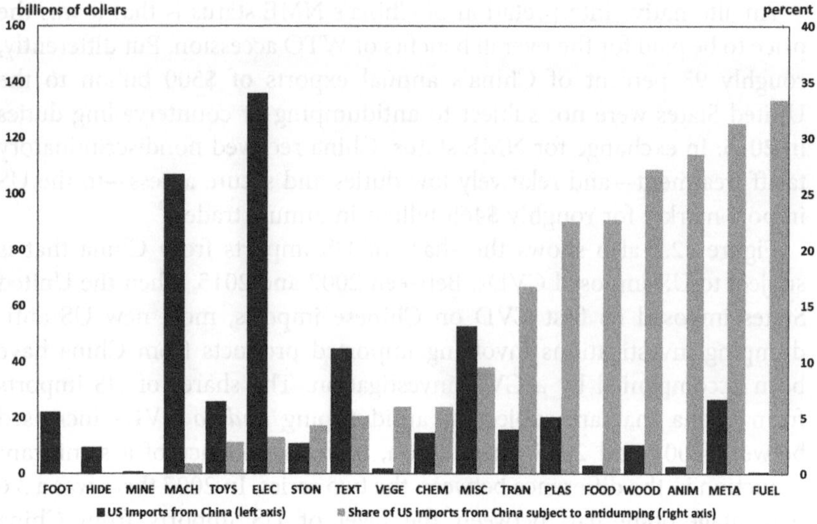

Figure 12.2 US goods imports from China and bilateral import share subject to antidumping in 2015, by sector.
Note: Shares are trade-weighted import coverage ratios following the methodology presented in Bown (2011). See Table 12.A1 in the Appendix for industry definitions
Source: Data in Bown (2016b) and six-digit Harmonized System trade data from UN Comtrade made available through World Integrated Trade Solution (WITS)

apparel and 3 percent of electronics and electronic machinery. And there were no US antidumping duties facing imports of footwear or minerals, and very little addressing machinery.

Trade restrictions and import levels are negatively correlated (the correlation is about –0.3). US imports from China tend to be smaller in sectors where there is more antidumping protection (in industries such as metals, wood products, plastic and rubber products, and animal and food products).[14] There is much less US antidumping protection in sectors with high levels of bilateral imports (textiles and apparel products, machinery, and electronics). These sectors cover more than half of US imports from China in 2015 but only about 20 percent of total US antidumping activity against China.

[14] The level of antidumping coverage of fuel products is high, despite the extremely low level of imports, because of import restrictions on foundry coke.

Any change in NME status would be expected to affect not only new dumping investigations involving China but also reviews of existing levels of applied duties. The Department of Commerce would eventually need to determine how the dozens of antidumping duties in place would be affected and whether and when they need to be recalculated.

12.5 How Large Are US Antidumping Duties on Imports from China?

The United States has historically imposed higher antidumping duties on imports from China than on imports from other trading partners (Table 12.2). Across all antidumping cases imposed as of 2015, US duties on China averaged 81.4 percent – more than 27 percentage points higher than duties on other trading partners (54.3 percent), most of which were treated as market economies. The difference is even larger when controlling for the product investigated (107.3 percent versus 58.0 percent). China would argue that it faced higher duties than other exporting countries because of the surrogate country discretion that NME treatment provides. The United States would argue that China faced higher duties because it was an NME.

The average US antidumping duty imposed on China has increased over time, as the United States began imposing such duties together with countervailing duties in 2007. The average US antidumping duty on China in antidumping cases that were jointly conducted with CVD investigations (96.4 percent) is more than twenty percentage points higher than the average US-imposed antidumping duty imposed without a CVD (72.1 percent).

The separate (and additive) US-imposed countervailing duty in these simultaneously conducted cases against China is also sizable. The thirty-three cases with a US-imposed CVD on imports from China had an average CVD of 83.8 percent, in addition to an average antidumping duty of 96.4 percent.[15]

Consider the implication of this last comparison. If a US change in China's NME status reduced the size of the average antidumping duty imposed, a large and independently determined US CVD – 83.8 percent on average as of 2015 – would remain in effect. And as Figure 12.1 indicates, an increasing share of US imports from China have also been

[15] The average US-imposed CVD against China is also considerably higher than the US-imposed CVDs on other trading partners (83.8 percent versus 30.7 percent).

Table 12.2 *US antidumping and countervailing duties applied in 2015*

Exporter	Number of cases	Average anti-dumping duty (percent)	Exporter	Number of cases	Average anti-dumping duty (percent)
All antidumping cases					
China			**Other trading partners**		
All cases involving China	89	81.4	All cases involving other trading partners	149	54.3
Cases involving only China	58	67.5	Cases not involving China at all	93	52.1
Cases involving China & others	31	107.3	Cases involving China & others	56	58.0
Antidumping only (no simultaneous CVD)					
China			**Other trading partners**		
All cases involving China	55	72.1	All cases involving other trading partners	111	54.4
Cases involving only China	37	69.9	Cases not involving China at all	64	50.0
Cases involving China & others	18	76.5	Cases involving China & others	47	60.5
Antidumping and CVD simultaneously					
China			**Other trading partners**		
All cases involving China	34	96.4	All cases involving other trading partners	38	54.2

Cases involving only China	21	63.3	Cases not involving China at all	29	57.0
Cases involving China & others	13	149.9	Cases involving China & others	9	45.0

Exporter	**Number of cases**	**Average CVD (percent)**	**Exporter**	**Number of cases**	**Average CVD (percent)**
All CVD cases					
China			**Other trading partners**		
All cases involving China	33	83.8	All cases involving other trading partners	27	30.7
Cases involving only China	30	79.3	Cases not involving China at all	25	31.8
Cases involving China & others	3	128.4	Cases involving China & others	2	17.5

Note: A case is defined at the country-product level (one case involving China may be associated with multiple cases associated with other trading partners also being investigated over the same product). The average duty is computed from the simple average of the final duty imposed at the final determination, as reported in the Federal Register; it does not include adjustments for administrative reviews.
Source: Data from Bown (2016b).

subject to US-imposed CVD protection – 4.7 percent of total US imports from China in 2015 – and were thus covered by both antidumping and countervailing duties.

12.6 Retaliation and China's Policy Response If the United States Does Not Change Its Nonmarket Economy Status

The failure of the United States and other WTO members to come to a political settlement with China over the NME issue could lead to China's retaliation.

First, China has filed formal trade complaints against the United States – as well as the European Union – with the WTO.[16] Although it may take two to three years for the full legal process to be resolved – a panel report, an appeal, and a period to obtain legal authorization for retaliation – the United States, for example, could lose. If the United States did lose and still refused to bring its antidumping procedure into WTO conformity, the WTO could authorize China to retaliate. China would likely be authorized to do so by raising its import tariffs against the United States by an amount equivalent to the estimated annual value of lost Chinese exports to the US market due to NME status.[17] Furthermore, letting the WTO litigation simply run its course would place an enormous burden on the rules-based trading system, regardless of how the appellate body decides.

Second, China could engage in WTO-illegal retaliation. By taking matters into its own hands, it could impose losses more quickly on US exporters in the hope of speeding up US policy engagement.[18] One

[16] China filed these two disputes (DS515 and DS516) against the United States and European Union, respectively, in December 2016. For a discussion see Bown (2016c).

[17] Such a calculation would require estimates of counterfactual levels of Chinese exports to the United States in products affected by the WTO-inconsistent element of the antidumping restrictions. The task of the WTO would be to use an economic model to identify counterfactual levels of Chinese exports under an assumption that the United States had imposed WTO-consistent levels of antidumping duties instead. Bown and Brewster (2017) describe WTO methods to construct such estimates under a different type of WTO-inconsistent policy, related to a dispute between the United States, Canada, and Mexico over a regulation affecting beef and pork products.

[18] China has also shown its willingness to use antidumping to retaliate against the European Union. For example, when the European Union used antidumping against low-end steel fastener imports from China in 2009, China immediately responded with its own antidumping restrictions on high-end steel fasteners from the EU (Bown and Mavroidis, 2013). When the European Union initiated an antidumping case against cargo-scanning

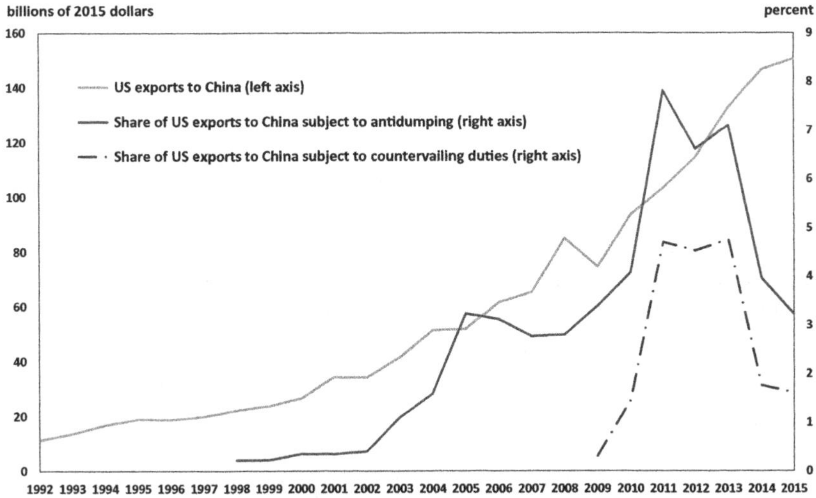

Figure 12.3 US goods exports to China and bilateral export share subject to antidumping and countervailing duties, 1992–2015.

Note: Shares are trade-weighted import coverage ratios, following the methodology in Bown (2011). China first applied a countervailing duty to imports from the United States in 2009

Source: Data in Bown (2016b) and six-digit Harmonized System trade data from UN Comtrade made available through World Integrated Trade Solution (WITS)

approach would be to resume an escalation of its own use of antidumping against the United States.

China implemented its own antidumping law in 1997. Although overall US exports to China increased considerably around China's 2001 WTO accession; only about 3 percent of US exports were subject to China-imposed antidumping as late as 2008 (Figure 12.3). China's use of antidumping against the United States at the time had been concentrated primarily in the chemicals sector.

Beginning in 2009, China started using antidumping more aggressively against exports from the United States overall and in new sectors. For the first time, China also applied CVDs against US exports it alleged were subsidized.

equipment from China in 2009, China initiated its own antidumping action over X-ray equipment from the EU (Moore and Wu, 2015).

China triggered antidumping decisions around major US trade policy announcements, such as the 2009 decision on a China-specific safeguard import restriction on tires and the 2010–11 decisions on the WTO dispute settlement activity.[19] It initiated antidumping investigations against US exports in new sectors, such as agriculture (e.g., chicken feet, dried distiller grains) and manufacturing (e.g., high-end specialty steel products, cars, optical fibers).

The share of total US exports to China subject to antidumping duties increased from 3 percent in 2008 to nearly 8 percent in 2011 (Figure 12.3). Those shares did finally fall and were back to 3 percent by 2015. However, China's removal of its import restrictions took place years after their original imposition, and only after the WTO ruled China's policies illegal under formal dispute settlement proceedings.[20]

While China's WTO-illegal antidumping duties were in effect, US companies suffered losses in export revenue. While illegal, a decision by China to return to WTO-inconsistent use of antidumping to address political concerns over NME status would be economically costly for the United States.

12.7 Conclusions

Even if China's NME status could be reduced to a purely bilateral issue between China and the United States, the political climate has not been ideal for the two countries to convene. The bruising US presidential election of 2016 brought into sharp relief the fact that the US population has been increasingly worried about globalization, including the effect of imports from China on the US labor market.[21] Furthermore, the Trump administration has signaled a potential major rethink on US trade policy

[19] See, for example, Bradsher (2009) and Shirouzu, Reddy, and Terlep (2011).

[20] In addition to the US disputes brought to the WTO over China–Autos (DS440), see the US disputes over antidumping in China–Broiler Products (DS427) and China–GOES (DS414). For legal-economic analysis of these three disputes, see Mitchell and Prusa (2016) and Prusa and Vermulst (2014, 2015).

[21] The magnitude of the blame placed on China (or trade more generally) for the labor market problems in the United States is excessive; automation and other shocks are more sizable contributors to dislocation. Even the largest estimates put imports from China as causing just 20 percent of US manufacturing job loss since 2001 (for a survey of the evidence, see Autor, Dorn, and Hanson 2016). Nevertheless, even a relatively modest negative impact of imports from China on US labor market outcomes would contribute to the toxic political climate toward trade.

overall, including its relationship toward the WTO and China, during its first few months in office (Bown, 2017). For its own part, China is struggling with its own slowing growth and a transition toward a more consumer-based and service-oriented economy. This transformation is expected to involve large-scale adjustment out of sectors that employ millions of Chinese workers, including in steel, where China as of 2016 had half of the world's production capacity.

Nevertheless, the United States, China, and the WTO system more broadly confront an important impasse that requires a political solution. The terms of China's 2001 WTO accession were silent on the criteria China would have to meet to graduate to market economy status as well as what would happen if China failed to meet them.

Most straightforward is management of the short-term trade tensions. The United States has been increasingly prepared for the day it must stop treating China as an NME in antidumping investigations. It has developed the ability to apply CVDs against implicitly subsidized imports from China when such imports cause injury to US companies. Indeed, as of 2015, US CVDs already covered two-thirds of the imports that antidumping duties address, and the share has been rising over time. This ability is likely to significantly offset any potentially disruptive effect on imports of granting market economy status. Even an immediate removal of all imposed antidumping duties on China – an outcome more extreme than elimination of NME status would necessitate – would imply that roughly 2.4 percent of China's exports – or $12 billion – would no longer be subjected to these import restrictions.

However, a longer-term agreement is needed to clarify the conditions under which countries like the United States could continue to access the surrogate-input methods that it applies to its imports from China under CVD law, without the threat of constant Chinese legal challenge at the WTO. Implementation of such an agreement could be possible through a WTO waiver.

The benefit to China of such a deal would be political: It would eliminate the stigma of NME status. The benefits to the United States would be twofold: It would retain sufficient trade policy flexibility to address future surges in imports, and it would also maintain access to the potential stick needed over the long term to enforce China's commitment to live up to the second objective.

Yet, the more difficult and systemically important question remains: How to come to a durable and mutually advantageous agreement on what it means for China to become sufficiently market oriented. This goes back to Jackson's original question of how market economies and nonmarket economies "interface." The details of such a deal would be complex and are well beyond the scope of this chapter. However, it is worth identifying some of the most critical elements, especially so as to clarify some of the key issues of interest of market-oriented WTO members such as the United States.

One important element is the need for increased Chinese transparency. Much of the tension between China and the United States arises from uncertainty, some of which could be eliminated with more information. Information is needed not only on China's government (direct) subsidies but also that might be used to independently determine whether what the United States alleges to be indirect subsidies are economically meaningful. The United States points to China's explicit plans for industrial policy, the role of the government and Chinese Communist Party officials in firm-level management decisions, and the continued impact of SOEs that provide excessively low-priced inputs to downstream industries. Additional transparency might be a tool that could help to assuage US concerns.

A new agreement could also usefully tackle related issues. It would certainly require fleshing out more explicit terms under which China would no longer be the target of specially designed import protection policies under antidumping or CVDs.[22] But it might also address the reality that even in market economies like the United States and European Union, trade-distorting subsidies continue to exist – e.g., Boeing/Airbus, agriculture – and thus China cannot be held to an unreasonable standard.

Such an agreement also requires earlier and more frequent feedback. The NME impasse flowed directly from the decision of the 2001 WTO accession to wait until the fifteen-year mark to provide China with a formal update. That turns out to have been an unproductive approach to managing long-run cooperation. While there are no signs that it is politically feasible, the most effective approach would be for the European Union and Japan to actually join the United States and negotiate jointly with China over this collection of issues, rather than playing (or being played) off one another.

[22] Bown and Crowley (2016, table 6) provide evidence that countries such as Japan and Korea are targeted with foreign antidumping much less frequently as of 2013 than in the 1990s.

Finally, a negotiated agreement would have other benefits leaving both market-oriented WTO members like the United States, but also China, better off. It might prevent significant Chinese retaliation from taking place outside of WTO rules, which has the potential to be very costly for the United States economy, and which could lead to a trade war.[23] Yet it is likely to be backed by reformers within China who have an independent economic interest. In addition to reducing trade tensions, an agreement would provide an external commitment device for China to undertake reforms to reduce state involvement in the economy – a move that would improve resource allocation, reduce waste, increase domestic productivity, and thus spur growth.

[23] See, for example, the simulations for the effect of China's tariff retaliation on the US economy presented in Noland et al. (2016).

Appendix

Table 12.A1 *Industry definitions and classifications*

Industry	Product	Harmonized system chapters
ANIM	Live animals and animal products	01–05
CHEM	Chemicals	28–38
ELEC	Electronics and electrical machinery	85
FOOD	Animal or vegetable oils and fats, prepared foodstuffs, beverages, tobacco	16–24
FOOT	Footwear	64–67
FUEL	Fuel	27
HIDE	Hides, skins	41–43
MACH	Machinery	84
META	Metals	72–83
MINE	Mineral products	25–26
MISC	Miscellaneous	90–94, 96–99
PLAS	Plastic, rubber	39–40
STON	Stone, glass	68–71
TEXT	Textiles, clothing	50–63
TOYS	Toys and sports equipment	95
TRAN	Transportation equipment	86–89
VEGE	Vegetable products	06–15
WOOD	Wood	44–49

Source: Own classification based on two-digit HS chapters.

13

A Time for Action

The WTO Must Change to Promote Regulatory Cooperation

THOMAS J. BOLLYKY AND PETROS C. MAVROIDIS

13.1 The Issue

Widespread recognition that international cooperation is needed does not in and of itself mean that it will occur. This was one of the lessons for trade integration in the interwar period, when governments were unable through proclamations and solo measures alone to arrest the cycle of retaliation that followed the US Smoot-Hawley Tariff Act of 1930, resulting in high tariff levels and rising tensions among the major powers. It is that experience that demonstrated the destructive potential of unilateralism in the trading system and led former US Secretary of State and Nobel Prize winner Cordell Hull and others to negotiate the General Agreement on Trade and Tariffs (GATT). Its rationale – or "GATT-think" – was that reciprocal liberalization would curb unilateral protection and the negative externalities that result from uncoordinated and nontransparent actions in a trading system with many partners (Bagwell and Staiger, 2002). In Hull's thinking, trade liberalization dovetailed with peace, which was his overarching ambition.

By any reasonable benchmark, GATT-think succeeded beyond expectation. This rules-based global trading system helped reduce tariffs and other border restraints and institutionalized global economic integration as a force for peace and prosperity. After the successful completion of eight rounds of multilateral trade talks, the average level of tariffs for Organisation for Economic Co-operation and Development (OECD) member countries fell to 3 percent; the average applied tariff in emerging economies like China and India is less than 10 percent (WTO, 2014). Membership in the GATT and its successor institution, the World Trade Organization (WTO), grew from 23 countries in 1947 to 164 nations today (WTO, 2016a). Trade liberalization and increased global economic integration, in the minds of some experts, have contributed to other important gains as well: fewer wars, and improved living standards in most nations of the world.[1]

It is fair to say that GATT's success in drastically reducing tariffs helped spur dramatic changes in the way the world trades. The relative importance of regulations and standards as determinants of market access grew. That importance has only increased with the subsequent disciplining of other border restraints on trade through the WTO Agreements on Customs Valuation, Import Licensing, and, more recently, on Trade Facilitation. At the same time, greater global economic integration, democratization, rising living standards, and increased awareness of risks have increased the demand for more regulations and rules as means of preserving and advancing social preferences on matters such as worker, environmental, and public health protection.[2] More trade occurs now via global value chains (GVCs), which rely on consistent, efficient, and adequate regulatory oversight to function.[3] The challenge of organizing consistent regulations is likely to grow with more products integrating value-added services and cross-border data flows – areas in which the WTO trade disciplines are few.

Already in 1970, Baldwin (1970) had persuasively argued that the "GATT-think" was ideally suited to curb border protection, but would need to adjust to a world of low/no tariffs when nontariff barriers (domestic policies) played a larger role in international commerce. The global trading system, however, has not adapted to these changes. The WTO still hews to the negative integration strategy of the GATT on regulations and social preferences, geared toward preventing domestic policies from being used to erode tariff concessions. This approach helped reduce explicitly protectionist regulations, but has done little to improve the international regulatory cooperation that is increasingly

[1] See Irwin, Mavroidis, and Sykes (2008), Pinker (2011, pp. 284–90, 341–2, 682–4), and Radelet (2015, pp. 258–9). Cordell Hull, one of the architects of the GATT trading regime, was awarded the Nobel Prize for Peace for his contributions.

[2] In this chapter, we define social preferences as fundamental interests that are not necessarily limited to a particular state. That definition distinguishes social preferences, which may transcend national boundaries, from the domestic policies of nation states or the transient negotiating demands, foreign policy goals, or bargaining positions that those states use to conduct foreign affairs. This definition draws loosely from the notion of preferences in Moravcsik (1997).

[3] Michael Porter popularized the value chain concept. His underlying notion was that a firm should focus on the stages and support functions in which that firm has a comparative advantage and outsource the rest. See Porter (1985a).

critical to freer trade. In the absence of that progress, countries are turning to bilateral and regional preferential trade agreements (PTAs) to deepen their integration on regulatory matters. Businesses and consumers are relying on private or nonprofit organization standards and third-party certifications to enforce social preferences and quality requirements. The resulting cacophony of rules and private standards has increased compliance costs and undermined effective international regulatory oversight. Popular support for liberalization of trade is already diminishing in many countries; that decline may accelerate without efforts to ensure that more trade also means better public health and a more protected environment.

It goes without saying that we should not need to relearn the lesson of the interwar era that unnecessary harm can result from uncoordinated and nontransparent actions in a global trading system with many partners and no strong institutional support. More international cooperation would improve the consistency, efficiency, and adequacy of regulations, which is in the mutual interest of trade officials and regulators alike. This, however, does not mean more international regulatory cooperation will spontaneously occur.

We believe that here, the WTO has an important role to play. Regulatory agencies are domestic in their orientation and their international cooperation initiatives often lack the funding, high-level political support, and urgency that trade negotiations can provide. Bilateral and regional PTAs are advancing international regulatory cooperation beyond disciplines on nondiscrimination, but most exclude many of the lower-income nations engaged in GVCs. While developing countries have been able to reduce tariffs unilaterally to better attract GVC investment, the options for doing so in the regulatory context are limited. Pursuing regulatory cooperation on a multilateral basis and within the WTO avoids the need for multiple, parallel cooperation initiatives between the various sets of regulatory agency counterparts and trading partners involved in a GVC. It also takes advantage of the emphasis on rules-based, nondiscriminatory trade and process for regulatory convergence, albeit rudimentary, that already exist at the WTO.

We further take the view that, to advance this cause, we need a new WTO-think, a strategy that is better suited to the present challenges of the global economy. This strategy remains rooted in the original rationale of the GATT of reducing the negative externalities of unilateral action and solving important international coordination challenges, but is more inclusive of regulators and nonstate actors and more flexible and positive in its means. To do this, we advocate that the WTO should embrace the confluence of shared social preferences and trade, where it exists, as a motivation for advancing international regulatory cooperation. We also recommend that the WTO rethink its corporate governance along the lines of variable geometry, an idea outlined in Lawrence (2006) and Hoekman and Mavroidis (2015c). Building on that work, we develop a workable mechanism for multilateralizing the progress being made on regulatory cooperation initiatives at the sub-WTO level. We also propose changes to WTO rules to facilitate the use of plurilateral agreements where consensus across members is not yet possible.

13.2 The Way We Were: GATT-Think

GATT-think is the answer to the question that many economists once asked: Why do we need trade agreements? There are economic benefits of eliminating protectionist policies, many argued, irrespective of whether other nations do the same. For this reason, some economists have characterized the multilateral trade system as enlightened mercantilism, a framework of rules and reciprocal liberalization that creates political trade-offs and domestic lobbies for making the tariff reductions that governments should already do for economic reasons.[4]

Yet, there are good reasons why some nations might want to protect.[5] Proponents of the terms of trade theory, for example, argue that those who have the bargaining power to do so can profit from imposing tariffs that reduce the world price to their advantage.[6] Economic history is full of examples of tariff impositions for various reasons.[7] Absent international agreement, (some) nations might have little incentive to eliminate protection. Indeed, following seventy years now of uninterrupted multilateral trade liberalization, unilateral reduction of tariffs continues to be the exception rather than the rule. Further, there are virtues of international agreements beyond the creation of political trade-offs and domestic lobbies for lower tariffs. Rules-based, reciprocal liberalization

[4] In other words, the prospect of tariff reductions in other nations helps generate enough support from domestic export-minded interests to overcome the domestic opposition to lower tariffs and the possibility of increased imports. See Krugman (1991, 1997).

[5] Regan (2006) cites revenue-raising, socially valued redistribution, and correcting externalities, including those affecting infant industries, as among the "perfectly proper" goals for protection.

[6] See Johnson (1953). Also see Bagwell and Staiger (2002).

[7] An extreme example is the US Morrill Tariff (1861), which raised revenue for the upcoming war in the United States.

provides predictability, prevents backsliding, and creates forward momentum for deeper economic integration. By drawing more countries into a rules-based system, multilateral trade agreements create static and dynamic efficiencies of scale.

The genius of the GATT lies with its approach to disciplining protection. Instead of seeking to define and prohibit protectionism in all its potential forms, the GATT channels protectionism from outright import quotas (that it outlaws per se) toward a less pernicious and more transparent form of protection (tariffs) and making it negotiable.[8] Once bound, tariff levels may only decrease. The requirement for nondiscriminatory application of domestic ("behind the border") policies was an insurance policy intended to prevent the use of regulatory measures to replace, and thereby erode, tariff concessions. Having the outcome of tariff negotiation extend to all GATT members on a nondiscriminatory basis created a powerful incentive for other nations to participate in the system. Enforceable dispute resolution kept them following the rules. So if negotiations persisted and succeeded, protection would gradually become extinct. Or, at least, this was the idea.[9]

Note also that the negotiators were determined to avoid a repeat of the escalating tariffs and trade wars that had characterized the interwar period. Tariffs levels had receded some by the time that GATT negotiations began, but the average tariff was still 22 percent in 1947.[10]

The negotiating record amply supports the view that the intent of the GATT framers was to reduce negative externalities that may result from uncoordinated and nontransparent use of protectionist measures in a trading system with many partners. Tariffs and import quotas were the quintessential instruments in this context, and it is only natural that these two instruments attracted the bulk of attention by the trading nations that convened the London Conference in 1946 that eventually led to the signing of the GATT. The limited rules on regulations and other

8 There remains no operational definition of protectionism in international law.

9 The GATT discipline is discussed in detail in Jackson (1969) and Baldwin (1971). Mavroidis (2016b) adds to the case law during the GATT and the WTO years. The GATT-think did not totally solve the problem of defining "protection." It requested from judges (panels) to come up with a workable definition every time they would be asked to pronounce whether domestic policies had been applied in a nondiscriminatory (e.g., nonprotectionist) manner. Alas, this is an area where panels did not manage to rise to the challenge.

10 Tariffs levels had receded some by the time that GATT negotiations began, but the average tariff was still 22 percent in 1947. See Bown and Irwin (2016). Also see Irwin et al. (2008) explaining that the fight against the UK imperial preferences was a major target of the US negotiators.

nontariff measures that exist in the GATT play a supporting role in that effort. The framers were well aware of the risk of policy substitution in this arrangement, for some of the brightest minds of that generation participated in the negotiation of the GATT (see Irwin et al., 2008). Thus, commitments on domestic policies were necessary; otherwise the value of tariff bindings would be easily eroded. What does it mean to bind customs duties, if domestic taxes (to consumers) and subsidies (to producers) are left unconstrained? The discipline on domestic policies, however, was softer. Those adhering to the GATT had to promise to place domestic and imported competing goods at equal footing. Nondiscrimination was thought to be an adequate insurance policy against erosion of the value of tariff bindings.[11] Tariffs, a negotiable instrument, remained as the only permitted means to protect domestic producers.

13.2.1 Agreed Neutral Tariff Classifications

The GATT focused on negotiation of tariffs, and outlawed recourse to (import and export) quotas. It did not have to be this way. Nations could have agreed to negotiate on trade volumes rather than on tariffs. The pioneering work of Krueger (1964), and Bhagwati (1965) has helped us understand why the GATT made an astute choice. Krueger first highlighted the important negative externalities associated with the administration of quota-based trade, if nondiscrimination continues to be relevant. Bhagwati added a different dimension. Even though one might theoretically be capable of establishing equivalence between say import quotas and import tariffs, the former provide an absolute threshold of permissible trade, whereas the "bite" of the latter will also depend on the pretax price of imported goods.

Rationally, thus, the GATT framers privileged a GATT negotiation whereby concessions would be expressed with respect to tariffs and not quotas. Through the GATT, tariff levels were reduced through reciprocal negotiations. To facilitate this tariff negotiation, a common description of goods for tariffs had to be invented, the successor of which is the current Harmonized Commodity Description and Coding System ("Harmonized System" or HS) classification.[12] This taxonomy provides a uniform classification of goods with numerical codes. A two-digit number refers

[11] The negotiating record is clear on this score. See Irwin et al. (2008). The WTO Appellate Body (AB) accepted as much in the WTO. See Appellate Body Report (WTO, 1996).

[12] The HS is governed by the International Convention on the Harmonized Commodity Description and Coding System, 1503 UNTS 167 (signed June 14, 1983) and maintained

to a family of goods (e.g., textiles), whereas a six-digit number, the maximum number of digits permitted in the HS system, identifies a particular species of that good at a more disaggregated level (e.g., shirts with polyester). The HS system classifies products according to their characteristics and properties. The end-use or the manufacturing methods used in production are not relevant, unless that end-use or manufacturing method had an impact on the product's properties. In other words, HS tariff classifications do not reflect social preferences (e.g., produced consistent with environmentally sustainable or labor-friendly standards), but rather product characteristics (e.g., cotton or polyester).

Again, it did not have to be this way. Tariff classifications can reflect social preferences. In fact, today, some national tariff classifications do. Article 3.3 of the International Convention on the Harmonized Commodity Description and Coding System ("HS Convention") allows for national subclassifications. The EU, and the USA and others negotiate at the eight-, ten- and higher-digit level classifications. These remain, however, national idiosyncratic classifications. The first attempt to design a tariff classification that includes social preferences – the WTO Environmental Goods Agreement (EGA) – is under way at the moment of writing. That classification will provide the basis for negotiating tariff reductions for products involving clean energy, energy efficiency, air pollution control, and environmental monitoring and analysis.

Trade in environmentally sustainable goods, however, was understandably not the most pressing problem that GATT negotiators were seeking to solve in the aftermath of World War II. The GATT was, of course, a gathering of more or less homogeneous players, the countries making for the Western world. Only Czechoslovakia, among the original signatories, belonged to the "Eastern bloc." It stayed on as an original signatory only because its transition to a centrally planned economy happened midway through the GATT negotiation.

13.2.2 Nontariff Measures and Concession Erosion

Without HS classifications that reflect social preferences, a GATT member that wishes to limit import of goods or services that contravene its environmental, food safety, and labor preferences has two choices. The government may block the imports at the border and, if challenged by another member, try to justify its action through recourse to general

by The World Customs Organization. More than 200 countries use the HS, which covers 5,000 commodity groups and more than 98 percent of the world's trade.

exceptions to the GATT (Article XX). Or, the regulating government could use a regulatory measure, such as a sales ban, and, if challenged, explain why that regulatory action is nondiscriminatory. Under the GATT, the first option offers no advantages at all. The burden of proof stays with the regulating state, and it still has to meet the nondiscrimination test embedded in the chapeau of Article XX of the GATT.[13] In the second case, the complainants have the associated burden of production of proof and persuasion.[14] Not surprisingly, GATT members prefer to impose regulatory measures that ban sales rather than imposing bans on imports.

The above seems to make good sense, and yet, the GATT framers did not address one key issue. The burden will fall to the GATT (and later the WTO) judge to determine whether the measure is nondiscriminatory. This means that WTO "judges" will have to design a "nondiscrimination" test. Since nondiscrimination is legalese for absence of protectionism, WTO judges will be called to design a test that will help distinguish protectionist from nonprotectionist policies. This is a tall order. Indeed, the advances in economic science notwithstanding, we still lack a reliable "protection meter." Bagwell and Staiger's (2002) "politically optimum" is hard to emulate in real world examples. Critics of the WTO case law on this score should keep this in mind.

The purpose of our chapter, however, is not to debate the quality of case law in this context, beyond noting that the exercise has been fraught (Mavroidis, 2016b). Defining "protection," especially in the regulatory context, is difficult and dependent on the activity and regulatory context. Trade effects could be the necessary and unintended by-product of pursuing an environmental or other legitimate social objective. A regulation, for example, that bans the sale of cars without a catalyst might be motivated by environmental concerns to reduce emissions. It will also exclude from the market all cars that do not carry a catalyst. Protectionist intent is difficult to reveal, since as in the prisoner's dilemma, the regulator, the possessor of

13 Although we still lack case law explicitly condoning this view, we believe that the better arguments side with the approach we advocate here. Otherwise, WTO Members would be allowed, for example, to punish imported goods for emitting carbon dioxide, while allowing their own producers to do so. The negotiating record of the GATT, as well as the current text of its first three provisions, leaves no doubt that this type of beggar-thy-neighbor policy was meant to be eliminated upon the signing of the agreement.

14 Viewed this way, it is remarkable that the USA defended its measures on US–Shrimp under Article XX rather than Article III of GATT, by adopting a sales ban on shrimps that were fished in a manner that prejudiced the life of sea turtles. See WTO (1998).

the private information, has little or no incentive to reveal the true intent of its actions (Bagwell and Staiger, 2002). Without a demonstrated intent to protect (and/or protectionist effect), many regulatory measures can be interpreted in multiple ways.

The GATT framers designed a remarkable contract that has withstood the test of time. The GATT framers devoted several provisions to the treatment of tariffs (Articles II, XXVIII, XXVIII *bis*, and indirectly VI, VII, VIII of GATT), but only one provision on the treatment of nontariff measures, namely, the nondiscrimination requirements in Article III. The agreement is largely unconcerned whether domestic policies and their underlying social preferences are pursued unilaterally. It also does not address the negative externalities for trade and effective regulation that may result from that uncoordinated action. Assuming that the regulator has adhered to the nondiscrimination principle, then affected trading nations will have to "bite the bullet," and accept the legitimacy of trade costs imposed on them.

In this system, the only possible line of attack against nondiscriminatory policies is offered by the so-called nonviolation complaints (NVCs) in Article XXIII.1(b) GATT. NVCs enable WTO Members to request compensation for trade damage inflicted upon them even through nondiscriminatory policies.[15] When the framers of the GATT realized that they could not foresee all possible expressions of policy substitution, they added this clause, which essentially requests regulators to compensate losers of policies that do not violate the letter, but only the spirit of the GATT. This is some consolation. In practice it has been successfully invoked in order to redress damage resulting from subsidization. In Japan–Film, the USA acting as complainant invoked this legal institution as means to redress damage it had allegedly suffered from the tolerance of restrictive business practices by the government of Japan. It did not manage to honor the associated burden of persuasion, and its complaint was rejected. With this we can close the parenthesis on NVCs, and return to nondiscrimination.

The nondiscrimination requirement on domestic policies in the GATT exhibits a binary function. Unless the regulatory standards of the importing state have been met, exporters will not access foreign markets even when duties are at zero level. Even excessive legislation, in principle, passes muster provided that it is nondiscriminatory. The GATT does not

[15] Mavroidis (2016b) reviews the literature on NVCs, and concludes that the most sophisticated arguments explaining NVCs have to do with contract incompletion and good faith.

attempt to rationalize domestic policies or facilitate their efficiency and effectiveness. As long as the same burden is imposed on domestic and foreign goods, measures satisfy the nondiscrimination requirement.[16]

With this in mind, one can legitimately ask whether the GATT framers could have done better? Perhaps, but it seems quite unlikely. Baldwin (1971) has persuasively argued that tariffs were high and regulation mostly nondiscriminatory in 1947 and, thus, it is understandable that domestic policies were not the focus of GATT framers.[17] Horn, Maggi, and Staiger (2010a) show that, when returns become diminishing, trade negotiators are apt to call it a day and leave it to subsequent negotiation(s) and/or adjudicators to "complete" the contract. Returns were becoming diminishing not only because it was difficult anyway to establish reciprocity between domestic nontariff measures, but also because of the "political" unwillingness to commit on domestic policies beyond nondiscrimination.

The focus, thus, on tariffs was not only rational. It was also politically commendable. Participating governments had little interest in limiting their freedom in areas like product safety for the sake of "a mere trade agreement" (see Bhagwati and Hudec, 1990). Social preferences and regulations did not fit easily with the notion of reciprocal negotiations central to the GATT. Workers' rights, competition policy, and other issues of economic and social regulation were to be taken up later in the International Trade Organization (ITO), of which the GATT was meant to be a part (see Slaughter, 1992). As years passed and the ITO was becoming a distant object in the horizon, countries became less willing to negotiate their domestic policies. Indeed, the 1955 Review Session of the GATT, which was supposed to be quite comprehensive, reflects no discussion on additional disciplines on domestic policies.

Even with this limited mandate, the GATT produced important benefits. These include binding the negotiated tariff reductions for an extended period, establishing the principle of nondiscrimination in international trade, improving the transparency and predictability of many trade policy measures, and providing a forum for future negotiations and

16 Grossman and Horn (2013) explain this point in detail. Case law has disturbed the balance struck by the GATT framers. At the end of the day, though, the absence of clear methodology and the commission of some judicial errors notwithstanding, more often than not the spirit of what we have described so far has been somewhat respected.

17 This was the case for various reasons. Tariffs represented the preferred instrument of protection, since they are a simple and efficient means to do so. Domestic regulation often addressed distortions irrespective of their origin. Furthermore, because tariffs could be used anyway, why should regulation of domestic policies be discriminatory?

for the peaceful resolution of bilateral disputes (see Bown and Irwin, 2016). The GATT is widely viewed as having facilitated the substantial reduction of tariffs – originally in higher-income nations, which included most of the original twenty-three GATT member countries, and subsequently around the world. It paved the way for negotiating disciplines on nontariff policies, which after the declines in tariffs, came to segment national markets from each other. The GATT had a like-minded group and a clear, agreed-upon goal back in the 1940s: to bring the tariffs down. Two things have changed ever since. First, the focus became blurred. Indeed, what should be the priority on nontariff measures (NTMs) even between the original twenty-three GATT member states? Second, once the 23 became 164, the homogeneity of membership was diluted with the increasing membership. The increase in numbers was, of course, a positive outcome of the GATT's success and a recognition of the potential benefits for more nations participating in a successful trade liberalization contract. The GATT's success, in other words, made life difficult for the WTO.

13.3 From GATT to the WTO

When the original member states signed the GATT in 1947, the objectives were a rules-based global trading system and fewer border restraints on trade. By the 1970s, both goals were well on their way to being achieved. Tariffs had declined dramatically, at least on the industrial goods on which higher-income countries were willing to negotiate. These gains were spurred by reciprocal concessions, extended by the nondiscrimination requirement, and enforced by dispute settlement under the GATT. Indeed, as Hudec's (1993) monumental study shows, the GATT dispute settlement system was an outlier in international relations. It functioned de facto as (almost) compulsory third-party adjudication. GATT "courts" (panels) would be routinely established at the wish of the complaining party, and the overwhelming majority of reports issued (approximately four-fifths of them) would become legally binding through the adoption process according to which the losing party would consent to the "adoption" of hostile reports issued by independent experts. There was, thus, guarantee that tariff commitments would be observed.

With lower tariffs, though, the role of regulations and standards as potential barriers to trade became more apparent (Baldwin, 1971). At the same time, new regulatory institutions arose and social preferences evolved, expanded, and were embedded in government policies in the decades following the postwar era (see Levi-Faur, 2005). With economic growth came an expansion of the middle class in many higher-income nations and a greater interest in quality of life concerns (see Ingelhart, 2000). New regulatory institutions and rules emerged on the safety of the workplace, the reliability of consumer products, the relations between employers and employees, the fairness of the market, the quality of air, water, and other environmental concerns, and various aspects of national life.

13.3.1 *From the Kennedy Round to the Tokyo Round*

Until the Kennedy Round in the mid-1960s, the GATT agenda was almost monopolized by negotiations on tariffs. Both incumbent member states and the "new kids on the block," the member states that would join either when trade rounds were initiated or in between rounds, would negotiate tariff reductions.

A tentative, but important shift of the multilateral trade agenda in the direction of addressing nontariff measures began in the Tokyo Round of the GATT (1973–9) and with the negotiation of "codes."[18] The Tokyo Round codes were plurilateral agreements negotiated and voluntarily adopted by only some GATT members. The Tokyo Round produced codes with new disciplines on nontariff issues including subsidies, government procurement, bovine meat, dairy, and technical barriers to the trade in goods (i.e., labeling, packaging, production, and product regulations and standards). There was no requirement to secure a "green light" from the GATT Membership in order to negotiate a code. An invitation was issued to all, but only the willing would go ahead and negotiate it. As the GATT was approaching 100 members, and its homogeneity was becoming a picture from the past, some felt that allowing members to pursue trade integration at different paces was the only feasible way forward. Third parties would not disadvantaged, at least not on paper.

With the start of the Uruguay Round in 1986, higher-income countries, which had already significantly reduced tariffs in their sectors of greatest interest, pushed for disciplines on the emerging priorities of their exporters, such as intellectual property rights and trade in services. Higher-income countries also wanted to update the Tokyo Round codes to address other areas of regulation and to ensure that all members adopted the codes as part of a single undertaking. In exchange, sectors that still had high tariffs and were not included in previous GATT rounds – agriculture,

[18] A more limited use of plurilateral codes began in the Kennedy Round of negotiations of the GATT in the 1960s, which, for example, produced a plurilateral code on antidumping.

clothing, and labor-intensive industrial goods – were put on the table to spur the interest of less wealthy countries and their lower-wage exporters. This deal was intended to generate momentum for future multilateral trade liberalization by broadening its focus, both in terms of increasing the number of member countries and the areas to be negotiated.

The WTO, which launched on January 1, 1995 after the Uruguay Round, can be seen as an effort to manage the success of the GATT. The results were mixed. More than seventy low- and middle-income countries joined the GATT/WTO since the start of the Uruguay Round. The goods sectors that remained stubbornly outside of the GATT were tamed with the signing of the Agreement on Agriculture, and the Agreement on Textiles and Clothing. With tariffs on their way out of most other sectors, the focus of the WTO shifted to nontariff measures and barriers, but its approach remained largely one of negative integration. Multilateral trade liberalization largely ground to a halt after the Uruguay Round; the current Doha Round has stalled since 2001.

WTO framers needed to ask two questions. First, why was single undertaking a necessity? Alas, the negotiating record does not reveal any information, other than mundane references to the need to ease transaction costs. There was, of course, an interest in having the targets of antidumping duties to join the Agreement on Antidumping. All WTO Members would have to abide by a much more demanding (than Article VI of GATT) framework. But does this logic apply to all Tokyo Round codes? One can legitimately take the opposite view. This is probably why a concession was made to the codes-approach through the introduction in the Uruguay Round of the possibility to sign plurilateral agreements.

Second, whether the approach to disciplining nontariff measures should change from GATT-think. Was the priority for disciplines on nontariff measures still ensuring against erosion of tariff concessions once global tariffs levels were relatively low and countries began unilaterally reducing tariff levels well beyond their bound levels? With the expansion of the GATT/WTO membership, should there be more positive integration of countries' regulatory objectives and social preferences into multilateral trade cooperation? WTO framers responded with the German word "jein," something between "ja" and "nein," as we explain in what follows.

13.3.2 *Tariff Classifications Revisited*

Recall that, as we have already explained above, there was no formal move toward greater accommodation of social preferences into the HS system, but countries have been moving in that direction. In the beginning, only the EU and United States had elaborate tariff classifications. Over the years, other WTO Members have begun to do the same. Expanded tariff classifications allow countries to target narrower classes of goods for preferential treatment, including those that reflect important social values. On the other hand, with more elaborate tariff classifications, WTO Members may advance demanding regulatory standards, which may reduce their possible sources of origin of those goods to a handful of more developed nations. The obligation to extend concessions on these regulation-informed tariff lines to other WTO member states on a nondiscriminatory (most-favored nation) basis may not mean much without a corresponding effort to improve their technical capacity to meet its requirements.

There is nevertheless an issue that has still to be addressed in an authoritative manner by the competent WTO bodies. National tariff classifications do not benefit from an irrefutable presumption of legality. They are WTO-compliant only if the classification meets the standard embedded in Article 3.3 of HS, which is that they are subclassifications of HS classifications at the six-digit level. Case law suggests that it may be permissible to include, inter alia, end-uses and consumer preferences in those subclassifications (see Mavroidis, 2016b, pp. 137ff.). Surprisingly, perhaps, there have been no disputes on this score yet, even though consumers and governments may have different preferences (otherwise there is no need to preempt consumers' choice through elaborate classifications). One reason for the lack of litigation may be the limited advantage afforded by using these classifications to reduce already low tariff levels.

Tariffs are still important in international trade. In some parts of the world (Brazil, China, India, Russia), considerable tariff advantages can still be granted. Even among WTO Members with the lowest tariff levels, high tariff advantages persist in some specific sectors (USA, textiles; EU, textiles, farm goods). There is no better argument in favor of this point than that offered by Limão (2016): the overwhelming majority of free trade areas (FTAs) signed even nowadays include a chapter on tariff preferences.

13.3.3 New Generation Agreements on NTMs

Following the successful conclusion of the Uruguay Round, the WTO has added two agreements (one new, one renewed) to its arsenal on regulations and other nontariff measures. The Agreement on Technical Barriers to Trade (TBT) is an update of the Tokyo Round agreement on the same subject, whereas the Agreement on Sanitary and Phytosanitary

(SPS) measures is a novelty that covers measures protecting human and animal health, and the environment from pests and diseases. The GATT also remained in place and covers transactions that do not fall under the SPS and the TBT Agreements. They are both colloquially referred to as "new generation" agreements, because of their new, when compared to the GATT, and more sophisticated approach regarding the disciplining of NTMs.

The TBT and SPS Agreements mostly function as an insurance policy to preserve the value of tariff concessions. This is particularly true for the SPS Agreement, which was included to guard against the EU common agricultural policy (CAP) through regulation. Various WTO Members fought long and hard to persuade the EU to reform its CAP. The last thing those members wished to see was the emergence of nontariff measures in lieu of the CAP's variable duties (again, see Limão, 2016).

Safeguarding the value of tariff concessions, though, does not exhaust the usefulness of the two agreements. The TBT and SPS Agreements do more than protect against erosion of tariff concessions. Both Agreements include provisions that promote consideration of the negative impact that unilateral or excessive exercise of regulatory authority might entail, but do not go so far as to oblige WTO Members to adopt a particular standard of protection or most efficient measure to achieve the stated social preference.

Let us start with the TBT Agreement. It recommends performance-over process-based measures, because there may be gains from having different approaches to meet regulatory objectives (see the Agreement on Technical Barriers to Trade). It requires governments to base their interventions on international standards, if the latter exist and are appropriate to the social preferences pursued.[19] The TBT Agreement requires adoption of measures necessary to achieve their objective and to be applied in a nondiscriminatory manner.[20] "Necessary" means that WTO Members must, when faced with regulatory alternatives that are equally efficient to achieve the stated social preferences, choose the measure that has less impact on the global volume of goods traded.[21] Both the TBT and SPS Agreements urge WTO Members to contemplate the necessity to intervene with their own regulatory measure in the first

[19] TBT Agreement, art. 2.4.
[20] TBT Agreement, art. 2.1, 2.2.
[21] See Mavroidis (2016c, pp. 493–4).

place.[22] This obligation is meant to reduce measures that unnecessarily duplicate the regulations of the exporting market or unnecessarily diverge from the international standard. For this reason, international standards are presumed necessary under the TBT Agreement.[23] Finally, the TBT includes a mix of legally binding obligations (like obligations to notify and explain national regulations) and a best efforts requirement to pursue mutual recognition, equivalency, and harmonization initiatives with other WTO Members.[24]

Let us move to the SPS Agreement now, which, arguably, goes even further. Besides fulfilling all the same requirements that are in the TBT Agreement, WTO Members must also adopt science-based measures and be consistent in formulating their policies.[25] A scientific basis is, of course, another indicator that a measure has not been enacted with protectionist intent. The consistency requirement reinforces that requirement, since it requires WTO Members to treat risks in a comparable manner.[26]

The provisions on necessity, science, consistency, and international standards in the TBT and SPS Agreements have served as additional proxies (besides the nondiscriminatory application of measures) for suppressing protectionist behavior, but seek to do more. These rules are also meant to discourage measures that have no disparate impact on imports, but are still excessive in achieving their intended regulatory objective.[27] There is little evidence, however, that these provisions have convinced countries not to adopt unilaterally regulatory measures that are duplicative, unnecessarily divergent, or inefficient. The WTO is still largely in a negative integration mode on regulatory measures and social preferences.[28] The WTO has only now started to take the first steps toward regulatory cooperation.

22 WTO (2012), paras 321–2.
23 TBT Agreement, art. 2.5.
24 TBT Agreement, art. 2.5–2.7.
25 SPS Agreement, art 2.2.
26 SPS Agreement, art. 2.3.
27 See Regan (2006) who describes the purpose of the TBT and SPS Agreements as restraining "domestically irrational" policies, a natural extension of the overall efforts to suppress protection.
28 Liberalization of investment is, of course, a mitigating factor, since foreign investors will lobby host governments and press for adoption of measures consistent with their regulatory interests. But it is only a mitigating factor.

13.4 Why Regulatory Cooperation?

The discussion so far points to gains to be had from cooperation on the regulatory front. In what follows, we analyze those potential gains and the extent to which the current WTO framework can support the pursuit of those gains. To do that, we will discuss in this section regulatory cooperation and its rising importance in international trade. In the next section, we will move to discuss the current WTO framework, and ask whether it can help, in its present form, WTO Members realize gains stemming from regulatory cooperation.

The term "regulatory cooperation" itself is not easy to define. It has been used to mean as little as dialogue and an agreement to notify and consult on a new or proposed regulatory measure or as much as to refer to an obligation to adopt international standards or to recognize or harmonize with another nation's laws.[29]

Why has the issue of international regulatory cooperation arisen at the WTO? Trade officials are interested in regulatory cooperation because there are few feasible alternatives for reducing the restraints that non-discriminatory regulations may impose on international commerce. Unlike tariffs, one cannot (and should not) eliminate regulations. Regulations are essential tools for promoting public health and safety, safeguarding the environment and rights of citizens, and ensuring the proper functioning of markets. Excessive, duplicative, or unnecessarily divergent regulations and conformity assessment procedures, however, can thwart the interoperability and effectiveness of regulatory systems, raise costs for businesses and citizens, and disadvantage foreign suppliers, which lack the inside knowledge of their counterparts (Sykes, 1999). Nondiscrimination, a key tenet of GATT-think, is limited in addressing this problem.

Prohibiting discriminatory nontariff barriers to trade ("negative integration") has helped open markets, but not yielded consistent, efficient, and effective oversight. OECD (2013b) has identified three categories of costs from international regulatory incoherence: (1) informational costs of identifying and understanding different regulations; (2) specification costs of complying with divergent and duplicative regulatory standards;

[29] The OECD categorizes international regulatory cooperation into: informal regulatory dialogue; nonbinding guidelines or principles; incorporation of international standards codes; transgovernmental networks of regulators; mutual recognition agreements; regional trade agreements with regulatory integration provisions; membership in intergovernmental organizations; formal regulatory cooperation agreements; and harmonization through supra-national or joint institutions (OECD, 2013a).

and (3) conformity assessment costs of demonstrating compliance with standards. Absent cooperation or the ability to pay these adjustment costs, foreign producers and suppliers, especially small and medium-sized enterprises, face market exclusion (see Maskus, Tsunehiro, and Wilson, 2005).

International regulatory incoherence, even when not directed against foreign producers, may occur and not be effectively restrained by the provisions in the SPS and TBT Agreements. There are three basic scenarios where this may occur. First, regulatory authorities may impose duplicative rules and conformity assessment procedures. This scenario may result from lack of awareness or concern with the trade costs of these redundancies. National regulatory authorities are primarily accountable for fulfilling their mandate to domestic constituencies, not to foreign producers. Duplicative regulation may also arise when a national regulator lacks confidence in its foreign counterpart to monitor and enforce the rules competently. It may also be the product of rent-seeking, used to generate fees to support regulatory agencies and the staff salaries devoted to overseeing and enforcing the rule.

Second, regulatory authorities may impose divergent, but similarly stringent rules. This scenario is most likely to occur among states at similar levels of economic development. Even among otherwise like-minded democratic, advanced industrialized economies, regulatory differences are inevitable. Regulation starts out as the answer to a domestic problem, developed within a preexisting national regulatory framework. So, while the social preferences and attitudes toward risk may be similar in two countries, governments may still devise different rules and enforce them differently because they are better suited to their particular institutional structures and rulemaking procedures (Drezner, 2008).

Third, regulatory authorities may impose divergent rules and conformity assessment procedures with different levels of stringency. This scenario is most likely to occur with states at different levels of economic development. At low levels of income, citizens and their governments tend to prioritize economic growth and efficiency over stringent domestic regulatory oversight (Drezner, 2008). As personal incomes increase, many lower-income nations are working to raise regulatory standards and improve oversight, especially over goods and services destined for export, but face capacity, resource, and governance challenges in doing so.[30]

[30] See World Bank (2006), describing a two-tier regulatory model in which products for export are fairly well regulated, but those for domestic consumption are not.

The regulatory incoherence in each of these scenarios does not run afoul of WTO restrictions on discriminatory measures or the provisions in the TBT and SPS Agreements on using necessary, science-based, and consistent regulatory measures and international standards where appropriate. In other words, the reasons for the incoherence are not necessarily protectionist or even domestically irrational, but the outcome remains inefficient for trade and, often, for achieving effective international regulatory oversight. The TBT and SPS Agreements include mutual recognition and equivalence provisions to help address the problem, but they are limited to best endeavours.[31]

It is in these scenarios where international regulatory cooperation is necessary. Dialogues and cooperation agreements, for instance, can help improve transparency, sensitize trading nations to others' needs and costs, and advance coordination among regulators and between regulators, businesses, and trade officials.[32] Peer-to-peer regulatory networks, consensus best practice guidelines and principles, and intergovernmental organizations promote work sharing and build regulatory and enforcement capacity, making it cheaper for nations to adopt policy reforms and maintain consistent regulatory oversight.[33] At the same time, mutual recognition agreements and regional trade deals can help increase the benefits of adopting convergent, adequate, and efficient regulations and conformity assessment by reinforcing their link to market access.[34]

31 TBT Agreement, art. 2.7; SPS Agreement, art. 4.

32 Examples of dialogues include the Transatlantic Business Dialogue (TABD) and the Transatlantic Consumer Dialogue (TACD). Examples of cooperation agreements include the Canada–US Regulatory Council (RCC) and the Rapid Alert System for Nonfood Dangerous Products (RAPEX), established pursuant to the EU–China Regulatory Cooperation Framework.

33 Examples of peer-to-peer regulatory networks include the Basel Committee on Banking Supervision and the Africa Medicines Regulatory Harmonization initiative. The Asia-Pacific Economic Cooperation (APEC) forum and the OECD put forward a frequently cited voluntary checklist to promote regulatory quality and efficiency. See OECD (2005b, pp. 1–36). Other institutions besides APEC and OECD involved in promoting regulatory cooperation and common standards include the International Organization for Standardization (ISO).

34 Examples of mutual recognition agreements include the Trans-Tasman Mutual Recognition Agreement, which has had the notable output of the Food Standards Australia/New Zealand (FSANZ), an effort to cooperate on the development of food standards before the adoption of national standards. Examples of regional trade agreements include the Comprehensive Economic and Trade Agreement (CETA), a pending deal between Canada and the EU with extensive provisions on product standards, mutual recognition, and regulatory cooperation.

13.4.1 Regulatory Cooperation in the WTO

We now shift gears and ask whether the WTO regime, as it now is, can help facilitate international regulatory cooperation. In other words, the subject matter of this discussion is whether the WTO can already now, without any amendment, help address the scenarios where regulatory incoherence persists.

13.4.1.1 Cooperation on NTMs in the WTO

Undeniably, the WTO has taken some tentative steps toward establishing regulatory cooperation with the advent of the TBT and the SPS Agreements.[35] Both agreements include various measures aiming to promote regulatory transparency and adoption of measures, such as international standards, which are not unilaterally defined. These disciplines are meant to curtail beggar-thy-neighbor national measures among trading nations. These agreements also facilitate trade and regulatory objectives by providing predictability for exporters and investors and simplifying regulatory compliance.[36]

Both agreements also provide a procedure for raising specific trade concerns (STCs), a more intensive avenue for engagement on NTMs that stops short of formal dispute settlement. STCs are formal requests for clarification by a WTO Member regarding another member state's TBT- or SPS-related measure, whether that measure was notified or if the other member state learned of measure without notification. STCs could lead to informal settlement or provide the basis for a formal dispute.[37] STCs represent a form of cooperation at the very beginning of the spectrum that could lead to common rules. Since the advent of the WTO, there has been an upward trend in the STCs filed annually, from four in 1995 to eighty-five in 2014 (Wijkström, 2015).

And one should not forget that WTO Members further discuss issues regarding the administration of regulatory measures in the committees created under the aegis of the SPS and TBT Agreements. Annex 3 of the

[35] This issue is discussed in detail in Mavroidis and Wolfe (2015).

[36] SPS Agreement, art. 2.3, 3, 5.4; TBT Agreement, Art. 2.2, 2.4, 2.8; General Agreement on Trade in Services, Apr. 15, 1994, Marrakesh Agreement Establishing the World Trade Organization, Annex 1B, The Legal Texts: The Results of the Uruguay Round of Multilateral Trade Negotiations 284 (1999), 1869 UNTS 183 [hereinafter GATS], Art 2.2, 2.3, 5.6.

[37] Transparency and dispute settlement are complements as they are substitutes. Once aware of a measure, a WTO Member might drop its original complaint. It could also take the view that it has a strong case before a WTO panel.

TBT Agreement includes the Code of Good Practice (CGP) for the Preparation, Adoption, and Application of Standards, which encourages standard-setting bodies to be transparent and promulgate nondiscriminatory, performance-based, and nonduplicative standards. In 2000, the WTO Committee on Technical Barriers to Trade (TBT Committee) agreed to additional principles for the work of international standard-setting bodies, which include transparency, openness, and an impartial and consensus-driven approach that promotes effective and relevant standards and incorporates the concerns of developing countries (WTO, 2000). The TBT Committee has also promoted the use of good regulatory practices in workshops and in its fifth triennial review.[38] These practices promote the exchange of information and more coordination among regulators, standard-setting bodies, and trade officials. In 2014, the SPS Committee launched a mechanism to mediate rising trade tensions over food safety and animal–plant health measures.[39]

At this stage, it is difficult to evaluate the impact of WTO efforts on regulatory cooperation, but one should probably not expect too much. Without a greater mandate and more institutional support, these WTO efforts seem more likely to serve as guidelines for unilateral actions by members, rather than the first step toward establishing a forum for cooperation between members.

13.4.1.2 Cooperation Regarding Tariff Classifications

Tariff classifications, as we have seen, were historically either harmonized (HS), or unilaterally defined (when recourse was being made to eight-or-more-digit classifications). Recently, however, a version of regulatory cooperation at the WTO has been taking place in the realm of tariff classifications as well. Although not formally under the auspices of the WTO, for the time being at least, negotiations of the EGA, which we briefly referred to above, were launched in July 2014.[40] The purpose of

[38] See, e.g., Committee on Technical Barriers to Trade, Summary Report of the WTO TBT Workshop on Good Regulatory Practice (G/TBT/W/287), World Trade Organization, adopted June 6, 2008, 1–28; WTO Committee on Technical Barriers to Trade, Fifth Triennial Review of the Operation and Implementation of the Agreement on Technical Barriers to Trade under Article 15.4 (G/TBT/26), adopted November 19, 2009, 5–6.

[39] For more details, see WTO News, "Steps Officially Agreed for Mediating Food Safety, Animal–Plant Health Friction," www.wto.org/english/news_e/news14_e/sps_10sep14_e.htm (visited September 19, 2016).

[40] Seventeen countries are participating in the negotiation: Australia; Canada; China; Chinese Taipei (Taiwan); Costa Rica; European Union; Hong Kong, China; Iceland;

the negotiation is to agree on preferential tariffs for goods that protect the environment. To do this, negotiators have to agree on classifications that reflect regulatory processes that promote environmental protective goods and provide tariff advantages to those goods that conform to the agreed process.

At the moment of writing it is unclear whether the EGA will be a multilateral, a plurilateral, or a critical mass agreement under WTO rules.[41] The fact that only seventeen countries are participating in the negotiations so far cannot itself be taken as an indication of the eventual format. Some developing members, though, might find it a daunting task to join in an agreement that conditions preferential tariff treatment upon meeting demanding environmental standards.

Irrespective of the final resolution on this issue, what matters for the purposes of our discussion is that the EGA marks the first case of regulatory cooperation in the realm of tariff classifications.

13.5 Asymmetric Players and Regulatory Cooperation

The EGA is no anomaly; it is rather a sign of the times. A number of FTAs have been signed between homogenous players that contain elaborate clauses regarding regulatory cooperation. The advances on this front in the TBT and SPS Agreements notwithstanding, there is still a lot that can be done on this front at the WTO as well.

13.5.1 Changing Patterns in World Trading

The fact is that the way the world trades is changing. Not only are trade barriers now predominantly nontariff measures, there are also fewer goods and services that originate from any one country or any one supplier. More trade occurs via GVCs, in which different firms in different countries undertake different parts of the process of producing a good or service. GVCs started in the 1960s when international companies took advantage of lower tariffs, the containerization of shipping, and better information and communication technologies to slice up and outsource parts of their manufacturing supply chains to lower-cost,

Israel; Japan; Korea; New Zealand; Norway; Singapore; Switzerland; Turkey; United States of America.

[41] This term refers to agreements concluded between producers representing a certain (important) percentage of world production of the negotiated good(s).

specialist suppliers abroad. In the 1990s and 2000s, the shift to GVCs expanded to services and to sectors ranging from food production to medical R&D. With the 2008 global economic crisis, GVCs evolved again, becoming more regional and reorienting around large emerging economies with rising production capabilities and more domestic consumer demand (Gereffi, 2014). The inputs and components in GVCs comprise 56 percent of the global goods trade and 73 percent of the services trade (WTO, 2011b).

The rise of GVCs is of course due to the fact that trade conducted through GVCs has had significant benefits.[42] Unbundling affords businesses the opportunity to scale economies, implement just-in-time production, and greater flexibility in meeting consumer demand. Consumers gain more affordable goods and services. GVCs have contributed to the shift of employment in labor-intensive sectors away from higher-income nations – a painful and unsettling process for the workers and communities affected – but it has also created specialized, higher-wage jobs in those nations coordinating production networks and in product design, branding, and other large-margin activities. The unbundling of production has also reduced the barriers to lower-income countries competing in the world economy, enabling those nations to industrialize through GVCs and lift millions of their citizens out of poverty.

GVCs are endogenous in the sense that traders will pick their partners in light of various factors ranging from productivity gains to transaction costs. Antràs and Staiger (2012) explain why in this context domestic policies might matter more than when final goods are being traded. Labor legislation, antitrust policies, fiscal treatment, and other domestic policies will affect who will and who will not jump on the GVCs bandwagon (Antràs and Staiger, 2012). Sustaining and expanding the benefits of GVCs requires consistent, adequate, and efficient regulation, among the various GVCs partners. GVCs involve the cross-border movement of capital, knowledge, and intermediate services and parts. As the number of countries and cross-border transactions in GVCs multiply, so do the economic costs of inefficient, duplicative, and divergent regulations. The proliferation of uncoordinated regulations challenges even sophisticated multinationals. The high costs of regulatory compliance can keep small and medium-sized businesses out of GVCs altogether. Divergent rules on data storage and analysis and product

[42] See the excellent analysis of this issue in Hoekman (2014).

testing can act as localization requirements, making production in other jurisdictions infeasible (OECD, 2015d). According to the WTO World Trade Report (WTO, 2009), one-third of the global trade in goods (estimated $19.2 trillion in 2018) was affected by standards that differ across jurisdictions. Regulatory cooperation is more of an issue in today's trading realities than ever before.

Consistent, adequate, and efficient regulatory oversight is also important to the viability of GVCs as a means of economic development. Goods and services must ultimately satisfy the social preferences of consumers and the standards of national regulatory authorities and retailers in end-user markets. Inability to comply reliably with food safety rules, labor standards, or environmental requirements can lead to border detentions and import bans, liability and reputational damage, and contractual penalties for manufacturers and suppliers. It can deter foreign direct investment in countries. Particularly in export-driven lower-income economies, the costs of regulatory noncompliance can be significant. In the context of GVCs, adequate, consistent regulatory oversight no longer just ensures social preferences; it is an investment in economic development and trade facilitation.[43]

But there is more. Health, labor, financial, and environmental policymakers likewise have an interest in adequate, consistent, and collaborative international regulation. In the GVC context, regulatory agencies cannot do their jobs without the help of their counterparts. Imports that the US Food and Drug Administration (USFDA) regulates, for example, have grown nearly sixfold (from 6 million to 35 million shipments) over the twelve years and now involve more than 300,000 facilities in more than 150 different countries (USFDA, 2012). There are legal and practical limits on inspecting such a multitude of producers and suppliers. Border and port surveillance can supplement but not replace oversight, control, and surveillance by local regulators and industry. In sectors involving global public goods – such as stemming climate change, financial contagion, or pollution – regulatory objectives cannot be met without international coordination. International collaboration helps regulators gather information and share best regulatory practices and tools, building their knowledge base for effective regulation.[44] For all these reasons, and in many sectors, regulatory oversight in one country increasingly depends

[43] See Henson (2003), World Bank (2005), Maertens and Swinnen (2009b), and National Academy of Sciences (2012).

[44] See De Búrca, Keohane, and Sabel (2014), Sabel and Victor (2015).

on the adequacy and consistency of regulatory oversight in other countries (Bollyky, 2009, 2012, 2015).

13.5.2 Positive Integration Recommended

If internationally consistent, efficient, and adequate regulatory oversight provides compound benefits, it may seem unnecessary for governments to engage international regulatory cooperation to achieve it. Why then don't governments undertake the necessary regulatory reforms unilaterally? Here, a partial analogy to GATT-think helps demonstrate the need for international regulatory cooperation and the reasons why negotiators and regulators need to pursue that objective together.

There are regulatory reforms that government may undertake unilaterally that benefit trade. Countries may increase their export competitiveness by unilaterally adopting good regulatory practices (OECD, 2002, 2005c). Improving the quality, transparency, and predictability of regulatory measures helps domestic actors and importers alike (Jacobs and Ladegaard, 2010). Over time, adoption of administrative law practices like regulatory impact assessment might also assist exporters if it brings the trade and regulatory communities closer and sensitizes both sides to each other's concerns (Coglianese, 2016).

Yet, as in GATT-think, structured international regulatory cooperation provides benefits that may not be easily achieved unilaterally: predictability, greater accountability for backsliding, iterative engagement on deepening integration, and gains in efficiencies from increased scale (Irwin, 2015). Regulations are also not like tariffs, which emerging economies have effectively liberalized unilaterally in order to attract GVC-related investment (Baldwin, 2010). Regulations are dynamic, with rules and their enforcement changing in response to emerging political and market demands. Unilateral adoption of good regulatory practices can only do so much to spur freer trade if other nations also do not reciprocate and maintain the internationally consistent, adequate measures and shared conformity assessments that both exporters and regulators need in this GVC-dominated economy (Bollyky, 2012).

Further, international, rules-based cooperation has an important role in improving domestic decision-making. Even in democratic governments, domestic interests may undermine or subvert good regulatory practices such as the obligation to provide notice and comment and assess the cost-benefits of proposed rules. The accountability and transparency that comes with iterative international regulatory engagement on shared goals provides an important restraint on that occurring.

As in GATT-think, international agreements to advance regulatory cooperation also may create the political support and domestic constituencies for making the necessary policy reforms. In this context, trade and regulators need each other.

Trade negotiators are unlikely to advance their priorities on improved international regulatory coherence without the support and active participation of regulatory officials. The reasons are twofold. First, consistent, efficient regulatory oversight depends as much on how rules are interpreted and enforced as the rules themselves. Even with the support of a country's leadership, it is difficult in a top-down approach to mandate and maintain iterative, cooperative behavior. Meaningful, sustained progress is more likely if the objective is addressing transnational regulatory priorities as well as facilitating international commerce.

Second, without the engagement of regulatory authorities, concerns about diminishing cherished social preferences would make the already difficult politics of trade liberalization unworkable. Fears over food safety and genetically modified organisms have driven a fierce backlash in the EU against the Trans-Atlantic Trade and Investment Partnership (TTIP) negotiations. Popular support for greater global economic integration is more likely to occur in a regulator-supported effort to ensure that freer trade also results in safer goods, a more protected environment, and more assured public health and welfare.

Conversely, regulatory cooperation initiatives have better prospects if pursued in partnership with trade officials and aligned with the needs of exporters and their governments. Here too, the reasons are twofold.

First, regulatory agencies are chronically underfunded and domestic in their orientation. Few of these agencies have the resources, staff, and mandate to pursue international cooperation and capacity building. Trade talks provide the structure, resources, and high-level political commitment that international regulatory dialogues often lack.

Second, advancing international cooperation in regulatory dialogues alone is unlikely to exploit the opportunity that the rise of GVCs presents. The challenge of achieving international cooperation is greatest in areas where (1) regulatory regimes are mature and (2) the responsible agencies in large-consumer markets disagree (Drezner, 2008). Even non-substantive changes, such as adoption of common forms or sharing of inspection reports, impose adjustment costs on regulatory agencies with well-established systems in that area. The adoption of international standards in many heavily regulated sectors has been slow and in high-income countries, such as the United States, poor (see Roberts and Josling, 2011). Regulator-to-regulator dialogues such as the International Conference on Harmonization of Technical Requirements for Registration of Pharmaceuticals for Human Use can make progress, but have required decades to do so (Institute of Medicine [IOM], 2013).

The rise of GVCs provides a powerful, but time-limited incentive for regulatory agencies to incur adjustment costs in order to spread their norms and standards to the many other countries involved in producing goods and services for import in their markets. The incentive exists because adoption of common rules and certification regimes helps spread those rules internationally, by making it easier for exporters and investors in third-party countries to achieve economies of scale by complying with regulations in multiple large consumer markets.[45]

That incentive is time-limited because it may become harder to drive adoption of international norms as emerging economies grow and their consumer markets become a bigger target for exporters. Further growth and a shift to more domestic consumption in emerging economies are positive trends, but adding more large-consumer markets will make reaching agreement on regulatory standards harder, especially in the absence of an effective multilateral institutional support. The emerging trends of large multinational companies localizing production in big end-use markets (Immelt, 2016) and the increasing reliance of these companies on private standards, third-party certifications, and proprietary quality management systems only compound that challenge.

13.5.3 *Where Regulatory Cooperation Happens*

Our discussion so far has focused on the inadequacy of the current WTO regime to address regulatory cooperation comprehensively, and the reasons why it should do so. But there is one additional piece in this jigsaw puzzle: regulatory cooperation at the sub-WTO level. There is no better argument that the WTO does not do enough in the realm of regulatory cooperation and social preferences than the proliferation of PTAs that seek to address these topics. In 1990, there were approximately 70 active PTAs; today there are more than 500 (Limão, 2016). The explosive growth in the number of PTAs began with the end of the

[45] See Vogel (1995), Greenhill, Mosely, and Prakash (2009) and Maertens and Swinnen (2009a), for further discussion.

Uruguay Round and the increased relative importance of NTMs as potential restraints on trade (see Mavroidis and Sapir, 2015). Roughly sixty PTAs have terms that go beyond the WTO TBT commitments; fifty have SPS commitments that exceed those in WTO agreements (WTO, 2011b). Countries with more extensive participation in GVCs are more likely to enter into these "deep integration" PTAs and more likely to reap the benefits of doing so (Orefice and Rocha, 2011).

The four major PTAs under negotiation at the time of writing – the Regional Comprehensive Economic Partnership (RCEP), the Trans-Pacific Partnership (TPP), the Trade in Services Agreement (TISA), and the TTIP – all include efforts to advance regulatory cooperation beyond disciplines on nondiscrimination. Serious regulatory cooperation also occurs in the ISO and other standard-setting institutions that include trade facilitation and promoting common standards in their mandate.

To date, the most ambitious regulatory cooperation efforts have occurred in PTAs among like-minded nations with regional ties. The EU has pursued regulatory integration among its twenty-eight member states through a wide variety of means including mutual recognition, harmonization, and cooperative approaches such as joint reviews. The United States has launched regulatory cooperation councils with Canada and Mexico (Steger, 2012). More of the CETA, the proposed deal between Canada and the EU, is devoted to product regulation, mutual recognition, and regulatory cooperation than to reducing tariffs and other border restraints.[46]

These arrangements also solve at the international plane a problem of absence of coordination at the domestic plane. Whereas the mandate for regulators is primarily domestic in orientation, trade officials are charged with looking for market access in foreign markets. There is a natural disconnect between these two government functions, which are only starting to be more aligned with the rise of GVCs. And yet, there is so much to win if more cooperation between them can be advanced. Trade talks, for example, can facilitate work-sharing and iterative engagement among regulators that can stretch their scarce resources and improve regulation, while also reducing the trade costs of duplicative testing and inspections. To be sure, some of this engagement already has found its place in the TBT and SPS Agreements, but not nearly enough. First, this is so because regulatory cooperation is confined to the subject matter of

[46] The fate of this agreement is now in doubt at the time of writing, with opposition in the Wallonia region of Belgium (The Economist, 2016b).

these two agreements, and not to the universe of domestic regulation. Second, for the reasons mentioned above, the current framework does not do enough to facilitate cooperation among national regulators on consistent, efficient, and adequate regulatory oversight. Trade officials likewise have a lot to learn from interacting with their colleagues in national regulatory offices. This form of cooperation will help them better assess the consistency of national policies with WTO obligations, as it will help them get better acclimatised with divergent regulations. Thus, to provide but an illustration, the Regulatory Cooperation Council between the USA and Canada helps advance cooperation not only between US and Canadian officials, but among US (and Canadian) officials belonging to different domestic agencies.

While having like-minded states often helps advance regulatory cooperation, it is possible to achieve among heterogeneous trading partners as well. Developing countries have agreed to environmental commitments in PTAs, when those states have not exhibited similar eagerness to do so at the multilateral level.[47] One reason might be the additional trade gains afforded in a PTA. The intensity of cooperation may differ, however, among heterogeneous trade partners. Like-minded trading partners have proven more willing to agree to binding disciplines than unlike-minded players.[48] Still, nonbinding commitments may help sensitize trading partners to the worries of their counterparts, encourage information exchange on the rationale for a regulatory intervention, and to set the stage for more rigorous cooperation in the future.

The prospects for regulatory cooperation are not limitless even when pursued with like-minded partners. Policy independence and regulatory sovereignty were among the reasons (along with anti-immigration) cited in the United Kingdom's June 2016 vote to exit the EU.[49] The 2007 initiative by Australia and New Zealand to create a joint regulatory agency for medicines and medical devices failed (Australian Government Department of Health: Therapeutic Goods Administration, 2007). Previous initiatives to improve EU–US regulatory cooperation made little progress (Akhtar and Jones, 2014). The near-term prospects for a successful conclusion of the TTIP talks do not look good at the time of writing.

[47] See, e.g., the US–Peru Free Trade Agreement, Chapter 18 (2006) as an illustration of this effect.

[48] Horn, Mavroidis, and Sapir (2010b) offer some examples to this effect.

[49] See The Economist (2016a).

And there are tangible results. Where regulatory cooperation has occurred, however, it has brought real benefits to like-minded trade and regulatory partners. Association of Southeast Asian Nations (ASEAN) countries have used mutual recognition agreements (MRAs) and cooperation on standards, technical regulations, and conformity assessment to promote themselves successfully as a GVC hub (WTO, 2011b). Transatlantic cooperation initiatives may have led to few regulatory changes, but they have helped reduce trade friction (Ahearn, 2009). The China–EU RAPEX, initially spurred by trade concerns, has investigated and helped constructively resolve thousands of product safety concerns.

13.5.4 The Limits of Cooperation within PTAs

Deep integration PTAs can provide for intense regulatory cooperation, and, of course, not entirely outside the ambit of the WTO, since free trade areas and customs unions operate within the four corners of the multilateral trading system. But, it is still important to "multilateralize" the progress on international regulatory cooperation occurring in PTAs and regional economic communities and bring it into the WTO. Here is why.

PTAs are a second-best solution to the problem of achieving freer trade and better regulation because these agreements do not encompass the range of countries in global commerce.[50] The organization of production and trade into international value chains and networks means that end products are affected by many regulatory jurisdictions. Those jurisdictions are diverse, including nations at different stages of economic development and some with relatively nascent regulatory agencies.[51] Agreements with rules that do not span all these economies cannot effectively advance global integration and efficiency, particularly in sectors dominated by GVCs and dependent on cross-border data flows and digital commerce.

Pursuing international regulatory cooperation on a multilateral basis within the WTO offers important advantages. It avoids the need to introduce multiple parallel discussions among regulatory and trading

[50] PTAs with countries at different stages of economic development tend to have less integration on TBT and SPS regulation. See WTO (2011b) at 141–2.

[51] Baldwin (2012) provides examples of the range and diversity of countries in GVCs and their degree of engagement.

partner counterparts. It also takes advantage of the process for regulatory convergence, albeit rudimentary, that is already in place at the WTO.

Many developing countries, especially the lowest-income nations, are not included in RCEP, TPP, or the other PTAs with ambitious commitments on regulatory cooperation and coordination. The EU has agreements that include regulatory cooperation with African countries, but those are generally not binding (Horn et al., 2010b). The PTAs that involve low- and middle-income countries do not include particularly "deep" or enforceable regulatory commitments that go beyond those in WTO agreements (again, see WTO, 2011b). There has been some targeted engagement between the trade and regulatory agencies of varying levels of economic development, especially on food safety and in the APEC forum, but progress has been slow.[52] The relative lack of engagement of lower-income nations in PTAs and other meaningful international regulatory cooperation initiatives is important because the avenues for unilateral liberalization are limited in the regulatory context.

We need to move beyond the current framework; we need to establish a new framework for regulatory cooperation within the WTO.

13.6 WTO Version 2.0

In a global economy increasingly dominated by GVCs, picking between freer trade and better regulation is increasingly a false choice. Pursuing regulatory cooperation as a strategy for trade liberalization (and vice versa) offers a more promising way for policymakers and negotiators to advance both economic objectives and social preferences on worker safety, a cleaner environment, and healthier, more sustainable products. It is the present alternative – trade officials and regulators operating unilaterally and in parallel – that leaves the fulfillment of those social preferences more at risk and international commercial goals unmet.

In this environment, the original precepts of GATT-think – reducing the negative externalities that result from uncoordinated and nontransparent actions in a trading system with many partners – remains as relevant as ever. But, the corporate governance of the GATT/WTO must change to reflect the decline in tariffs and the other traditional barriers to commerce and the emerging challenges of advancing trade, regulation cooperation, and social preferences in a global economy dominated by

[52] APEC Food Safety Cooperation Forum (FSCF), www.foodstandards.gov.au/science/international/apec/Pages/default.aspx (visited September 19, 2016).

GVCs. We refer to this integration strategy as the "new WTO-think." In what follows, we explore the parameters of that concept, and provide our "nudge" for a serious discussion on WTO institutional reform.

13.6.1 *The Corporate Governance of the WTO: Time for a Change*

We have established in the preceding discussion that the rules and procedures of the WTO were designed for a different global economy in which mostly finished goods moved across national borders. With the rise of GVCs, tariffs and other border restraints matter less and the protection of investments and intellectual property, and free flow of components, services, and people matters more. As a result, the rules and the institutions that support that trade must also evolve.

A focus on market access, simple and broadly applied rules, and dispute resolution will not advance the deeper integration that is increasingly required in the world economy. Nondiscrimination and reciprocity cannot assure market access when it is conditioned upon satisfying country-specific regulatory standards and social preferences. The availability of binding dispute resolution will do little to attract the active engagement of regulatory authorities in international cooperation, when those regulatory authorities have bitterly resented past WTO reviews of their choices.

13.6.2 *WTO 2.0*

While the negative integration approach of the GATT/WTO may be less relevant, the role for the multilateral trade institution remains critical and unlikely to be supplanted by PTAs. By this, we do not want to introduce a firewall between PTAs and the WTO. To the contrary, WTO 2.0 could benefit from solutions already agreed at the PTA level. Ideally we would like to introduce an osmosis mechanism between PTAs and the WTO. In fact, a very recent WTO publication follows exactly this line of thinking when arguing that the challenge for the WTO in the near future will be to emulate at the multilateral level the best practices observed in the PTA context (Rohini, 2016). Implicit in this thesis is that the WTO should be strengthened and supported.

The challenge is doing so at a time when global economic power is increasingly diffuse and there is little appetite for empowering a supranational institution to reduce the market-segmenting effects of regulatory policies and social preferences. (Hoekman, 2016). This will require supplementing the traditional approach of the GATT/WTO – fixed, universal rules subject to binding dispute resolution – with the opportunities for interested members to pursue shared social preferences, plurilateral agreements, and outside partnerships, and to multilaterize the regulatory cooperation occurring via PTAs and regional economic communities.

13.6.2.1 Divergent Social Preferences: A Cost and a Benefit

Advancing international trade liberalization has emerged as an important way to pursue social preferences. The reverse is also becoming true.[53] To provide but an example, WTO Members with strong safety social nets might find it easier to sell trade liberalization to their domestic constituents than their counterparts with no protection for the weaker social groups. The WTO should embrace and reinforce this positive link between trade and social preferences, wherever it exists, to advance multilateral agreements on regulatory cooperation.

An increasing number of PTAs, particularly those involving the United States and the EU, advance social preferences such as labor and environmental protections, human rights, rule of law, and other aspects of public governance.[54] The trend began with the North American Free Trade Agreement (NAFTA) as a way to resolve political differences in the United States over trade. In the most recent iteration, the TPP, many of the labor and environmental measures are enforceable and subject to dispute resolution. Promoting social preferences as part of PTAs spreads the benefits of trade liberalization, discourages the worst mistreatment of workers and the environment, and builds public support for trade deals (Elliott, 2012).

Conversely, the desire to advance shared social preferences has also spurred interested states to pursue trade initiatives in sectors of concern. The EU, for example, established a Forest Law Enforcement Governance and Trade Initiative to engage lower-income nations in promoting trade in legal timber, to increase the market demand for sustainable forestry, and to reduce the supply of illegally harvested timber (Shaffer, 2015).

[53] See Friedman (2005) on bidirectional links between economic growth and advancing moral benefits such as improving the environment, reducing poverty, promoting democracy, and making for a more open and tolerant society.

[54] We reference here PTAs that the EU has entered into with other nations, not the EU integration process itself.

Shared preferences provide the basis for establishing a broad framework of shared goals that may attract the active support and participation of regulators. These regulators, in turn, have the sector-specific understanding and mandate to implement, monitor, and maintain meaningful cooperation (see De Búrca et al., 2014). The alternative of advancing internationally consistent, efficient, and effective regulations without embracing a larger role for social preferences and norms in WTO agreements seems hopeless.

It is probably commonplace but worth repeating that trade disciplines, like most laws and regulations, are generally less effective when they require taking iterative, positive action instead of barring unwanted behavior. Compliance with the notification or technical transfer requirements in trade agreements, for example, has been poor (Maskus, 2012). Mandating that regulators cooperate or consider the trade impact of their proposed rules is likely to be less effective than providing a workable framework for interested states to advance shared social preferences and consistent, effective, and efficient oversight in commercially important sectors.

We have already explained that the WTO has taken a tentative step in this direction with the EGA. This plurilateral agreement is to be concluded between the EU, United States, China, and fourteen other WTO Members accounting for nearly 90 percent of the world's trade in environmental goods. The core of the agreement is the objective to reduce tariffs on a list of fifty-four environmental goods identified by the APEC forum (APEC Leaders Declaration, 2012).

In addition to embracing the social preferences of interested members to advance trade and regulatory goals, the EGA negotiation sets two other precedents that should be more widely embraced: the renewed use of WTO plurilateral agreements and the effort to multilateralize progress that occurred first on a bilateral or regional basis.

13.6.2.2 Multispeed Trade Integration

The WTO counts 164 members. They represent a very heterogeneous whole, ranging from Switzerland, Norway and Liechtenstein to the least developed countries in the sub-Saharan Africa. The social preferences of each member are, of course, defined endogenously and depend, in part, on the capacity of each member to finance the necessary regulatory policies to give effect to those preferences. Regulations reflect the culture, religion, the particulars of the legal system, and the relative homogeneity of that society. Whereas some social concerns are almost universal (climate change), others are quite local (pollution of a lake shared between two WTO Members). Under these circumstances, it is highly unlikely that regulatory cooperation will involve all its members.

The current WTO-think is based on the idea of "single undertaking," in which all members adopt agreements. The WTO, with the exception of the Agreement on Government Procurement (GPA), has, for all practical purposes, moved away from the Tokyo Round model of plurilateral integration. True, four plurilateral agreements had been signed during the Uruguay Round. Two of them are by now defunct though, and the usefulness of the Agreement on Civil Aviation is at best questionable in light of the fact that its disciplines are reproduced in the Agreement on Subsidies and Countervailing Measures. This leaves us with only the GPA as a legitimate plurilateral agreement.

Some criticized this Tokyo Round model of integration as increasing transaction costs for WTO Members. This was a rushed judgment. Yes, different WTO Members undertook different obligations in the Tokyo Round. But the advantage of that approach was the increased legitimacy. Each trading nation agreed to the commitments with which it could live. What we recommend here is, in a nutshell, a return to that approach, at least on the issue of regulatory cooperation.

The WTO should encourage the formation of plurilateral agreements, a design that, unlike free trade areas, keeps the umbilical cord between international regulatory cooperation and the multilateral trading regime tight. Intense regulatory cooperation is taking place within free trade areas, especially among like-minded partners. In light of this, it appears that trading nations gave up on the Tokyo Round approach of codes too soon. Those codes evolved at a moment when WTO agreements on nontariff barriers became a pressing issue, and when agreement across all GATT members would have been impossible. That same dynamic is even more pronounced today.

The advantages of WTO plurilateral agreements over PTAs are that the former provide greater transparency, input, and an explicit path to accession to nonparty WTO Members in the future. They are also less likely than PTAs to impose negative externalities on third countries (Hoekman and Mavroidis, 2015a, 2015b).

Currently, there are two ways in which a subset of WTO Members may undertake additional commitments and trade liberalization – critical mass agreements (CMAs) and plurilateral agreements (PAs). A CMA, as we have already discussed, is an agreement in which negotiated disciplines apply only to a subset of WTO Members, but its benefits are implemented on a most-favored nation (MFN) basis and, thus, must apply to all WTO Members. The significant advantage of CMAs is that these agreements do not require unanimous approval of the full WTO membership. The disadvantages of CMAs are that they allow free-riders and MFN disciplines are an uneasy fit with forms of cooperation that depend on like-minded regulatory agencies with similar capacities (again, see Bollyky, 2015).

In contrast, neither the benefits nor the commitments undertaken in PAs extend to nonsignatories. The major other advantage of PAs is, unlike CMAs, clear legal authority exists to extend and deepen WTO commitments on regulatory matters in areas other than services. The major disadvantage of PAs, however, is that their incorporation into the WTO must occur "exclusively by consensus" of the full membership, which greatly undermines the value of proceeding on a plurilateral basis.

For PAs to become a functional and feasible approach for advancing deeper regulatory cooperation at the WTO, Article X:9 of the WTO Agreement must be amended to no longer require approval of PAs by the full membership. In order to secure the necessary support for that amendment, WTO Members should also agree to binding principles limiting the use of PAs. These principles should include assurances that nonsignatories will not be compelled to adopt PAs at a later date. The principles should also provide that Members may join PAs later with the same conditions that applied to the original signatories and require implementation support to be provided for least developed member countries (see Lawrence, 2006). Requiring the creation of an observer status for nonparticipating WTO Members would also ensure the nonparticipating WTO Members have full transparency and can raise concerns.

The choice of topic for PAs should be member-state driven and reflect the need for interested governments to advance shared social preferences and efficient and effective regulatory oversight as part of global economic integration. This is most likely to occur in GVC-dominated sectors that depend on internationally consistent, adequate, and efficient standards for both freer trade and more effective regulatory oversight, such as automobiles, chemicals, and consumer goods (Bollyky, 2015). Another promising area is digital trade in goods and services, where regulatory paradigms are less entrenched in many countries and the adequacy and effective oversight of privacy, security, consumer protection, and contract enforcement depend on international cooperation and consistency (Manyika et al., 2016).

We should also note that the design of PAs should, of course, depend on the sector and the objectives for trade and regulatory cooperation. The WTO GATS provides a potentially useful model for a rolling process of rulemaking in a still novel area. The contribution of the GATS was to expand the coverage of services in the multilateral trading system but to do so in a way that afforded flexibility to countries undertaking new commitments.

This approach might involve a baseline set of rules and a venue for engagement on regulatory transparency, information sharing, and explanations of new rules. The agreement should establish priorities and transparent procedures but otherwise be left broad, allowing member countries the flexibility to collaborate on emerging challenges. It might operate in a hub-and-spoke model and include voluntary, topic-specific, regulator-led working groups for interested members to negotiate deeper forms of regulatory cooperation (Stewart, 2016). The hub, perhaps a Committee of participating member states with observer member states present, should: prepare common technical regulations and standards; recommend adoption of international standards; and promote the sharing of surveillance data and inspection reports through the development of confidentiality arrangements. The substance of these recommendations and proposals should be generated through the ad hoc, regulator-led working groups. These groups should be open to consultation with nonstate actors and experts. The recommendations and proposals of the Committee should be made public and subject to notice and comment.[55]

We should finally note that maintaining the sovereignty and local accountability of national regulatory authorities will be essential to the success. Agreed-upon regulatory cooperation measures should not have binding domestic legal effect. Thereby, where new legislation is required to implement such measures, opportunity for parliamentary scrutiny is assured. Participating member states should, however, commit to decide on whether to adopt these joint recommendations within a fixed period of time and to provide a written, detailed explanation when deciding not to do so. Given the relative novelty of regulatory cooperation and sensitivities around policy independence, subjecting the agreement to WTO dispute resolution would likely only discourage participation and inclusion of strong provisions in this area.

13.6.2.3 Expanding Partnerships

The state-to-state nature of WTO operations is increasingly outdated. Even a brief perusal of PTAs suffices for the reader to understand that a

[55] Bollyky (2012) makes similar recommendations with regard to what would have been a "twenty-first century approach" to regulatory coherence in the TPP.

lot more is requested from business and civil society in this context. Public-private partnerships are now common in investment projects and in GVCs. The WTO needs to play a larger role in working with partners to create the broadly supported governance frameworks that can advance international regulatory cooperation in the areas that most affect trade and investment (see Hoekman and Mavroidis, 2015c).

Keep in mind that regulatory cooperation is not the exclusive mandate of the WTO. Many other institutions, including the OECD, Food and Agriculture Organization of the United Nations, World Economic Forum, World Health Organization, and the International Centre for Trade and Sustainable Development, are in this space and can take the lead in setting substantive norms. The World Bank, regional development banks, and donors such as the Bill and Melinda Gates Foundation are all supporting regulatory cooperation initiatives and might offer financial resources for capacity building, policy dialogue, and monitoring here too.

We thus recommend greater engagement of the WTO with business organizations and civil society as particularly important for its future relevance. Firms participate in and manage GVCs, engage in private and nongovernmental international standard-setting initiatives, and support corporate social responsibility and capacity-building programs. Civil society, nongovernmental institutions, and academic institutions have expertise and the deep understanding of local circumstances to contribute agenda setting and ongoing problem solving.

13.6.2.4 Multilateralizing Progress in PTAs

Recent WTO publications propose multilateralizing the best practices observed in PTAs (Acharya, 2016). We agree. The WTO needs a mechanism to "multilateralize" the important regulatory cooperation that will inevitably happen in smaller clubs of like-minded countries, such as PTAs or regional economic communities.[56] Multilateralizing that progress would reduce business costs, expand regulatory cooperation and fulfillment of shared social preferences, and unlock the welfare benefits of trade liberalization in both the WTO and the PTAs.[57]

[56] For similar suggestions see Baldwin, Evenett, and Low (2009) and Trachtman (2007).

[57] Baldwin et al. (2009) note that the EU has a similar "clubs within the club" approach with its Closer Cooperations, or Enhanced Cooperations. See also Wolfe (2011), who expresses a similar view regarding the role of the OECD, as an institution that shapes but, unlike the WTO, does not codify trade law. PTAs codify trade law, of course, but may be able to shape the multilateral process as well.

One idea could be to initiate automatic negotiations any time a fixed number of countries belonging to the three distinct WTO groups (developed; developing; and least developed countries) entered into comparable arrangements on regulatory cooperation in separate agreements. Another idea would be to tie those automatic negotiations to the adoption of regulatory cooperation in a PTA covering a high percentage (such as 85 percent or more) of global trade in a goods or services sector.

13.7 Conclusion

Can the WTO evolve? The institution remains a product of the post–World War II, Bretton Woods era, created by a coalition of powerful states, and vested with their authority to act as their agent in addressing well-defined coordination and governance problems emerging from their interdependence. Like many of its sister institutions from this era, such as the World Bank, the International Monetary Fund, the United Nations and its agencies such as the World Health Organization, the WTO has struggled as power dispersed to a greater number of states and nonstate interests and broad-based consensus became harder to reach. It is no answer to state that the WTO will evolve because it must to survive. This has been true for many post–World War II era intergovernmental institutions for decades. Many have not and may never evolve.

The emergence of GVCs, however, provides the WTO with an opportunity. In the sectors where this production model dominates, GVCs create a potential alignment of the interests of a wide diversity of states and nonstate actors interested in freer trade, better regulation, and broader economic development. PTAs, standard-setting organizations, and regulator-to-regulator initiatives are making important progress in advancing the international regulatory cooperation needed in the GVC era. That progress is limited, however, because these arrangements do not encompass the full range of countries in global commerce.

This chapter advocates changes in the corporate governance of the GATT/WTO to reflect the decline in tariffs and border restraints to commerce and the emerging challenges of advancing trade, regulation cooperation, and social preferences in a global economy dominated by GVCs. Together, these changes form a positive integration strategy that we refer to as the new WTO-think. This strategy remains rooted in the original rationale of the GATT (or GATT-think) of reducing the negative externalities of unilateral action and solving important international coordination challenges, but is more inclusive of regulators and nonstate actors and more flexible and positive in its means. In particular, the WTO should embrace the confluence of shared social preferences and trade, where it exists, as a motivation for advancing international regulatory cooperation. It should multilateralize the important regulatory cooperation occurring in smaller clubs of like-minded countries and adopt changes to facilitate the use of PAs where agreement across all WTO Members is not yet possible.

While making these corporate governance changes will not be easy, they are feasible. There are precedents to draw upon from the Tokyo Round codes. The GATS and, more recently, the EGA negotiations offer potential lessons for tackling other regulatory cooperation changes at the WTO.

GVCs provide an opportunity for the WTO to evolve. As GVCs become less inclusive and more regional in nature, reaching consensus among the relevant actors will only become harder. The time to act is now.

REFERENCES

Acharya, R. (2016). *Regional Trade Agreements and the Multilateral Trading System*. Geneva: Cambridge University Press and the WTO.

Ahearn, R. J. (2009). *Transatlantic Regulatory Cooperation: Background and Analysis*. Washington, DC: Report for Congress, Congressional Research Service, 16–17.

Aichele, R., G. Felbermayr, and I. Heiland (2014). "Going Deep: The Trade and Welfare Effects of TTIP." Cesifo Working Paper No. 5150. Center for Economic Studies and Ifo Institute.

Akhtar, S. I. and V. C. Jones (2014). *Transatlantic Trade and Investment Partnership (TTIP) Negotiations*. Washington, DC: Report for Congress, Congressional Research Service, 26–8.

Allee, T. and M. Elsig (2019). "Are the Contents of International Treaties Copied-and-Pasted? Unique Evidence from Preferential Trade Agreements." *International Studies Quarterly* https://doi.org/10.1093/isq/sqz029.

Allee, T. and A. Lugg (2016). "Who Wrote the Rules for the Trans-Pacific Partnership?" *Research and Politics*, 1–13 (April–June).

Allee, T., M. Elsig, and A. Lugg (2017b). "Is the European Union Trade Deal with Canada New or Recycled? A Text-as-Data Approach." *Global Policy*, 8(2): 246–52.

(2017a). "The Ties between the World Trade Organization and Preferential Trade Agreements: A Textual Analysis." *Journal of International Economic Law*, 20(2): 333–63.

Allio, L. (2015). "Ex Post Evaluation of Regulation: An Overview of the Notion and of International Practices." In OECD (Ed.), *Regulatory Policy in Perspective: A Reader's Companion to the OECD Regulatory Policy Outlook 2015*. Paris: OECD Publishing.

Anliker, M. (2016). "Non-preferential Rules of Origin: High Level Assessment." Report. PricewaterhouseCoopers.

Antràs, P. and R. W. Staiger (2012). "Offshoring and the Role of Trade Agreements." *American Economic Review*, 102(7): 3140–83.

Antràs, P., D. Chor, T. Fally, and R. Hillberry (2012). "Measuring the Upstreamness of Production and Trade Flows." *The American Economic Review*, 102(3): 412–16.

APEC Leaders Declaration (2012). List of Environmental Goods, Annex C.

Arkolakis, C., A. Costinot, and A. Rodríguez-Clare (2012). "New Trade Models, Same Old Gains?" *American Economic Review*, 102(1): 94–130.

Arvíus, C. and L. Jachia (2015). *Regulatory Cooperation: A Wikihow*. E15 Initiative, Geneva.

Australian Government Department of Health: Therapeutic Goods Administration (2007). "Australia New Zealand Therapeutic Products Authority (ANZTPA) Postponed" [Press Release]. www.tga.gov.au/Media-Release/Australia-New-Zealand-Therapeutic-Products-Authority-Anztpa-Postponed.

Autor, D., D. Dorn, and G. Hanson (2016). "The China Shock: Learning about Labor Market Adjustment to Large Changes in Trade." *Annual Review of Economics*, 8(1): 205–40.

Ayres, I. and J. Braithwaite (1992). *Responsive Regulation: Transcending the Deregulation Debate*. Oxford: Oxford University Press.

Bacchetta, M., J. Richtering, and R. Santana (2012). "How Much Light Do WTO Notifications Shed on NTMs?" In O. Cadot and M. Malouche (Eds.), *Non-Tariff Measures: A Fresh Look at Trade Policy's New Frontier*. Washington, DC: World Bank, Centre for Economic Policy Research, Chapter 2.

Baccini, L., A. Dür, and Y. Haftel (2014). "Imitation and Innovation in International Governance: The Diffusion of Trade Agreement Design." In A. Dür and M. Elsig (Eds.), *Trade Cooperation: The Purpose, Design and Effects of Preferential Trade Agreements*. Cambridge: Cambridge University Press.

Backer, K. D. and S. Miroudot (2013). "Mapping Global Value Chains." OECD Trade Policy Papers No. 159. Paris: OECD Publishing. http://dx.doi.org/10.1787/5k3v1trgnbr4-En.

Bagwell, K. and R. W. Staiger (2002). "Economic Theory and the Interpretation of GATT/WTO." *The American Economist*, 46(2): 3–19.

Bagwell, K., C. P. Bown, and R. W. Staiger (2016). "Is the WTO Passé?" *Journal of Economic Literature*, 54(4): 1125–31.

Bair, J. (2005). "Global Capitalism and Commodity Chains: Looking Back, Going Forward." *Competition and Change*, 9(2): 153–80.

Baker, S. R., N. Bloom, and S. J. Davis (2016). "Measuring Economic Policy Uncertainty." *The Quarterly Journal of Economics*, 131(4): 1593–636.

Baldwin, R. E. (1970). *Non-tariff Distortions in International Trade*. Washington, DC: Brookings Institution.

(1971). "Determinants of the Commodity Structure of US Trade." *American Economic Review*, 61(1): 126–46.

(2010). "Unilateral Tariff Liberalization." NBER Working Paper No. 16600.

(2012). "Global Supply Chains: Why They Emerged, Why They Matter, and Where They Are Going." CTEI Working Paper 2012–13. Geneva: Centre for Trade and Economic Integration (Demonstrating Range and Diversity of Countries in GVCs and Their Degree of Engagement).

(2014). *Multilateralising 21st Century Regionalism*. Global Forum on Trade, OECD.

Baldwin, R. E. and D. Jaimovich (2012). "Are Free Trade Agreements Contagious?" *Journal of International Economics*, 88(1): 1–16.

Baldwin, R. E., S. Evenett, and P. Low (2009). "Beyond Tariffs: Multilateralising Non-tariff RTA Commitments." In R. Baldwin and P. Low (Eds.), *Multilateralising Regionalism: Challenges for the Global Trading System*. Cambridge: Cambridge University Press, 79–141.

Baldwin, R. E., J. F. Francois, and R. Portes (1997). "The Costs and Benefits of Eastern Enlargement: The Impact on the EU and Central Europe." *Economic Policy*, 12(24): 125–76.

Baltagi, B. H., P. Egger, and M. Pfaffermay (2003). "A Generalized Design for Bilateral Trade Flow Models." *Economics Letters*, 80(3): 391–7.

Bao, X. and L. D. Qiu (2010). "Do Technical Barriers to Trade Promote or Restrict Trade? Evidence from China." *Asia-Pacific Journal of Accounting and Economics*, 17: 253–80.

Basedow, R. and C. Kauffmann (2016). "International Trade and Good Regulatory Practices: Assessing the Trade Impacts of Regulation." OECD Regulatory Policy Working Paper 4. Paris: OECD Publishing.

Bchir, M. H., Y. Decreux, J.-L. Guérin, and S. Jean (2002). "MIRAGE, a Computable General Equilibrium Model for Trade Policy Analysis." CEPII Working Paper No. 2002–17.

Beghin, J., A. C. Disdier, and S. Marette (2015). "Trade Restrictiveness Indices in the Presence of Externalities: An Application to Non-tariff Measures." *Canadian Journal of Economics/Revue Canadienne d'économique*, 48(4): 1513–36.

Beghin, J., A. C. Disdier, S. Marette, and F. van Tongeren (2012). "Welfare Costs and Benefits of Non-tariff Measures in Trade: A Conceptual Framework and Application." *World Trade Review*, 11(3): 356–75.

Bekkers, E. and H. Rojas-Romagosa (2019). "The Welfare Effects of FTAs in Quantitative Trade Models: A Comparison of Studies about TTIP." *World Economy*, 42(1): 87–121.

Bekkers, E., J. Francois, and M. Manchin (2012). "Import Prices, Income, and Inequality." *European Economic Review*, 56(4): 848–69.

Bekkers E., J. Francois, and H. Rojas-Romagosa (2018). "Melting Ice Caps and the Economic Impact of Opening the Northern Sea Route." *The Economic Journal*, 128(610): 1095–127 (May).

Bennard, L. and K. Dickinson (2011). "Incorporating Evaluation into the Regulatory Process." Duke Environmental Economics Working Paper Series 11.

Berden, K. and J. Francois (2015). "Quantifying Non-tariff Measures for TTIP." In D. S. Hamilton and J. Pelkmans (Eds.), *Rule-Makers or Rule-Takers? Exploring the Transatlantic Trade and Investment Partnership*. Brussels and

Washington, DC: Centre for European Policy Studies (CEPS) and Center for Transatlantic Relations (CTR).
Bergh, A. and T. Nilsson (2010). "Do Liberalization and Globalization Increase Income Inequality?" *European Journal of Political Economy*, 26(4): 488–505.
Bertoletti, P. and F. Etro (2016). "Monopolistic Competition When Income Matters." *The Economic Journal*, 127(603): 1217–43.
Bhagwati, J. (1965). "On the Equivalence of Tariffs and Quotas." In R. E. Baldwin et al. (Eds.), *Trade, Growth, and the Balance of Payments*. Chicago: Rand McNally, 53–67.
Bhagwati, J. and R. E. Hudec (1990). *Aggressive Unilateralism: America's 301 Trade Policy and the World Trading System*. Ann Arbor: University of Michigan Press.
Blackhurst, R., A. Enders, and J. F. Francois (1996). "The Uruguay Round and Market Access: Opportunities and Challenges for Developing Countries." In W. Martin and A. Winters (Eds.), *The Uruguay Round and the Developing Countries*. Cambridge: Cambridge University Press.
Blanka, K., A. Palerm, and S. Thomsen (2010). "OECD's FDI Restrictiveness Index: 2010 Update." OECD Working Papers on International Investment. Paris: OECD Publishing.
Blonigen, B. A. and T. J. Prusa (2016). "Dumping and Antidumping Duties." In K. Bagwell and R. W. Staiger (Eds.), *The Handbook of Commercial Policy, Volume 1B*. Amsterdam: Elsevier/North Holland, 107–59.
Bollyky, T. J. (2009). *Global Health Interventions for Food and Drug Safety*. Washington, DC: Center for Strategic and International Studies.
(2012). "Regulatory Coherence in the TPP Talks." In C. L. Lim, D. K. Elms, and P. Low (Eds.), *The Trans-Pacific Partnership: A Quest for a Twenty-First Century Trade Agreement*. Cambridge: Cambridge University Press, 171–86.
(2015). *A Role for the WTO on Regulatory Coherence*. E15 Initiative, Geneva.
Borchert, I., B. Gootiiz, and A. Mattoo (2011). "Services in Doha: What's on the Table." In W. Martin and A. Mattoo (Eds.), *Unfinished Business? The WTO's Doha Agenda*. Washington, DC: World Bank/CEPR, 115–43.
(2012). "Guide to the Services Trade Restrictions Database." World Bank Policy Research Working Paper No. 6108, Washington, DC.
(2014). "Policy Barriers to International Trade in Services: Evidence from a New Database." *The World Bank Economic Review*, 28(1): 162–88.
Bown, C. P. (2007). "Global Antidumping Database Version 3.0." World Bank Policy Research Working Paper No. 3737, Washington, DC.
Bown, C. P. (2011). "Taking Stock of Antidumping, Safeguards and Countervailing Duties, 1990–2009." *World Economy*, 34(12): 1955–98.
(2016a). "Should the United States Recognize China as a Market Economy?" Peterson Institute for International Economics Policy Brief No. 16-24, December.

(2016b). "Temporary Trade Barriers Database." Washington, DC: World Bank. http://econ.worldbank.org/ttbd.

(2016c). "The Perils of Shifting China's 'Market Economy' Dispute to the WTO." *World Politics Review*, December 21.

Bown, C. P. (Ed.) (2017). *Economics and Policy in the Age of Trump*. London: CEPR Press.

Bown, C. P. and R. Brewster (2017). "US–COOL Retaliation: The WTO's Article 22.6 Arbitration." *World Trade Review*, 16(2): 371–94.

Bown, C. P. and M. A. Crowley (2013a). "Self-Enforcing Trade Agreements: Evidence from Time-Varying Trade Policy." *American Economic Review*, 103(2): 1071–90.

(2013b). "Import Protection, Business Cycles, and Exchange Rates: Evidence from the Great Recession." *Journal of International Economics*, 90(1): 50–64.

(2016). "The Empirical Landscape of Trade Policy." In K. Bagwell and R. W. Staiger (Eds.), *The Handbook of Commercial Policy, Volume 1A*. Amsterdam: Elsevier/North Holland.

Bown, C. P. and D. A. Irwin (2016). "The GATT's Starting Point: Tariff Levels Circa 1947." In M. Elsig, B. Hoekman, and J. Pauwelyn (Eds.), *Assessing the World Trade Organization: Fit for Purpose?* Cambridge: Cambridge University Press.

Bown, C. P. and P. C. Mavroidis (2013). "One (Firm) Is Not Enough: A Legal-Economic Analysis of EC-Fasteners." *World Trade Review*, 12(2): 243–71.

Bown, C. P. and R. McCulloch (2009). "US-Japan and US-China Trade Conflict: Export Growth, Reciprocity, and the International Trading System." *Journal of Asian Economics*, 20(6): 669–87.

Bradsher, K. (2009). "China Moves to Retaliate against US Tire Tariff." *New York Times*, September 13.

Braithwaite, J. and P. Drahos (2000). *Global Business Regulation*. Cambridge: Cambridge University Press.

Bratt, M. (2017). "Estimating the Bilateral Impact of Nontariff Measures on Trade." *Review of International Economics*, 25(5): 1105–29.

Büthe, T. and W. Mattli (2011). *The New Global Rulers: The Privatization of Regulation in the World Economy*. Princeton, NJ: Princeton University Press.

Cadot, O. and L. Y. Ing (2016). "How Restrictive Are ASEAN's RoOs?" *Asian Economic Papers*, 15(3): 115–34.

Cadot, O., M. Malouche, and S. Sáez (2012). *Streamlining Non-tariff Measures – A Toolkit for Policy Makers*. Washington, DC: World Bank.

Cadot, O., C. Carrere, J. De Melo, and B. Tumurchudur (2006). "Product-Specific Rules of Origin in EU and US Preferential Trading Arrangements: An Assessment." *World Trade Review*, 5(2): 199–224.

Caliendo, L. and F. Parro (2015). "Estimates of the Trade and Welfare Effects of NAFTA." *Review of Economic Studies*, 82(1): 1–44.

Caron, J., T. Falley, and J. M. Markusen (2014). "International Trade Puzzles: A Solution Linking Production and Preferences." *The Quarterly Journal of Economics,* 129(3): 1501–52.

Carrère, C., A. Grujovicz, and F. Robert-Nicoud (2015). "Trade and Frictional Unemployment in the Global Economy." CEPR Discussion Paper No. 10692. Centre for Economic Policy Research.

Caves, D. W., L. R. Christensen, and W. E. Diewert (1982). "Multilateral Comparisons of Output, Input, and Productivity Using Superlative Index Numbers." *The Economic Journal,* 92(365): 73–86.

Choi, Y. C., D. Hummels, and C. Xiang (2009). "Explaining Import Quality: The Role of Income Distribution." *Journal of International Economics,* 77(2): 265–75.

Chor, D., K. Manova, and Z. Yu (2014). "The Global Production Line Position of Chinese Firms." Industrial Upgrading and Urbanization Conference, Stockholm, Vol. 28.

Christen, E., J. Francois, and B. Hoekman (2012). "Computable General Equilibrium Modeling of Market Access in Services." In P. B. Dixon and D. W. Jorgenson (Eds.), *Handbook of Computable General Equilibrium Modeling.* Amsterdam: Elsevier.

Ciuriak, D., A. Dadkhah, and J. Xiao (2016). "Taking the Measure of the TPP as Negotiated." SSRN Working Papers. Available at SSRN: https://ssrn.com/abstract=2743009.

(2017). "Quantifying the Comprehensive and Progressive Agreement for Trans-Pacific Partnership." *East Asian Economic Review,* 21(4): 343–84.

Coe, D. T., E. Helpman, and A. W. Hoffmaister (1997). "North-South R&D Spillovers." *Economic Journal,* 107(440): 134–49.

Coglianese, C. (2016). "Measuring Regulatory Excellence." In Cary Coglianese (Ed.), *Achieving Regulatory Excellence.* Washington, DC: Brookings Institution Press.

Conconi, P., M. García-Santana, L. Puccio, and R. Venturini (2018). "From Final Goods to Inputs: The Protectionist Effect of Rules of Origin." *American Economic Review,* 108(8): 2335–65.

Corporate Europe Observatory (2015). "Regulatory Cooperation in TTIP: United in Deregulation." April. Brussels. https://corporateeurope.org/international-trade/2015/04/regulatory-cooperation-ttip-united-deregulation.

(2016). "Dangerous Regulatory Duet – How Transatlantic Regulatory Cooperation under TTIP Will Allow Bureaucrats and Big Business to Attack the Public Interest." January. Brussels. https://corporateeurope.org/sites/default/files/attachments/regulatoryduet_en021.pdf.

Cosar, K., N. Guner, and J. R. Tybout (2016). "Firm Dynamics, Job Turnover, and Wage Distributions in an Open Economy." *American Economic Review,* 106(3): 625–63.

Crivelli, P. and S. Inama (2018). "Comparative Analysis of RoO in Recent FTAs." UNCTAD and EUI, Excel Workbook and Related Tables. In Progress.

Crozet, M., E. Milet, and D. Mirza (2016). "The Impact of Domestic Regulations on International Trade in Services: Evidence from Firm-Level Data." *Journal of Comparative Economics*, 44(3): 585–60.

Dalgin, M., V. Trindade, and D. Mitra (2008). "Nonhomothetic Preferences, and Trade: A Gravity Approach." *Southern Economic Journal*, 74(3): 747–74.

Davies, G. (2016). "The Global Pivot towards Fiscal Policy." *Financial Times*, 25 September.

De Almeida, F. M., W. Da Cruz Vieira, and O. M. Da Silva (2012). "SPS and TBT Agreements and International Agricultural Trade: Retaliation or Cooperation?" *Agricultural Economics*, 43(2): 125–32.

De Búrca, G., R. O. Keohane, and C. Sabel (2014). "Global Experimentalist Governance." *British Journal of Political Science*, 44: 477–86.

Deardorff, A. (1998). "Determinants of Bilateral Trade: Does Gravity Work in a Neoclassical World?" In J. Frankel (Ed.), *The Regionalization of the World Economy*. Chicago: University of Chicago Press, 7–32.

Deardorff, A. V. and R. M. Stern (1997). "Measurement of Non-tariff Barriers." OECD Economics Department Working Paper No. 179. Paris: OECD Publishing.

Department of Commerce (2006a). "The People's Republic of China (PRC) Status As a Non-Market Economy (NME)." A-570-901 Investigation Public Document, May 15. Washington, DC.

(2006b). "Antidumping Duty Investigation of Certain Lined Paper Products from the People's Republic of China ('China'). China's Status as a Non-Market Economy ('NME')." A-570-901 Investigation Public Document, August 30. Washington, DC.

(2007). "Countervailing Duty Investigation of Coated Free Sheet Paper from the People's Republic of China. Whether the Analytical Elements of the *Georgetown Steel* Opinion Are Applicable to China's Present-Day Economy." Document C-570-907, March 29. Washington, DC.

Disdier, A., L. Fontagne, and M. Mimouni (2008). "The Impact of Regulations on Agricultural Trade: Evidence from the SPS and TBT Agreements." *American Journal of Agricultural Economics*, 90(2): 336–50.

Drezner, D. W. (2008). *All Politics Is Global: Explaining International Regulatory Regimes*. Princeton, NJ: Princeton University Press.

Dunlop, C. and C. Radaelli (Eds.) (2016). *Handbook of Regulatory Impact Assessment*. Cheltenham: Edward Elgar.

Dür, A., L. Baccini, and M. Elsig (2014). "The Design of International Trade Agreements: Introducing a New Dataset." *The Review of International Organizations*, 9(3): 353–75.

Eaton, M., B. Leatherbarrow, Z. Shapiro, J. Signoret, and J. Vila-Goulding (2013). "The CoRe NTMs Database Version 2: A Compilation of Reported

Non-Tariff Measures." US International Trade Commission Working Paper No. 2013-01A.

ECORYS (2009). "Non-tariff Measures in EU-US Trade and Investment: An Economic Analysis." Report Prepared by Koen G. Berden, Joseph F. Francois, Saara Tamminen, Martin Thelle, and Paul Wymenga for the European Commission, Reference OJ 2007/S180-219493, ECORYS Nederland BV.

Ederington, J. and M. Ruta (2016). "Non-tariff Measures and the World Trading System." World Bank Policy Research Working Paper No. 7661, Washington, DC.

Edwards, S. (1998). "Openness, Productivity and Growth: What Do We Really Know?" *The Economic Journal*, 108(447): 383–98.

Egan, M. and J. Pelkmans (2015). "TTIP's Hard Core – Technical Barriers to Trade and Standards." Paper No. 13 in the CEPS-CTR Project "TTIP in the Balance" and CEPS Special Report No. 117. Brussels: Centre for European Policy Studies.

Egger, P., M. Larch, and K. E. Staub (2012). "Trade Preferences and Bilateral Trade in Goods and Services: A Structural Approach." CEPR Discussion Paper No. 9051. Centre for Economic Policy Research.

Egger, P., J. F. Francois, M. Manchin, and D. Nelson (2015). "Non-tariff Barriers, Integration and the Transatlantic Economy." *Economic Policy*, 30(83): 539–84.

Elliott, K. A. (2012). "Labor Standards and the TPP." In C. L. Lim, Deborah K. Elms, and Patrick Low (Eds.), *The Trans-Pacific Partnership: A Quest for a Twenty-First Century Trade Agreement*. Cambridge: Cambridge University Press, 200–10.

Estevadeordal, A. (1999). "Negotiating Preferential Market Access: The Case of NAFTA." INTAL ITD Working Paper No. 3. Institute for the Integration of Latin America and the Caribbean and the Integration, Trade and Hemispheric Issues Division of the Integration and Regional Programs Department of the IDB.

Estevadeordal, A. and K. Suominen (2004). "Rules of Origin in FTAs in Europe and the Americas: Issues and Implications for EC–Mercosur Interregional Association Agreement." INTAL ITD Working Paper No. 15. Institute for the Integration of Latin America and the Caribbean and the Integration, Trade and Hemispheric Issues Division of the Integration and Regional Programs Department of the IDB.

(2006). "Mapping and Measuring Rules of Origin around the World." In Olivier Cadot, Antoni Estevadeordal, Akiko Suwa-Eisenmann, and Thierry Verdier (Eds.), *The Origin of Goods: Rules of Origin in Regional Trade Agreements*. Oxford: Oxford University Press, 69–113.

Estevadeordal, A., J. Harris, and K. Suominen (2009). "Multilateralizing Preferential Rules of Origin around the World." Inter-American Development Bank Working Paper No. 137.

European Commission (2013). "Transatlantic Trade and Investment Partnership: The Economic Analysis Explained." Technical Report. European Commission.

Evenett, S. and J. Fritz (2015a). *Throwing Sand in the Wheels: How Foreign Trade Distortions Slowed LDC Export-Led Growth*. London: CEPR Press.

(2015b). *The Tide Turns? Trade, Protectionism, and Slowing Global Growth*. London: CEPR Press.

(2016). *Global Trade Plateaus*. London: CEPR Press.

Evenett, S. and B. Hoekman (2005). "Government Procurement: Market Access, Transparency, and Multilateral Trade Rules." *European Journal of Political Economy*, 21(1): 163–83 (March).

Feenstra, R. C. (1994). "New Product Varieties and the Measurement of International Prices." *American Economic Review*, 84(1): 157–77.

Feenstra, R. C., R. Inklaar, and M. P. Timmer (2015). "The Next Generation of the Penn World Table." *American Economic Review*, 105(10): 3150–82, www.ggdc.net/pwt (accessed May 24, 2019).

Felbermayr, G., B. Heid, and S. Lehwald (2013a). "Transatlantic Trade and Investment Partnership (TTIP): Who Benefits from a Free Trade Deal?" Report, Global Economic Dynamics (GED). Bertelsmann Foundation.

Felbermayr, G., B. Heid, M. Larch, and E. Yalcin (2015). "Macroeconomic Potentials of Transatlantic Free Trade: A High Resolution Perspective for Europe and the World." *Economic Policy*, 30(83): 491–537.

Felbermayr, G., M. Larch, L. Flach, E. Yalcin, and S. Benz (2013b). "Dimensionen und Auswirkungen eines Freihandelsabkommens Zwischen der EU und den USA." Studie im Auftrag des Bundesministeriums für Wirtschaft und Technologie, Endbericht, CES-IFO.

Fieler, A. (2011). "Nonhomotheticity and Bilateral Trade: Evidence and a Quantitative Explanation." *Econometrica*, 79(4): 1069–1101.

Fontagné, L., A. Guillin, and C. Mitaritonna (2011). "Estimations of Tariff Equivalents for the Services Sectors." CEPII Working Paper No. 2011-24.

Fontagné, L., J. Gourdon, and S. Jean (2013). "Transatlantic Trade: Whither Partnership, Which Economic Consequences?" CEPII Policy Brief No. 1.

Foster-McGregor, N., J. Pöschl, and R. Stehrer (2014). "Capacities and Absorptive Barriers for International R&D Spillovers through Intermediate Inputs." Working Paper No. 108. The Vienna Institute for International Economic Studies, wiiw.

Francois, J. (1997). "External Bindings and the Credibility of Reform." In A. Galal and B. Hoekman (Eds.), *Regional Partners in Global Markets*. Cambridge: Cambridge University Press.

(2001). "Trade Policy Transparency and Investor Confidence – The Implications of an Effective Trade Policy Review Mechanism." *Review of International Economics*, 9(2): 303–16.

Francois, J. F. and B. Hoekman (1999). "Estimates of Barriers to Trade in Services." Working Paper. Erasmus University, Tinbergen Institute.

(2010). "Services Trade and Policy." *Journal of Economic Literature*, 48: 1–51.

Francois, J. and S. Kaplan (1996). "Aggregate Demand Shifts, Income Distribution, and the Linder Hypothesis." *The Review of Economics and Statistics*, 244–50.

Francois, J. and M. Manchin (2016). "Technical Note on Services NTM Database." Technical Paper for EC Project PRONTO under the European Union's Seventh Framework Programme for Research, Technological Development and Demonstration under grant agreement No. 61350. Downloadable at: https://prontonetwork.org/database/resources/papers/WB%20Services%20NTM%20database.pdf.

Francois, J. and W. Martin (1997). "Bindings and Rules as Trade Liberalization." In Keith E. Maskus, Peter Hooper, and Edward E. Leamer (Eds.), *Quiet Pioneering: Robert Stern and His International Economic Legacy*. Ann Arbor: University of Michigan Press.

(2003). "Formula Approaches for Market Access Negotiations." *The World Economy*, 26(1): 1–28.

(2004). "Commercial Policy Variability, Bindings, and Market Access." *European Economic Review*, 48(3): 665–79.

Francois, J., B. Hoekman, and D. Nelson (2015). "TTIP, Regulatory Diversion and Third Countries." In M. Akman, S. Evenett, and P. Low (Eds.), *Catalyst? TTIP's Impact on the Rest*. London: CEPR Press.

Francois, J., B. Hoekman, and J. Woerz (2007). "Does Gravity Apply to Nontangibles: Trade and FDI Openness in Services." Plenary Paper, 2007 European Trade Study Group Conference.

Francois, J., M. Manchin, H. Norberg, O. Pindyuk, and P. Tomberger (2013). "Reducing Transatlantic Barriers to Trade and Investment: An Economic Assessment." Final Project Report, Prepared under Implementing Framework Contract TRADE10/A2/A16. London: CEPR.

Frankel, J. A. and D. Romer (1999). "Does Trade Cause Growth?" *American Economic Review*, 89(3): 379–99.

Friedman, B. (2005). *The Moral Consequences of Economic Growth*. New York: Knopf.

Gawande, K., B. Hoekman, and Y. Cui (2015). "Global Supply Chains and Trade Policy Responses to the 2008 Financial Crisis." *World Bank Economic Review*, 29(1): 102–28.

Gereffi, G. (1994). "The Organization of Buyer-Driven Global Commodity Chains: How US Retailers Shape Overseas Production Networks." In G. Gereffi and M. Korzeniewicz (Eds.), *Commodity Chains and Global Capitalism*. Westport, CT: Praeger.

(2014). *A Global Value Chain Perspective on Industrial Policy and Development in Emerging Markets*. Mimeo.

Gereffi, G. and T. Sturgeon (2013). "Global Value Chain-Oriented Industrial Policy: The Role of Emerging Economies." In D. K. Elms and P. Low (Eds.), *Global Value Chains in a Changing World*. Geneva: World Trade Organization.

Gereffi, G., J. Humphrey, and T. Sturgeon (2005). "The Governance of Global Value Chains." *Review of International Political Economy*, 12(1): 78–104.

Ghodsi, M. (2018). "Determinants of Specific Trade Concerns Raised on Technical Barriers to Trade EU versus Non-EU." *Empirica*, 45(1): 85–138 .

Ghodsi, M. M. and J. J. Michalek (2016). "Technical Barriers to Trade Notifications and Dispute Settlement within the WTO." *Equilibrium. Quarterly Journal of Economics and Economic Policy*, 11(2): 219–49.

Ghodsi, M., J. Gruebler, and R. Stehrer (2016a). "Estimating Importer-Specific Ad Valorem Equivalents of Non-tariff Measures." Working Paper No. 129. The Vienna Institute for International Economic Studies, wiiw.

Ghodsi, M., O. Reiter, and R. Stehrer (2015). "Compilation of a Database for Non-tariff Measures from the WTO Integrated Trade Intelligence Portal (WTO I-TIP)." Mimeo. The Vienna Institute for International Economic Studies, wiiw.

Ghodsi, M., J. Gruebler, O. Reiter, and R. Stehrer (2016b). "The Evolution of Non-tariff Measures and Their Diverse Effects on Trade." Mimeo. The Vienna Institute for International Economic Studies, wiiw.

Goldberg, P. and G. Maggi (1999). "Protection for Sale: An Empirical Investigation." *American Economic Review*, 89(5): 1135–55.

Goldberg, P. and N. Pavcnik (2007). "Distributional Effects of Globalization in Developing Countries." *Journal of Economic Perspectives*, 45(1): 39–82.

Gootiiz, B. and A. Mattoo (2017). "Services in the Trans-Pacific Partnership: What Would Be Lost?" World Bank Policy Research Working Paper No. 7964, Washington, DC.

Greenhill, B., L. Mosely, and A. Prakash (2009). "Trade-Based Diffusion of Labor Rights: A Panel Study, 1986–2002." *American Political Science Review*, 103: 669–90.

Greenpeace (2016). "TTIP Leaks." www.ttip-leaks.org (accessed October 11, 2016).

Grossman, G. M. and E. Helpman (1993). *Innovation and Growth in the Global Economy*. Cambridge, MA: MIT Press.

Grossman, G. M. and H. Horn (2013). "Why the WTO? An Introduction to the Economics of Trade Agreements." In H. Horn and P. C. Mavroidis (Eds.), *Legal and Economic Principles of World Trade Law*. Cambridge: Cambridge University Press, 9–66.

Grosso, M. G., F. Gonzales, S. Miroudot, H. K. Nordås, D. Rouzet, and A. Ueno (2015). "Services Trade Restrictiveness Index (STRI): Scoring and Weighting Methodology." OECD Trade Policy Paper No. 177. Paris: OECD Publishing.

Gulen, H. and M. Ion (2015). “Policy Uncertainty and Corporate Investment.” *The Review of Financial Studies*, 29(3): 523–64.

Handley, K. (2014). “Exporting under Trade Policy Uncertainty: Theory and Evidence.” *Journal of International Economics*, 94(1): 50–66.

Harrison, A. (1996). “Openness and Growth: A Time-Series, Cross-Country Analysis for Developing Countries.” *Journal of Development Economics*, 48(2): 419–47.

Head, K. and T. Mayer (2010). “Illusory Border Effects: Distance Mismeasurement Inflates Estimates of Home Bias in Trade.” In S. Brakman and P. Van Bergeijk (Eds.), *The Gravity Model in International Trade: Advances and Applications*. Cambridge: Cambridge University Press.

(2014). “Gravity Equations: Workhorse, Toolkit, and Cookbook.” In G. Gopinath, E. Helpman, and K. Rogoff (Eds.), *Handbook of International Economics*, Vol. 4. Amsterdam: Elsevier, 131–95.

Henson, Spencer (2003). “Food Safety Issues in International Trade (Brief 5).” In Laurian J. Unnevehr (Ed.), *Food Safety in Food Security and Food Trade*. Washington, DC: International Food Policy Research Institute.

Hertel, T. (2013). “Global Applied General Equilibrium Analysis Using the Global Trade Analysis Project Framework.” In P. Dixon and D. Jorgenson (Eds.), *Handbook of Computable General Equilibrium Modeling*. Amsterdam: Elsevier.

Hertel, T. W. and M. E. Tsigas (1997). “Structure of GTAP.” In T. W. Hertel (Ed.), *Global Trade Analysis: Modeling and Applications*. Cambridge: Cambridge University Press.

Hoekman, B. (1996). “Assessing the General Agreement in Trade in Services.” In W. Martin and A. Winters (Eds.), *The Uruguay Round and the Developing Countries*. Cambridge: Cambridge University Press.

(2008). “The General Agreement on Trade in Services: Doomed to Fail? Does It Matter?” *Journal of Industry, Competition and Trade*, 8(3): 295–318.

(2014). “Supply Chains, Mega-regionals and Multilateralism: A Road Map for the WTO.” London: CEPR Press, https://voxeu.org/sites/default/files/file/WTO_Roadmap.pdf.

(2015). “Fostering Transatlantic Regulatory Cooperation and Multilateralization.” *Journal of International Economic Law*, 18: 609–24.

(2016). “‘Behind the Border’ Policies: Regulatory Cooperation and Trade Agreements.” In Bernard Hoekman and Carlos A. Primo Braga (Eds.), *Future of the Global Trade Order*. Lausanne: European University Institute and IMD, 69–96.

Hoekman, B. and M. Kostecki (2009). *The Political Economy of the World Trading System*, 3rd ed. Oxford: Oxford University Press.

Hoekman, B. and P. Mavroidis (2015a). *Regulatory Spillovers and the Trading System: From Coherence to Cooperation*. E15 Initiative, Geneva.

(2015b). "Embracing Diversity: Plurilateral Agreements and the Trading System." *World Trade Review*, 14(1): 101–16.

(2015c). "WTO 'à la Carte' or 'Menu du Jour'? Assessing the Case for More Plurilateral Agreements." *European Journal of International Law*, 26(2): 319–43.

(2015d). *World Trade Organization (WTO): Law, Economics, and Politics*, 2nd ed. New York: Routledge.

Hopkins, T. K. and I. Wallerstein (1977). "Patterns of Development of the Modern World-System." *Review of the Fernand Braudel Center*, 111–45.

Horn, H., G. Maggi, and R. Staiger (2010a). "Trade Agreements as Endogenously Incomplete Contracts." *American Economic Review*, 100(1): 394–419.

Horn, H., P. Mavroidis, and A. Sapir (2010b). "Beyond the WTO? An Anatomy of the US and EU Preferential Trade Agreements." *The World Economy*, 33: 1565–88.

Hudec, R. E. (1993). *Enforcing International Trade Law*. London: Butterworths.

Hummels, D. and P. L. Klenow (2005). "The Variety and Quality of a Nation's Trade." *American Economic Review*, 95(3): 704–23.

Immelt, J. (2016). "The World I See." Text of Commencement Address to New York University Stern School of Business. http://fortune.com/2016/05/20/ge-immelt-globalization/.

Inama, S., E. Vermulst, and P. Eeckhout (2009). "Nonpreferential Origin Rules in Antidumping Law and Practice." In K. Bagwell, G. Bermann, and P. Mavroidis (Eds.), *Law and Economics of Contingent Protection in International Trade*. Cambridge: Cambridge University Press, 276–308.

Inglehart, R. (2000). "Globalization and Postmodern Values." *The Washington Quarterly*, 23(1): 215–28.

Institute of Medicine (IOM) (2013). *International Regulatory Harmonization Amid Globalization of Drug Development: Workshop Summary*. Washington, DC: The National Academies Press.

Ip, G. (2016). "Central Banks Are Losing Their Edge." *Wall Street Journal*, September 21.

Irwin, D. (2015). *Free Trade under Fire*. Princeton, NJ: Princeton University Press.

Irwin, D., P. Mavroidis, and A. O. Sykes (2008). *The Genesis of the GATT*. Cambridge: Cambridge University Press.

ITC (2014). "Classification of Trade Obstacles for the TOA Platform." Geneva: International Trade Centre, May.

ITC (2015). "The Invisible Barriers to Trade – How Businesses Experience Non-Tariff Measures." International Trade Centre Technical Paper No. MAR-15-326.E, Geneva.

ITC (2016). "Procedural Obstacles." www.intracen.org/itc/market-info-tools/non-tariff-measures/procedural-obstacles/ (accessed April 20, 2016).

Jackson, J. H. (1969). *World Trade and the Law of GATT*. Indianapolis, IN: Bobbs-Merrill.

(1989). *The World Trading System: Law and Policy of International Economic Relations*. Cambridge, MA: MIT Press.

Jacobs, S. and P. Ladegaard (2010). *Regulatory Governance in Developing Countries*. Washington, DC: International Finance Corporation.

Jafari, Y. and D. G. Tarr (2017). "Estimates of Ad Valorem Equivalents of Barriers against Foreign Suppliers of Services in Eleven Services Sectors and 103 Countries." *The World Economy*, 40(3): 544–73.

Jaumotte, F., S. Lall, and C. Papageorgiou (2013). "Rising Income Inequality: Technology, or Trade and Financial Globalization?" *IMF Economic Review*, 61(2): 271–309.

Johnson, H. G. (1953). "Optimum Tariffs and Retaliation." *Review of Economic Studies*, 1: 142–53.

Kee, H. L., A. Nicita, and M. Olarreaga (2008). "Import Demand Elasticities and Trade Distortions." *The Review of Economics and Statistics*, 90(4): 666–82.

(2009). "Estimating Trade Restrictiveness Indices." *Economic Journal*, 119(534): 172–99.

Kimura, F. and H. H. Lee (2006). "The Gravity Equation in International Trade in Services." *Review of World Economics*, 142(1): 92–121.

Koske, I., I. Wanner, R. Bitetti, and O. Barbiero (2014). "The 2013 Update of the OECD Product Market Regulation Indicators: Policy Insights for OECD and Non-OECD Countries." OECD Economics Department Working Papers. Paris: OECD Publishing.

Krueger, A. O. (1964). "The Political Economy of Rent Seeking Society." *American Economic Review*, 64: 291–303.

Krugman, Paul R. (1991). "The Move toward Free Trade Zones." *Economic Review*, 5–24 (November).

Krugman, Paul (1997). "What Should Trade Negotiators Negotiate About?" *Journal of Economic Literature*, 35: 113–20.

Lanz, R. and A. Maurer (2015). "Services and Global Value Chains: Servicification of Manufacturing and Services Networks." *Journal of International Commerce, Economics and Policy*, 6(3): 1550014.

Lardy, N. R. (2014). *Markets over Mao: The Rise of Private Business in China*. Washington, DC: Peterson Institute for International Economics.

Lawrence, R. Z. (2006). "Rule Making amidst Growing Diversity: A Club-of-Club Approach to WTO Reform and New Issue Selection." *Journal of International Economic Law*, 9(4): 823–35.

(2013). *When the Immovable Object Meets the Unstoppable Force: Multilateralism, Regionalism and Deeper Integration*. E15 Initiative, Geneva.

Lee, J. and P. Swagel (2000). "Trade Barriers and Trade Flows across Countries and Industries." *The Review of Economics and Statistics*, 79(3): 372–82.

Lesser, C. (2007). "Do Bilateral and Regional Approaches for Reduction Technical Barriers to Trade Converge towards the Multilateral Trading System?" Trade Policy Working Paper No. 58. Paris: OECD Publishing.

Levi-Faur, David (2005). "The Global Diffusion of Regulatory Capitalism." *The Annals of the American Academy of Political and Social Science*, 598: 12–32.

Lim, C. G. and P. McNelis (2014). "Income Inequality, Trade and Financial Openness." Fordham University Schools of Business Research Paper No. 2425068.

Limão, N. (2016). "Preferential Trade Agreements." In Kyle Bagwell and Robert W. Staiger (Eds.), *Handbook in Commercial Policy*. New York: Oxford University Press.

Lumenga-Neso, O., M. Olarreaga, and M. Schiff (2005). "On Indirect Trade-Related R&D Spillovers." *European Economic Review*, 49(7): 1785–98.

Maertens, M. and J. Swinnen (2009a). "Food Standards, Trade, and Development." *Review of Business and Economics*, LIV(3): 313–26.

(2009b). "Trade, Standards, and Poverty: Evidence from Senegal." *World Development*, 34: 161–78.

Majone, G. (1994). "The Rise of the Regulatory State in Europe." *West European Politics*, 17: 77–101.

(1997). "From the Positive to the Regulatory State: Causes and Consequences of Changes in the Mode of Governance." *Journal of Public Policy*, 17: 139–67.

Malyshev, N. and C. Kauffmann (2015). *International Regulatory Co-operation: The Menu of Approaches*. E15 Initiative, Geneva.

Manyika, J., S. Lund, J. Bughin, J. Woetzel, K. Stamenov, and D. Dhingra (2016). *Digital Globalization: The New Era of Global Flows*. McKinsey Global Institute, February.

Markusen, J. R. (2013). "Putting Per-Capita Income Back into Trade Theory." *Journal of International Economics*, 90(2): 255–65.

Maskus, K. (2012). *Private Rights and Public Problems: The Global Economics of Intellectual Property in the 21st Century*. Washington, DC: Petersen Institute of International Economics.

Maskus, K., O. Tsunehiro, and J. S. Wilson (2005). "The Cost of Compliance with Product Standards for Firms in Developing Countries: An Econometric Study." World Bank Policy Research Working Paper No. 3590. Washington, DC.

Mavroidis, P. (2016a). *Regulatory Cooperation: Lessons from the WTO and the World Trade Regime*. E15 Initiative, Geneva.

(2016b). *The Regulation of International Trade. Vol. 1: GATT*. Cambridge, MA: MIT Press.

(2016c). *The Regulation of International Trade: Vol. 2: The WTO Agreements on Trade in Goods*. Cambridge, MA: MIT Press.

Mavroidis, P. and A. Sapir (2015). "Dial PTAs for Peace: The Influence of Preferential Trade Agreements on Litigation between Trading Partners." *Journal of World Trade*, 49: 351–74.

Mavroidis, P. and R. Wolfe (2015). "From Sunshine to a Common Agent: The Evolving Understanding of Transparency in the WTO." *Brown Journal of World Affairs*, XXI: 117–30.

Mayer, T. and S. Zignago (2006). "Notes on CEPII's Distances Measures." Paris: CEPII.

Mendes, J. (2015). "Regulatory Cooperation under TTIP: Democracy on This Side of the Bridge." Verfassungsblog.

Metzenbaum, S. (1998). *Making Measurement Matter: The Challenge and Promise of Building a Performance-Focused Environmental Protection System*. Washington, DC: Brookings Institute.

Miller, R. E. and U. Temurshoev (2017). "Output Upstreamness and Input Downstreamness of Industries/Countries in World Production." *International Regional Science Review*, 40(5): 443–75.

Miroudot, S. and K. Pertel (2015). "Water in the GATS: Methodology and Results." OECD Trade Policy Papers No. 185. Paris: OECD Publishing, October.

Miroudot, S. and B. Shepherd (2014). "The Paradox of Preferences: Regional Trade Agreements and Trade Costs in Services." *The World Economy*, 37(12): 1751–72.

Miroudot, S., D. Rouzet, and F. Spinelli (2013). "Trade Policy Implications of Global Value Chains: Case Studies." OECD Trade Policy Papers No. 161. Paris: OECD Publishing. http://dx.doi.org/10.1787/5k3tpt2t0zs1-en.

Mitchell, Andrew and Thomas J. Prusa (2016). "China-Autos: Haven't We Danced This Dance Before?" *World Trade Review*, 15(2): 303–25.

Molina, A. C. and V. Khoroshavina (2015). "TBT Provisions in Regional Trade Agreements: To What Extent Do They Go Beyond the WTO TBT Agreement?" Staff Working Paper No. ERSD-2015-09. Geneva: World Trade Organization.

Monteagudo, J., A. Rutkowski, and D. Lorenzani (2012). "The Economic Impact of the Services Directive: A First Assessment Following Implementation." European Economy: Economic Papers No. 456.

Moore, Michael O. and M. Wu (2015). "Antidumping and Strategic Industrial Policy: Tit-for-Tat Trade Remedies and the China–X-Ray Equipment Dispute." *World Trade Review*, 14(2): 239–86.

Moore, M. O. and M. Zanardi (2011). "Trade Liberalization and Antidumping: Is There a Substitution Effect?" *Review of Development Economics*, 15(4): 601–19.

Moravcsik, A. (1997). "Taking Preferences Seriously: A Liberal Theory of International Politics." *International Organization*, 51: 513–53.

Mustilli, F. (2015). "Estimating the Economic Gains of TTIP." *Intereconomics*, 50(6): 321–7.

Narlikar, A., M. Daunton, and R. Stern (Eds.) (2012). *The Oxford Handbook of the World Trade Organization*. Oxford: Oxford University Press.

National Academy of Sciences (2012). *Ensuring Safe Foods and Medical Products through Stronger Regulatory Systems Abroad. Committee on Strengthening Core Elements of Regulatory Systems in Developing Countries*. Board on Global Health; Board on Health Sciences Policy; Institute of Medicine. Washington, DC: National Academies Press.

Nicoletti, G., S. Scarpetta, and O. Boylaud (1999). "Summary Indicators of Product Market Regulation with an Extension to Employment Protection Legislation." *SSRN Electronic Journals*, May. doi:10.2139/ssrn.201668.

Nishioka, S. and M. Ripoll (2012). "Productivity, Trade and the R&D Content of Intermediate Inputs." *European Economic Review*, 56(8): 1573–92.

Noland, M., G. Hufbauer, S. Robinson, and T. Moran (2016). "Assessing Trade Agendas in the US Presidential Campaign." PIIE Briefing 16-6. Washington, DC: Peterson Institute for International Economics.

OECD (2002). *Regulatory Policies in OECD Countries: From Interventionism to Regulatory Governance*. Paris: OECD.

(2005a). *OECD Best Practice Principles for Regulatory Policy: The Governance of Regulators*. Paris: OECD.

(2005b). *APEC-OECD Integrated Checklist on Regulatory Reform*. Paris: OECD.

(2005c). *Guiding Principles of Regulatory Quality and Performance*. Paris: OECD.

(2012). *Recommendation of the Council on Regulatory Policy and Governance*. Paris: OECD.

(2013a). *International Regulatory Co-operation: Addressing Global Challenges*. Paris: OECD.

(2013b). *Interconnected Economies: Benefiting from Global Value Chains*. Paris: OECD.

(2015a). "Benefits from Trade-Related International Regulatory Cooperation – A Theoretical Framework" (TAD/TC/WP/RD(2015)5). Paris: OECD.

(2015b). *OECD Regulatory Policy Outlook 2015*. Paris: OECD.

(2015c). *2014 OECD Regulatory Indicators Survey*. Paris: OECD.

(2015d). *Inclusive Global Value Chains: Policy Options in Trade and Complementary Areas for GVC Integration by Small and Medium Enterprises and Low-Income Developing Countries*. Paris: OECD.

Office of the United States Trade Representative (2017). "The Trans-Pacific Partnership." www.ustr.gov (accessed February 10, 2017).

Orefice, G. and N. Rocha (2011). "Deep Integration and Production Networks: An Empirical Analysis." World Trade Organization Staff Working Paper No. ERSD-2011-11.

Otsuki, T., J. S. Wilson, and M. Sewadeh (2001). "Saving Two in a Billion: Quantifying the Trade Effect of European Food Safety Standards on African Exports." *Food Policy*, 26(5): 495–514.

Pelkmans, J., A. Lejour, L. Schrefler, F. Mustilli, and J. Timini (2014). "EU-US Transatlantic Trade and Investment Partnership: Detailed Appraisal of the European Commission's Impact Assessment." Ex-Ante Impact Assessment Unit Study, European Parliamentary Research Service, European Parliament.

Piermartini, R. and M. Budetta (2006). "A Mapping of Regional Rules on Technical Barriers to Trade." Mimeo. Geneva: World Trade Organization.

(2009). "A Mapping of Regional Rules on Technical Barriers to Trade." In A. Estevadeordal, K. Suominen, and R. Tech (Eds.). *Regional Rules in the Global Trading System*. Cambridge: Cambridge University Press.

Pinker, Steven. (2011). *The Better Angels of Our Nature, Why Violence Has Declined*. New York: Penguin Books.

Politico (2016). "Full Transcript: First 2016 Presidential Debate." September 27. www.politico.com (accessed December 13, 2018).

Porter, M. E. (1985a). "Technology and Competitive Advantage." *Journal of Business Strategy*, 5(3): 60–78.

(1985b). *Competitive Advantage: Creating and Sustaining Superior Performance*. New York: Freepress.

Prusa, T. J. and E. Vermulst (2013). "United States: Definitive Anti-dumping and Countervailing Duties on Certain Products from China: Passing the Buck on Pass-Through." *World Trade Review*, 12(2): 197–234.

(2014). "China: Countervailing and Anti-dumping Duties on Grain Oriented Flat-Rolled Electrical Steel from the United States: Exporting US AD/CVD Methodologies through WTO Dispute Settlement?" *World Trade Review*, 13(2): 229–66.

(2015). "China: Anti-dumping and Countervailing Duty Measures on Broiler Products from the United States: How the Chickens Came Home to Roost." *World Trade Review*, 14(2): 287–335.

Radelet, S. (2015). *The Great Surge*. New York: Simon and Schuster.

Regan, D. H. (2006). "What Are Trade Agreements For? – Two Conflicting Stories Told by Economists with a Lesson for Lawyers." *Journal of International Economic Law*, 9(4): 951–88.

Renda, A. (2015). "Regulatory Impact Assessment and Regulatory Policy." In OECD (Ed.), *Regulatory Policy in Perspective: A Reader's Companion to the OECD Regulatory Policy Outlook 2015*. Paris: OECD Publishing.

Reuters (2016). "Tens of Thousands Protest in Europe against Atlantic Free Trade Deals." September 17. www.reuters.com (accessed November 16, 2016).

Roberts, D. and T. Josling (2011). *Tracking the Implementation of Internationally Agreed Standards in Food and Agricultural Production*. Washington, DC: International Food and Agricultural Trade Policy Council.

Rodriguez, F. and D. Rodrik (2001). "Trade Policy and Economic Growth: A Skeptic's Guide to the Cross-National Evidence." In *NBER Macroeconomics Annual 2000*, Vol. 15. Cambridge, MA: MIT Press, 261–338.

Rodrik, D. (1991). "Policy Uncertainty and Private Investment in Developing Countries." *Journal of Development Economics*, 36(2): 229–42.

(1992). "The Limits of Trade Policy Reform in Developing Countries." *The Journal of Economic Perspectives*, 6(1): 87–105.

(2015). "The War of Trade Models." Dani Rodrik's weblog (rodrik.typepad .com). May 4.

Rohini, A. (Ed.) (2016). *Regional Trade Agreements and the Multilateral Trading System*. Geneva: Cambridge University Press and the WTO.

Rosendorff, B. P. (1996). "Voluntary Export Restraints, Antidumping Procedure, and Domestic Politics." *The American Economic Review*, 86(3): 544–61.

Rouzet, D. and S. Miroudot (2013). "The Cumulative Impact of Trade Barriers along the Value Chain: An Empirical Assessment Using the OECD Inter-Country Input-Output Model." In 16th Annual Conference on Global Economic Analysis.

Roy, M. (2011). "Services Commitments in PTAs: An Expanded Dataset." WTO Working Paper No. ERSD-2100-18.

Sabel, C. F. and D. G. Victor (2015). "Governing Global Problems under Uncertainty: Making Bottom-Up Climate Policy Work." *Climatic Change*, 136: 1–13.

Sauvé, P. (1995). "The General Agreement on Trade in Services: Much Ado about What?" In D. Schwanen (Ed.), *Trains, Grains, and Automobiles: Canada and the Uruguay Round*. Toronto: C. D. Howe Institute.

Scharpf, F. (1999). *Regieren in Europa – Effektiv und Demokratisch?* Frankfurt: Campus.

(2003). "Problem-Solving Effectiveness and Democratic Accountability in the EU." MPifG Discussion Paper No. 3.

Shaffer, G. (2015). "How the World Trade Organization Shapes Regulatory Governance." *Regulation and Governance*, 9: 1–15.

Shirouzu, N., S. Reddy, and S. Terlep (2011). "US-China Trade Spat Escalates to Autos." *Wall Street Journal*, December 15.

Slaughter, A. M. (1992). "Regulating the World: Multilateralism, International Law, and the Projection of the New Deal Regulatory State." In John Ruggie (Ed.), *Multilateralism Matters: The Theory and Praxis of an Institutional Form*. New York: Columbia University Press, 125–56.

Smith, J. M. (2013). *US Trade Remedy Laws and Nonmarket Economies: A Legal Overview*. CRS Report for Congress RL33976 (January 31). Washington, DC: Congressional Research Service.

Steger, D. P. (2012). "Institutions for Regulatory Cooperation in 'New Generation' Economic and Trade Agreements." *Legal Issues of Economic Integration*, 39: 109–26.

Stewart, R. B. (2016). "State Regulatory Capacity and Administrative Law and Governance under Globalization." New York University School of Law, Institute for International Law and Justice Working Paper No. 2016/1.

Stolper, W. F. and P. A. Samuelson (1941). "Protection and Real Wages." *The Review of Economic Studies*, 9(1): 58–73.

Swedish Board of Trade (2016). *Protectionism in the 21st Century*. Stockholm: National Board of Trade.

Swedish Board of Trade and UNCTAD (2018). *The Use of the EU's Free Trade Agreements Exporter and Importer Utilization of Preferential Tariffs*. Stockholm: National Board of Trade.

Sykes, A. O. (1999). "The (Limited) Role of Regulatory Harmonization in International Goods and Service Markets." *Journal of International Economic Law*, 2(1): 49–70.

Tarasov, A. (2012). "Per Capita Income, Market Access Costs, and Trade Volumes." *Journal of International Economics*, 86(2): 284–94.

The Economist (2013). "Transatlantic Trade Talks: Opening Shots." July 6, Print Edition.

(2016a). "Dreaming of Sovereignty." March 10, Print Edition.

(2016b). "Wallonia Is Adamantly Blocking the EU's Trade Deal with Canada." October 22, Print Edition.

The Guardian (2015). "What Is TTIP? The Controversial Trade Deal Proposal Explained." July 3, Print Edition.

(2016). "Belgian Politicians Drop Opposition to EU-Canada Trade Deal," October 27, www.theguardian.com (accessed November 15, 2016).

The New York Times (2017). "Trump Abandons Trans-Pacific Partnership, Obama's Signature Deal." January 23. www.nytimes.com (accessed January 30, 2017).

Timmer, M., A. A. Erumban, R. Gouma et al. (2012). "The World Input-Output Database (WIOD): Contents, Sources and Methods." IIDE Discussion Papers No. 20120401. Institute for International and Development Economics.

Trachtman, J. P. (2007). "International Trade: Regionalism." In Andrew T. Guzman and Alan O. Sykes (Eds.), *Research Handbook in International Economic Law*. Northampton, MA: Edward Elgar, 151–76.

Trefler, D. (1993). "Trade Liberalization and the Theory of Endogenous Protection: An Econometric Study of U.S. Import Policy." *Journal of Political Economy*, 101(1): 138–60.

Turnovsky, S. and J. Rojas-Vallejos (2016). "The Distributional Consequence of Tariff Liberalization: Consumption versus Investment Tariff Reduction." Working Paper.

UNCTAD (2009). *Non-Tariff Measures: Evidence from Selected Developing Countries and Future Research Agenda*. Geneva: United Nations.

(2015). *International Classification of Non-Tariff Measures*. Geneva: United Nations. UNCTAD/DITC/TAB/2012/2/Rev.1.

(2016). *Guidelines to Collect Data on Official Non-Tariff Measures*. Geneva: United Nations. UNCTAD/DITC/TAB/2014/4.

US Food and Drug Administration (2012). Global Engagement Report. Silver Spring, MD: US Food and Drug Administration, 2. wayback.archive-it.org/7993/20171101214953/https://www.fda.gov/downloads/AboutFDA/ReportsManualsForms/Reports/UCM298578.pdf.

Vandenbussche, H. and M. Zanardi (2008). "What Explains the Proliferation of Antidumping Laws?" *Economic Policy*, 23(53): 94–138.

Van Tongeren, F., J. Beghin, and S. Marette (2009). "A Cost-Benefit Framework for the Assessment of Non-Tariff Measures in Agro-Food Trade." OECD Food, Agriculture and Fisheries Papers No. 21. Paris: OECD Publishing.

Vogel, D. (1995). *Trading Up: Consumer and Environmental Regulation in a Global Economy*. Cambridge, MA: Harvard University Press.

Walsh, K. (2006). "Trade in Services: Does Gravity Hold? A Gravity Model Approach to Estimating Barriers to Services Trade." Working Paper. Department of Economics & Institute for International Integration Studies, Trinity College, Dublin.

Wijkström, E. (2015). *The Third Pillar: Behind the Scenes, WTO Committee Work Delivers*. E15 Initiative, Geneva.

Wolf, M. (2015). "The Embattled Future of Global Trade Policy." *The Financial Times*, May 12.

Wolfe, R. (2011). "The OECD Contribution to the Evolution of 21st Century Trade Law." *George Washington International Law Review*, 43: 277–93.

World Bank (2005). "Food Safety and Agricultural Health Standards: Challenges and Opportunities for Developing Country Exports." Report No. 31207.

(2006). "China's Compliance with Food Safety Requirements for Fruits and Vegetables: Promoting Food Safety, Competitiveness and Poverty Reduction." Beijing/Washington, DC: World Bank.

(2010). "Investing across Borders 2010: Indicators of Foreign Direct Investment Regulation in 87 Economies." Washington, DC: World Bank.

(2016). "World Development Indicators." Washington, DC: World Bank.

WTO (1996). "Japan – Taxes on Alcoholic Beverages." WT/DS8/AB/R, WT/DS10/AB/R, WT/DS11/AB/R, adopted November 1, 1996, DSR 1996:I, 97.

(1998). *United States – Import Prohibition of Certain Shrimp and Shrimp* Products, Appellate Body Report, WT/DS58/AB/R, adopted November 6, 1998, DSR 1998:VII, p. 2755.

(2000). TBT Committee Decision on Principles for the Development of International Standards, Guides and Recommendations with Relation to Articles 2, 5, and Annex 3 of the TBT Agreement Contained in Annex 2 of G/TBT/1/Rev. 12.

(2001). "Accession of The People's Republic of China: Decision of 10 November 2001." Document WT/L/432. Geneva: World Trade Organization.

(2009). "World Trade Report 2009: Trade Policy Commitments and Contingency Measures." Geneva: World Trade Organization.

(2010). "United States: Definitive Anti-dumping and Countervailing Duties on Certain Products from China." Report of the Panel. Document WT/DS379/R. Geneva: World Trade Organization.

(2011a). "Compilation of Sources on Good Regulatory Practice." Document G/TBT/W/341. Geneva: World Trade Organization.

(2011b). "World Trade Report 2011: The WTO and Preferential Trade Agreements: From Co-existence to Coherence." Geneva: World Trade Organization.

(2012). United States – Measures Concerning the Importation, Marketing and Sale of Tuna and Tuna Products, Appellate Body Report, WT/DS381/R, adopted May 16, 2012, paras 321–2.

(2014). "World Trade Report 2014 – Trade and Development: Recent Trends and the Role of the WTO." Geneva: World Trade Organization.

(2015). "I-TIP Services: User Guide." Geneva: World Trade Organization.

(2016a). "Accessions: Afghanistan to Become 164th WTO Member on 29 July 2016." World Trade Organization, June 29.

(2016b). "Report to the TPRB from the Director-General on Trade-Related Developments (mid-October 2015 to mid-May 2016)." Geneva: World Trade Organization.

(2016c). "Disputes by Agreement." November 2017. www.wto.org (accessed November 17, 2017).

(2016d). "Integrated Trade Intelligence Portal." November 2017. www.wto.org (accessed November 17, 2017).

Wu, M. (2016). "The 'China, Inc.' Challenge to Global Trade Governance." *Harvard International Law Journal*, 57(2): 261–324.

Yotov, Y. V., R. Piermartini, J. A. Monteiro, and M. Larch (2016). *An Advanced Guide to Trade Policy Analysis: The Structural Gravity Model.* Geneva: World Trade Organization.

Young, A. (2016). "Not Your Parents' Trade Politics: The Transatlantic Trade and Investment Partnership Negotiations." *Review of International Political Economy*, 23(3): 345–78.

INDEX

accountability, 180, 323–4
ad-valorem equivalents (AVEs)
cumulative in GVCs, 75–7
free trade agreements and, 101
gravity approach to, 53
for NTMs, 67, 68, 71, 73–5, 95–7, 97–9*f*, 114–15
percentage calculation, 210
trade costs calculations, 101–10
of TTIPs, 119–21
African, Caribbean, and Pacific (ACP) countries, 216
African Growth and Opportunities Act (AGOA), 235
Agreement on Antidumping, 311
Agreement on Civil Aviation, 333
Agreement on Government Procurement (GPA), 129, 333
Agreement on Rules of Origin (ARO), 212–13
Agreement on Sanitary and Phyto-sanitary (SPS) measures, 312–14, 318–19
Agreement on Subsidies and Countervailing Measures, 333
Agreement on Technical Barriers to Trade (TBT), 312–14, 318–19
agricultural regulatory decisions, 181
Aichele et al. case, 112–13, 116–17, 123
Aid for Trade resources, 192
antidumping
Agreement on Antidumping, 311
imports and, 285–9, 286*f*, 288*f*
overview of, 280–5
size of, 289–92, 290–1it
APEC-OECD Integrated Checklist on Regulatory Reform, 203
ASEAN Trade in Goods Agreement (ATIGA), 4, 186
ASEAN Work Program, 188
Asia-Pacific Economic Cooperation (APEC) Forum, 329
Association of Southeast Asian Nations (ASEAN) countries, 215, 328

bilateral industry-level imports, 287–8
bilateral restrictiveness index (BRI), 67, 71–3, 75, 78–84, 92–5, 94–5*t*
bilateral trade agreements, 11, 18, 301
binary variables, 28
bottom-up trade cost calculations, 106–10
Brazil, 182
Buy America provisions, 129

Cambodian export costs, 188
Cambodian National Trade Repository, 187
Canada-EU Trade Agreement (CETA), 6, 213, 216, 247–50
Canada-US Trade Agreement (CUSTA), 216
Carrère et al. case, 113, 117, 123
categorical variables, 28
Centre for Economic Policy Research (CEPR), 132
CEPII study, 111, 115, 121–2
CEPR Study, 110–11, 121
change of tariff classification (CTC), 215–16, 229
change of tariff subheading (CTSH), 229–30
China, 6, 209

China-Specific Safeguards Database (CSGD), 21–2
China's NTM strategy for WTO accession
  introduction to, 277–9
  summary of, 294–7, 298*t*
  US antidumping and imports, 285–9, 286*f*, 288*f*
  US antidumping law and, 280–5
  US antidumping size, 289–92, 290–1*t*
  US nonmarket economy status, 292–4, 293*f*
Code of Good Practice (CGP) for the Preparation, Adoption and Application of Standards, 319
Committee on Rules of Origin (CRO), 215
Committee on Sanitary and Phytosanitary Matters, 271
Committee on Technical Barriers to Trade, 319
commodity chains, 68–9
common agricultural policy (CAP), 313
Common Market for Eastern and Southern Africa (COMESA), 215
Comprehensive and Progressive Agreement on Trans-Pacific Partnership (CPTPP), 49
Comprehensive Economic and Trade Agreement (CETA), 246–50, 256–74, 260–1*f*, 326
COMPTRADE data, 158
computed indicators, 29
concession erosion, 305–9
convergence in rules of origin, 218–32, 221–7*t*, 222–7*t*
corporate governance of WTO, 330
countervailing duties (CVDs), 279–89, 286*f*, 288*f*, 293
coverage ratio overview, 155–8
critical mass agreements (CMAs), 333–4
cross-border sales, 1

de-regulation era, 195
democratization, 300
developing countries NTM reforms, 191
Development Research Group of the World Bank, 22
dispute resolution enforcement, 303
dispute settlement system, 66, 309
divergence in rules of origin, 218
Doha Round, 51
drafting of NTM reforms, 192
duty-free, quota-free (DFQF), 212

Economy-wide regulations (PMR), 19
effectively applied rates (AHS), 78
Egger et al. case, 111–12, 116, 122
enlightened mercantilism, 302
Environmental Goods Agreement (EGA), 305, 332
Estevadeordal index, 230–1
EU Market Access Database (MADB), 26
European Commission, 200–2, 256
European Committee for Electrotechnical Standardization (CENELEC), 273
European Committee for Standardization (CEN), 273
European Free Trade Association (EFTA), 216
European Union (EU), 4, 27, 232
Everything But Arms (EBA), 235
ex post evaluations and trade considerations, 196–8, 202–3

Federal Administrative Procedure Act (LFPA), 182
Federal Commission on Regulatory Improvement (COFEMER), 182
Felbermayr et al. case, 112, 115, 122
Fontagné et al. case, 114–15
Food and Agriculture Organization of the United Nations Statistics (FAOSTAT), 78
foreign commercial interests, 129, 132–3, 138–9
foreign direct investment (FDI), 252
foreign equity, 20–1, 28, 43
Forest Law Enforcement Governance and Trade Initiative, 331
Francois et al. case, 113–14
free trade agreements (FTAs), 100–10
free trade areas (FTAs), 312

G-20 Leaders, 133, 138, 147
General Agreement on Trade and Tariffs (GATT)
  China and, 278
  classifications revisited, 311–12
  concession erosion, 305–9
  Environmental Goods Agreement, 305
  evolution of WTO, 309–14
  introducing GATT-think, 299–302
  introduction to, 7
  Mexico joining of, 51
  neutral tariff classifications, 304–5
  new generation of agreements on NTMs, 312–14
  overview of GATT-think, 302–9
  rules of origin and, 211–12
  Tokyo Round codes, 310–11
General Agreement on Trade in Services (GATS)
  market access in services, 49–50, 52–3
  negotiations to expand, 49
  NTMs and, 14, 19
  role of, 334–5
Generalized System of Preferences (GSP) scheme, 215
Global Antidumping Database, 21–2
global commodity chains (GCC), 68–9
Global Countervailing Duties Database (GCVD), 21–2
global economic integration, 300
global financial crisis (2008-2009), 131–2
Global Safeguards Database (GSGD), 21–2
Global Trade Alert (GTA)
  classification and reported measures, 138–40
  data collection on, 131–40
  government intervention, 135–6
  introduction to, 4, 22–3, 31, 128–31
  policy scope, 133–5
  public procurement policy change, 140–8, 142–5*t*
  summary of, 148–9
Global Trade and Financial Architecture (GTFA), 22
global trade liberalization, 1
global trade policy, 81, 88, 96
global value chains (GVCs)
  cumulative AVEs in, 75–7
  data on, 77–8
  increased trade from, 300, 320–3, 330
  introduction to, 1, 3, 7
  literature on, 67–70
  methodology, 71
  in non-tariff measures, 65–7
globalization process, 69
good regulatory practices (GRP)
  ex post evaluations and trade considerations, 196–8, 202–3
  future outlook, 204–5
  guidelines for, 207–8
  introduction to, 5, 193–4
  limitations of, 198
  methods of assessments, 202
  in practice, 199–204
  regulatory impact assessments, 196, 199–204
  rise of, 194–5
  stakeholder consultations, 197–8
  stakeholder engagement, 203–4
  systematic assessment of trade impacts, 199–200
  in theory, 194–8
  types of assessments, 200–2
  WTO role in, 194, 201, 205–6, 211–14, 323–5
government intervention in Global Trade Alert, 135–6
government NTM reforms, 191
Government Procurement (GPA), 129
Great Depression, 131–2
gross domestic product (GDP), 71, 159–61, 166, 169
GTAP-8 database, 110, 112
GTAP-9 database, 112

Harmonization Work Programme (HWP), 211, 213–14, 216, 219
Harmonized Commodity Description and Coding System, 210, 304–5

harmonized rules of origin (HRO), 216
Harmonized System (HS) 6-digit products, 71
high-skill labour (HS), 88
Hull, Cordell, 299

impact assessments in NTMs, 100–10, 180
Import Licensing Procedures (ILP) Agreement, 184–5
import measures, 15
import quotas, 303–4
import restrictions, 1, 285, 294–5
information and telecommunication (ICT) services, 69
Information Technology Agreement (ITA), 228
input legitimacy, 195
international agreements, 18, 22–3, 255, 302, 324
international competitiveness, 1, 201
International Conference on Harmonization of Technical Requirements for Registration of Pharmaceuticals for Human Use, 325
international cooperation, 2, 278, 299, 301, 324, 330, 334
International Electrotechnical Commission (IEC), 273
International Organization for Standardization (ISO), 273, 326
international regulatory incoherence, 315–17
International Trade Commission, 285
international trade flows, 1
International Trade Organization (ITO), 308
Internet regulation, 19
introduction to, 6
inventories of legislation, 16–22
Investing Across Border (World Bank), 18, 21
Investment Policy Hub (UNCTAD), 21

Jackson, John H., 278, 295–6
Japan-Film, 307

labour productivity growth, 3
LDC DFQF programs, 218
least-developed countries (LDCs), 212
legal form of entry/restrictions, 20
legal inflation, 108
less than fair value (LTFV), 281–2
liberalization of trade, 301
licensing limits, 20
living standards, 300

macroeconomic policy, 128
management of NTM reforms, 191–2
Market Access Database (MADB), 31
market access in services
  data on, 52–4
  estimating equations, 54–6, 56*t*
  introduction to, 2, 48–50
  results and discussion, 57–61, 57*t*, 59–60*t*
  uncertainty and, 50–1
mega-regional trade agreements, 256–74
Mexico, 51, 182–3
most-favored nation (MFN) principle of WTO
  equal treatment and, 32
  estimating equations, 54–6, 56–7*t*, 57–61, 59–60*t*
  international agreements and, 18
  rates of, 74, 78
  regulatory inventories and, 16–22
  rules of origin and, 228
  WTO and, 334
Multi-Agency Support Team (MAST) for NTMs
  classification of, 14–16, 15*t*, 18, 24–6
  coverage of sectors, 37–9
  introduction to, 11–12
  types of measures, 35–9, 36*t*, 38*t* 40*t*
multilateral trade liberalization, 311, 333
multinational corporations (MNCs), 198, 325
multispeed trade integration, 332–5
mutual recognition agreements (MRAs), 328

national coordination mechanisms, 181–4
national ministries/administrations, 18
National Trade Facilitation Committee, 188
National Trade Repositories (NTRs), 186, 188–9
national welfare maximisation, 196
neo-liberal macroeconomic paradigm, 195
non-discrimination in GATT-think, 304, 315
non-discriminatory NTMs, 65, 306–8
non-homotheric preferences, 153–5
Non-manufacturing sector regulations (NMR), 19
non-market economy (NME) status, 6
non-preferential rules of origin, 209, 243
non-tariff barriers (NTBs), 2, 6, 13
non-tariff measures (NTMs). *see also* China's NTM strategy for WTO accession; impact assessments in NTMs; market access in services; Multi-Agency Support Team (MAST) for NTMs; Stone-Geary preferences and NTMs
  AVEs for, 67, 68, 71, 73–5, 95–7, 97–9*f*, 114–15
  bilateral-trade restrictiveness indices, 71–3, 92–5, 94–5*t*
  challenges when applying databases, 39–42
  classification of, 13–16, 15*t*, 192
  collection of reforms, 192
  comprise of government initiatives, 27–8
  concession erosion and, 305–9
  data on, 77–8
  data sources, 16–28, 17*t*
  defined, 11
  economic effects of, 42
  geographic coverage, 31–3, 32*f*, 43
  global value chains and, 65–7
  impact assessments in NTMs, 100–10, 180
  impact on industrial productivity, 84–6
  implementation and enforcement, 41–2, 44
  import refusals, 27
  international agreements, 22–3
  introduction to, 2–5, 11–12
  inventories of legislation, 16–22
  literature on, 67–70
  methodology, 71
  new generation of agreements on, 312–14
  productivity results, 86–95, 87*t*, 89–90*t*
  reductions in TTIPs, 113–17
  regulatory systems of, 41
  restrictiveness of measures, 42–4
  review of legislation, 23
  rules of origin as, 228–32
  selected descriptive results, 78–84, 79*t*, 80–1*f*, 82–3*t*
  summary of, 42–6, 47*t*, 95–7, 97–9*f*, 127
  surveys and complaint protocols, 24–7
  time coverage, 33–5, 34–5*t*
  trade facilitation and compliance, 29–31, 30*t*
  type of information, 28–9
non-tariff measures (NTMs) reforms
  Cambodian export costs, 188
  international disciplines and principles, 184–6
  lessons learned about, 190–2
  national coordination mechanisms, 181–4
  trade facilitation and, 179–81
  World Bank support, 186–90
non-violation complaints (NVCs), 307
North American Free Trade Agreement (NAFTA)
  aim of RoO in, 228–9
  import-specific indexes, 113
  negotiations on, 215, 246
  overview of, 266–8, 267–8*f*
  political differences and, 331
  stability from, 51
NTM TRAINS database, 31, 33–9, 34–5*t*

Organisation for Economic Co-operation (OECD). *see also* Services Trade Restrictiveness Index
data collection for NTMs, 14
good regulatory practices, 194, 199–205
hierarchy of measures, 41
Product Market Regulation (PMR) database, 18–19
Regulatory Indicators Questionnaires, 18–19
Regulatory Indicators Survey, 199
trading environment indicators, 29
output legitimacy, 195

pan-European RoO model, 216, 229
peer-to-peer regulatory networks, 317
Penn World Tables (PWT), 78
plurilateral agreements (PAs), 11, 18, 310–11, 333–4
political level NTM reforms, 190–1
predicted welfare effects, 123–5, 124*f*
preferential rules of origin, 209, 235
preferential tariff rates (PRF), 74, 78
Preferential Trade Agreement (PTA)
evolution of, 253–6, 256*f*, 257–8*t*
increased use of, 301
introduction to, 5, 74
literature review, 250–3
mega-regional trade agreements, 256–74
multilateralizing progress in, 336–7
regulatory cooperation and, 325–9
role of, 205–6
rules of origin in, 211, 214–19, 217*t*, 233–4
summary of, 275–6
TBT *vs.* SPS, 246–50
TTIP overview, 268–71, 269–70*f*
WTO and, 325–31
procedural obstacles, 41
procurement discrimination, 147
Product Market Regulation (PMR) database, 18–19
product specific rules of origin (PSRO), 215, 220–8
protectionism, 131–2, 306–7, 314
publication of NTM reforms, 192

quantitative restrictions (QRs), 1, 48

Rapid Alert System for Food and Feed (RASFF), 27
Rapid Alert System for Nonfood Dangerous Products (RAPEX), 328
R&D spillovers, 70
re-regulation era, 195
reciprocal liberalization, 299, 302
reciprocal trade agreements, 211, 235
Regional Comprehensive Economic Partnership (RCEP), 326
regional value content (RVC), 229
Regulatory Burden Measurement Framework, 184
regulatory cooperation in WTO
defined, 315
international regulatory incoherence, 315–17
overview of, 318–20
regulatory divergence, 2, 5, 193–4, 196–8, 201, 204–5
regulatory environment, 18, 20, 193, 196–7
regulatory impact assessments (RIA), 196, 199–204
regulatory inventories, 16–22
Regulatory Reform Committee, 183
restrictions on foreign equity, 20
restrictions on operations, 20
rules of origin (RoO)
cumulation of, 240–1
determining convergence in, 218–32, 221–7*t*, 222–7*t*
draft taxonomy of, 235–45
introduction to, 5, 209–11
non-preferential rules of origin, 209, 243
as NTMs, 228–32
origin criterion, 235–9, 243–4
pan-European RoO model, 216, 229
preferential rules of origin, 209, 235
in Preferential Trade Agreement, 211, 214–19, 217*t*, 233–4

proof of direct shipment, 242–3
proof of origin, 241–5
in PTAs, 211, 214–19, 217*t*
summary of, 233–4
Transpacific Partnership and, 213, 217, 234

sanitary and phytosanitary (SPS) measures
domestic measures, 91
evolution of, 253–6, 256*f*, 257–8*t*
good regulatory practices and, 204–5
introduction to, 6, 246–50
literature review, 250–3
measures on the agri-food sector, 39
mega-regional trade agreements, 256–74
NAFTA overview, 266–8, 268*f*
NTMs and, 65, 184–5
in Stone-Geary preferences and NTMs, 151, 152*f*
summary of, 275–6
Transpacific Partnership overview, 261–6, 262*f*, 263*t*, 265*f*
TTIP overview, 268–71, 269–70*f*
US *vs.* EU draft proposals for TTIP, 271–4, 272*t*, 274*t*
at World Trade Organisation, 247–50, 248*f*
sector regulators, 19–20
sector-specific trade barriers, 111
self-declaration of origin, 215
Services Trade Restrictiveness Index (STRI)
estimating equations, 54–6, 56–7*t*, 57–61, 59–60*t*
overview of, 18–21, 31, 52–3
snapshot of services, 33–5
trade cost estimators, 108
as trade cost indicator, 108
Single Market, 53
Smoot-Hawley Tariff Act, 299
Southern African Development Community (SADC), 215
Southern Common Market (MERCOSUR), 215
specific trade concerns (STCs), 26–7, 66, 318
spillover effects in TTIP, 125–6
stakeholder consultations, 5, 195–8, 203–6
stakeholder engagement, 193, 203–4
Standard Cost Model (SCM), 183
"state of the art" of rules of origin, 219–20
State-Owned Assets Supervision and Administration Commission of the State Council (SASAC), 284
state-owned enterprises (SOEs), 194, 284
stock management programmes, 197
Stone-Geary preferences and NTMs
coverage ratio overview, 155–8
empirical specification and data, 158–61, 160*t*, 162–4*t*
introduction to, 150–3, 152*f*
non-homotheric preferences, 153–5
results of study, 161–76, 165*t*, 167–8*t*, 170*t*, 171–3*t*
summary of, 176
structural gravity (SG) models, 110
supply of services, 20
systematic assessment of trade impacts, 199–200

tariffs. *see also* General Agreement on Trade and Tariffs; non-tariff measures (NTMs)
classifications of, 311–12, 319–20
import tariffs, 304
neutral tariff classifications, 304–5
non-tariff barriers, 2, 6, 13
nondiscrimination in tariff bindings, 304
preferential tariff rates, 74, 78
reductions in, 1
Smoot-Hawley Tariff Act, 299
tax on investment returns, 50
technical barriers to trade (TBTs)
coverage ratios, 161
evolution of, 253–6, 256*f*, 257–8*t*
introduction to, 6, 246–50
literature review, 250–3
mega-regional trade agreements, 256–74
NAFTA overview, 266–8, 267*f*

technical barriers to trade (TBTs) (cont.)
NTMs and, 65–6
overview of, 91–2, 151, 159, 184–5
summary of, 275–6
trade policy measures, 81–4
Transpacific Partnership overview, 261–6, 262*f*, 263*t*, 265*f*
TTIP overview, 268–71, 269–70*f*
US *vs.* EU draft proposals for TTIP, 271–4, 272*t*, 274*t*
at World Trade Organisation, 247–50, 248*f*
technical capacity, 180, 312
Technical Committee on Rules of Origin (TCRO), 215
technical level NTM reforms, 191
technology spillovers, 70
Temporary Barriers of Trade Database (TBTD), 21–2
text, defined in regulations, 28
third channel coefficients, 95
Tokyo Round codes, 310–11, 333
top-down trade cost calculations, 108–10
trade agreements, 1, 48–50. *see also* North American Free Trade Agreement; Preferential Trade Agreement
bilateral trade agreements, 11, 18, 301
Canada-EU Trade Agreement, 6, 213, 216, 247–50
Canada-US Trade Agreement, 216
Comprehensive Economic and Trade Agreement, 246–50, 256–74, 260–1*f*, 326
free trade agreements, 100–10
mega-regional trade agreements, 256–74
reciprocal trade agreements, 211, 235
trade barriers
liberalization and, 49, 69
macroeconomic conditions and, 50
as nontariff measures, 320
overview of, 28, 33
reductions in, 181, 219
regulatory divergences, 193–4
sector-specific trade barriers, 111
trade cost calculations
gravity estimations, 117–19
NTM reduction with, 101–10
predicted welfare effects, 101, 123–5, 124*f*
reduction comparisons in TTIPs, 117–21
reductions *vs.* economic effects, 121–6
Trade Facilitation Agreement, 179–81, 184–6
trade impacts of regulations, 199–200
Trade in Services Agreement (TiSA), 49, 51, 326
Trade in Services Database, 52
trade liberalization, 69, 311, 329, 331–3
Trade Monitoring Database (WTO), 139
trade negotiations, 251–3, 301, 324
trade policy (TP), 12, 66, 75–7, 195
Trade Policy Review (TPR), 20, 23, 31, 33
Trade Policy Review Mechanism (TPRM), 23
trade-weighted coverage ratios, 158
Trans-Atlantic Trade and Investment Partnership (TTIP)
ad-valorem equivalents, 119–21
Aichele et al. case, 112–13, 116–17, 123
backlash over, 324
Carrère et al. case, 113, 117, 123
CEPII study, 111, 115, 121–2
CEPR Study, 110–11, 121
Egger et al. case, 111–12, 116, 122
expected welfare effects, 121–3
Felbermayr et al. case, 112, 115, 122
Fontagné et al. case, 114–15
Francois et al. case, 113–14
general characteristics, 110–13
good regulatory practices, 193
impact assessment studies on, 100–1
introduction to, 3, 6
negotiations for, 246, 326
NTM reductions, 113–17

overview of, 110–17, 268–71, 269–70*f*
protests against, 246–7
signing of, 246
spillover effects, 125–6
summary of, 127, 275–6
trade cost reduction comparisons, 117–26
US *vs.* EU draft proposals, 271–4, 272*t*, 274*t*
Transpacific Partnership (TPP)
bottom-up study on, 107
good regulatory practices and, 193, 206
NAFTA overview, 266–8
negotiations for, 326
overview of, 261–6, 262*f*, 263*t*, 265*f*
rules of origin and, 213, 217, 234
transparency, 20, 179–80, 323–4
Tripartite Free Trade Area, 26

UN COMTRADE database, 77, 136
uncertainty and market access, 50–1
UNCTAD-MAST system, 189
UNCTAD-TRAINS database, 106
United Nations Conference on Trade and Development (UNCTAD), 21
United Nations Economic and Social Commission for Asia and the Pacific (ESCAP), 29
United Nations International Trade Center (UNITC), 25–6
United States International Trade Commission (USITC), 28
Uruguay Round, 51, 311
US Food and Drugs Administration (FDA), 27
US International Trade Commission, 281–2
US nonmarket economy status, 292–4, 293*f*

World Bank
compliance standards and, 42
data collection for NTMs, 14
Development Research Group of, 22
hierarchy of measures, 41
Investing Across Borders, 18, 21
market access in services, 53
NTM reforms and, 186–92
Services Trade Restrictiveness Index, 18–21, 31, 52–3
Temporary Barriers of Trade Database, 21–2
Trade in Services Database, 52
trading environment indicators, 29
World Bank Doing Business Indicators, 29
World Input-Output Databases (WIOD), 69–74, 78, 82–3*t*
world input-output tables (WIOT), 77
World Trade Organization (WTO). *see also* China's NTM strategy for WTO accession; most-favored nation (MFN) principle of WTO
Agreement on Civil Aviation, 333
Agreement on Government Procurement, 4, 333
Agreement on Subsidies and Countervailing Measures, 333
Agreements on Customs Valuation, Import Licensing, 300
changing patterns in world trading, 320–3
Committee on Technical Barriers to Trade, 319
cooperation on NTMs, 318–19
cooperation on tariff classifications, 319–20
corporate governance of, 330
divergent social preferences, 331–2
evolution of, 309–14
expanding partnerships, 335–6
Global Trade Alert, 129
good regulatory practices, 194, 201, 205–6, 211–14, 323–5
institutional dimensions of, 7
international disciplines and principles, 184–6
introduction to, 18, 32, 299–302
literature review, 250–3
multi-speed trade integration, 332–5
new WTO think, 329–37
notifications, 23–4
positive integration and, 323–5
PTAs and, 325–31

World Trade Organization (WTO). (cont.)
regulatory cooperation, 315–29
specific trade concerns and, 26–7, 66
summary of, 337–8
TBT *vs.* SPS, 247–50, 248*f*, 253–6, 256*f*, 257–8*t*
technical barriers to trade and, 65–6
Trade Facilitation Agreement, 4
Trade Monitoring Database, 139
Trade Policy Review, 20, 23, 31 33
World War II, 194, 305
WTO Disputes Database (DSUD), 21–2

zero-for-zero sectoral agreements for chemical products, 228